FRANKLIN PARK PUB

W9-DDF-065

3/07

STOP!

This is the back of the book.
You wouldn't want to spoil a great ending!

This book is printed "manga-style," in the authentic Japanese right-to-left format. Since none of the artwork has been flipped or altered, readers get to experience the story just as the creator intended. You've been asking for it, so TOKYOPOP® delivered: authentic, hot-off-the-press, and far more fun!

DIRECTIONS

If this is your first time reading manga-style, here's a quick guide to help you understand how it works.

It's easy... just start in the top right panel and follow the numbers. Have fun, and look for more 100% authentic manga from TOKYOPOP®!

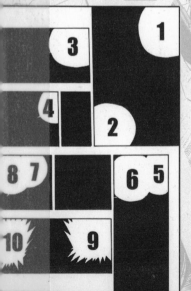

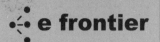

SMUGGLER

スマグラー

shohei manabe

真鍋昌平

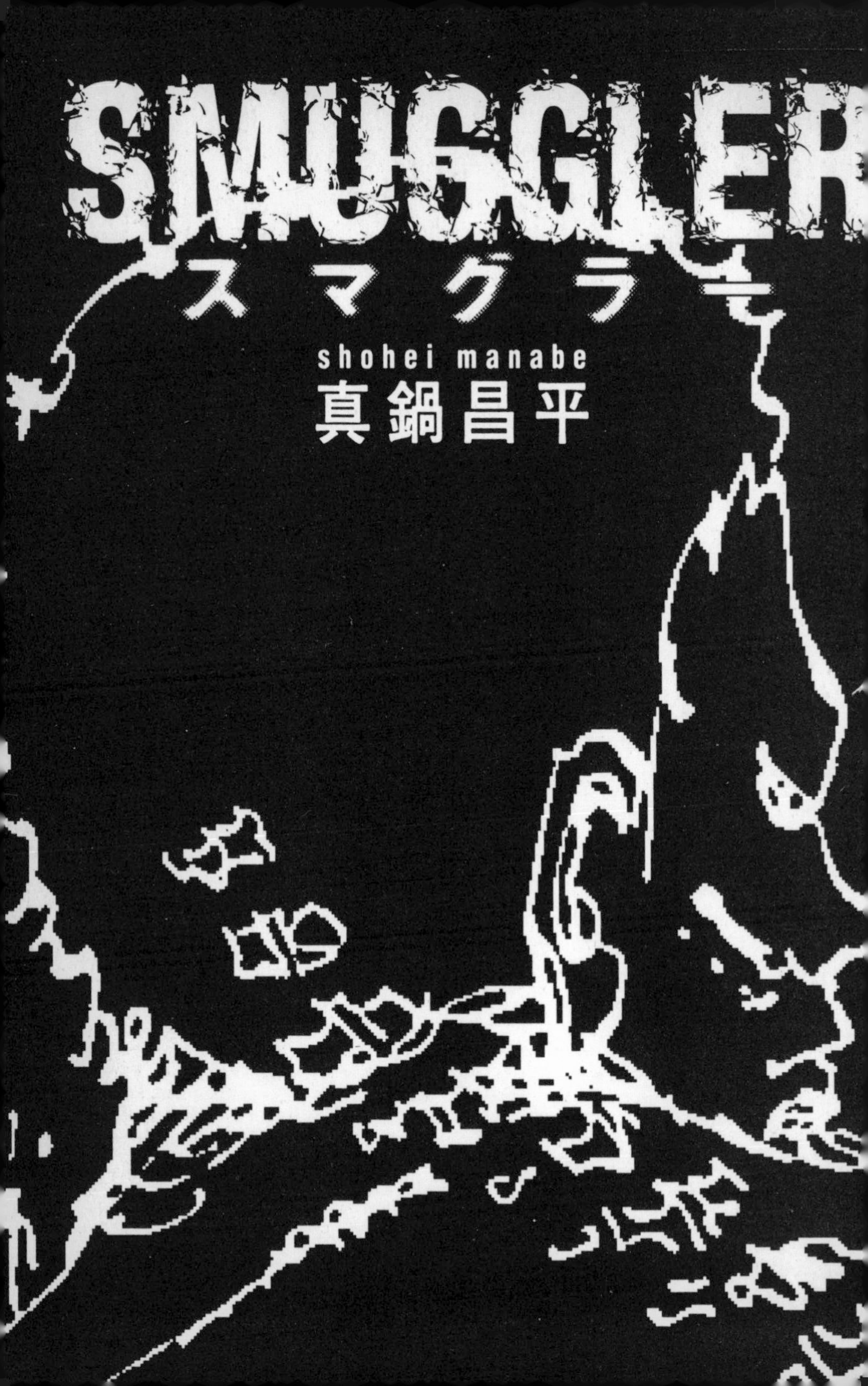

Smuggler Vol. 1
Created by Shohei Manabe

Translation - Sarah Backhouse
English Adaptation - Jay Antani
Copy Editor - Eric Althoff
Retouch and Lettering - Alyson Stetz
Production Artist - Ana Lopez
Cover Design - Thea Willis

Editor - Paul Morrissey
Digital Imaging Manager - Chris Buford
Production Managers - Jennifer Miller and Mutsumi Miyazaki
Managing Editor - Lindsey Johnston
VP of Production - Ron Klamert
Publisher and E.I.C - Mike Kiley
President and C.O.O. - John Parker
C.E.O. - Stuart Levy

A  Manga

TOKYOPOP Inc.
5900 Wilshire Blvd. Suite 2000
Los Angeles, CA 90036

E-mail: info@TOKYOPOP.com
Come visit us online at www.TOKYOPOP.com

ISBN:1-59532-150-0

First TOKYOPOP printing: January 2006
10 9 8 7 6 5 4 3 2 1
Printed in the USA

SMUGGLER

BY
SHOHEI MANABE

HAMBURG // LONDON // LOS ANGELES // TOKYO

Smuggler Character Chart

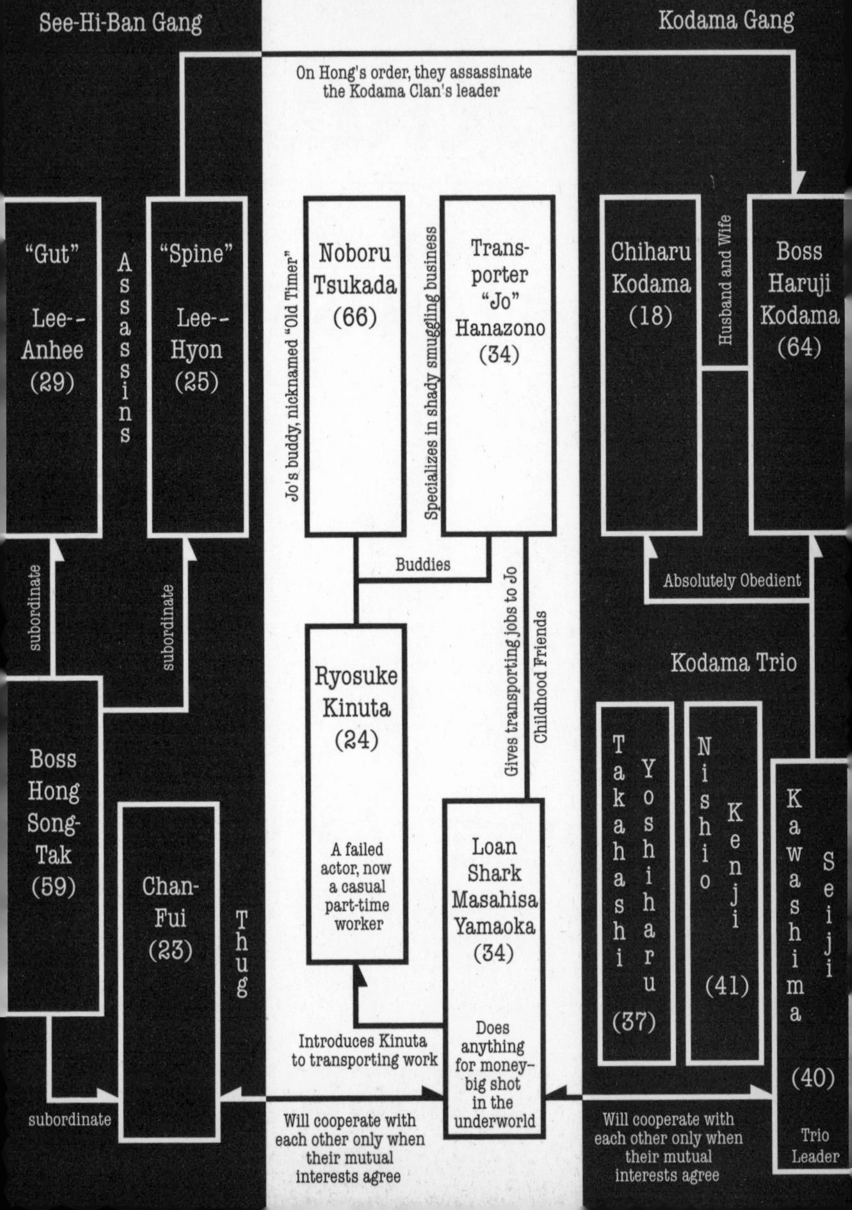
See-Hi-Ban Gang
Kodama Gang
On Hong's order, they assassinate the Kodama Clan's leader
"Gut" Lee--Anhee (29)
Assassins
"Spine" Lee--Hyon (25)
Jo's buddy, nicknamed "Old Timer"
Noboru Tsukada (66)
Specializes in shady smuggling business
Trans-porter "Jo" Hanazono (34)
Chiharu Kodama (18)
Husband and Wife
Boss Haruji Kodama (64)
subordinate
subordinate
Buddies
Absolutely Obedient
Kodama Trio
Gives transporting jobs to Jo
Childhood Friends
Ryosuke Kinuta (24)
A failed actor, now a casual part-time worker
Boss Hong Song-Tak (59)
Chan-Fui (23)
Thug
Loan Shark Masahisa Yamaoka (34)
Does anything for money-big shot in the underworld
Takahashi Yoshiharu (37)
Nishio Kenji (41)
Kawashima Seiji (40)
Trio Leader
Introduces Kinuta to transporting work
subordinate
Will cooperate with each other only when their mutual interests agree
Will cooperate with each other only when their mutual interests agree

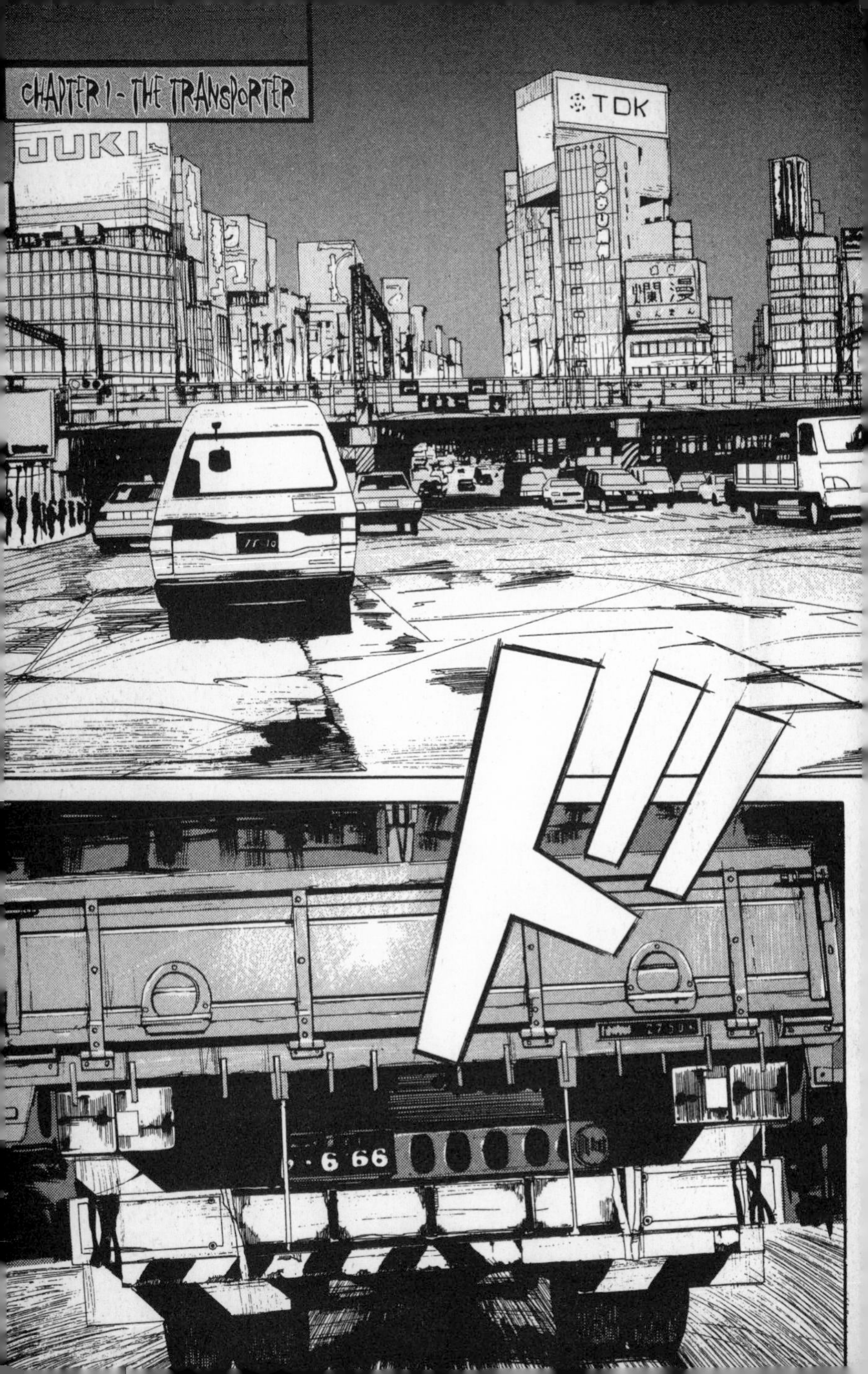
CHAPTER 1 - THE TRANSPORTER
TDK
爛漫
JUKI
ド

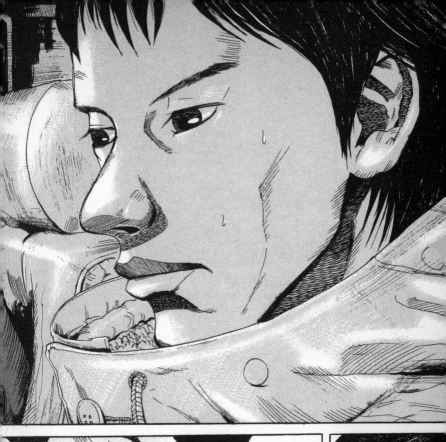

MANY COUNTRIES ARE IN A STATE OF FINANCIAL CRISIS, BUT...

...JAPAN'S IN ESPECIALLY BAD SHAPE, DON'T YOU THINK?

HERE THE RICH ARE GETTING RICHER AND THE POOR ARE GETTING POORER. IT'S EVEN WORSE THAN IN THE STATES.

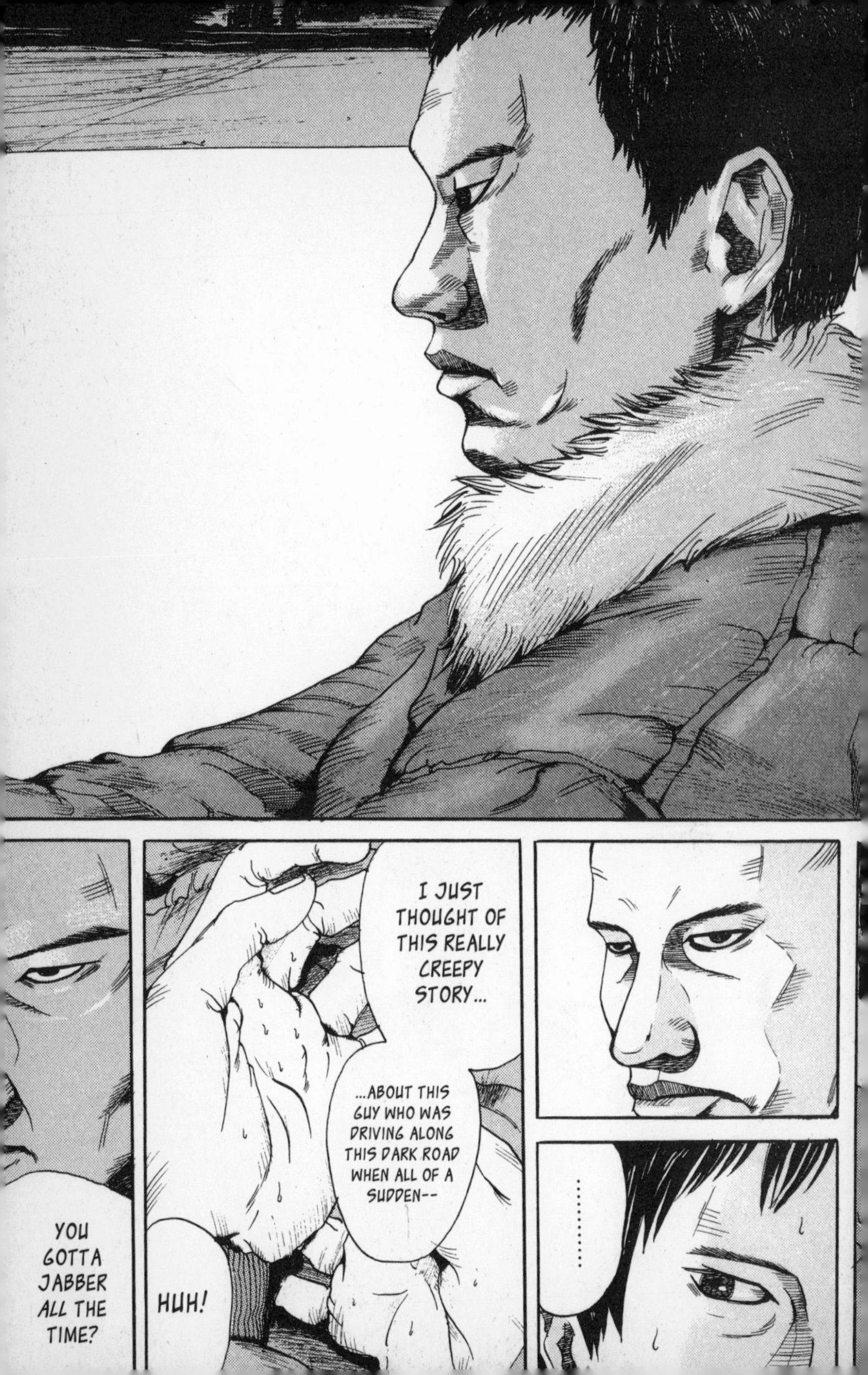
......
I JUST THOUGHT OF THIS REALLY CREEPY STORY...
...ABOUT THIS GUY WHO WAS DRIVING ALONG THIS DARK ROAD WHEN ALL OF A SUDDEN--
HUH!
YOU GOTTA JABBER ALL THE TIME?

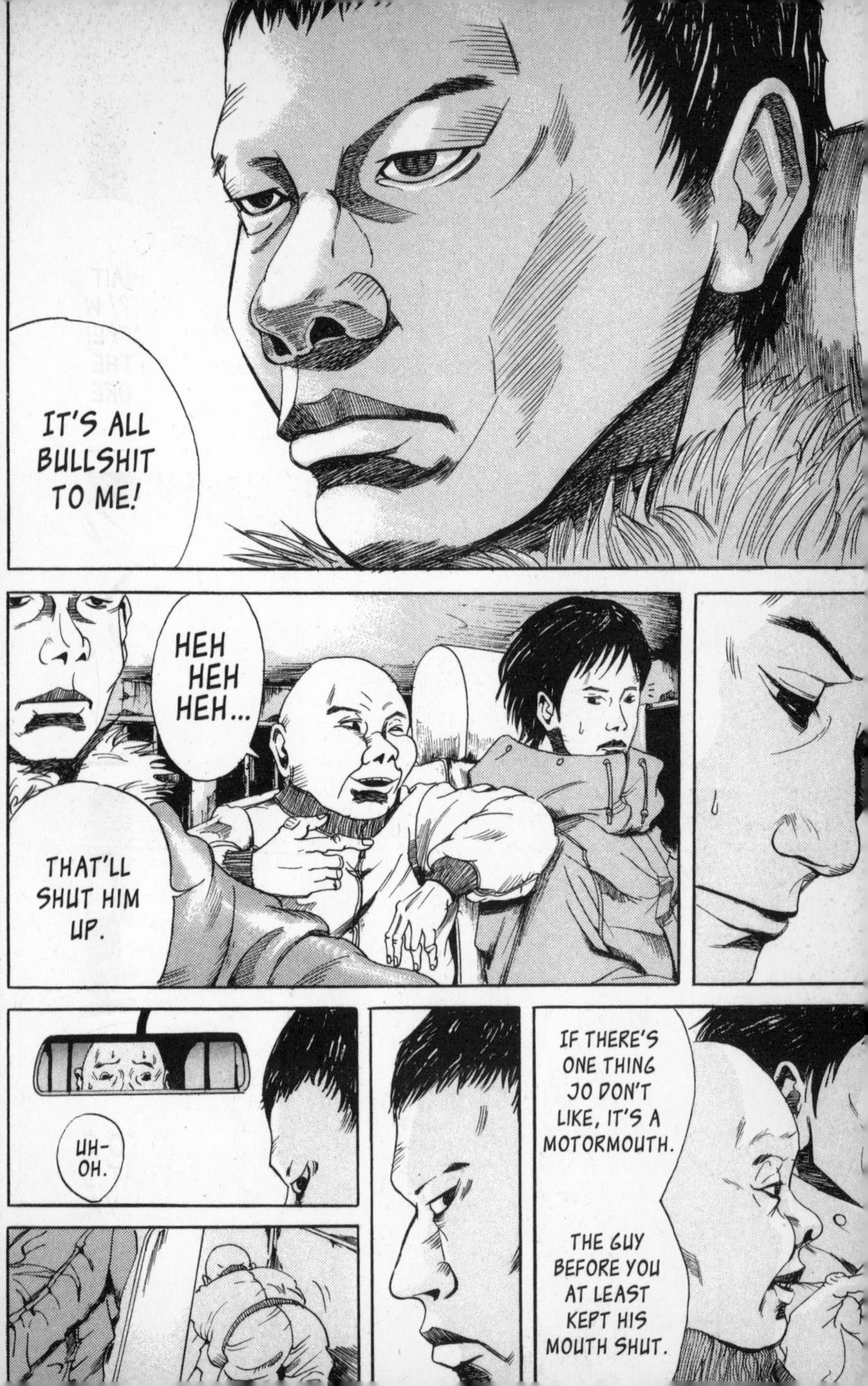
IT'S ALL BULLSHIT TO ME!
HEH HEH HEH...
THAT'LL SHUT HIM UP.
IF THERE'S ONE THING JO DON'T LIKE, IT'S A MOTORMOUTH.
THE GUY BEFORE YOU AT LEAST KEPT HIS MOUTH SHUT.
UH-OH.

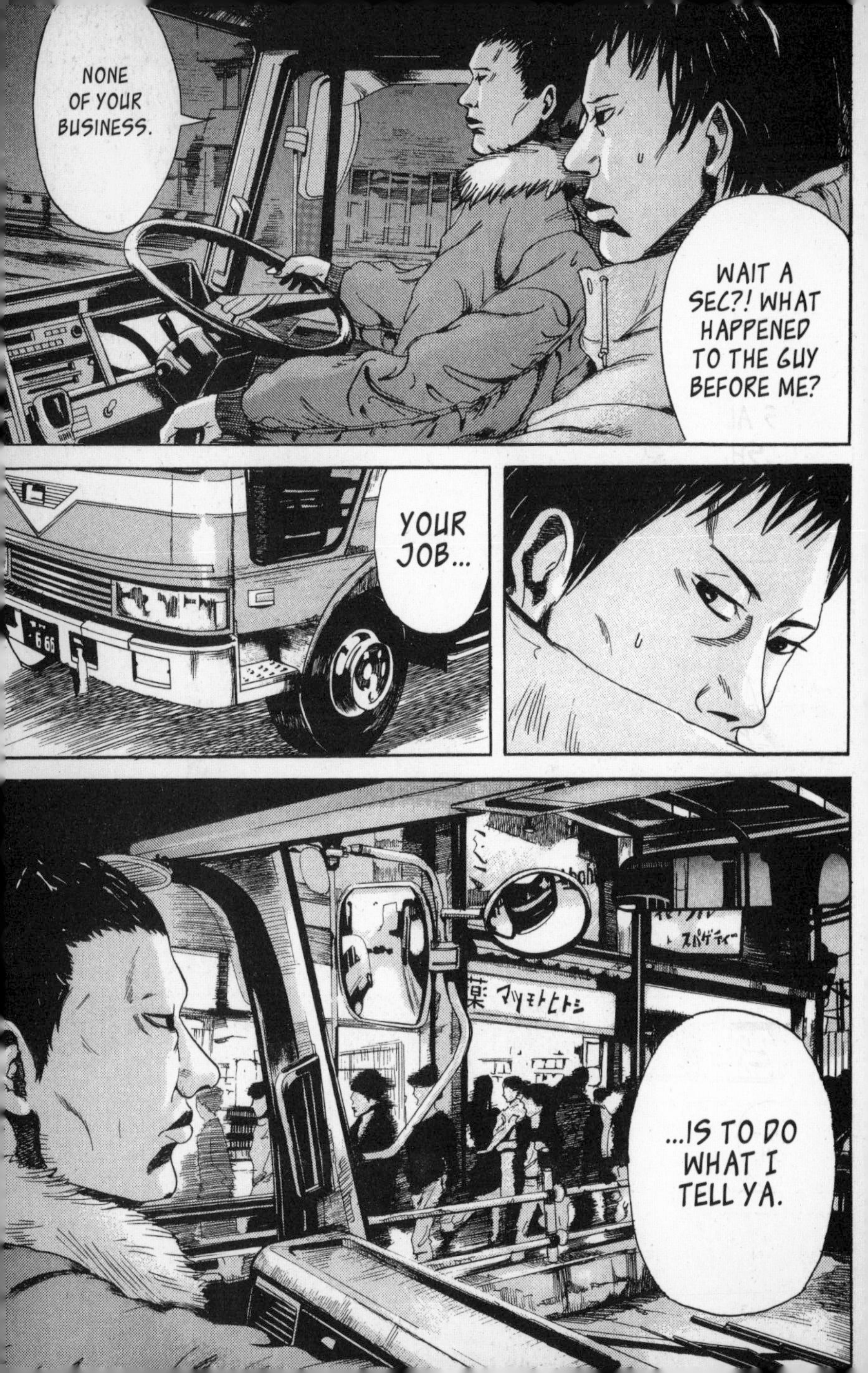
WAIT A SEC?! WHAT HAPPENED TO THE GUY BEFORE ME?
NONE OF YOUR BUSINESS.
YOUR JOB...
スパゲティー
薬 マツモトヒトシ
...IS TO DO WHAT I TELL YA.

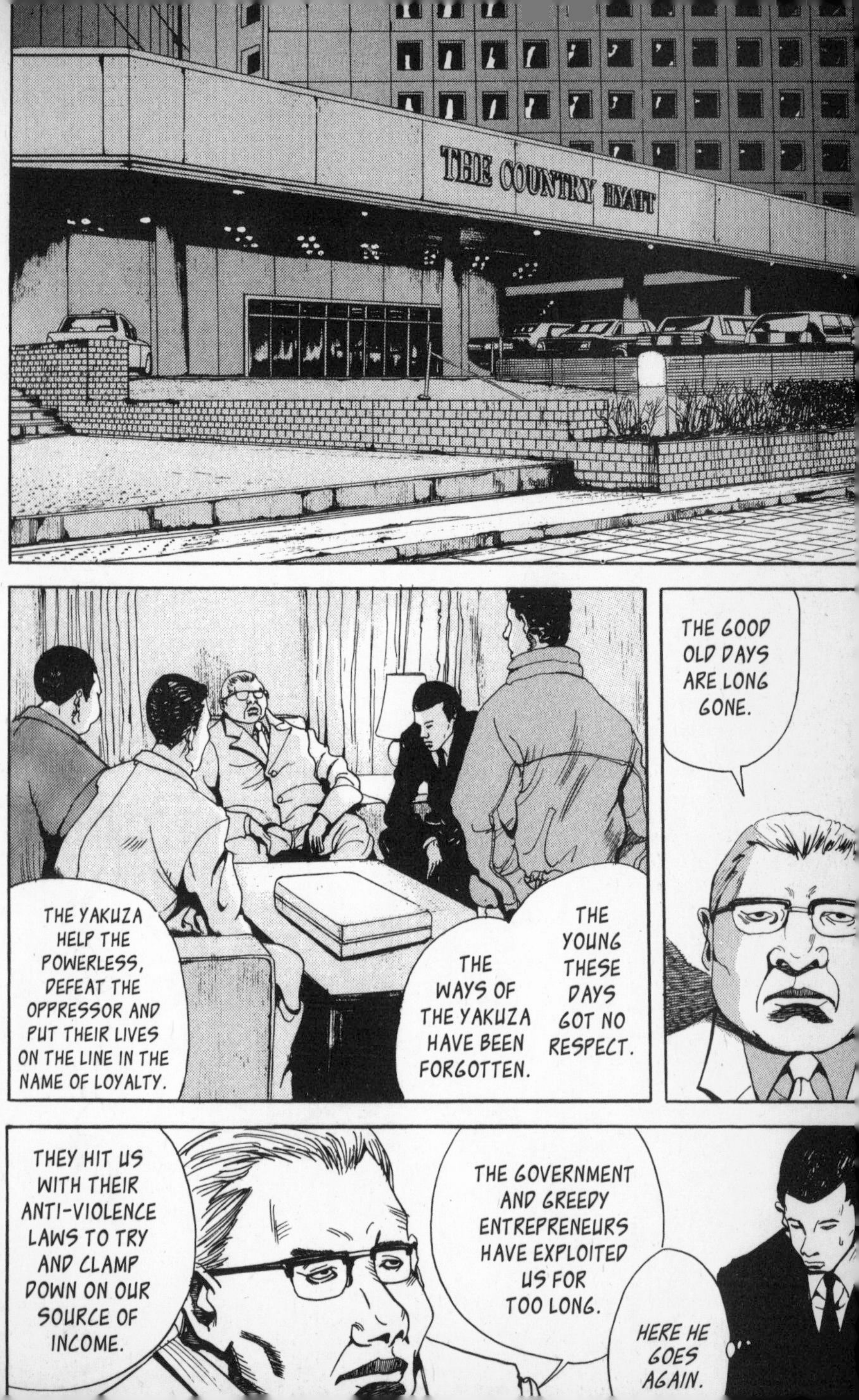
THE COUNTRY HYATT
THE GOOD OLD DAYS ARE LONG GONE.
THE YOUNG THESE DAYS GOT NO RESPECT.
THE WAYS OF THE YAKUZA HAVE BEEN FORGOTTEN.
THE YAKUZA HELP THE POWERLESS, DEFEAT THE OPPRESSOR AND PUT THEIR LIVES ON THE LINE IN THE NAME OF LOYALTY.
THE GOVERNMENT AND GREEDY ENTREPRENEURS HAVE EXPLOITED US FOR TOO LONG.
THEY HIT US WITH THEIR ANTI-VIOLENCE LAWS TO TRY AND CLAMP DOWN ON OUR SOURCE OF INCOME.
HERE HE GOES AGAIN.

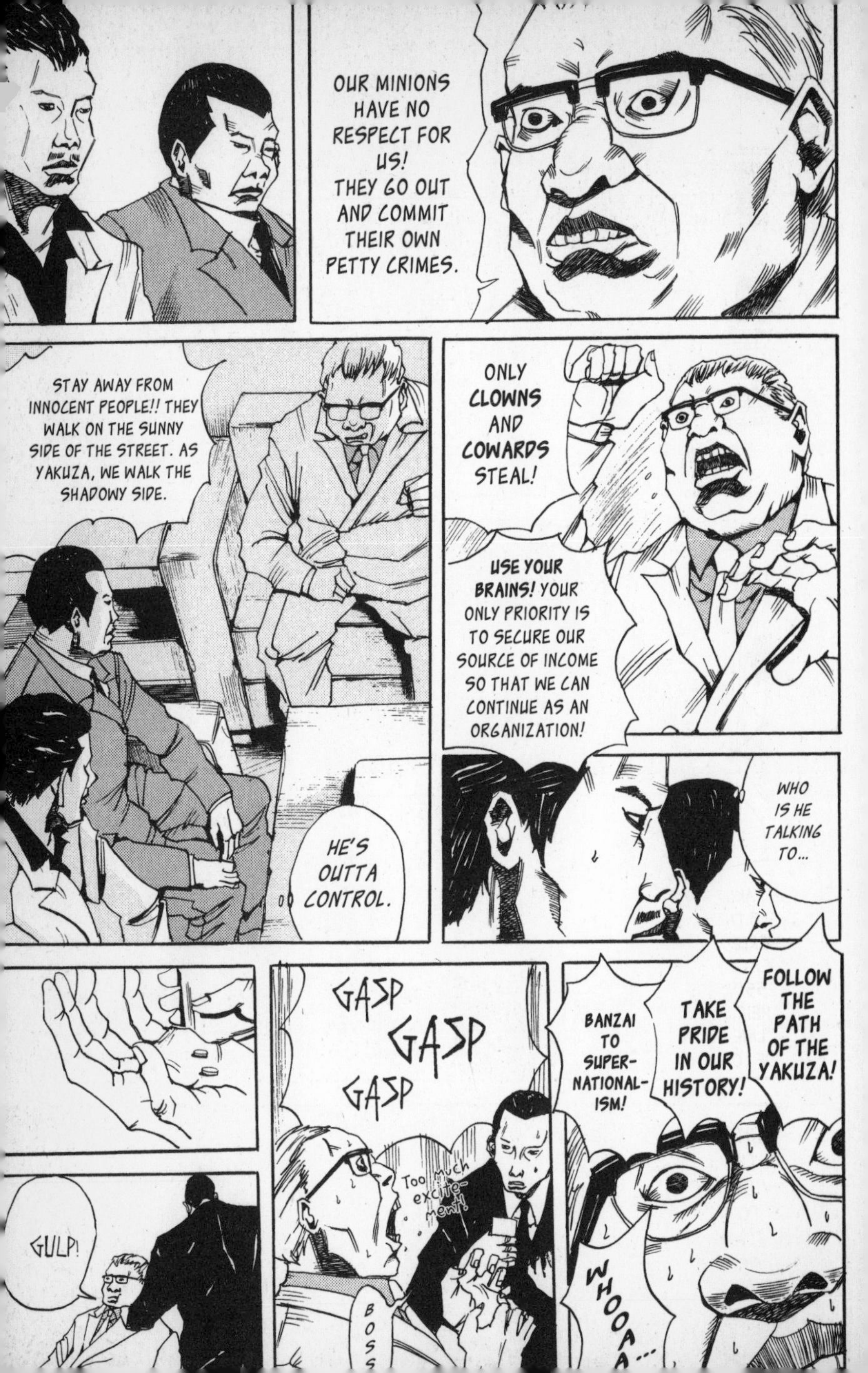
OUR MINIONS HAVE NO RESPECT FOR US!
THEY GO OUT AND COMMIT THEIR OWN PETTY CRIMES.
ONLY CLOWNS AND COWARDS STEAL!
USE YOUR BRAINS! YOUR ONLY PRIORITY IS TO SECURE OUR SOURCE OF INCOME SO THAT WE CAN CONTINUE AS AN ORGANIZATION!
WHO IS HE TALKING TO...
STAY AWAY FROM INNOCENT PEOPLE!! THEY WALK ON THE SUNNY SIDE OF THE STREET. AS YAKUZA, WE WALK THE SHADOWY SIDE.
HE'S OUTTA CONTROL.
FOLLOW THE PATH OF THE YAKUZA!
TAKE PRIDE IN OUR HISTORY!
BANZAI TO SUPER-NATIONAL-ISM!
WHOOAA...
GASP
GASP
GASP
Too much excite-ment!
BOSS
GULP!

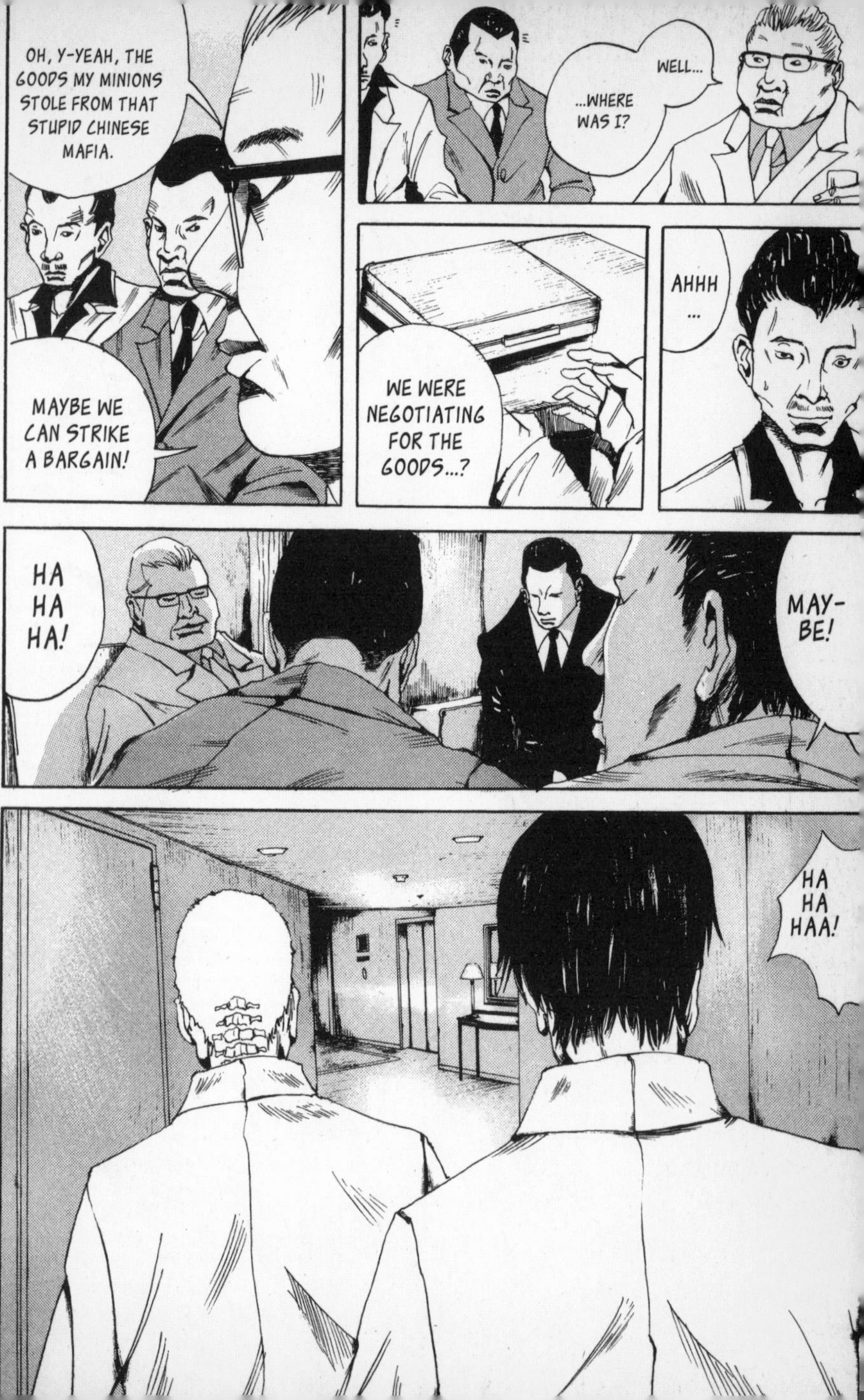
WELL...
...WHERE WAS I?
AHHH...
WE WERE NEGOTIATING FOR THE GOODS...?
OH, Y-YEAH, THE GOODS MY MINIONS STOLE FROM THAT STUPID CHINESE MAFIA.
MAYBE WE CAN STRIKE A BARGAIN!
MAY-BE!
HA HA HA!
HA HA HAA!

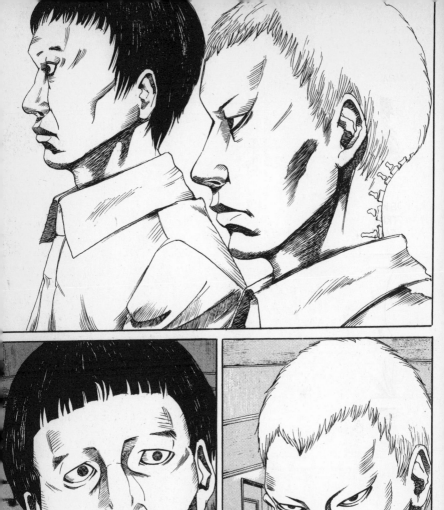

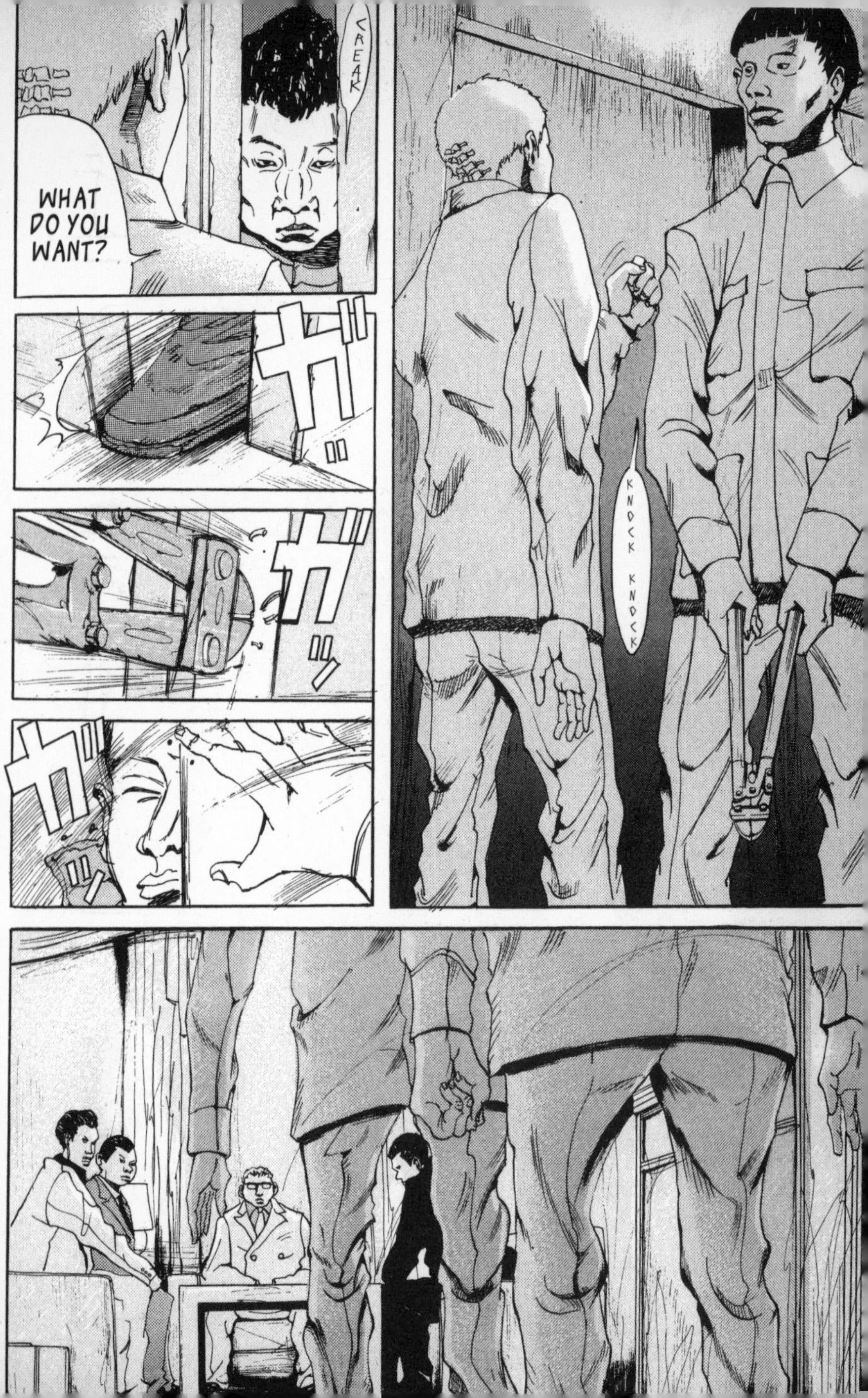

KNOCK KNOCK
CREAK
WHAT DO YOU WANT?
ガッ
ガッ
ガッ

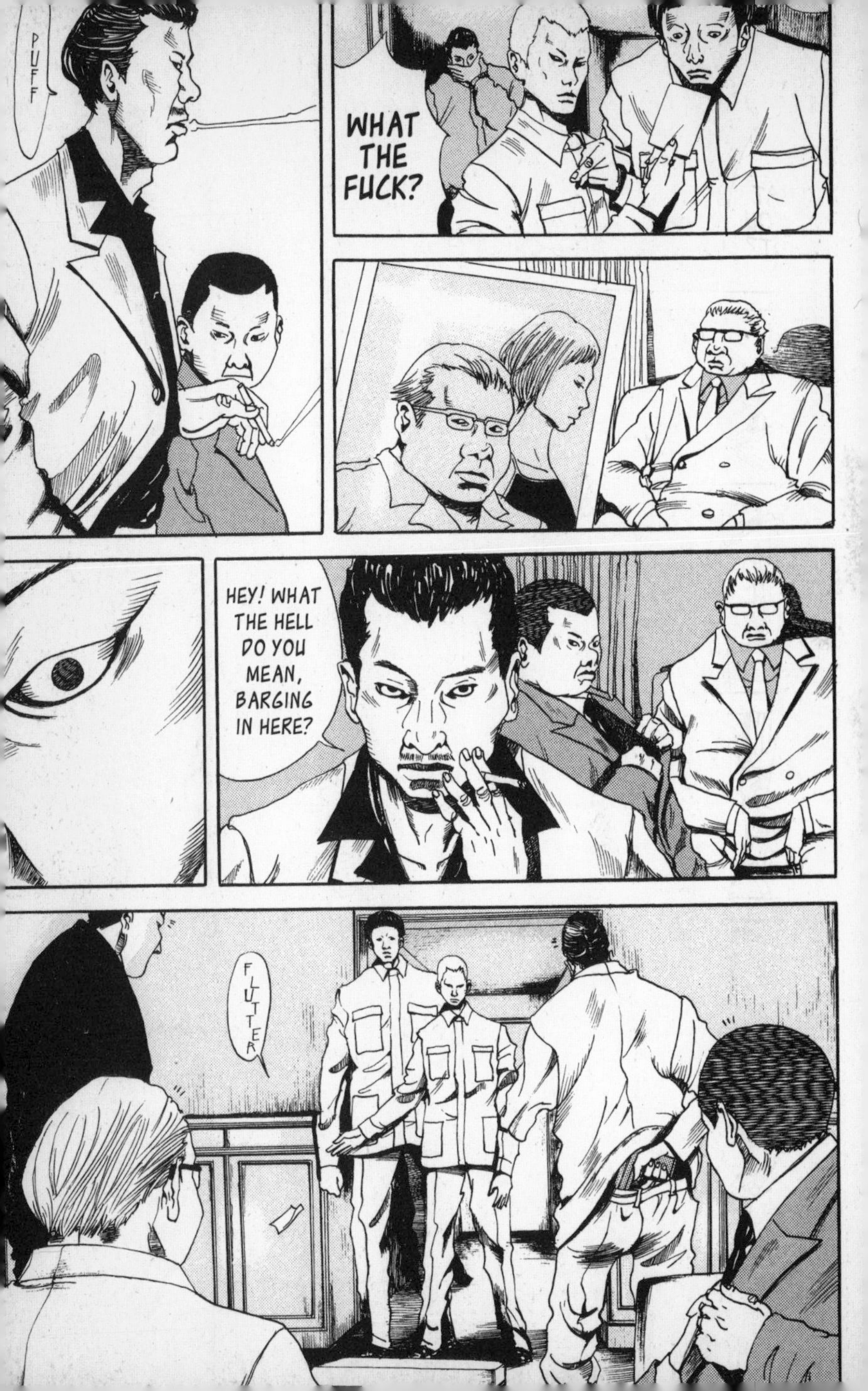
WHAT THE FUCK?
PUFF
HEY! WHAT THE HELL DO YOU MEAN, BARGING IN HERE?
FLUTTER

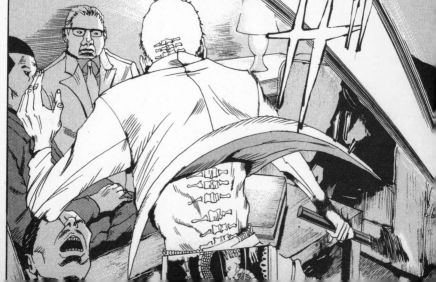

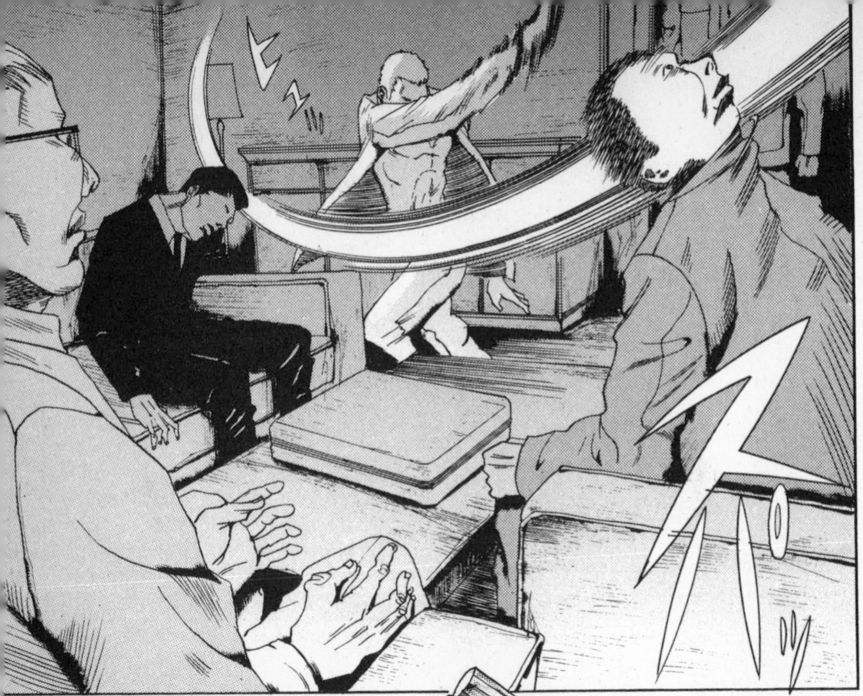
ヒュ
スパッ

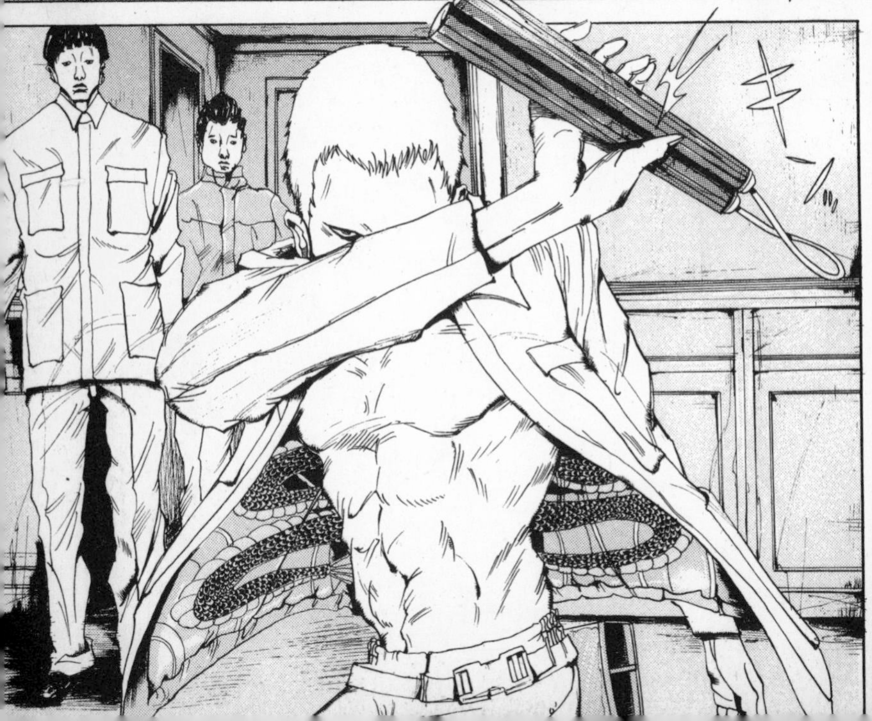
キン

LITTLE
SHIT!

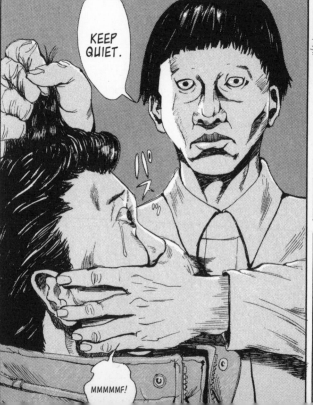

KEEP
QUIET.

MMMMMF!

AHHHHHH!

GAH!

SHUT UP!

AAAH!

AAAH!

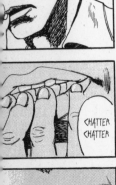

CHATTER CHATTER

YIKES!

SLIP

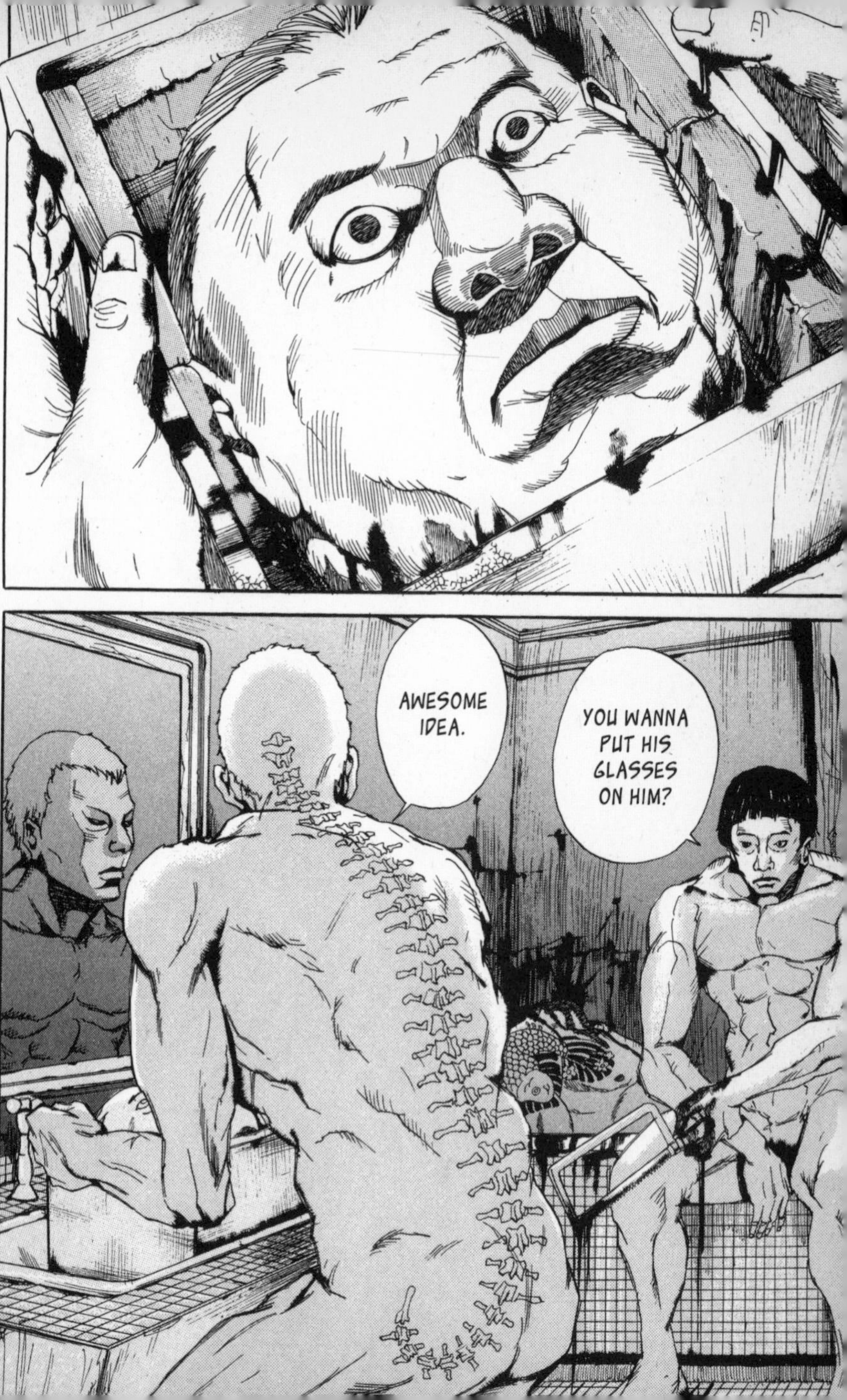
YOU WANNA PUT HIS GLASSES ON HIM?
AWESOME IDEA.

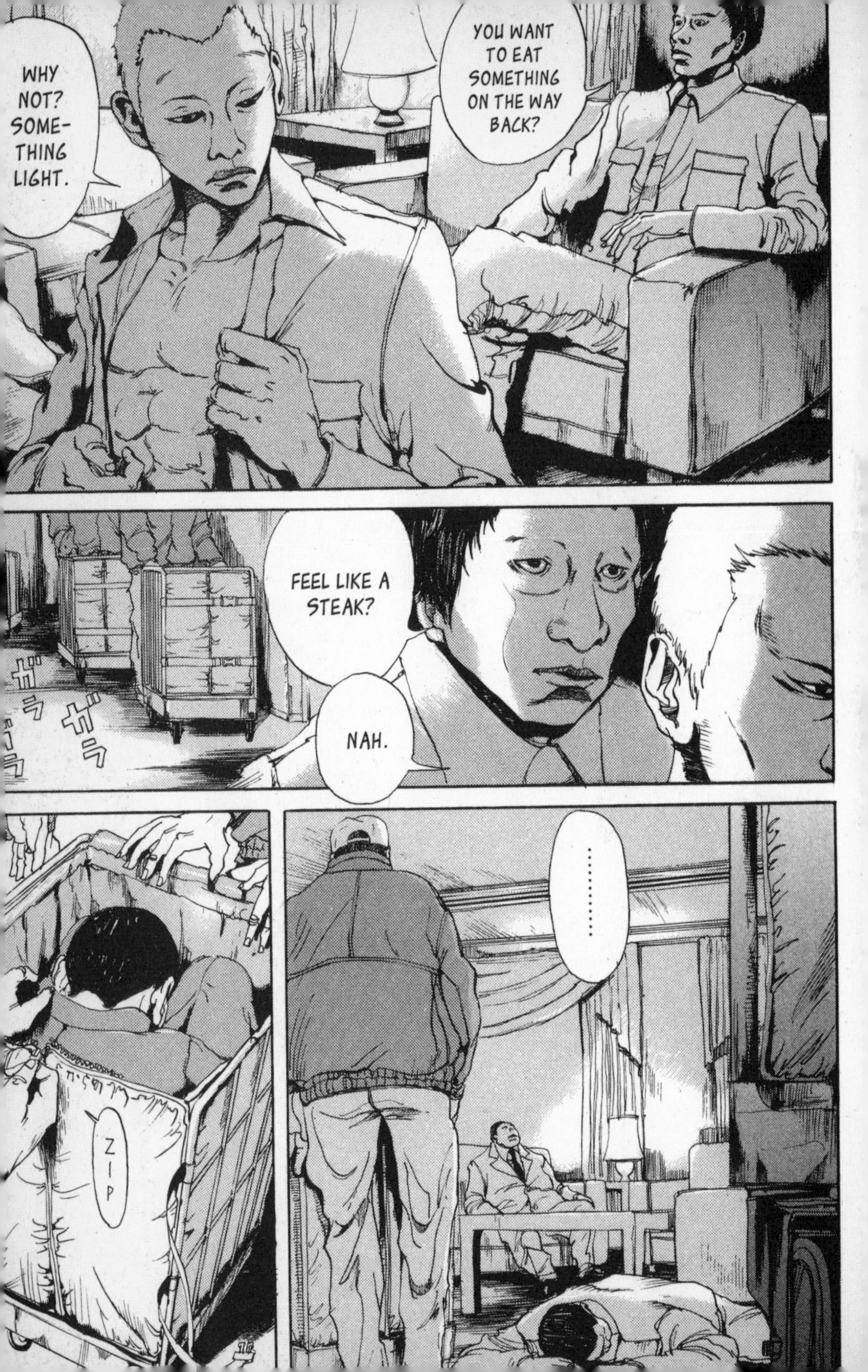
YOU WANT TO EAT SOMETHING ON THE WAY BACK?
WHY NOT? SOME-THING LIGHT.
FEEL LIKE A STEAK?
NAH.
ガラ ガラ
....
ZIP

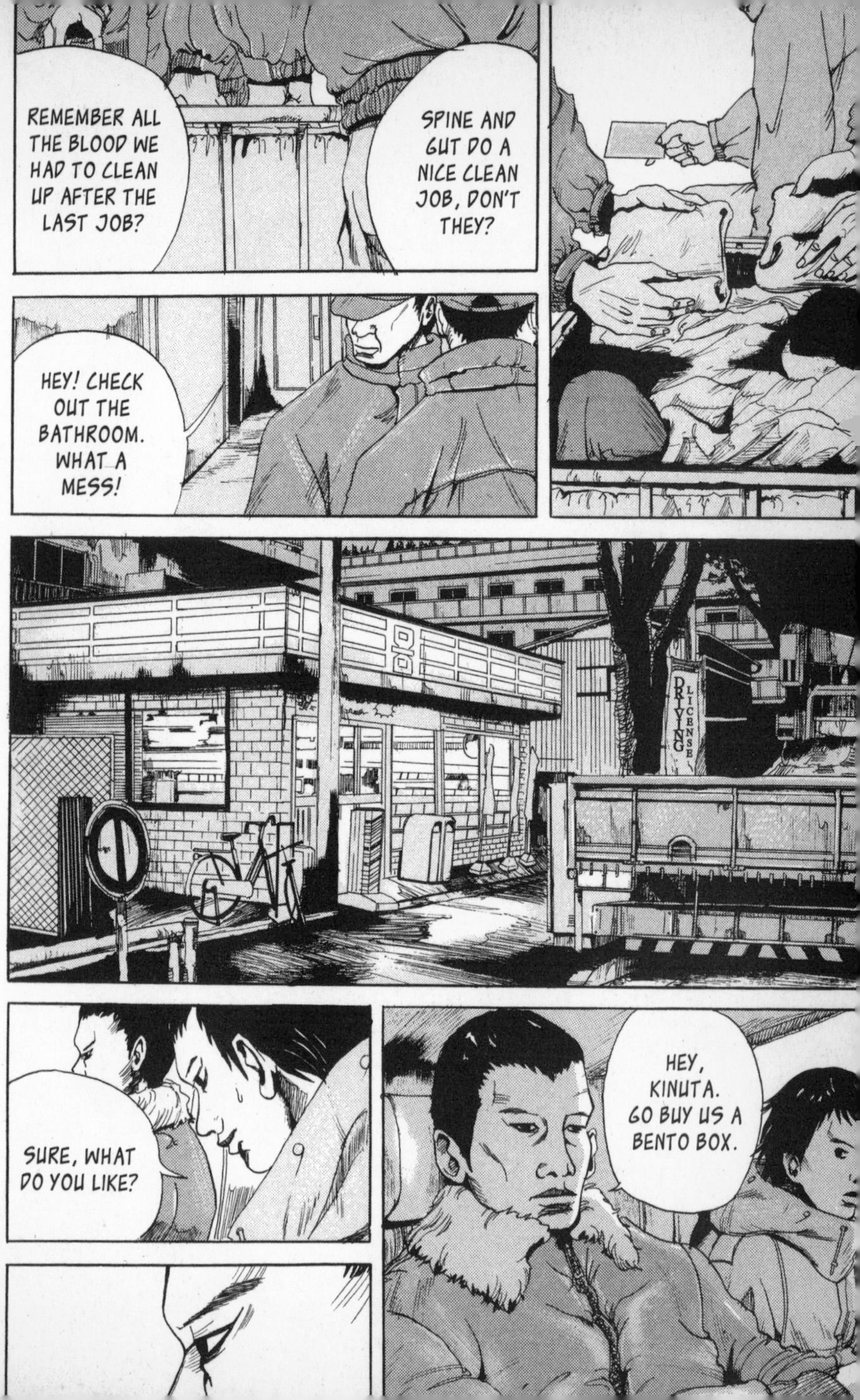
SPINE AND GUT DO A NICE CLEAN JOB, DON'T THEY?
REMEMBER ALL THE BLOOD WE HAD TO CLEAN UP AFTER THE LAST JOB?
HEY! CHECK OUT THE BATHROOM. WHAT A MESS!
DRIVING LICENSE
HEY, KINUTA. GO BUY US A BENTO BOX.
SURE, WHAT DO YOU LIKE?

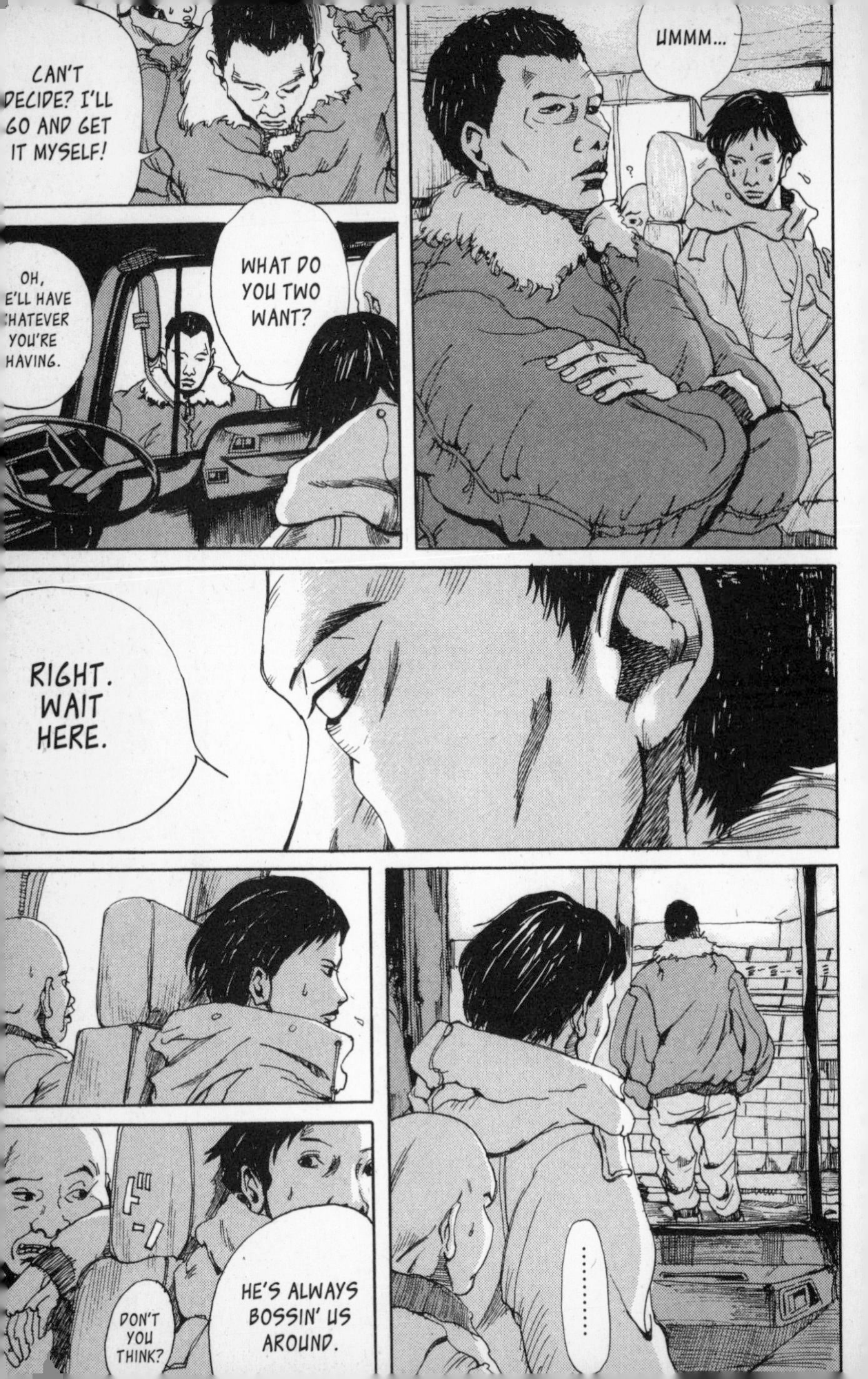
UMMM...
CAN'T DECIDE? I'LL GO AND GET IT MYSELF!
WHAT DO YOU TWO WANT?
OH, E'LL HAVE HATEVER YOU'RE HAVING.
RIGHT. WAIT HERE.
......
HE'S ALWAYS BOSSIN' US AROUND.
DON'T YOU THINK?

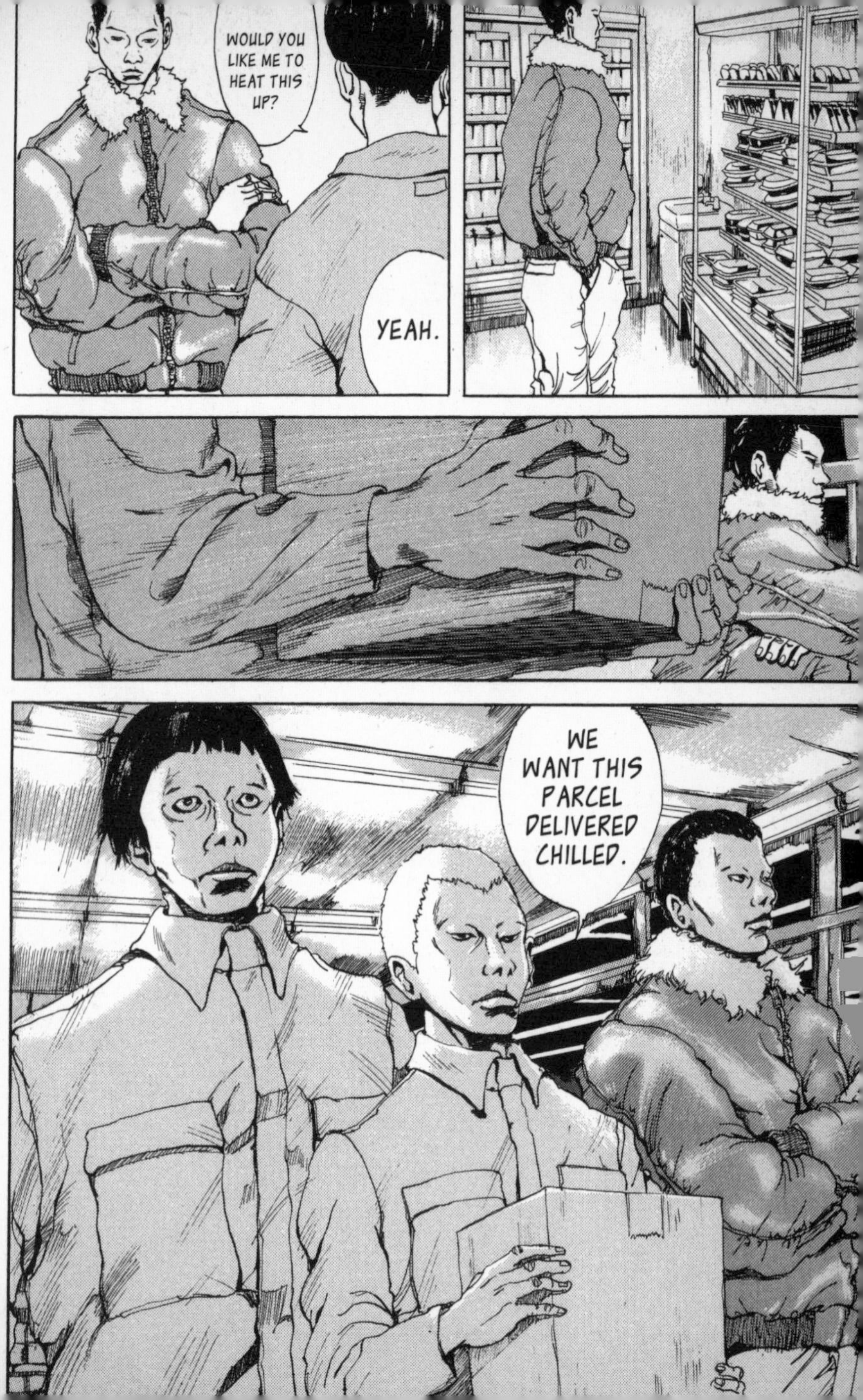
WOULD YOU LIKE ME TO HEAT THIS UP?
YEAH.
WE WANT THIS PARCEL DELIVERED CHILLED.

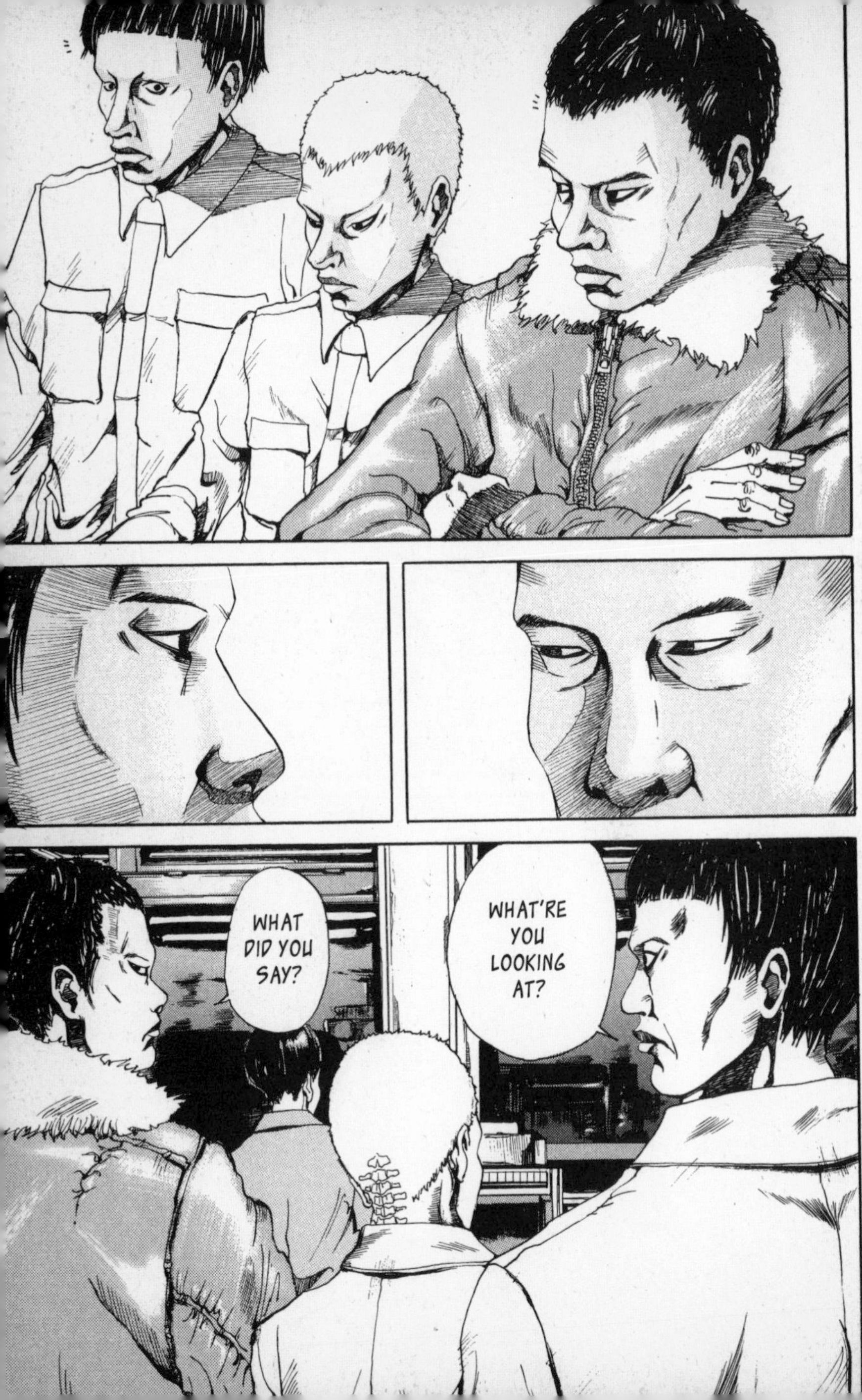
WHAT'RE YOU LOOKING AT?
WHAT DID YOU SAY?

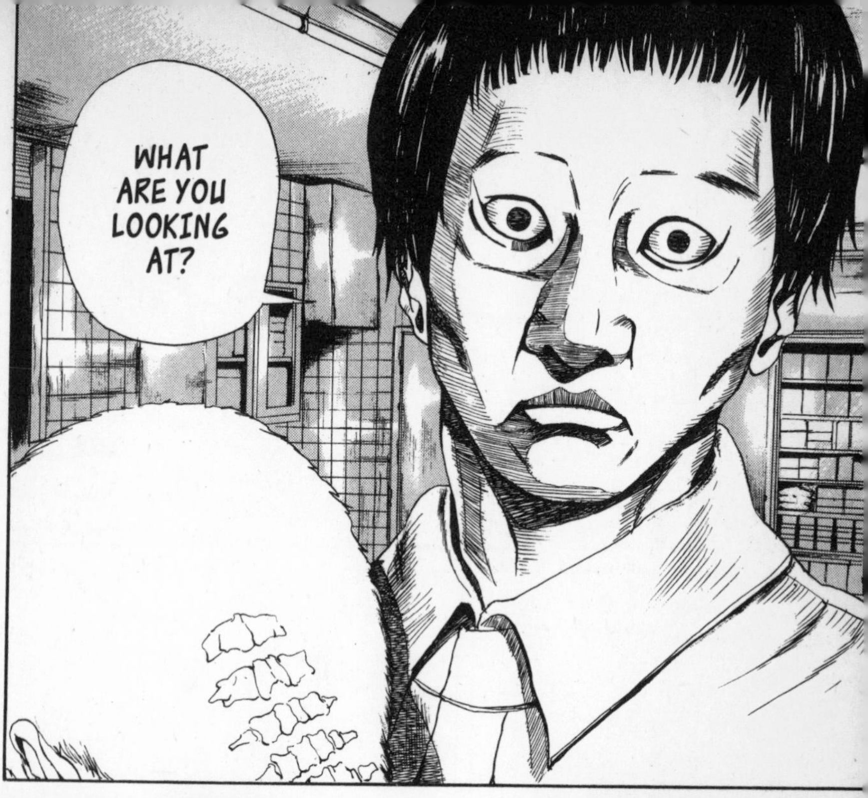
WHAT ARE YOU LOOKING AT?
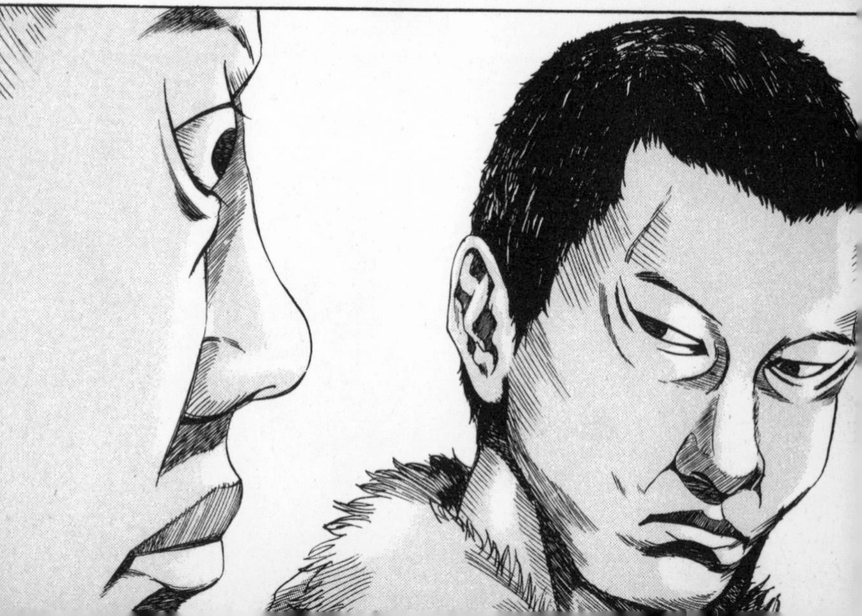

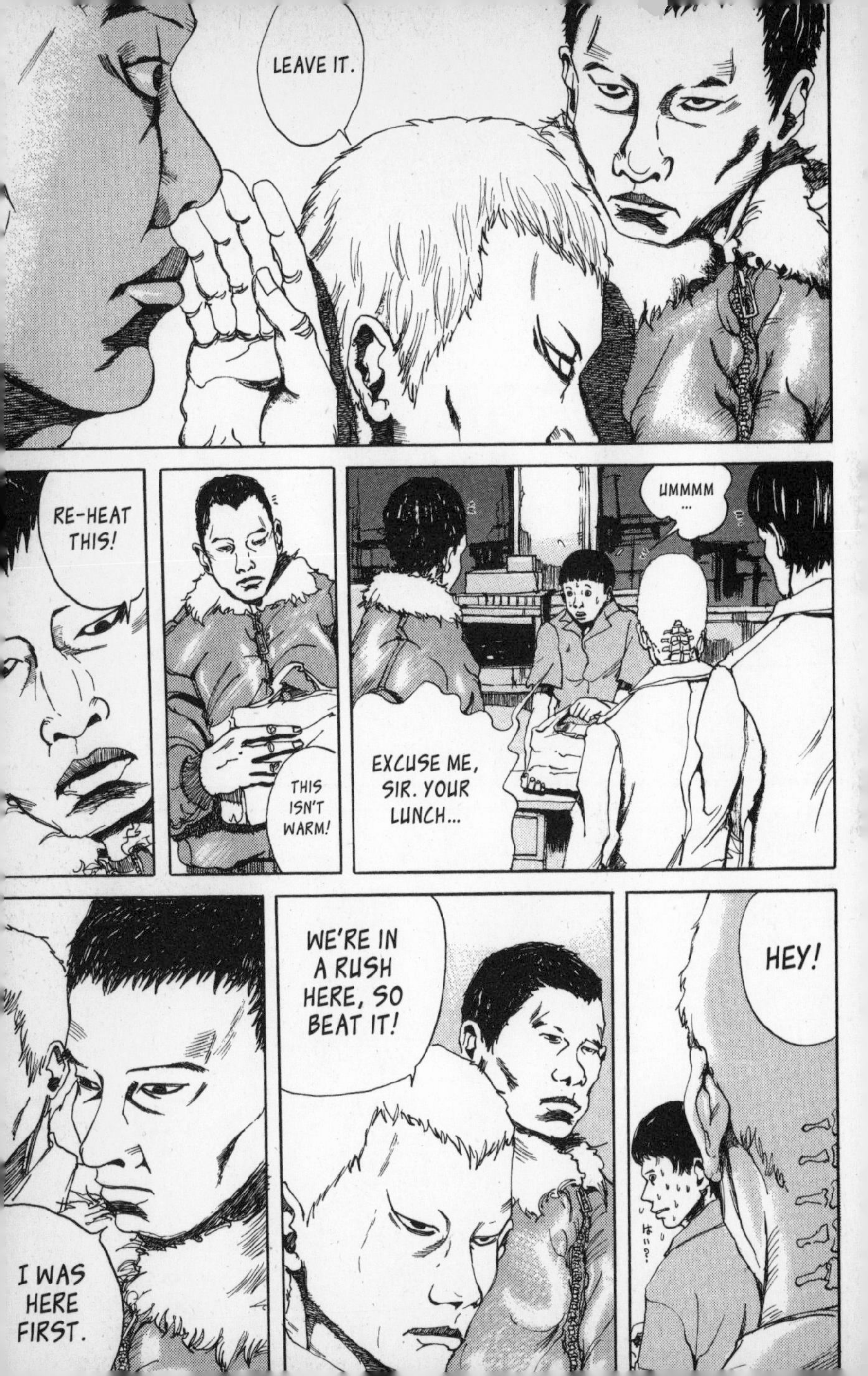
LEAVE IT.
UMMMM ...
EXCUSE ME, SIR. YOUR LUNCH...
THIS ISN'T WARM!
RE-HEAT THIS!
HEY!
WE'RE IN A RUSH HERE, SO BEAT IT!
I WAS HERE FIRST.

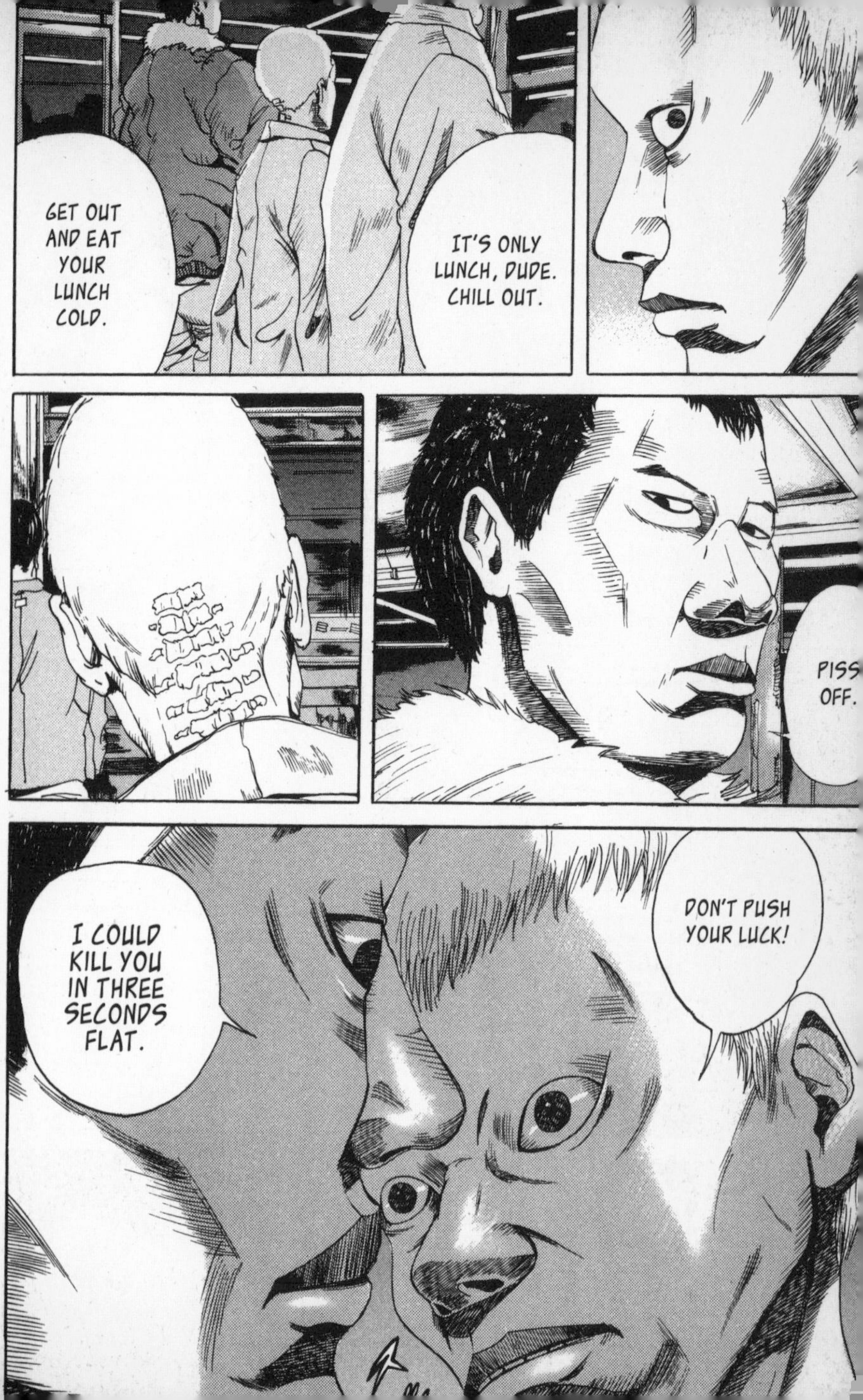
IT'S ONLY LUNCH, DUDE. CHILL OUT.
GET OUT AND EAT YOUR LUNCH COLD.
PISS OFF.
DON'T PUSH YOUR LUCK!
I COULD KILL YOU IN THREE SECONDS FLAT.

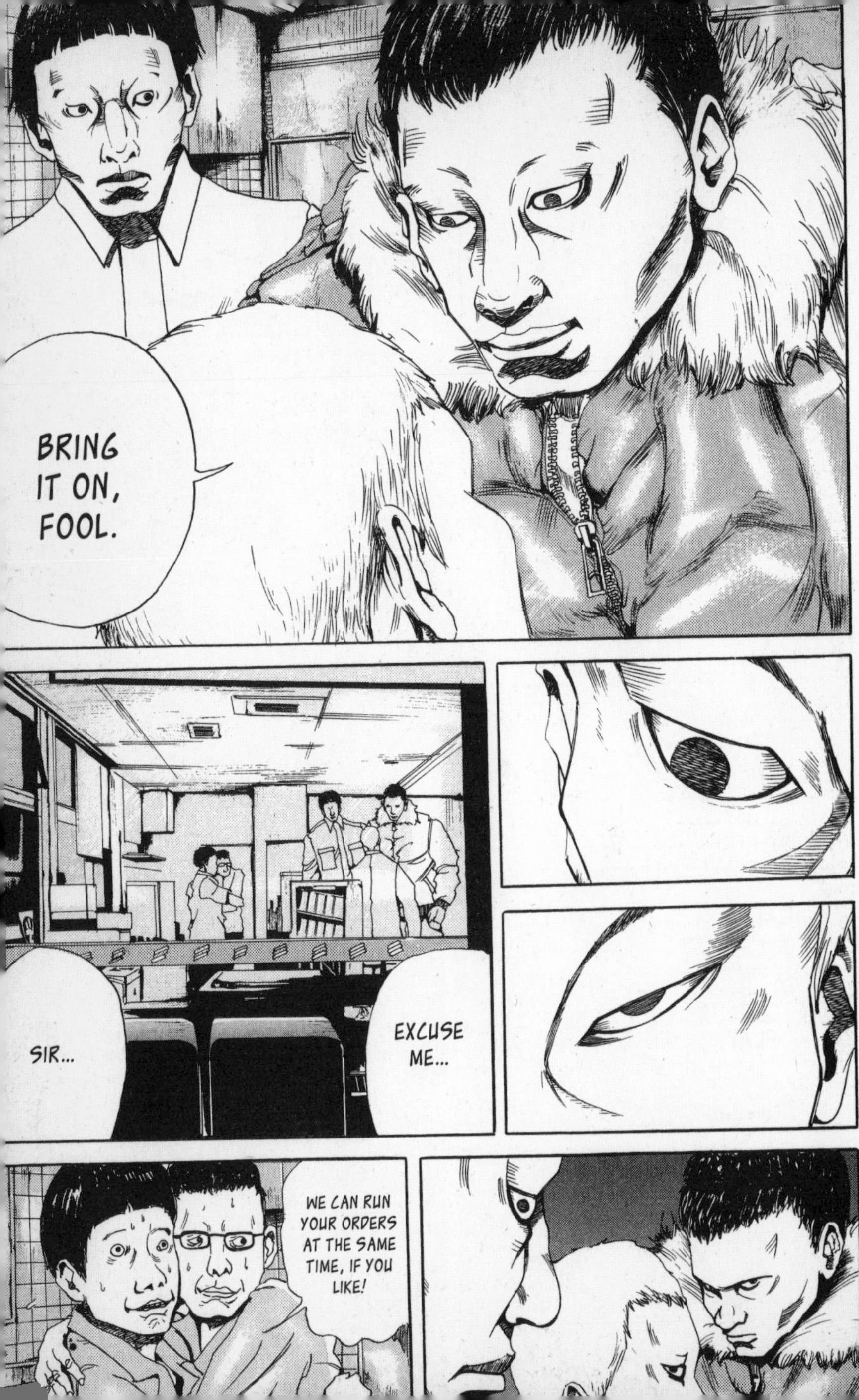
BRING IT ON, FOOL.
EXCUSE ME...
SIR...
WE CAN RUN YOUR ORDERS AT THE SAME TIME, IF YOU LIKE!

YOUR ASS
WAS SAVED BY
A COUPLE OF
GIRLIE-MEN.
REMEMBER THAT.

HEH
HEH!

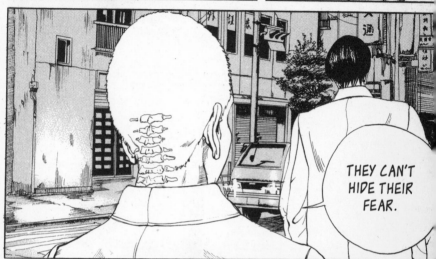

THEY CAN'T
HIDE THEIR
FEAR.

YOU SURE
TOOK A
WHILE. WHAT
HAPPENED?

NOTHING,
NOW SHUT
UP!

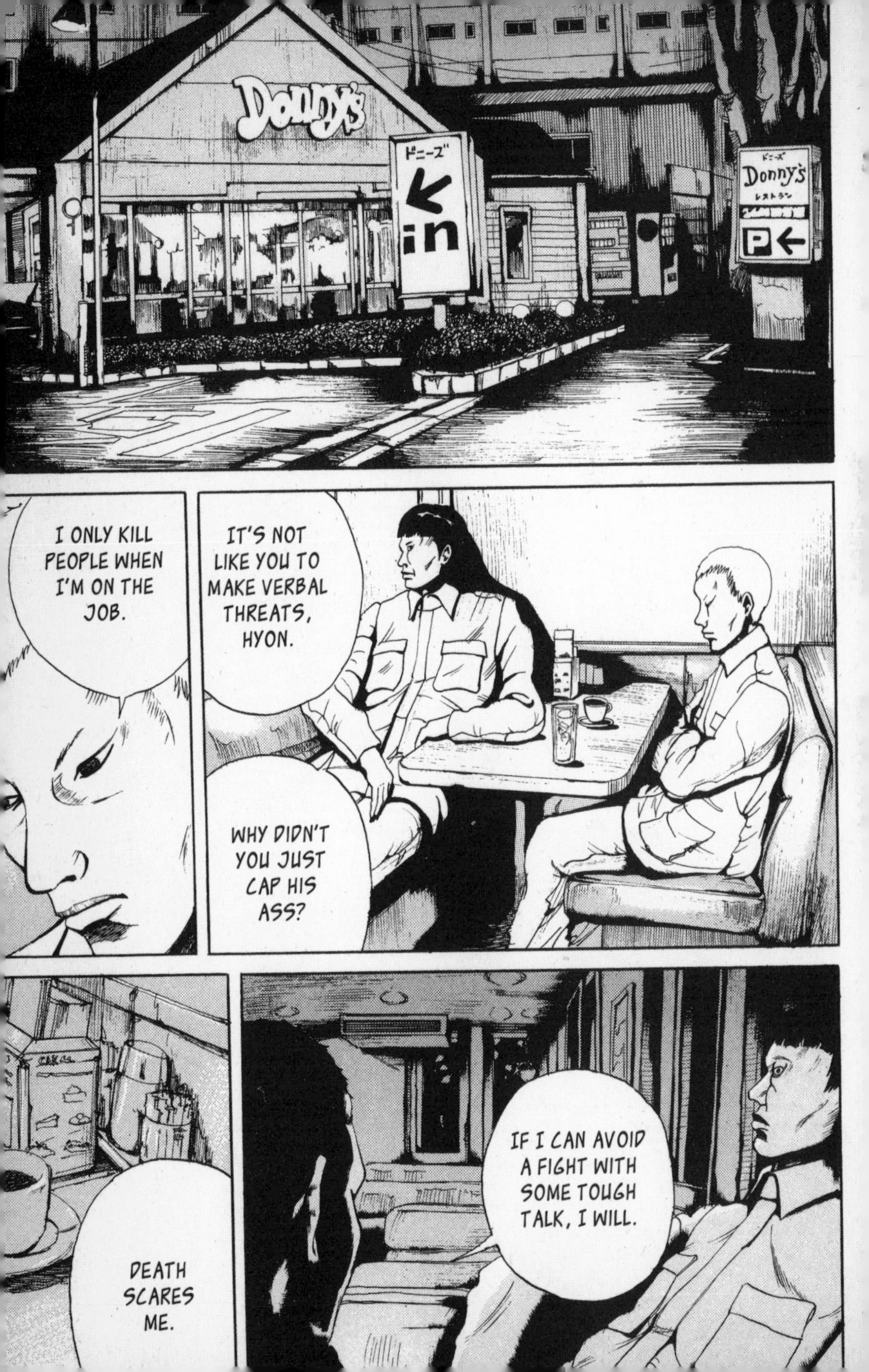
Donny's
ドニーズ
in
ドニーズ
Donny's
レストラン
P
IT'S NOT LIKE YOU TO MAKE VERBAL THREATS, HYON.
WHY DIDN'T YOU JUST CAP HIS ASS?
I ONLY KILL PEOPLE WHEN I'M ON THE JOB.
IF I CAN AVOID A FIGHT WITH SOME TOUGH TALK, I WILL.
DEATH SCARES ME.

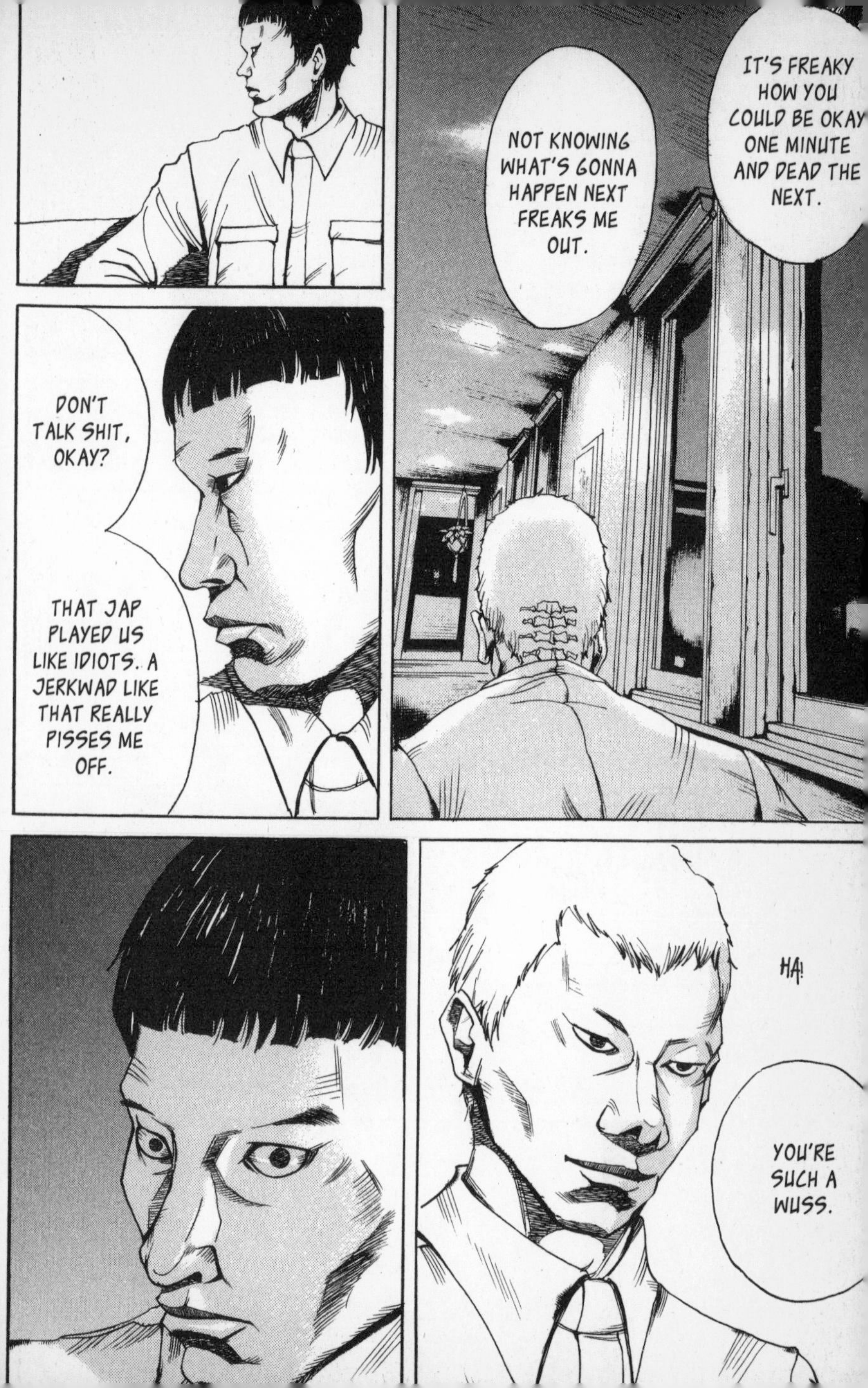
IT'S FREAKY HOW YOU COULD BE OKAY ONE MINUTE AND DEAD THE NEXT.
NOT KNOWING WHAT'S GONNA HAPPEN NEXT FREAKS ME OUT.
DON'T TALK SHIT, OKAY?
THAT JAP PLAYED US LIKE IDIOTS.. A JERKWAD LIKE THAT REALLY PISSES ME OFF.
HA!
YOU'RE SUCH A WUSS.

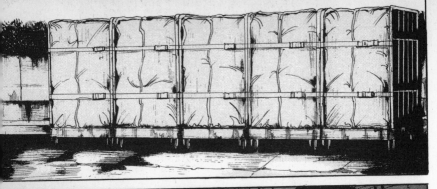

ZIP THE REST OF THAT UP!

KINUTA!

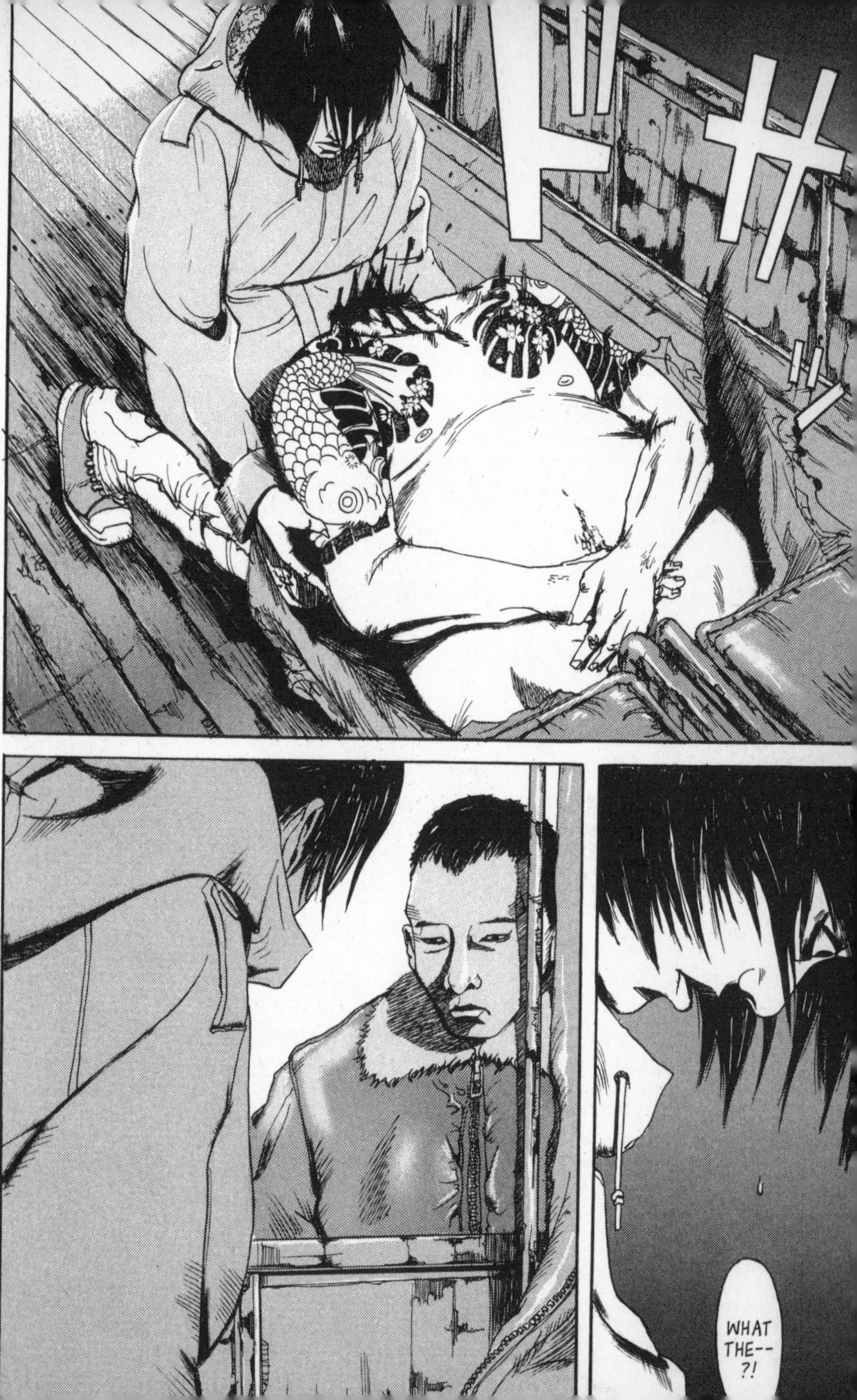
ドサ
WHAT THE-- ?!

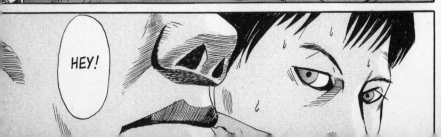

HEY!

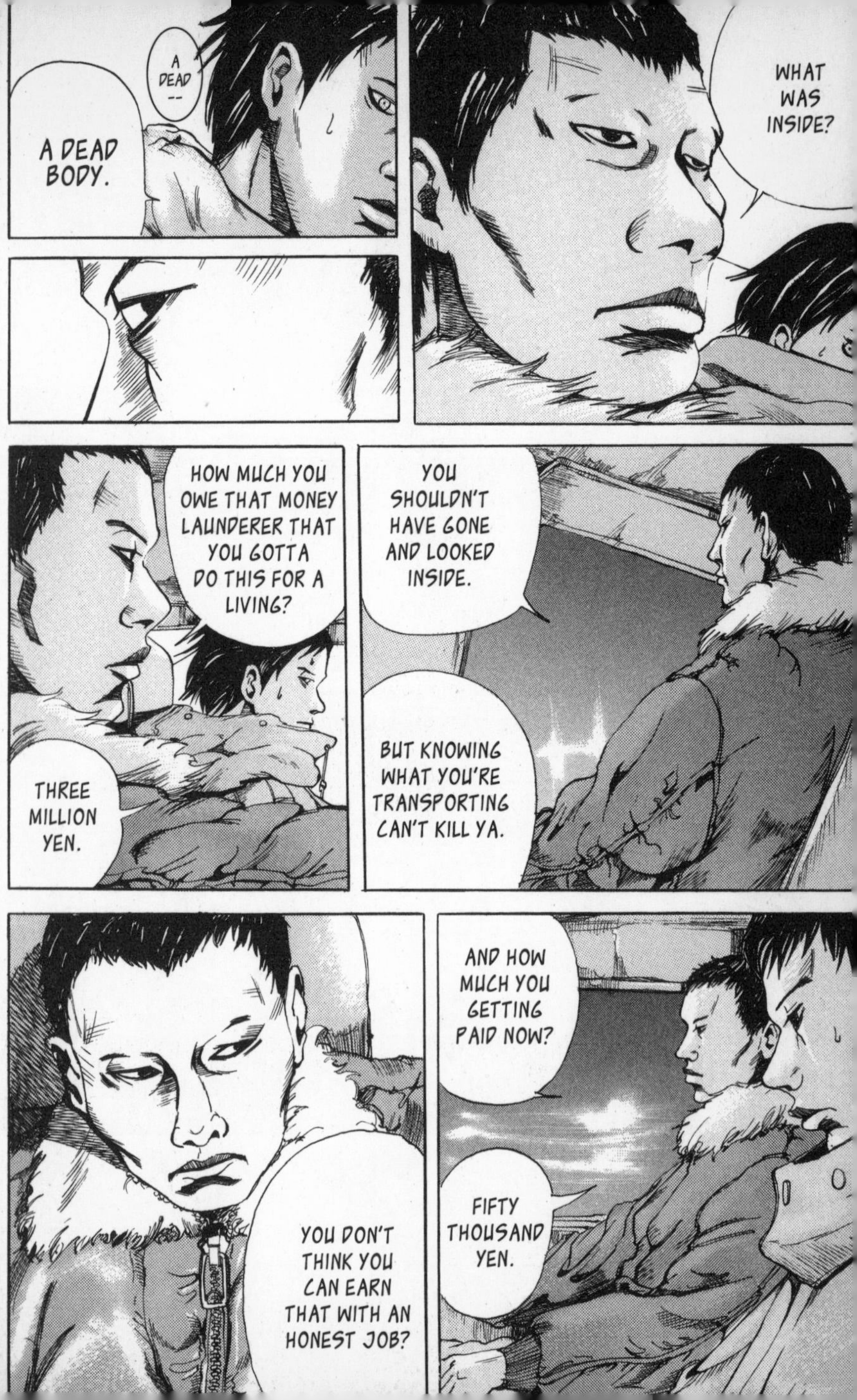
WHAT WAS INSIDE?
A DEAD --
A DEAD BODY.
YOU SHOULDN'T HAVE GONE AND LOOKED INSIDE.
BUT KNOWING WHAT YOU'RE TRANSPORTING CAN'T KILL YA.
HOW MUCH YOU OWE THAT MONEY LAUNDERER THAT YOU GOTTA DO THIS FOR A LIVING?
THREE MILLION YEN.
AND HOW MUCH YOU GETTING PAID NOW?
FIFTY THOUSAND YEN.
YOU DON'T THINK YOU CAN EARN THAT WITH AN HONEST JOB?

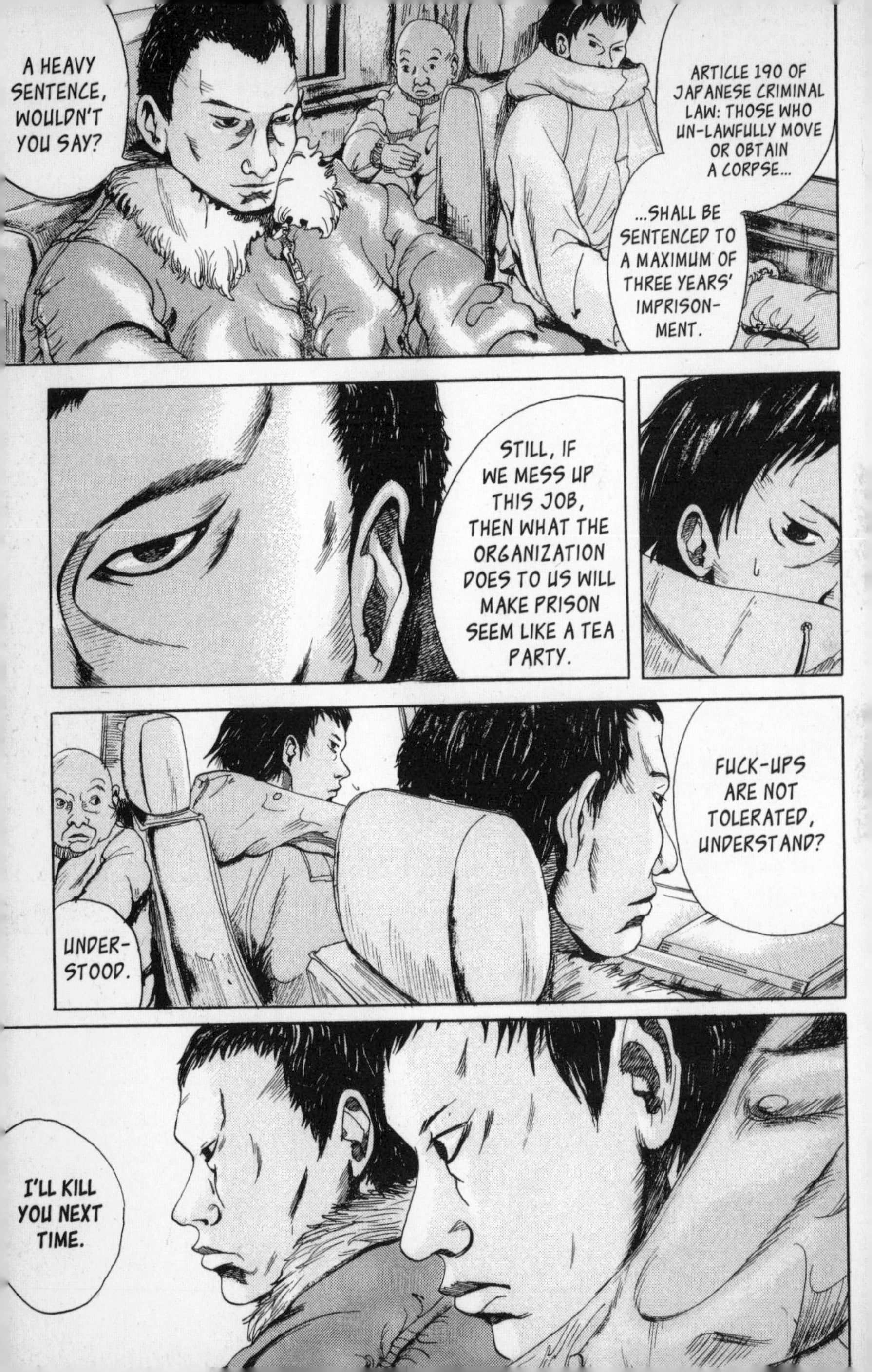
ARTICLE 190 OF JAPANESE CRIMINAL LAW: THOSE WHO UN-LAWFULLY MOVE OR OBTAIN A CORPSE...
...SHALL BE SENTENCED TO A MAXIMUM OF THREE YEARS' IMPRISON-MENT.
A HEAVY SENTENCE, WOULDN'T YOU SAY?
STILL, IF WE MESS UP THIS JOB, THEN WHAT THE ORGANIZATION DOES TO US WILL MAKE PRISON SEEM LIKE A TEA PARTY.
FUCK-UPS ARE NOT TOLERATED, UNDERSTAND?
UNDER-STOOD.
I'LL KILL YOU NEXT TIME.

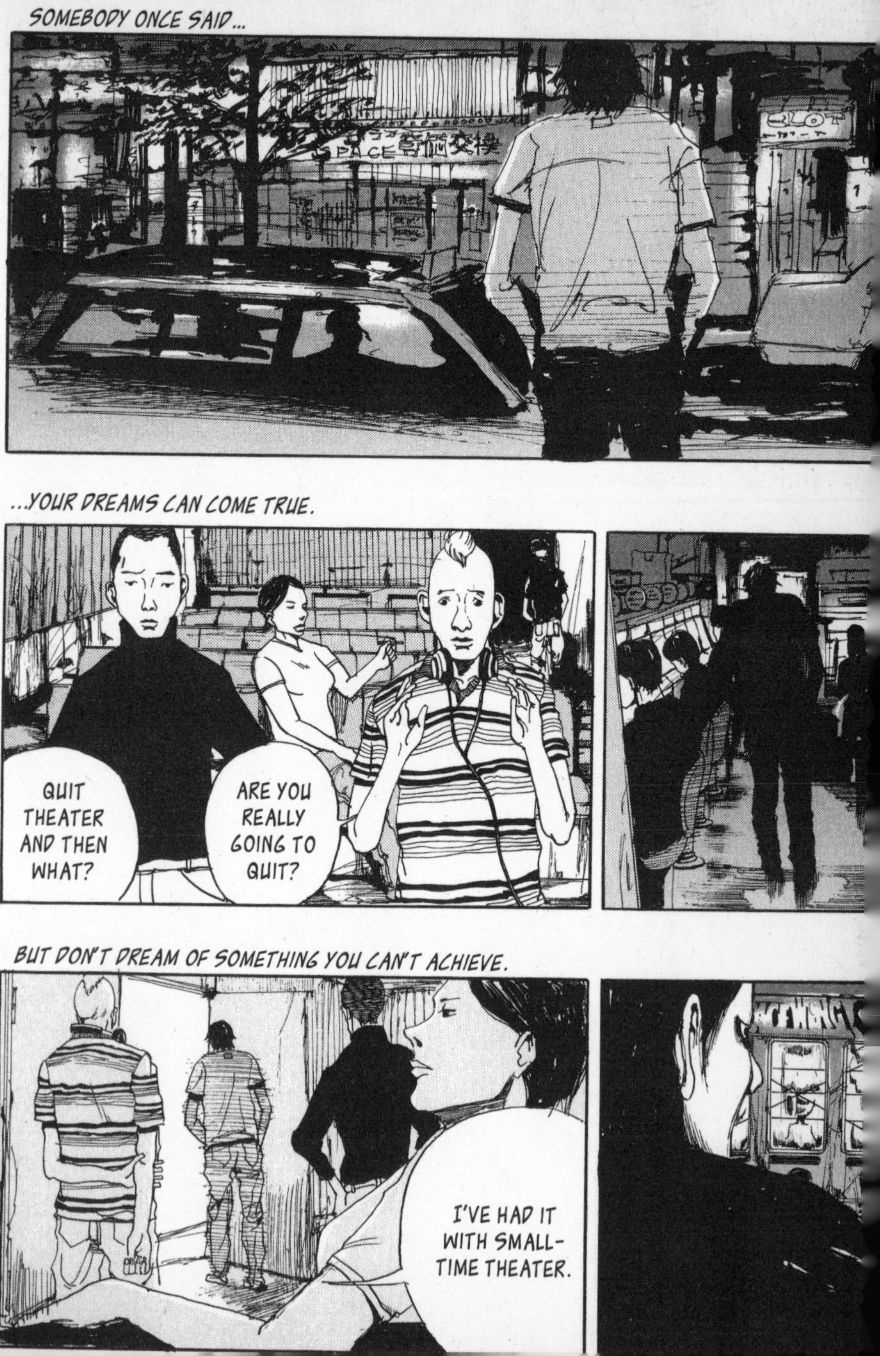
SOMEBODY ONCE SAID...
...YOUR DREAMS CAN COME TRUE.
ARE YOU REALLY GOING TO QUIT?
QUIT THEATER AND THEN WHAT?
BUT DON'T DREAM OF SOMETHING YOU CAN'T ACHIEVE.
I'VE HAD IT WITH SMALL-TIME THEATER.

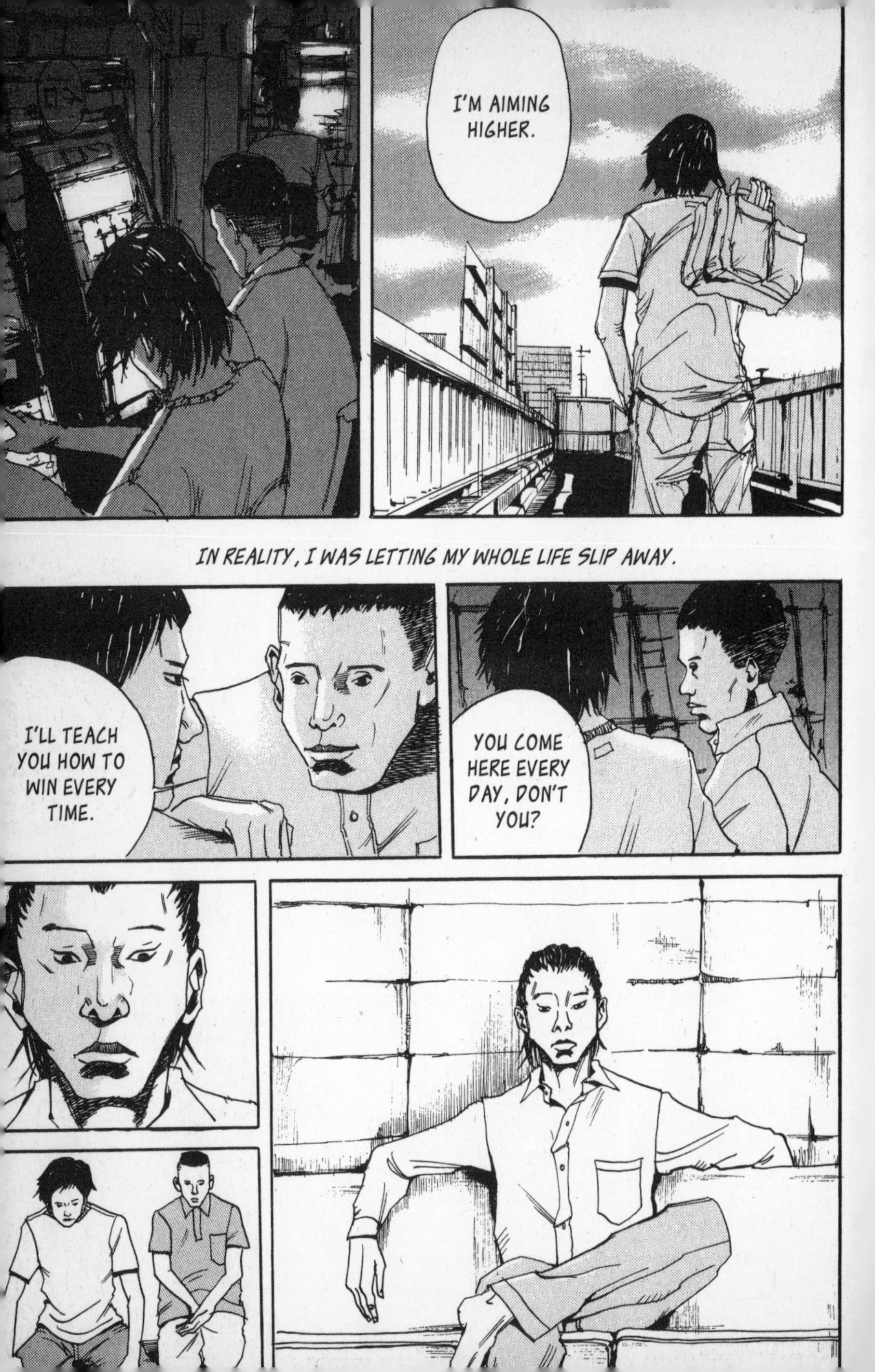
I'M AIMING HIGHER.
IN REALITY, I WAS LETTING MY WHOLE LIFE SLIP AWAY.
YOU COME HERE EVERY DAY, DON'T YOU?
I'LL TEACH YOU HOW TO WIN EVERY TIME.

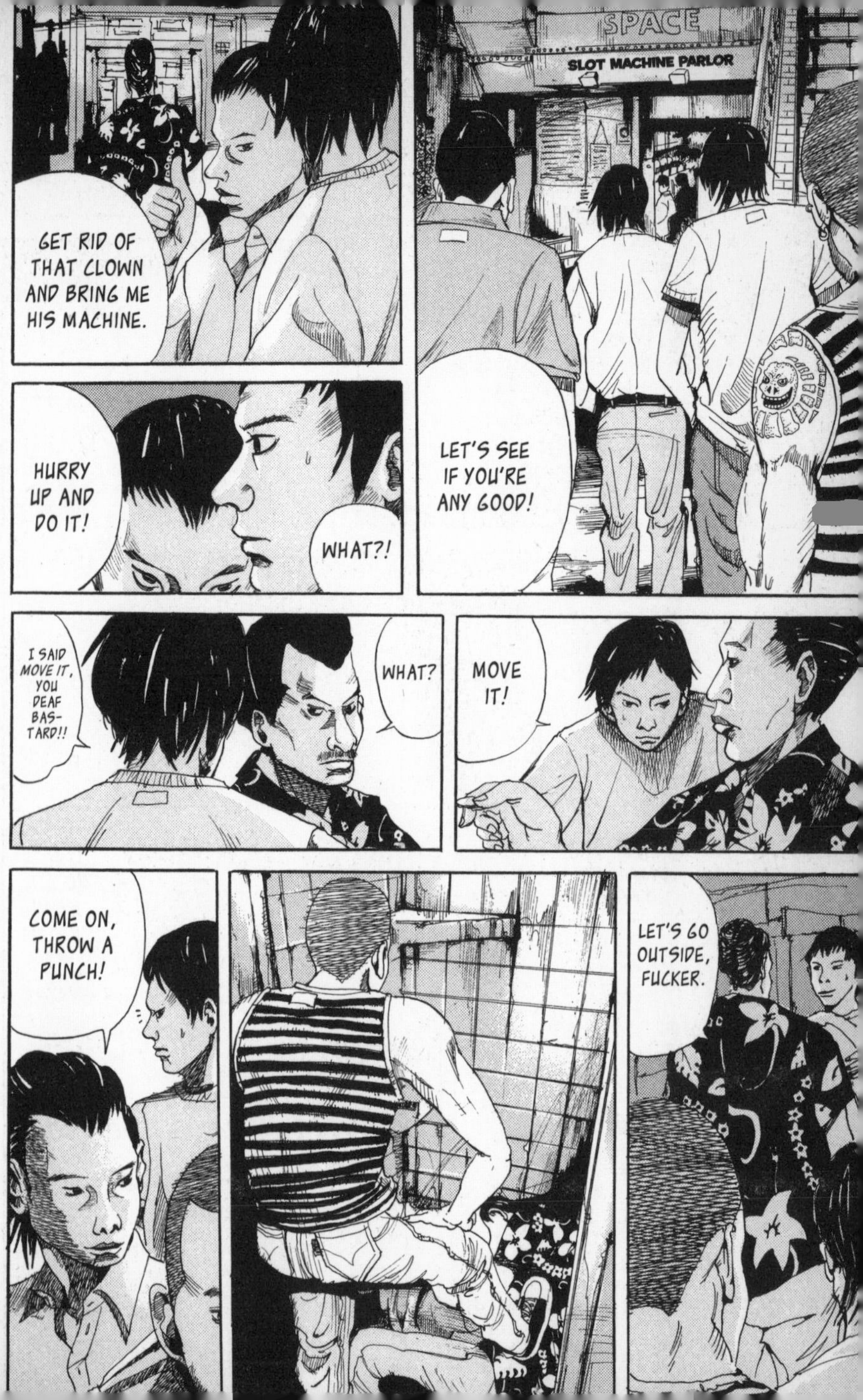
SPACE
SLOT MACHINE PARLOR
LET'S SEE IF YOU'RE ANY GOOD!
GET RID OF THAT CLOWN AND BRING ME HIS MACHINE.
HURRY UP AND DO IT!
WHAT?!
MOVE IT!
WHAT?
I SAID *MOVE IT*, YOU DEAF BAS-TARD!!
LET'S GO OUTSIDE, FUCKER.
COME ON, THROW A PUNCH!

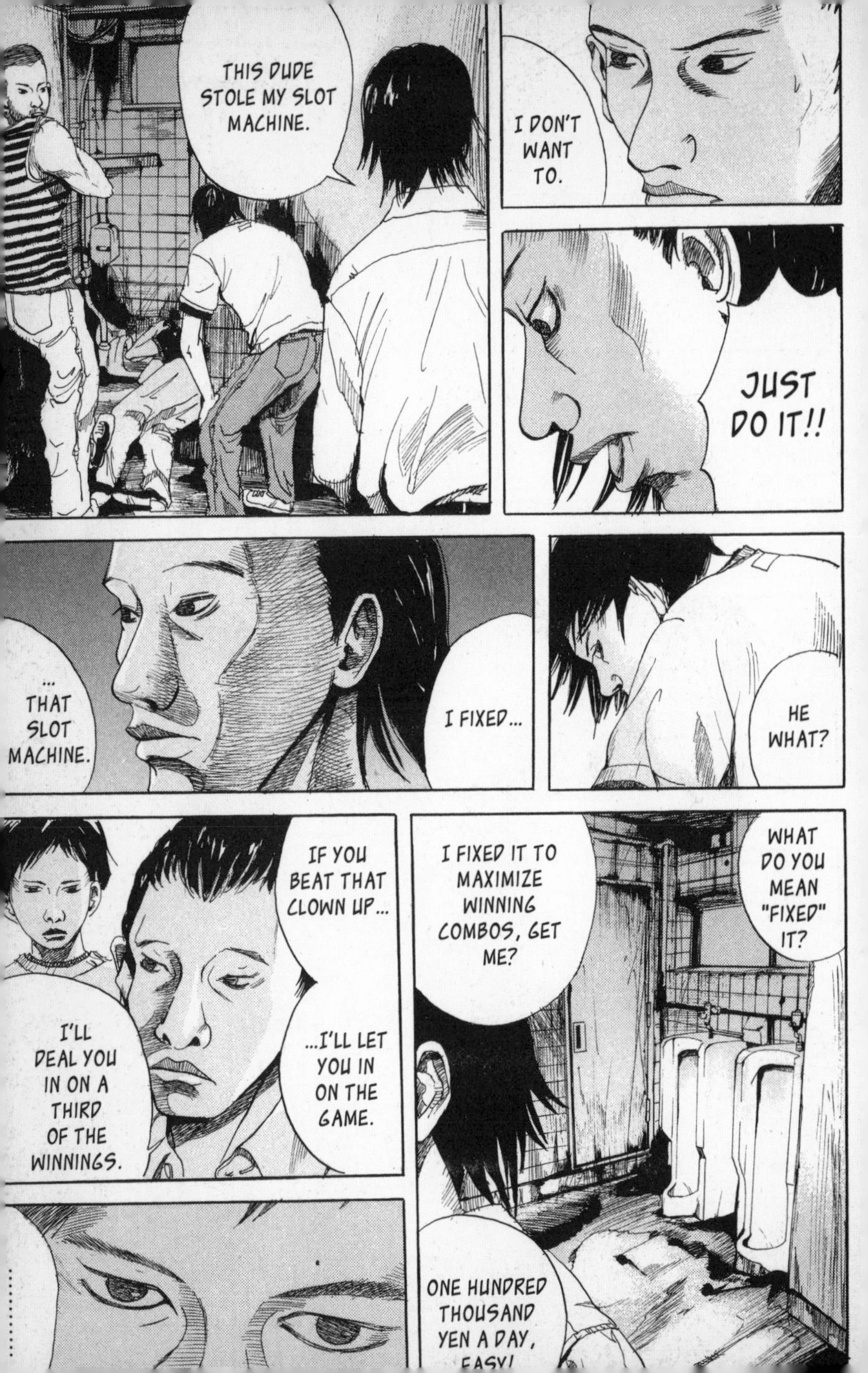
I DON'T WANT TO.
JUST DO IT!!
THIS DUDE STOLE MY SLOT MACHINE.
HE WHAT?
I FIXED...
... THAT SLOT MACHINE.
WHAT DO YOU MEAN "FIXED" IT?
I FIXED IT TO MAXIMIZE WINNING COMBOS, GET ME?
ONE HUNDRED THOUSAND YEN A DAY, EASY!
IF YOU BEAT THAT CLOWN UP...
...I'LL LET YOU IN ON THE GAME.
I'LL DEAL YOU IN ON A THIRD OF THE WINNINGS.

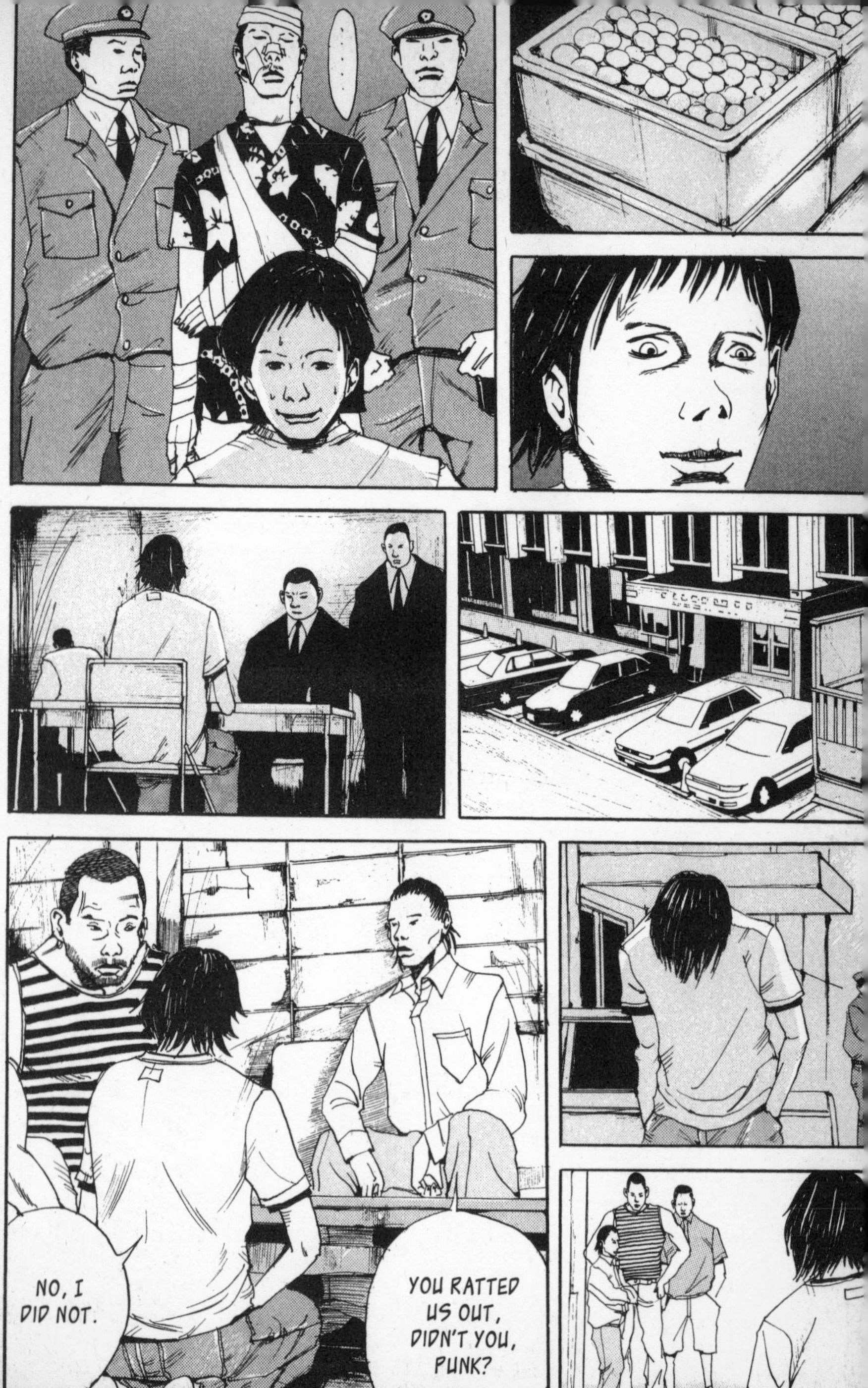
YOU RATTED US OUT, DIDN'T YOU, PUNK?
NO, I DID NOT.

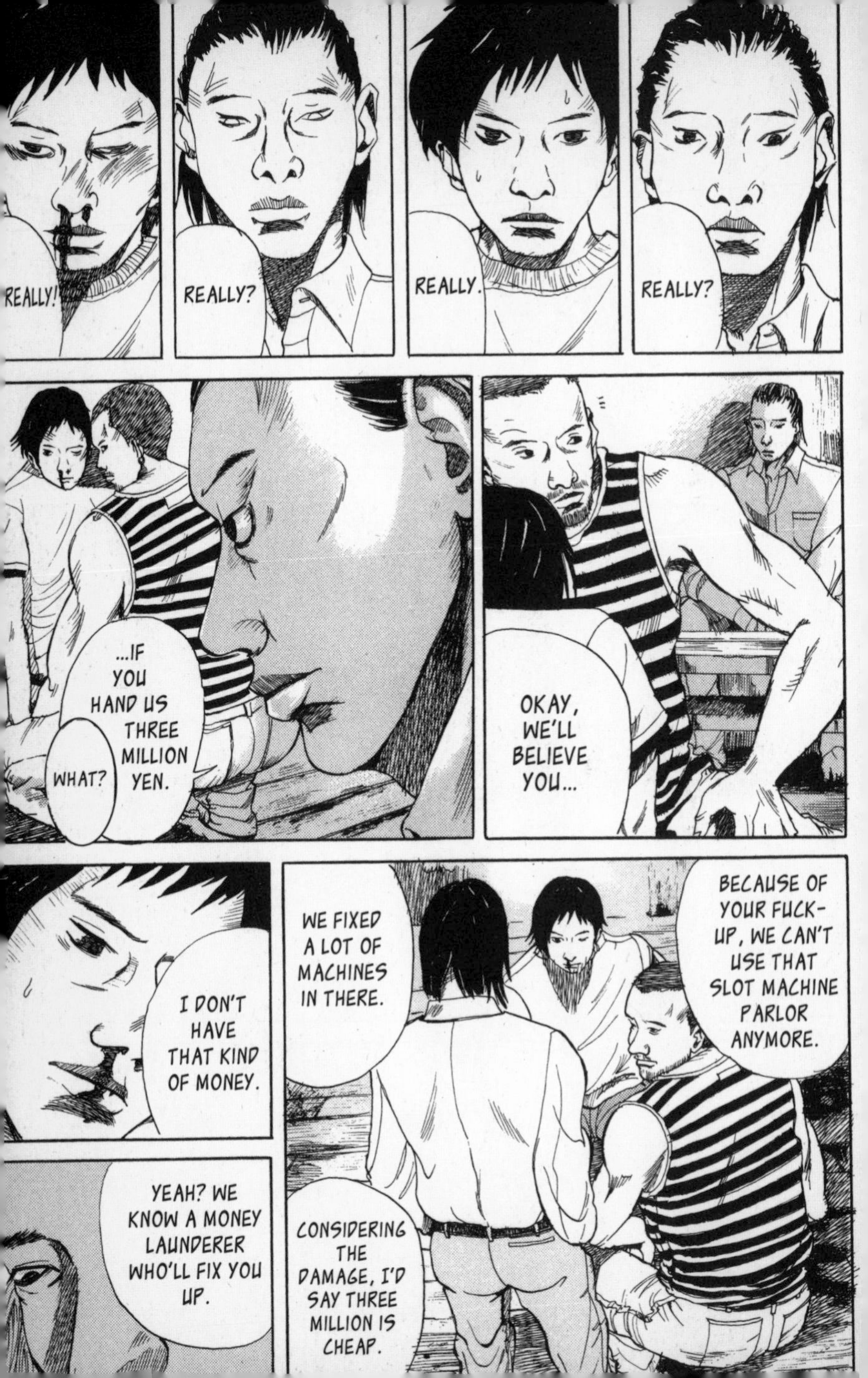
REALLY?
REALLY.
REALLY?
REALLY!
OKAY, WE'LL BELIEVE YOU...
...IF YOU HAND US THREE MILLION YEN.
WHAT?
BECAUSE OF YOUR FUCK-UP, WE CAN'T USE THAT SLOT MACHINE PARLOR ANYMORE.
WE FIXED A LOT OF MACHINES IN THERE.
CONSIDERING THE DAMAGE, I'D SAY THREE MILLION IS CHEAP.
I DON'T HAVE THAT KIND OF MONEY.
YEAH? WE KNOW A MONEY LAUNDERER WHO'LL FIX YOU UP.

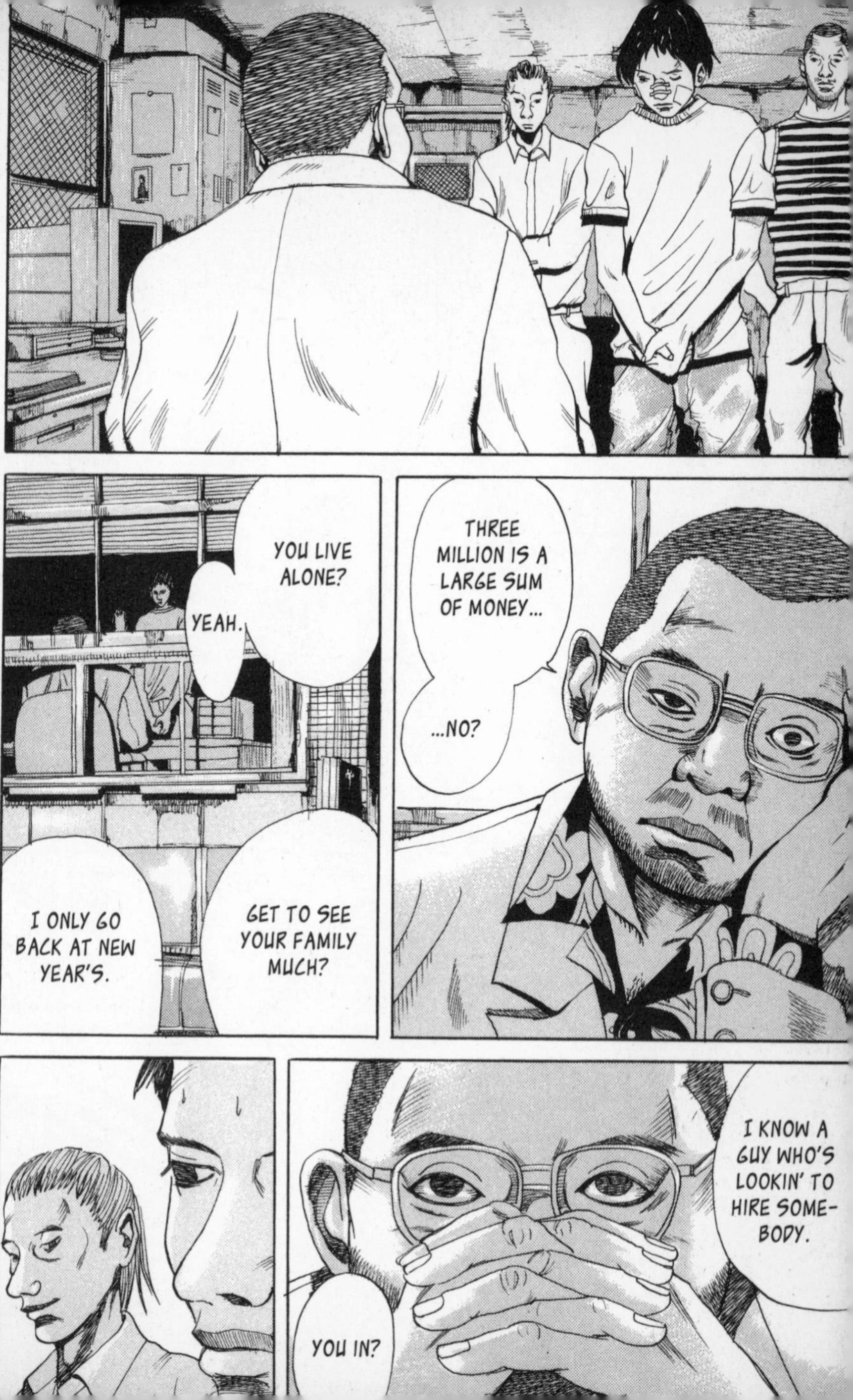
THREE MILLION IS A LARGE SUM OF MONEY...
...NO?
YOU LIVE ALONE?
YEAH.
GET TO SEE YOUR FAMILY MUCH?
I ONLY GO BACK AT NEW YEAR'S.
I KNOW A GUY WHO'S LOOKIN' TO HIRE SOME-BODY.
YOU IN?

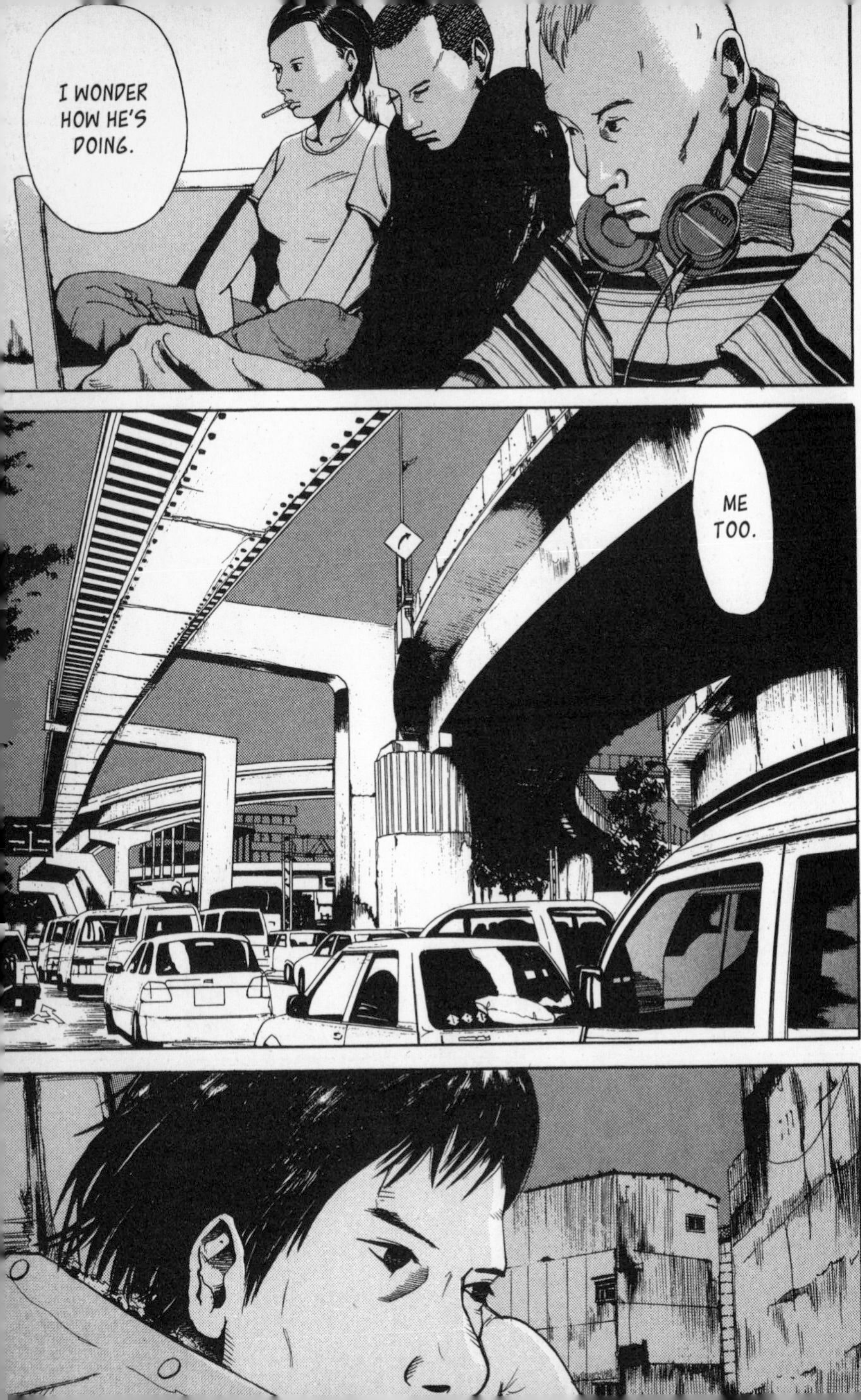
I WONDER HOW HE'S DOING.
ME TOO.

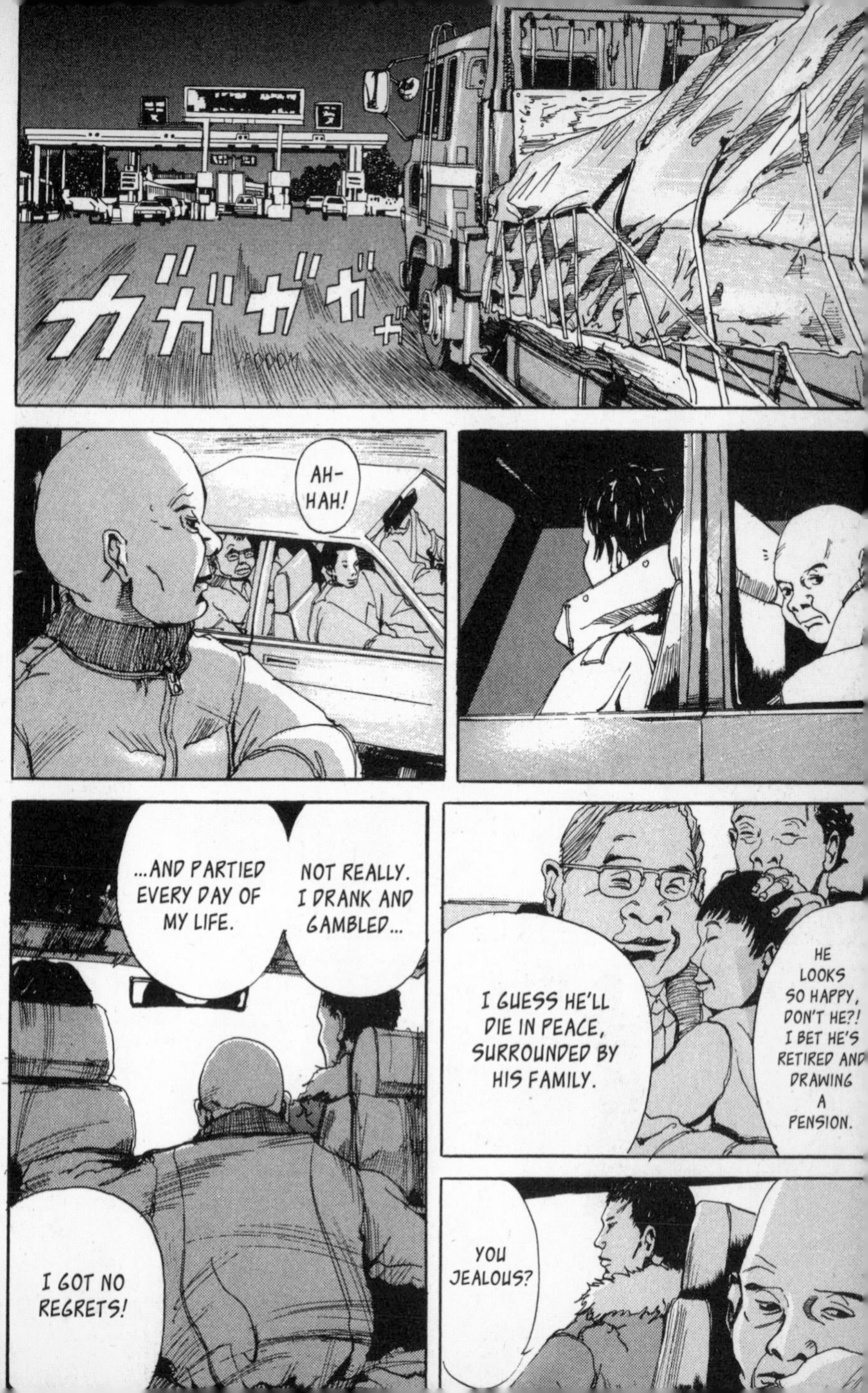
カガガガガ
VROOOM
AH-HAH!
HE LOOKS SO HAPPY, DON'T HE?! I BET HE'S RETIRED AND DRAWING A PENSION.
I GUESS HE'LL DIE IN PEACE, SURROUNDED BY HIS FAMILY.
YOU JEALOUS?
NOT REALLY. I DRANK AND GAMBLED...
...AND PARTIED EVERY DAY OF MY LIFE.
I GOT NO REGRETS!

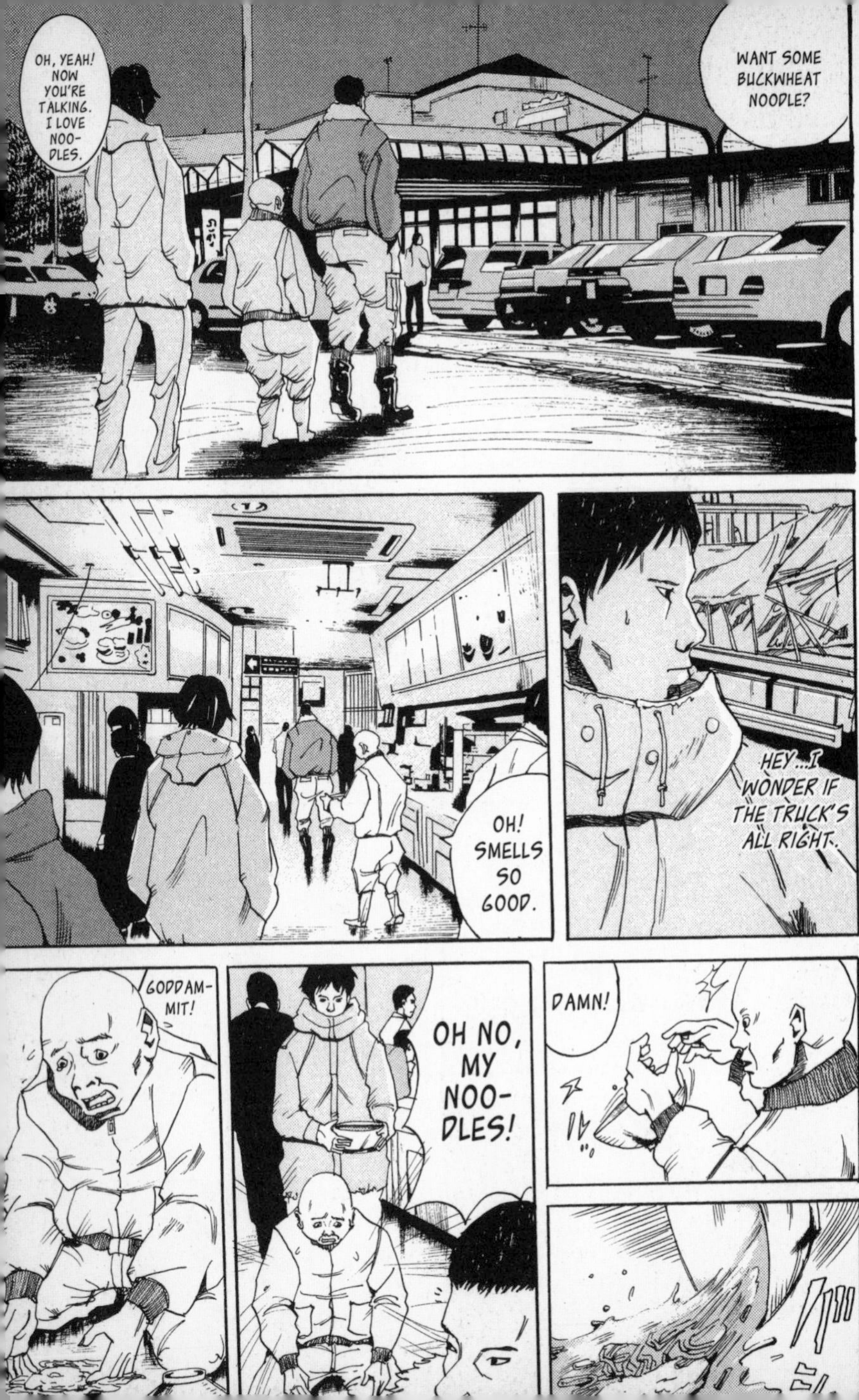
WANT SOME BUCKWHEAT NOODLE?
OH, YEAH! NOW YOU'RE TALKING. I LOVE NOO-DLES.
HEY...I WONDER IF THE TRUCK'S ALL RIGHT.
OH! SMELLS SO GOOD.
DAMN!
OH NO, MY NOO-DLES!
GODDAM-MIT!

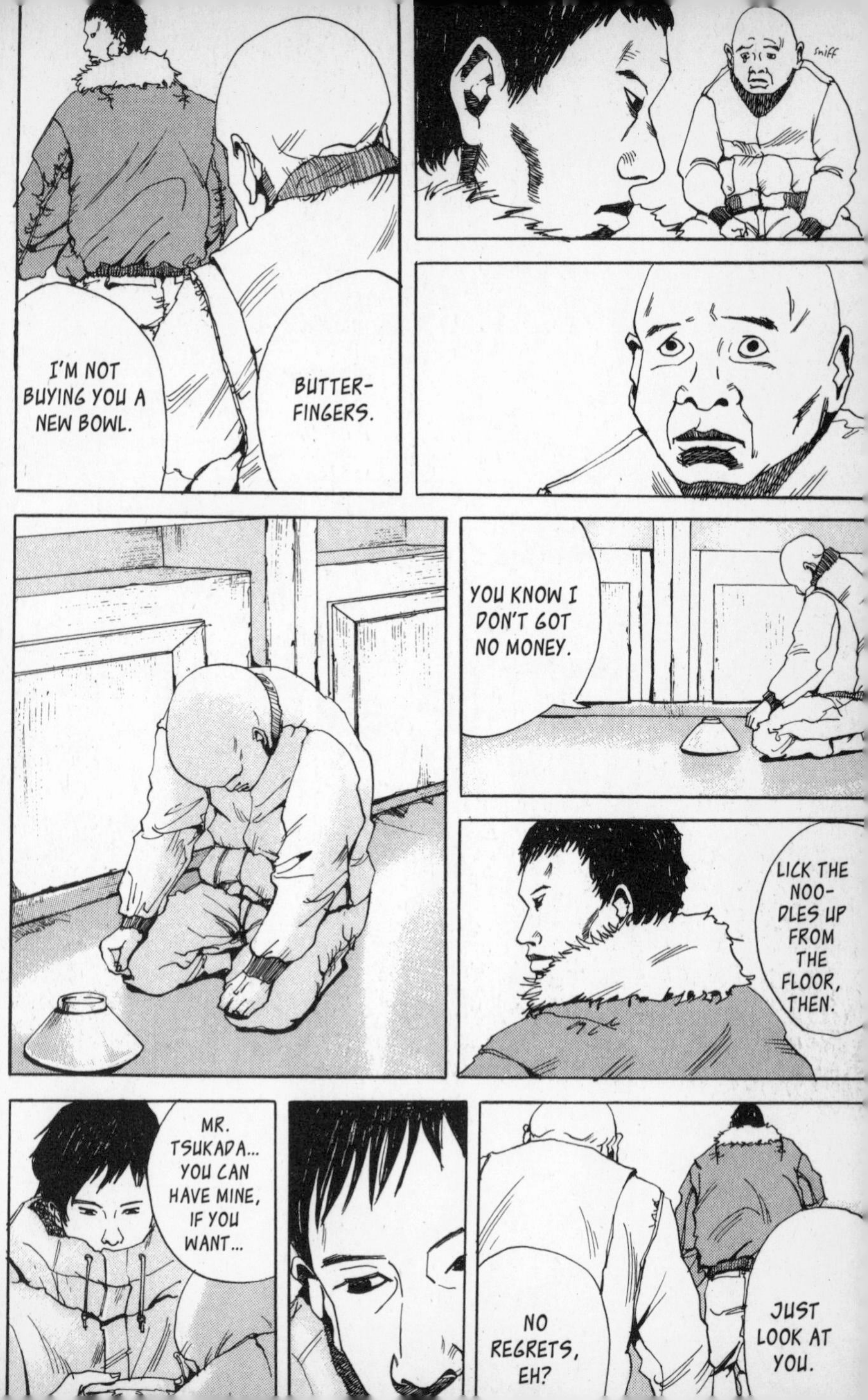
sniff
BUTTER-FINGERS.
I'M NOT BUYING YOU A NEW BOWL.
YOU KNOW I DON'T GOT NO MONEY.
LICK THE NOO-DLES UP FROM THE FLOOR, THEN.
JUST LOOK AT YOU.
NO REGRETS, EH?
MR. TSUKADA... YOU CAN HAVE MINE, IF YOU WANT...

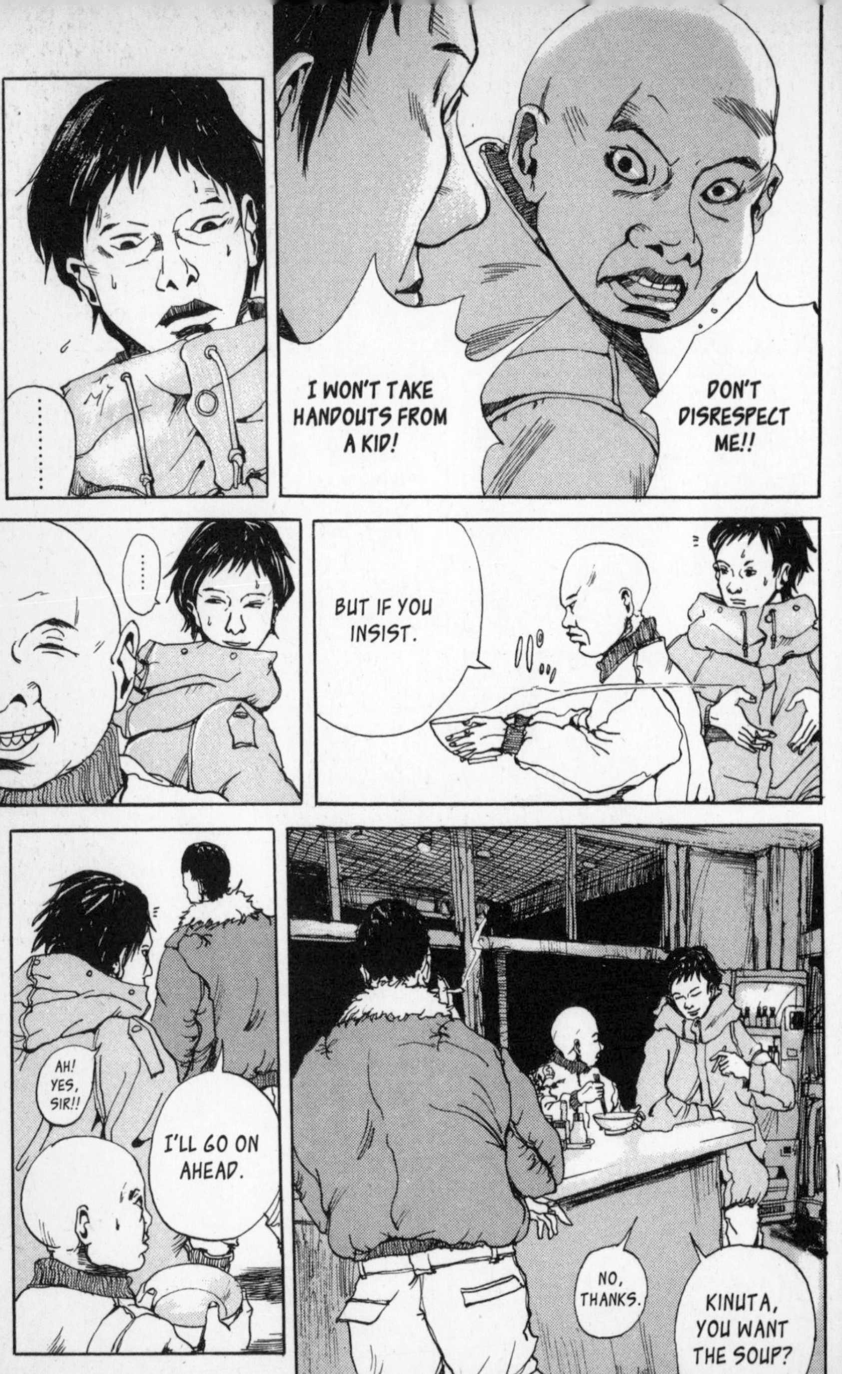
DON'T DISRESPECT ME!!
I WON'T TAKE HANDOUTS FROM A KID!
......
BUT IF YOU INSIST.
......
KINUTA, YOU WANT THE SOUP?
NO, THANKS.
I'LL GO ON AHEAD.
AH! YES, SIR!!

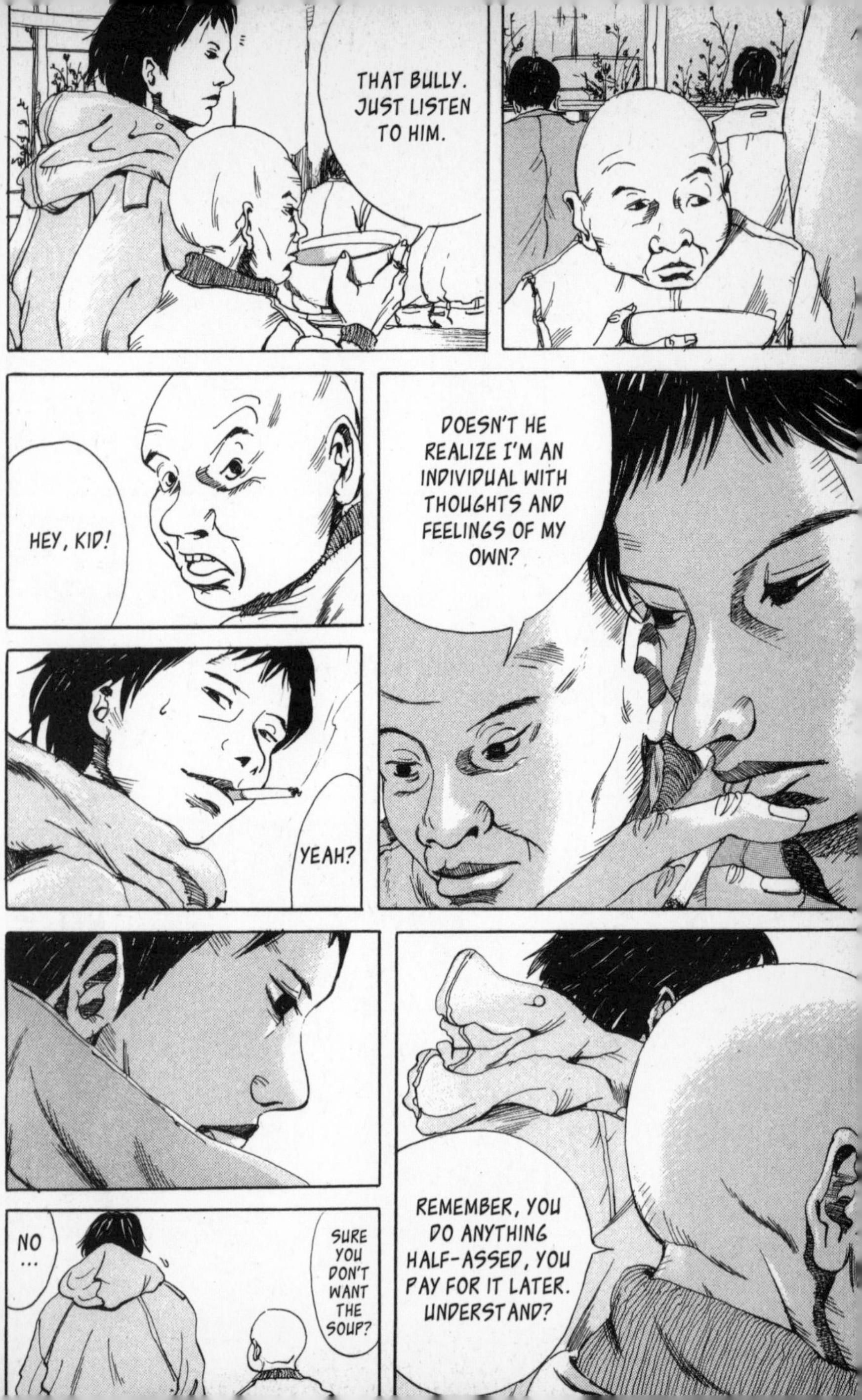
THAT BULLY. JUST LISTEN TO HIM.
DOESN'T HE REALIZE I'M AN INDIVIDUAL WITH THOUGHTS AND FEELINGS OF MY OWN?
HEY, KID!
YEAH?
REMEMBER, YOU DO ANYTHING HALF-ASSED, YOU PAY FOR IT LATER. UNDERSTAND?
SURE YOU DON'T WANT THE SOUP?
NO ...

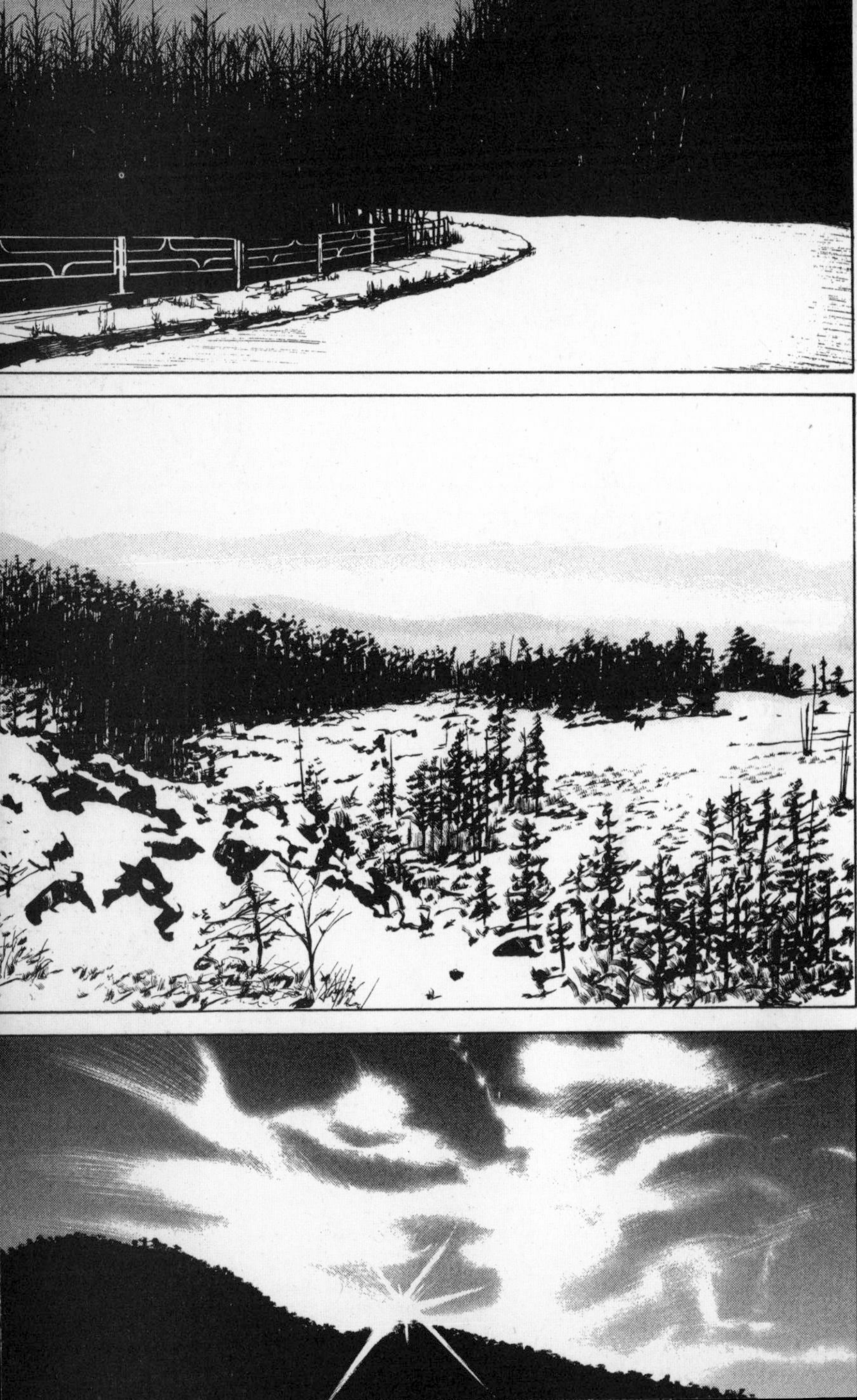

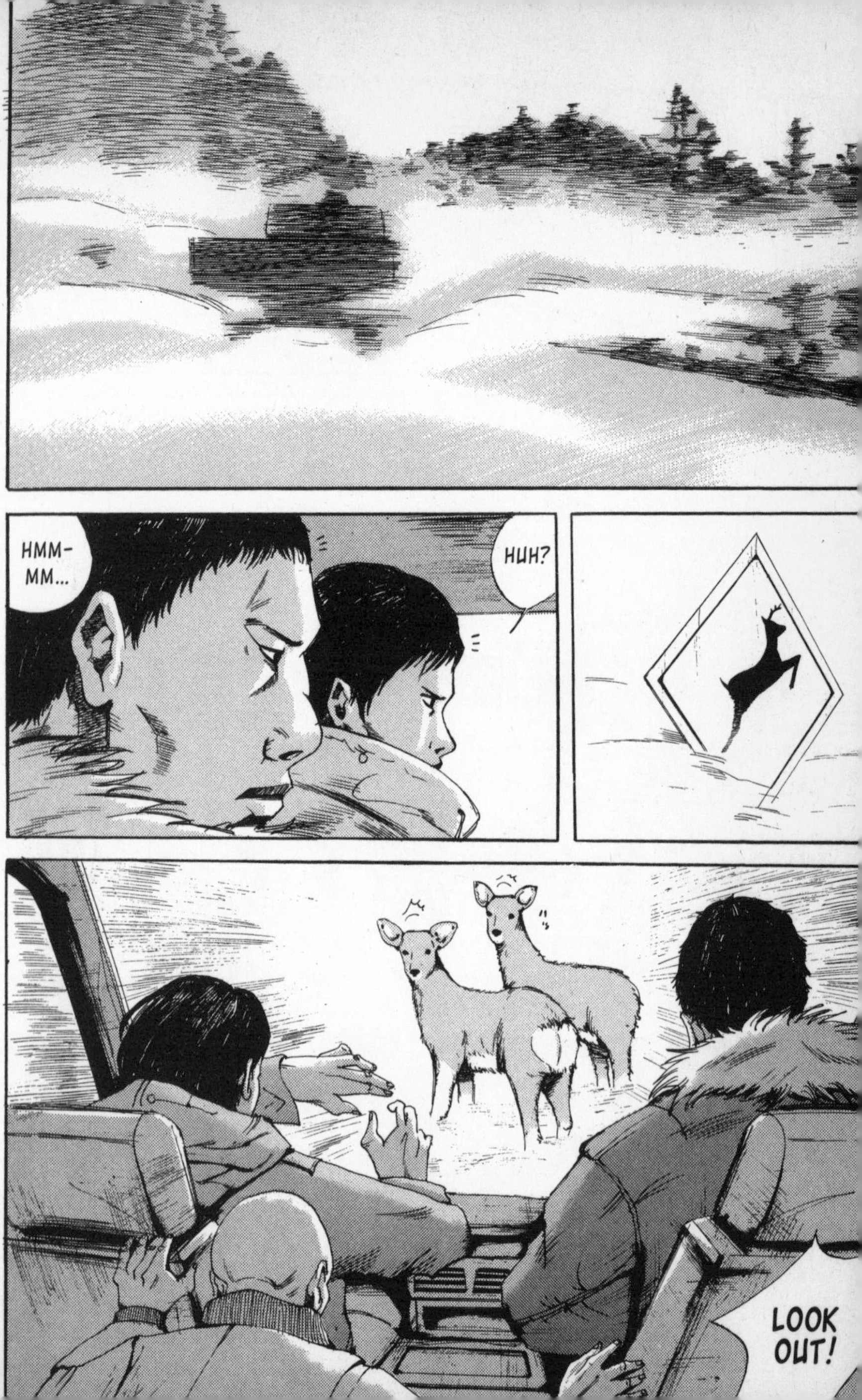
HUH?
HMM-MM...
LOOK OUT!

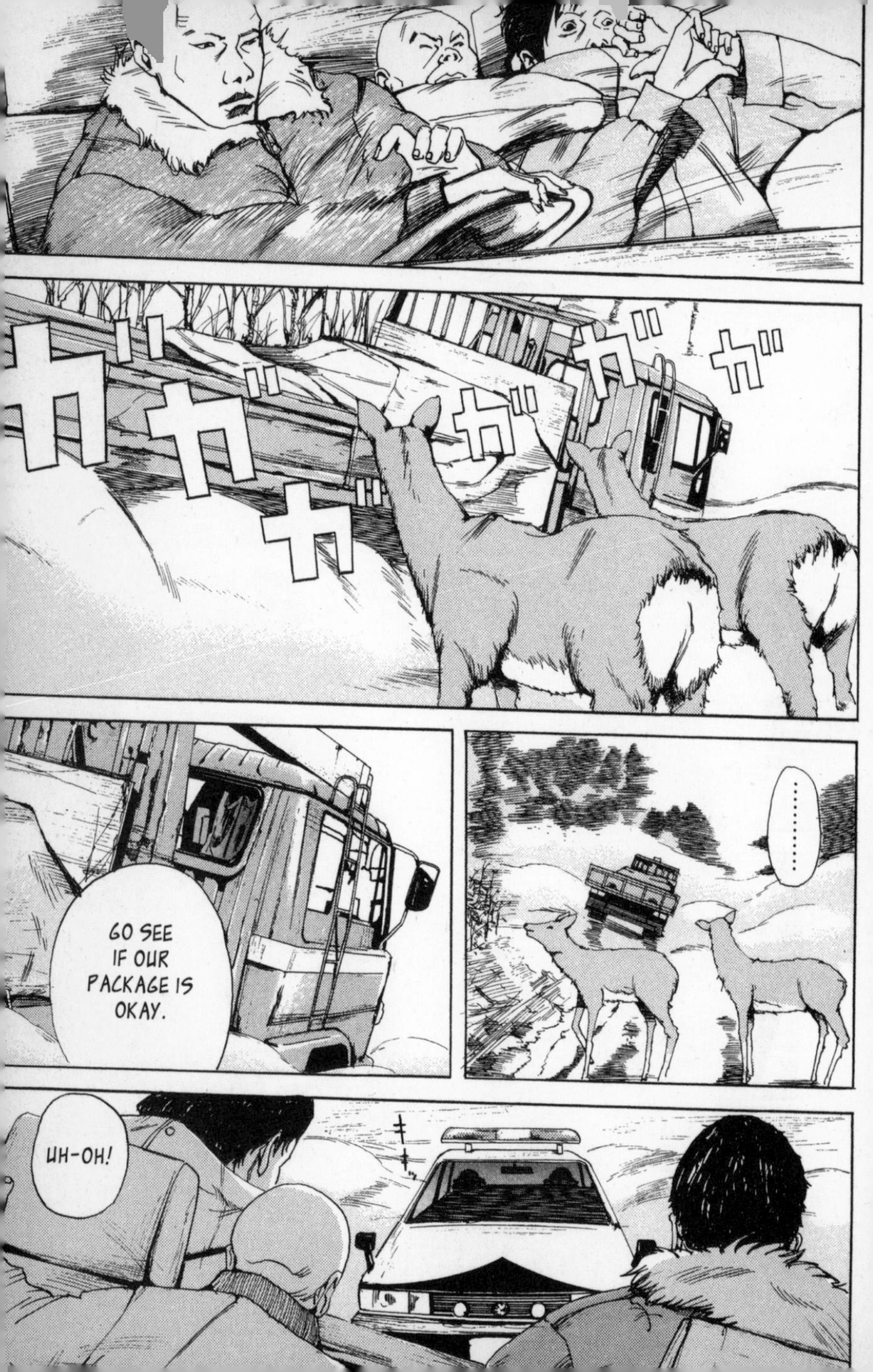
ガガガガガガ
……
GO SEE IF OUR PACKAGE IS OKAY.
UH-OH!

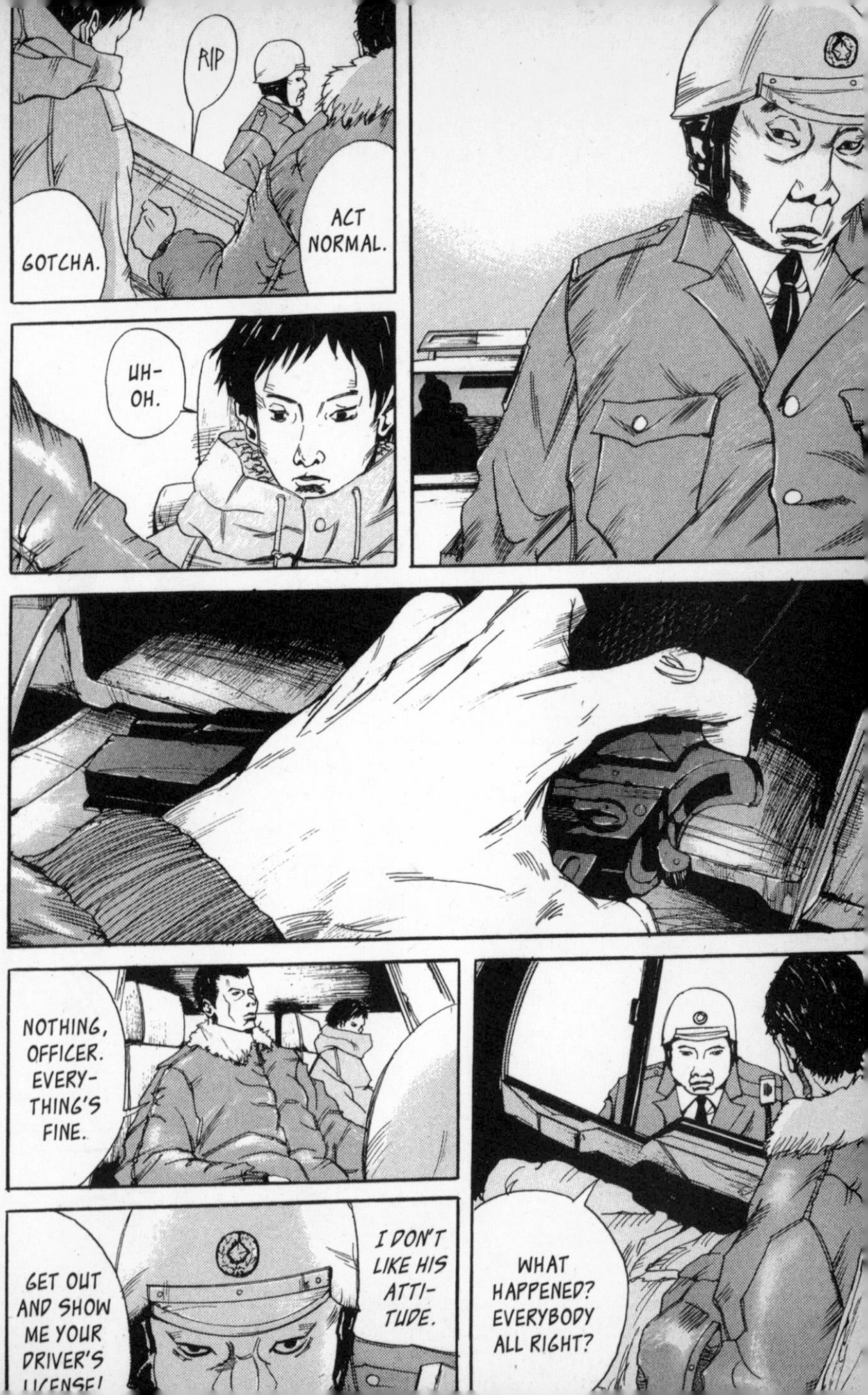
RIP
ACT NORMAL.
GOTCHA.
UH-OH.
WHAT HAPPENED? EVERYBODY ALL RIGHT?
NOTHING, OFFICER. EVERY-THING'S FINE.
I DON'T LIKE HIS ATTI-TUDE.
GET OUT AND SHOW ME YOUR DRIVER'S LICENSE!

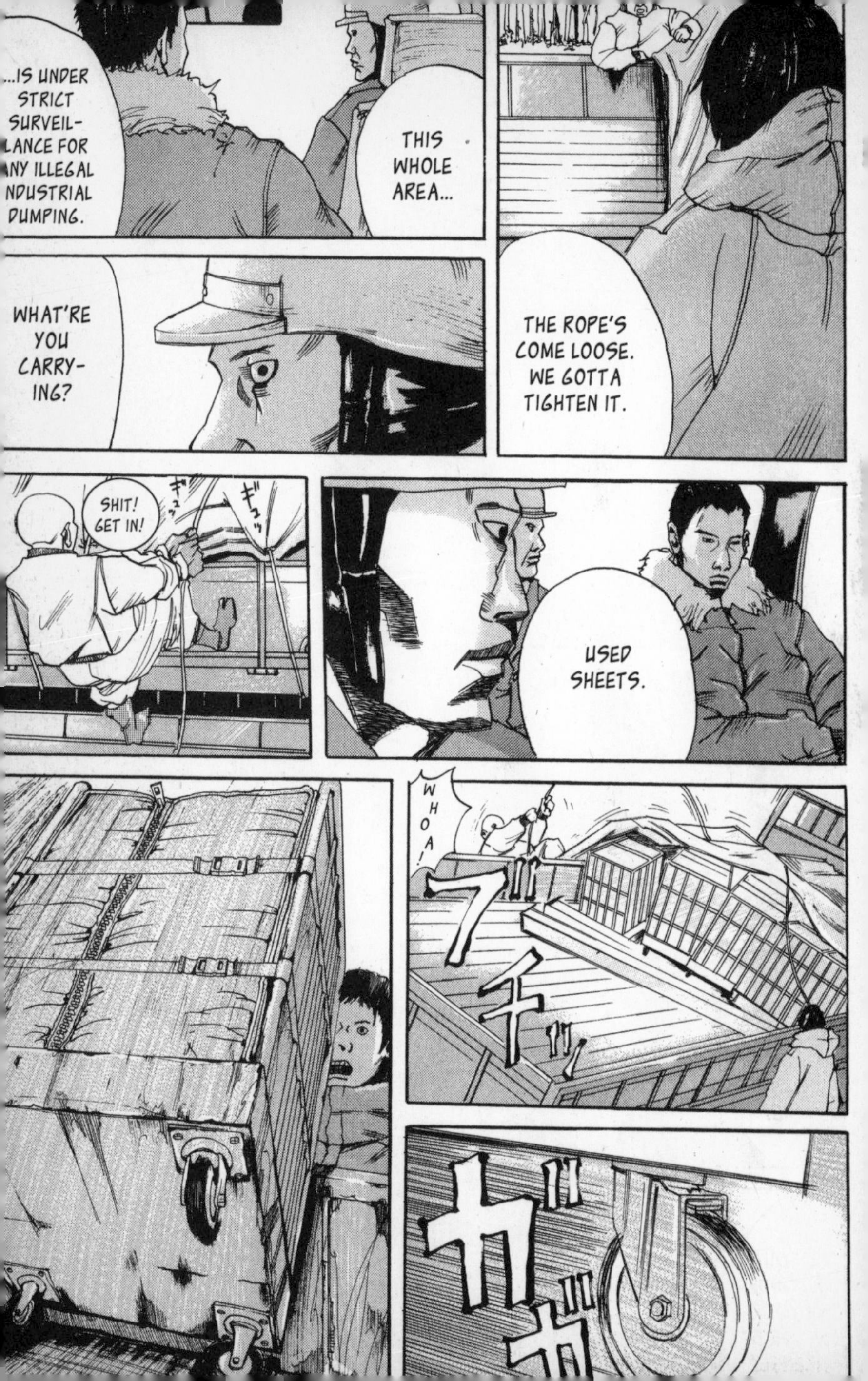
THIS WHOLE AREA...
...IS UNDER STRICT SURVEIL-LANCE FOR NY ILLEGAL NDUSTRIAL DUMPING.
THE ROPE'S COME LOOSE. WE GOTTA TIGHTEN IT.
WHAT'RE YOU CARRYING?
USED SHEETS.
ギュッ
SHIT! GET IN!
WHOA!
ガチッ
ガガ

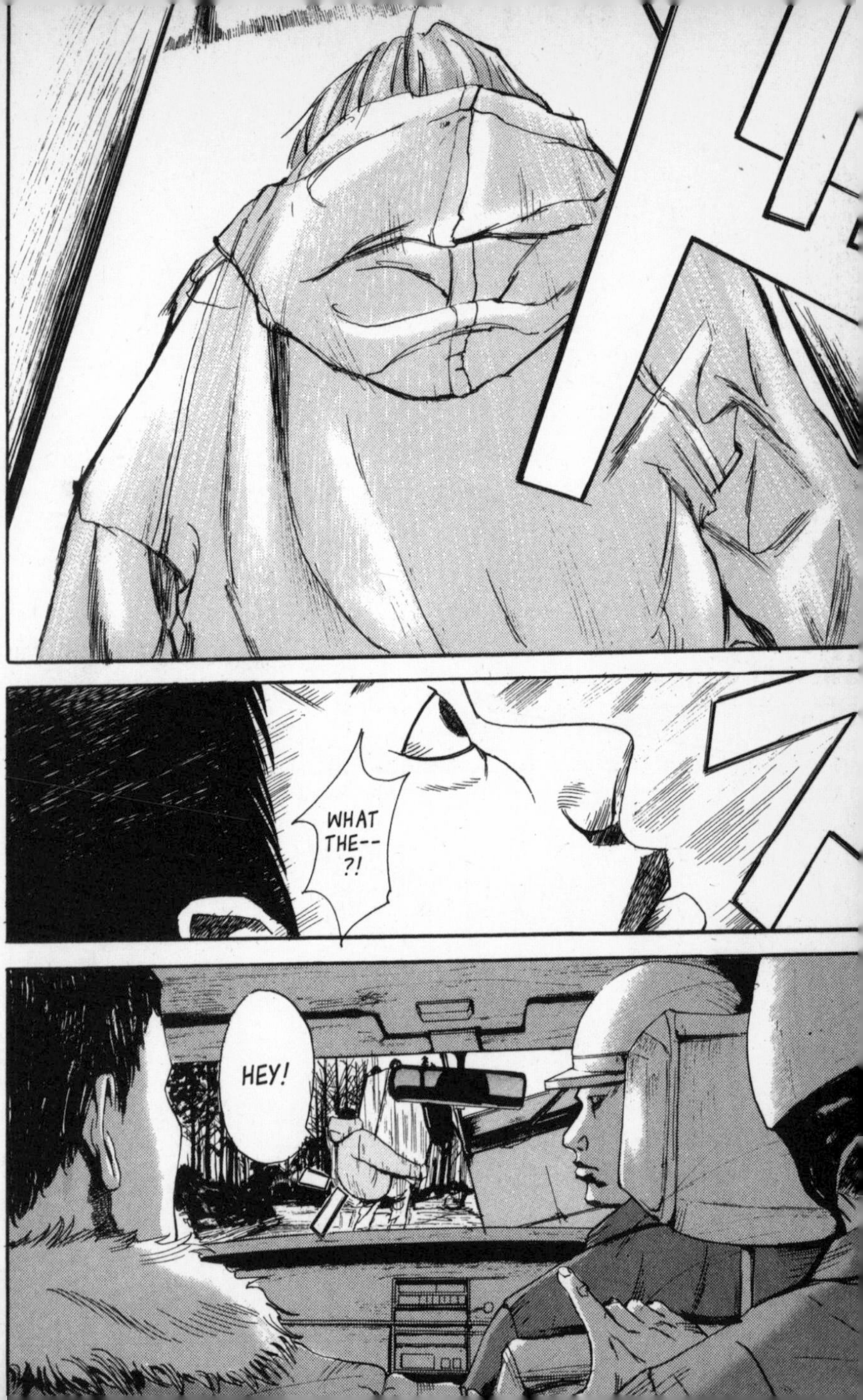
WHAT THE-- ?!
HEY!

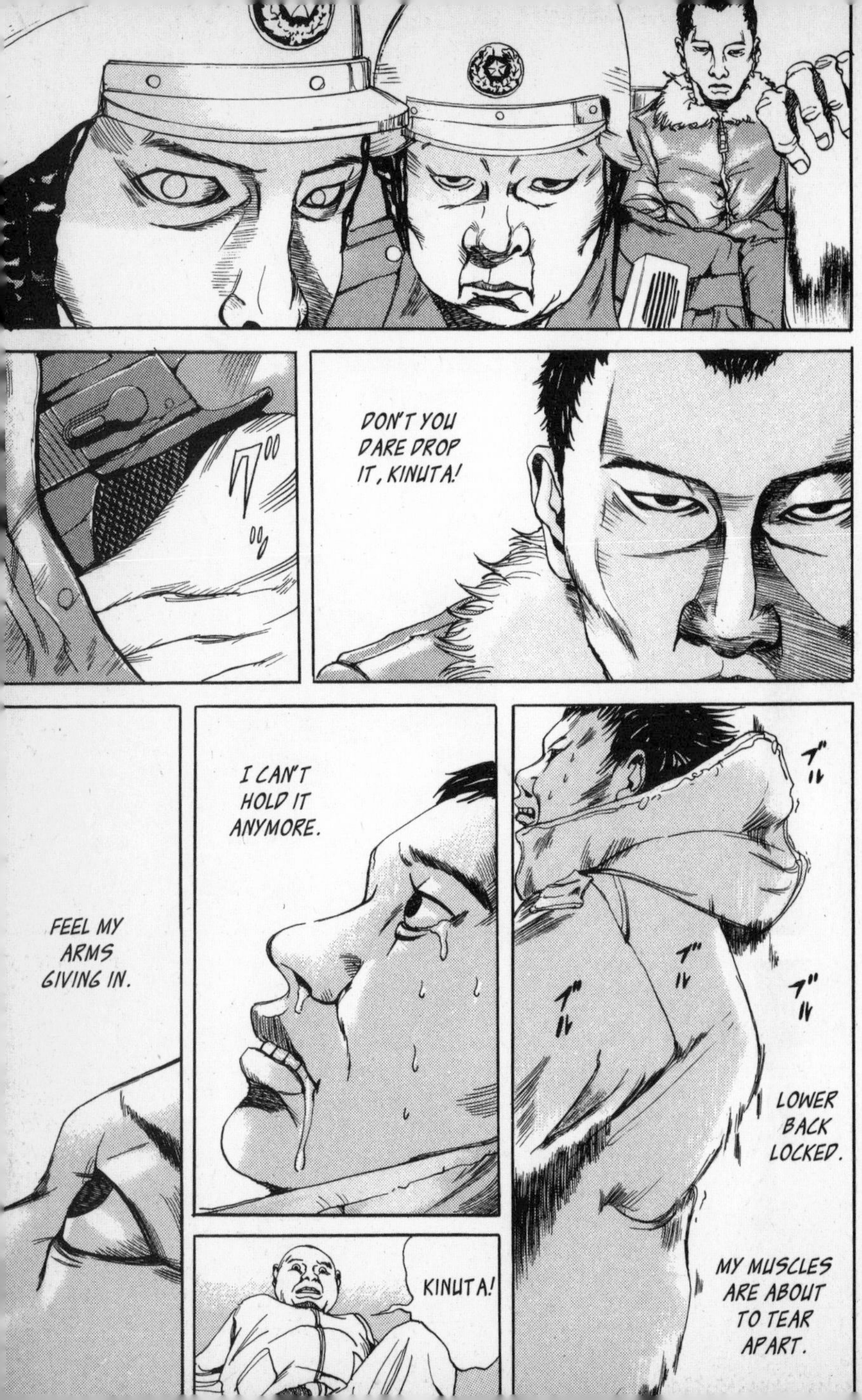
DON'T YOU DARE DROP IT, KINUTA!
ブル
ブル
ブル
ブル
LOWER BACK LOCKED.
MY MUSCLES ARE ABOUT TO TEAR APART.
I CAN'T HOLD IT ANYMORE.
KINUTA!
FEEL MY ARMS GIVING IN.

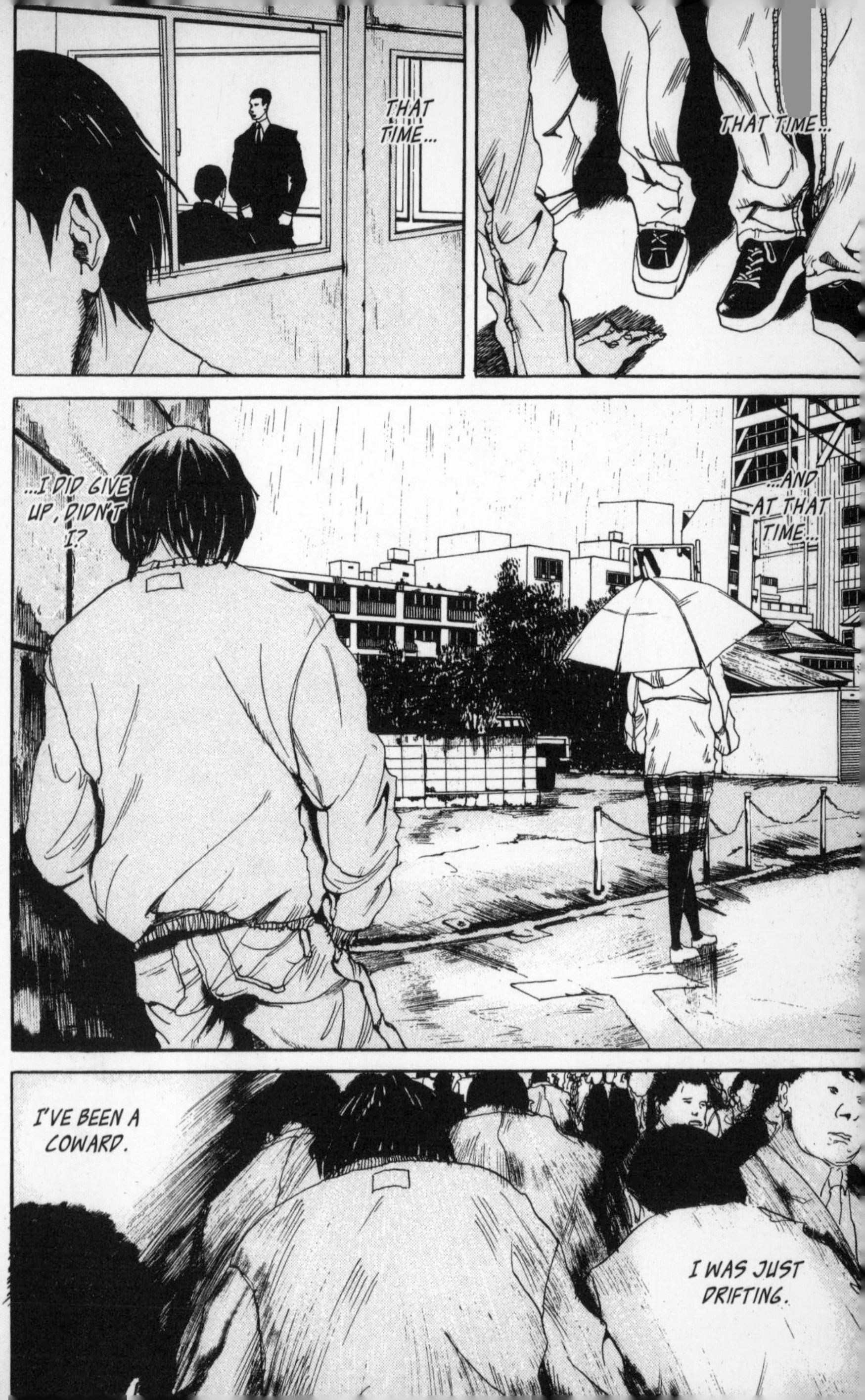
THAT TIME...
THAT TIME...
...AND AT THAT TIME...
...I DID GIVE UP, DIDN'T I?
I'VE BEEN A COWARD.
I WAS JUST DRIFTING.

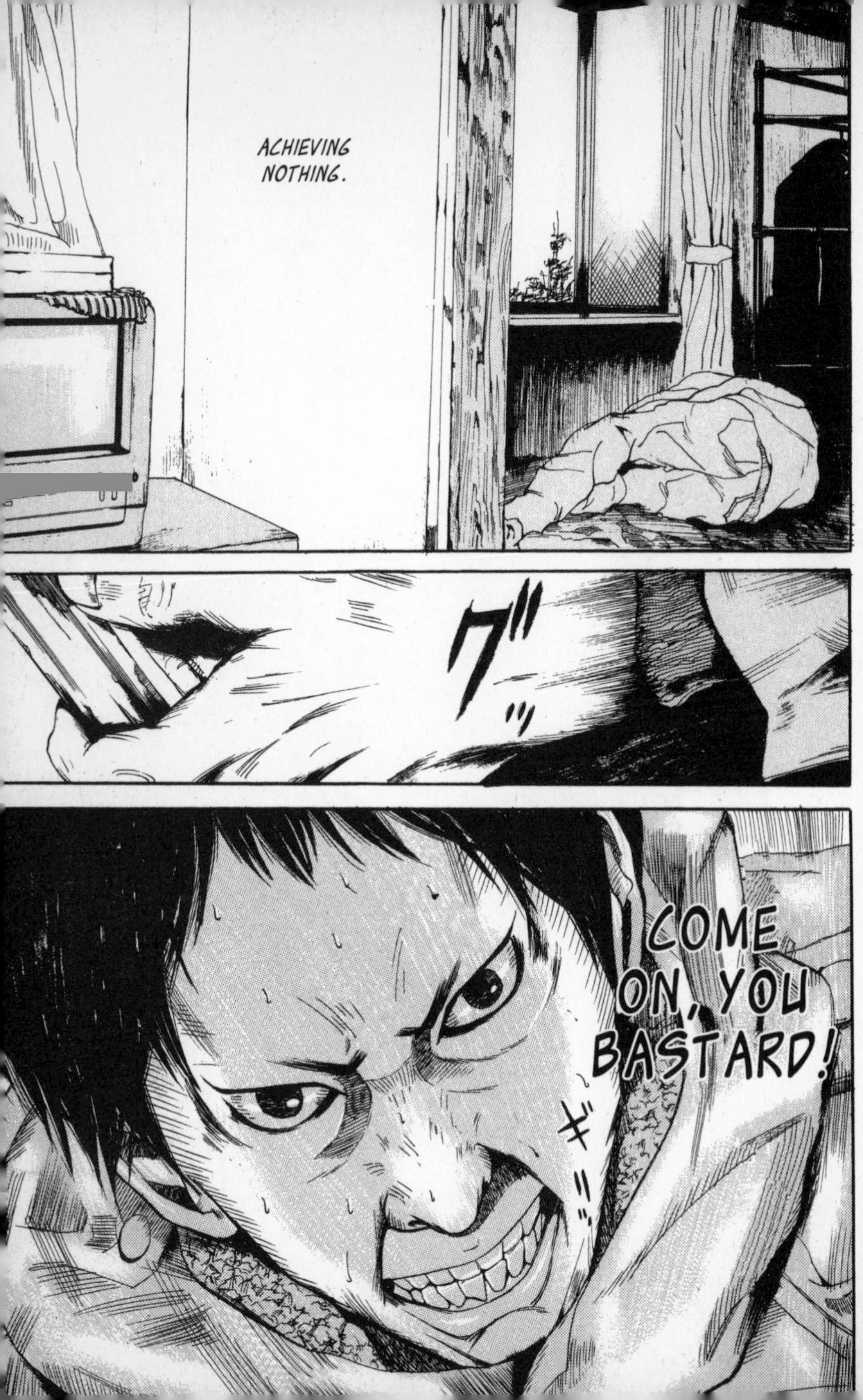
ACHIEVING NOTHING.
グッ
COME ON, YOU BASTARD!
ギリ

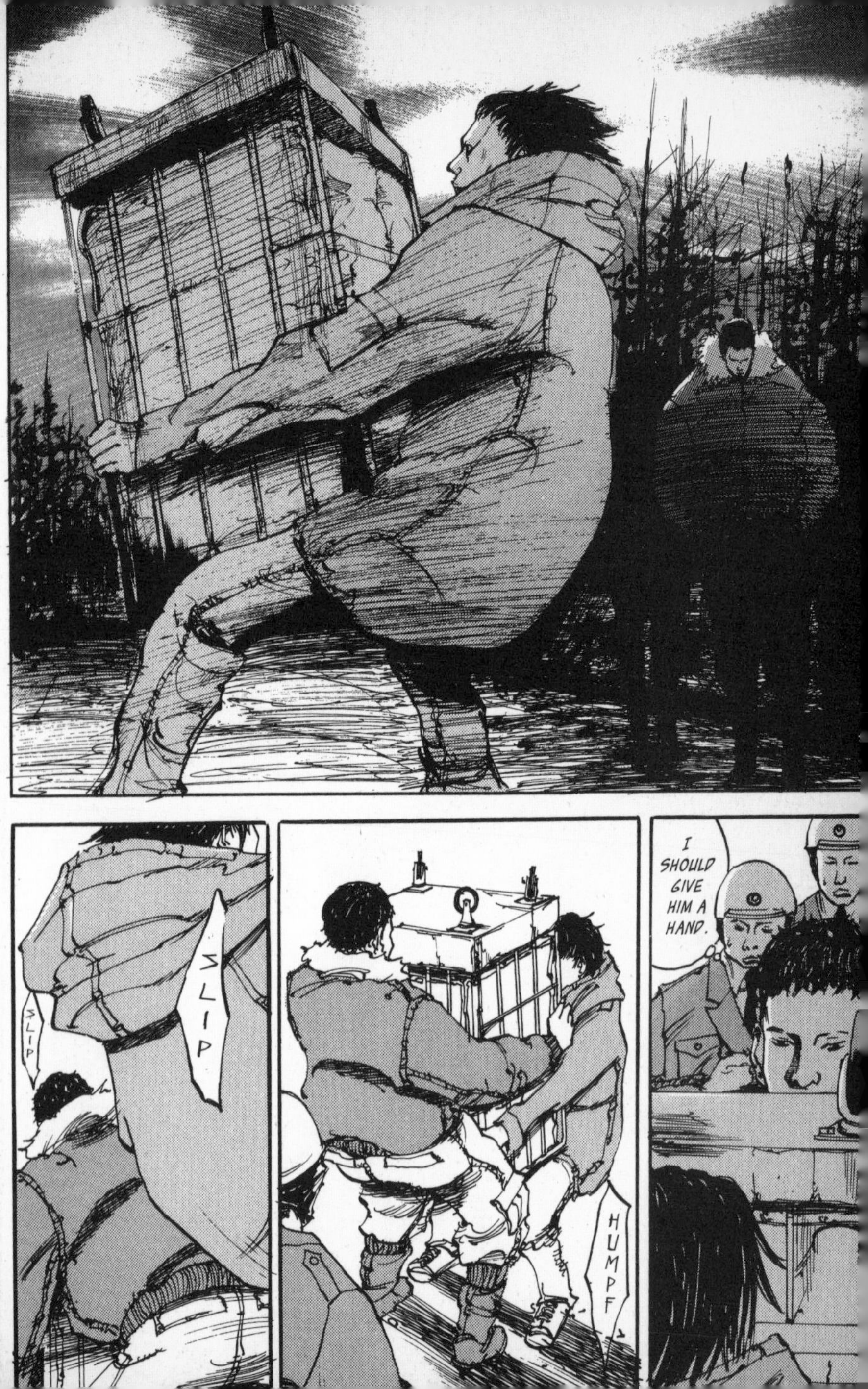
I SHOULD GIVE HIM A HAND.
HUMPF
SLIP
SLIP

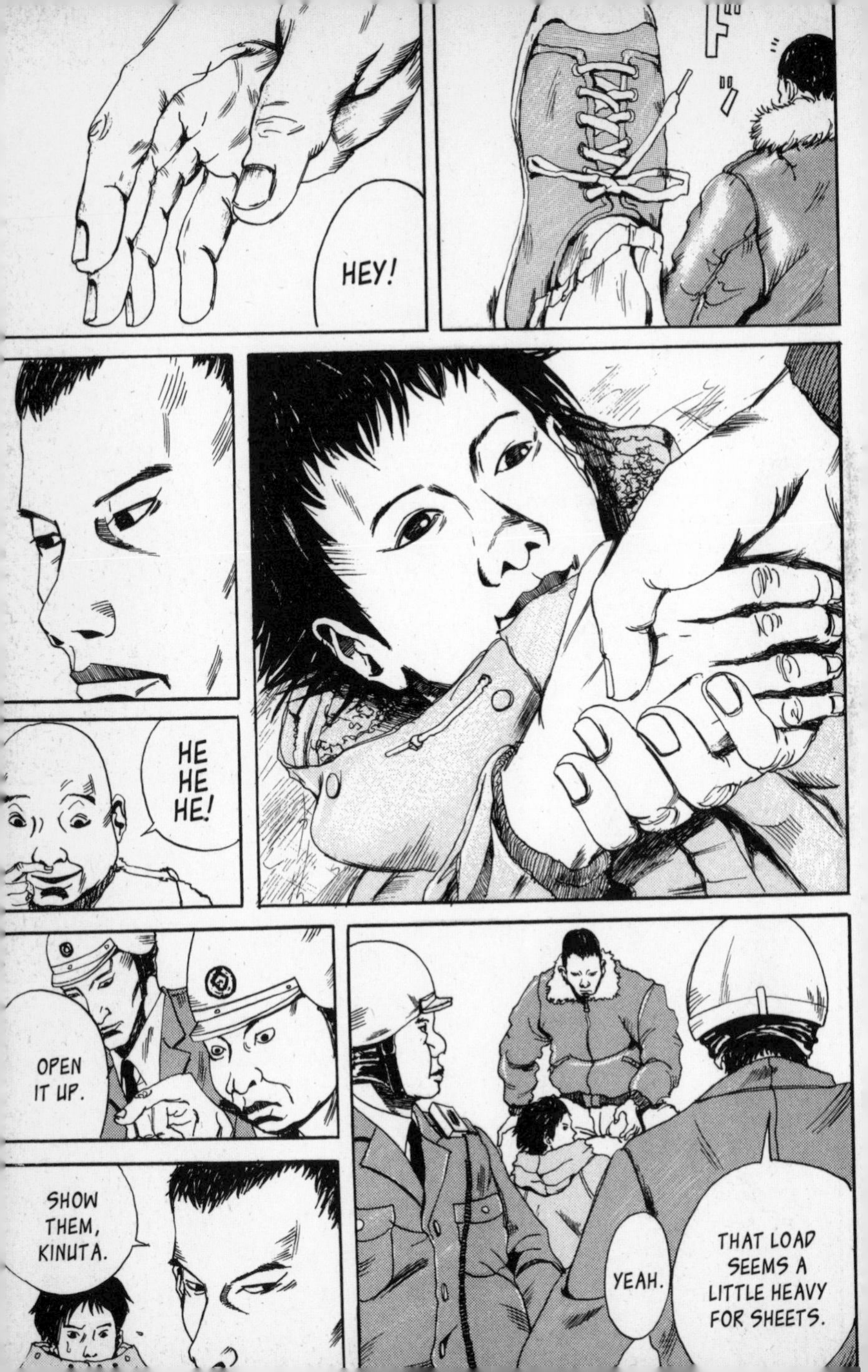
HEY!
HE HE HE!
THAT LOAD SEEMS A LITTLE HEAVY FOR SHEETS.
YEAH.
OPEN IT UP.
SHOW THEM, KINUTA.

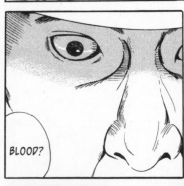

BLOOD?

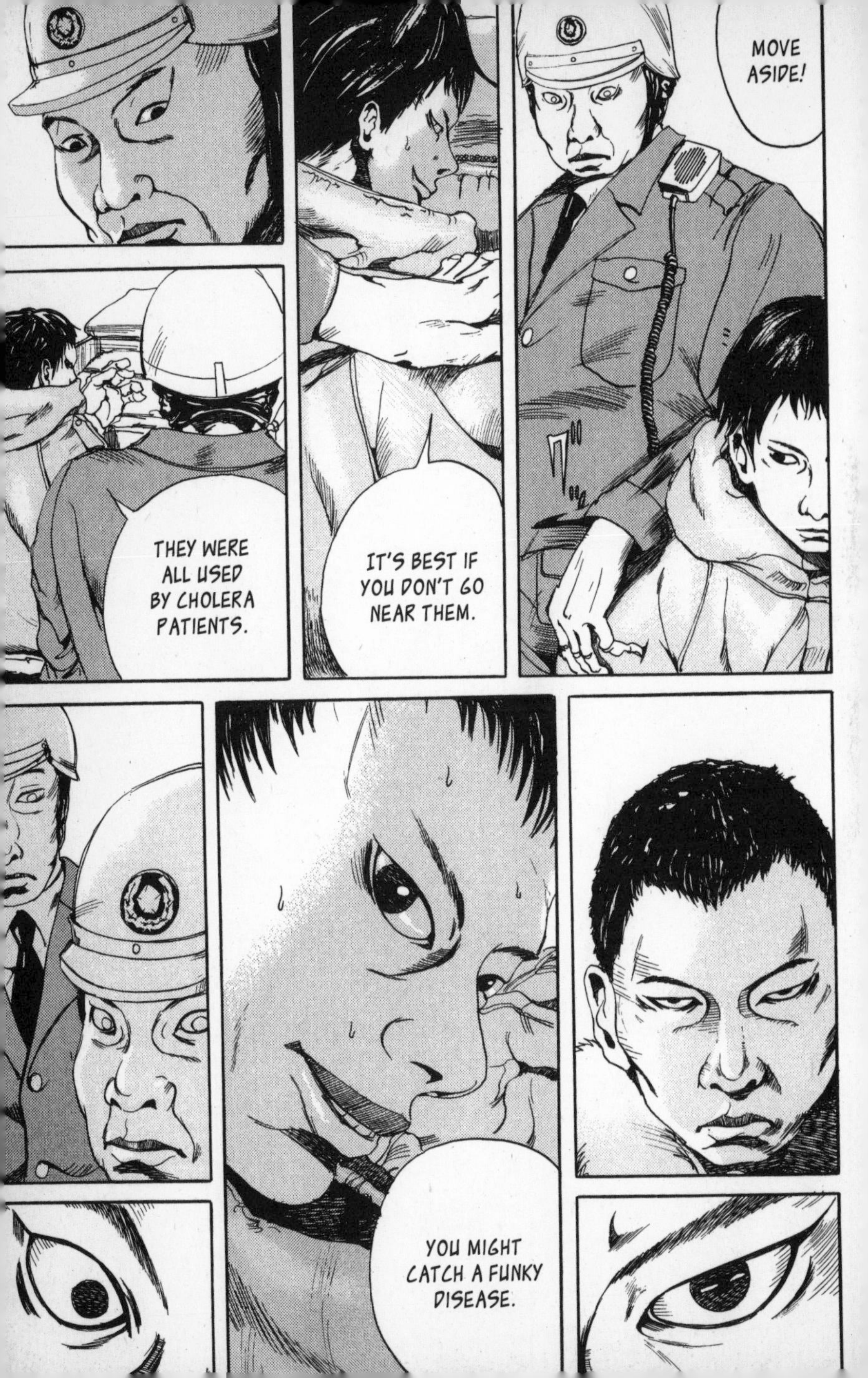
MOVE ASIDE!
IT'S BEST IF YOU DON'T GO NEAR THEM.
THEY WERE ALL USED BY CHOLERA PATIENTS.
YOU MIGHT CATCH A FUNKY DISEASE.

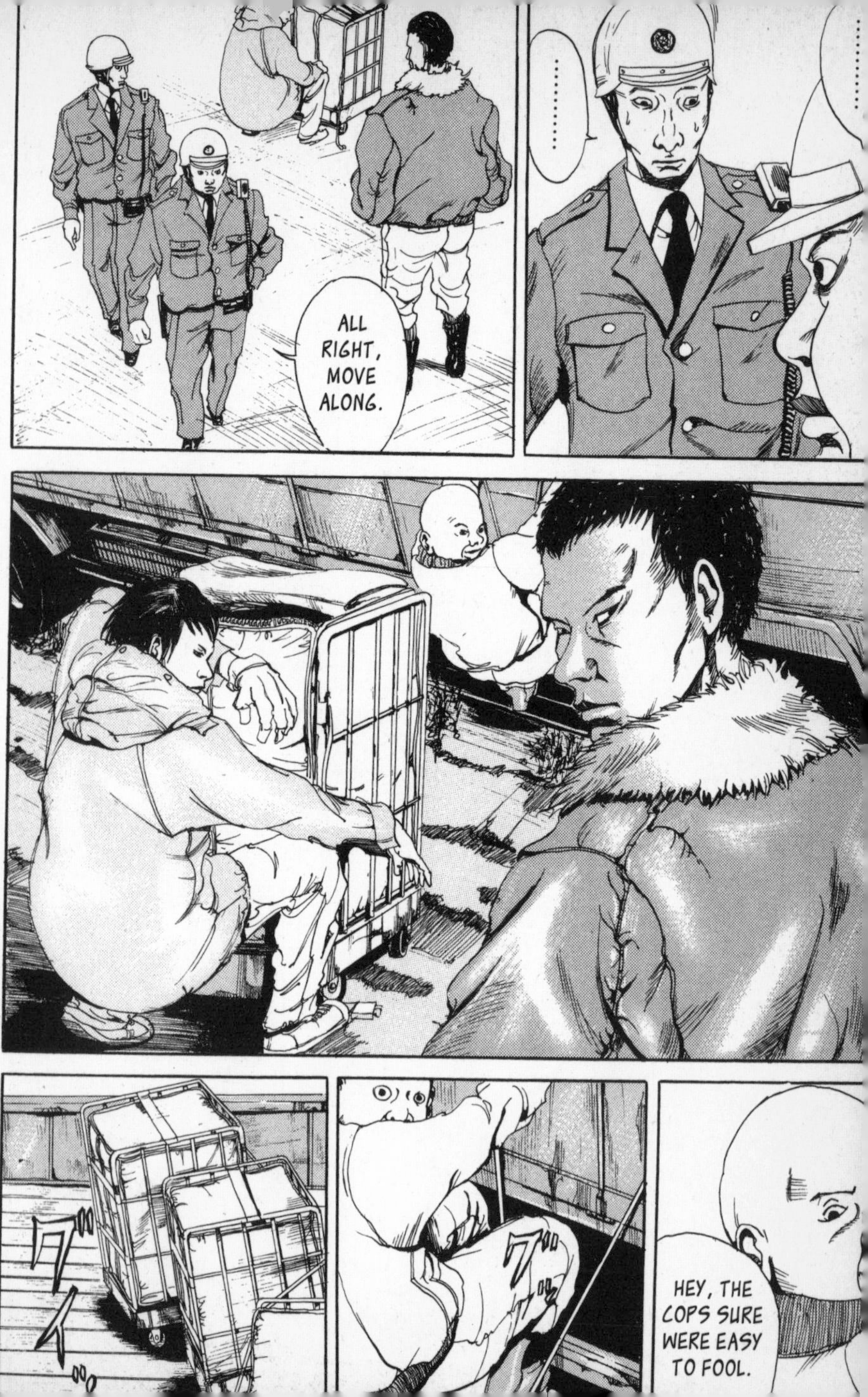
......
ALL RIGHT, MOVE ALONG.
HEY, THE COPS SURE WERE EASY TO FOOL.

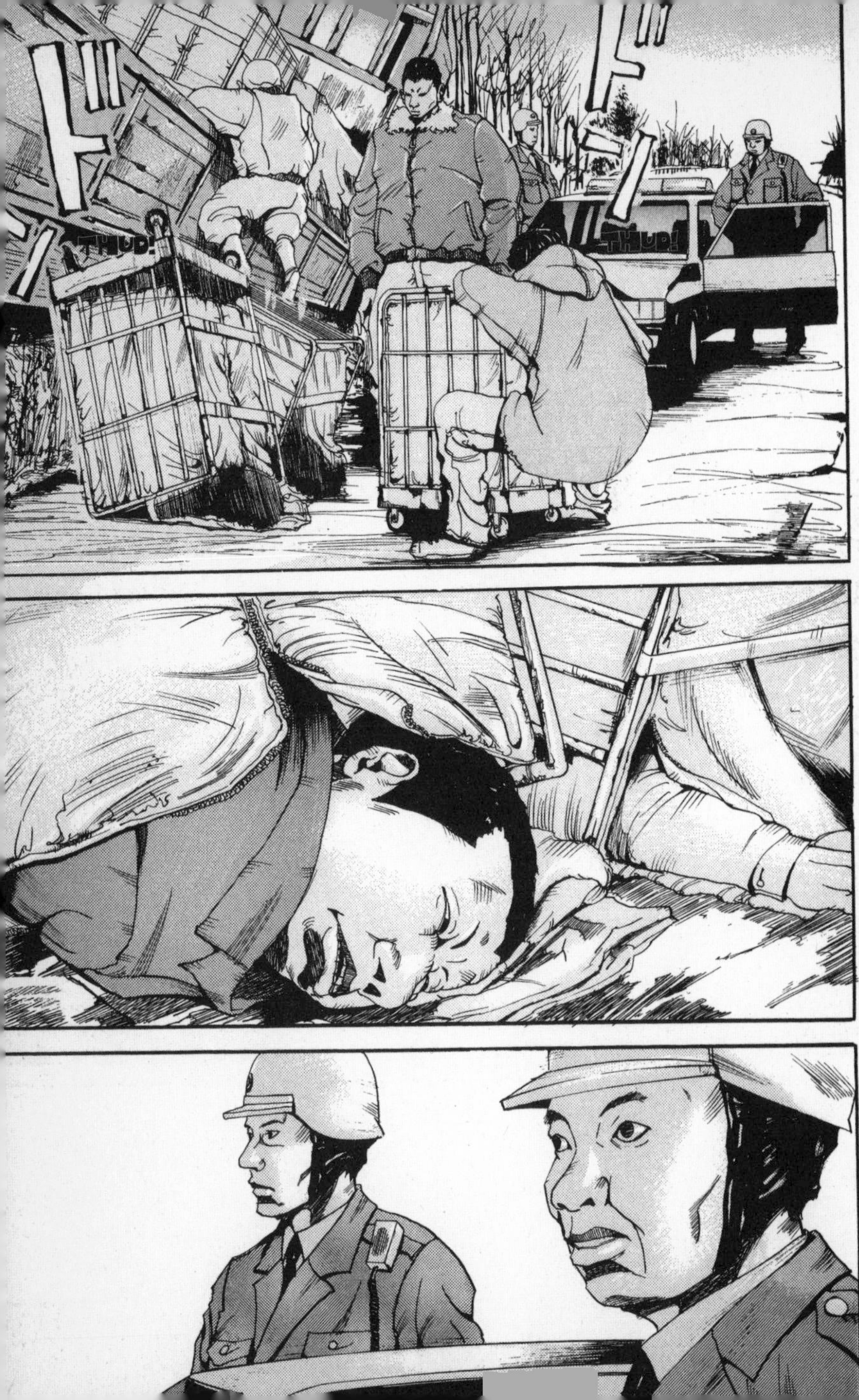
THUD!
THUD!

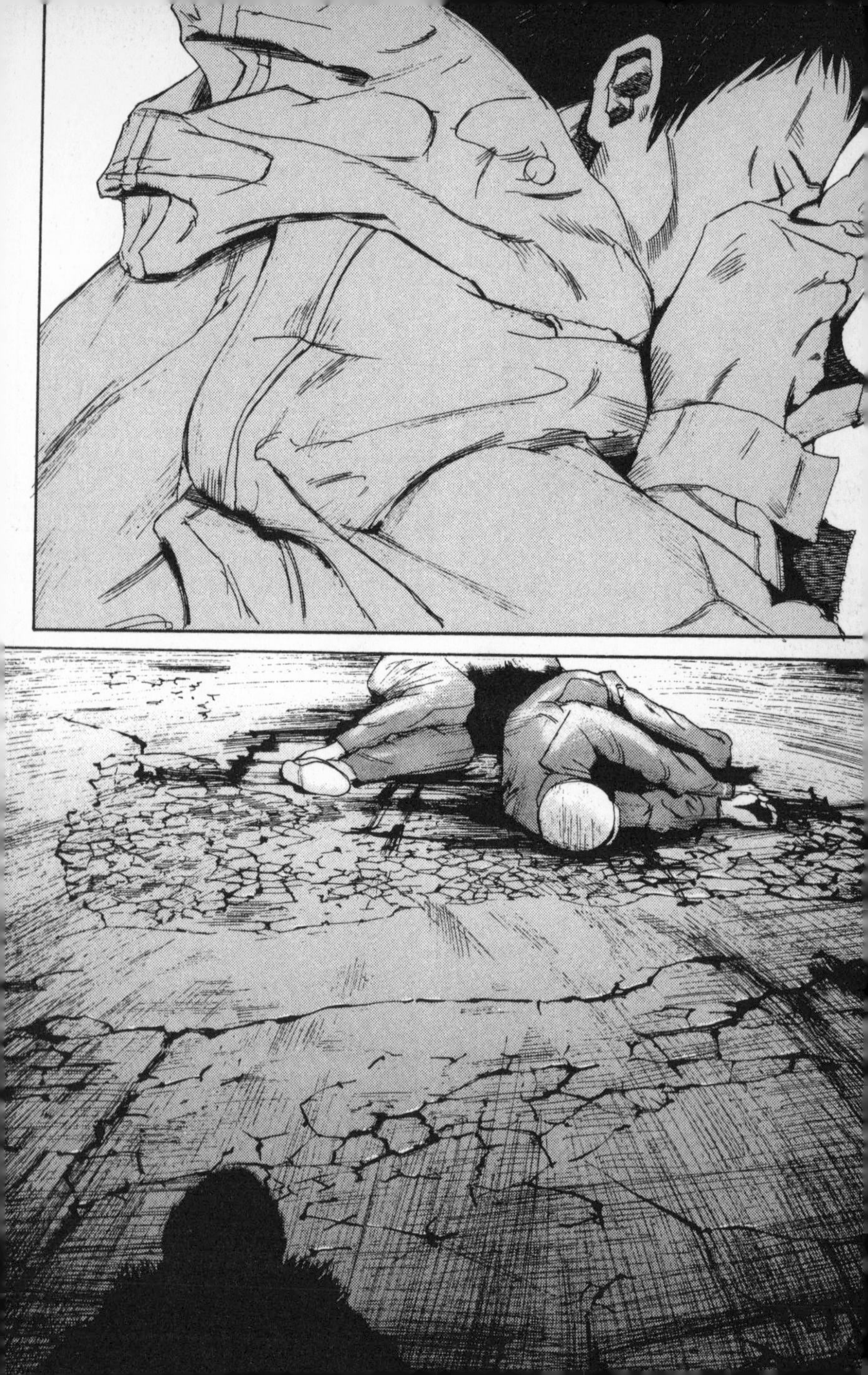

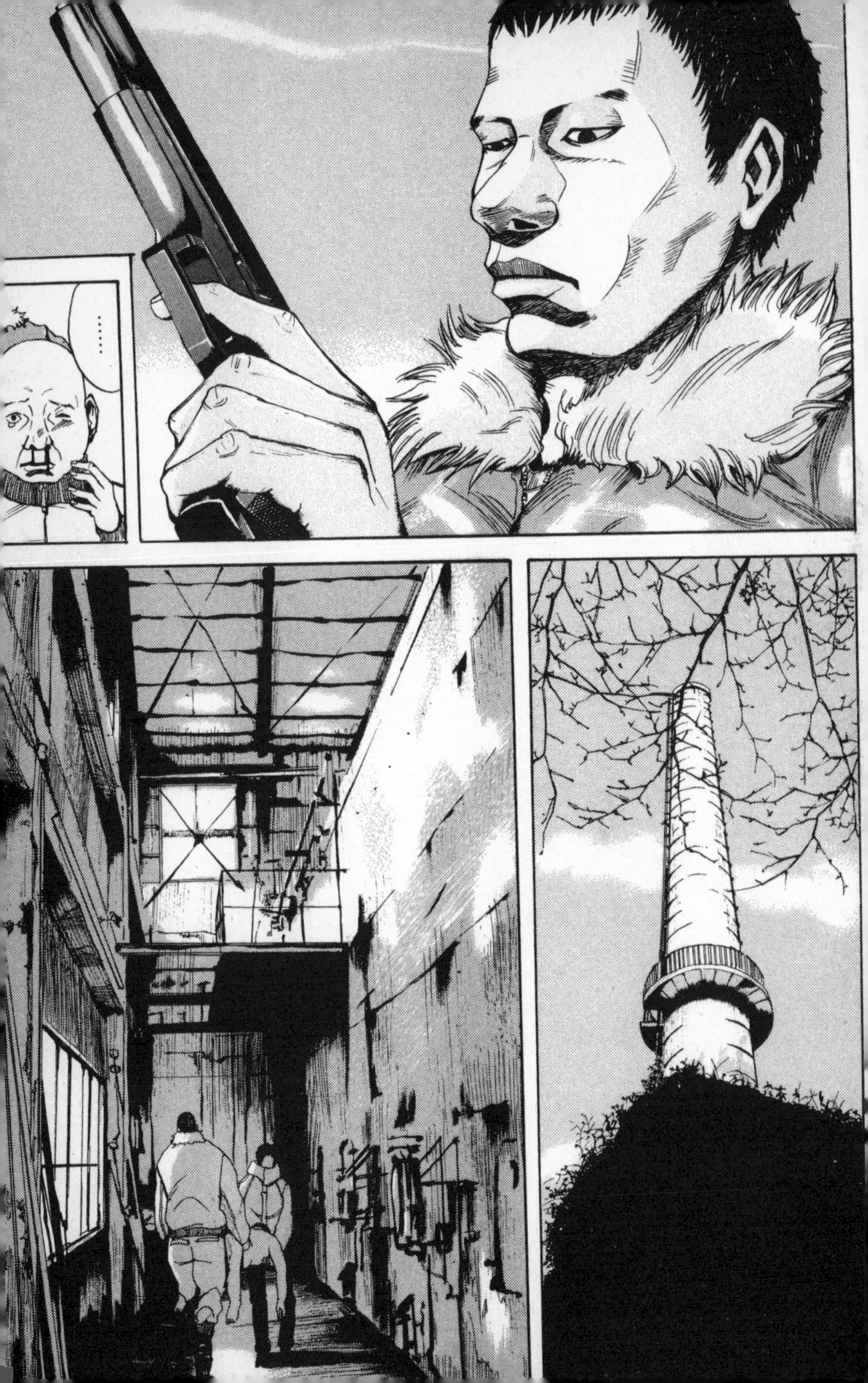
……

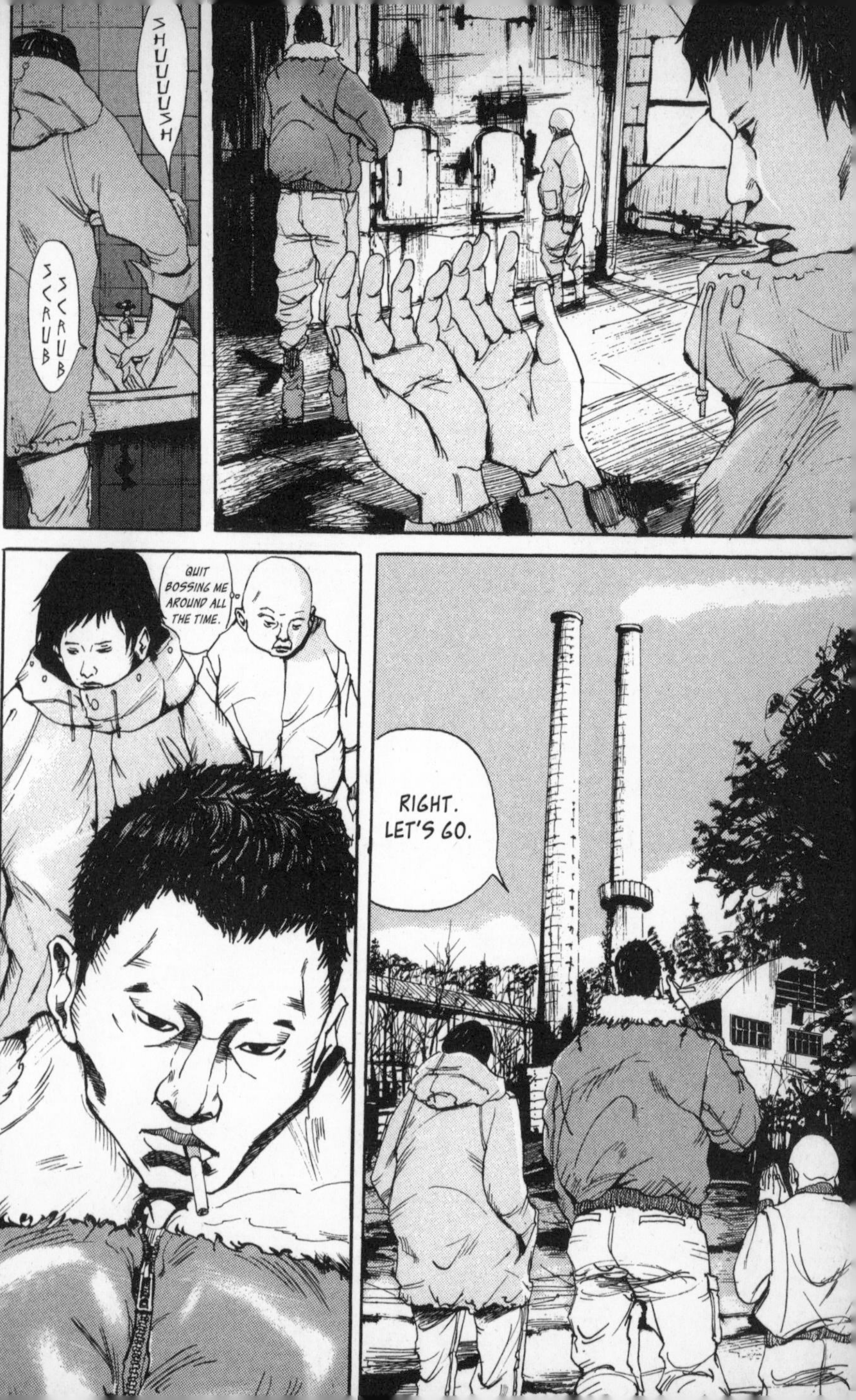
SHUUUUSH
SCRUB SCRUB
RIGHT. LET'S GO.
QUIT BOSSING ME AROUND ALL THE TIME.

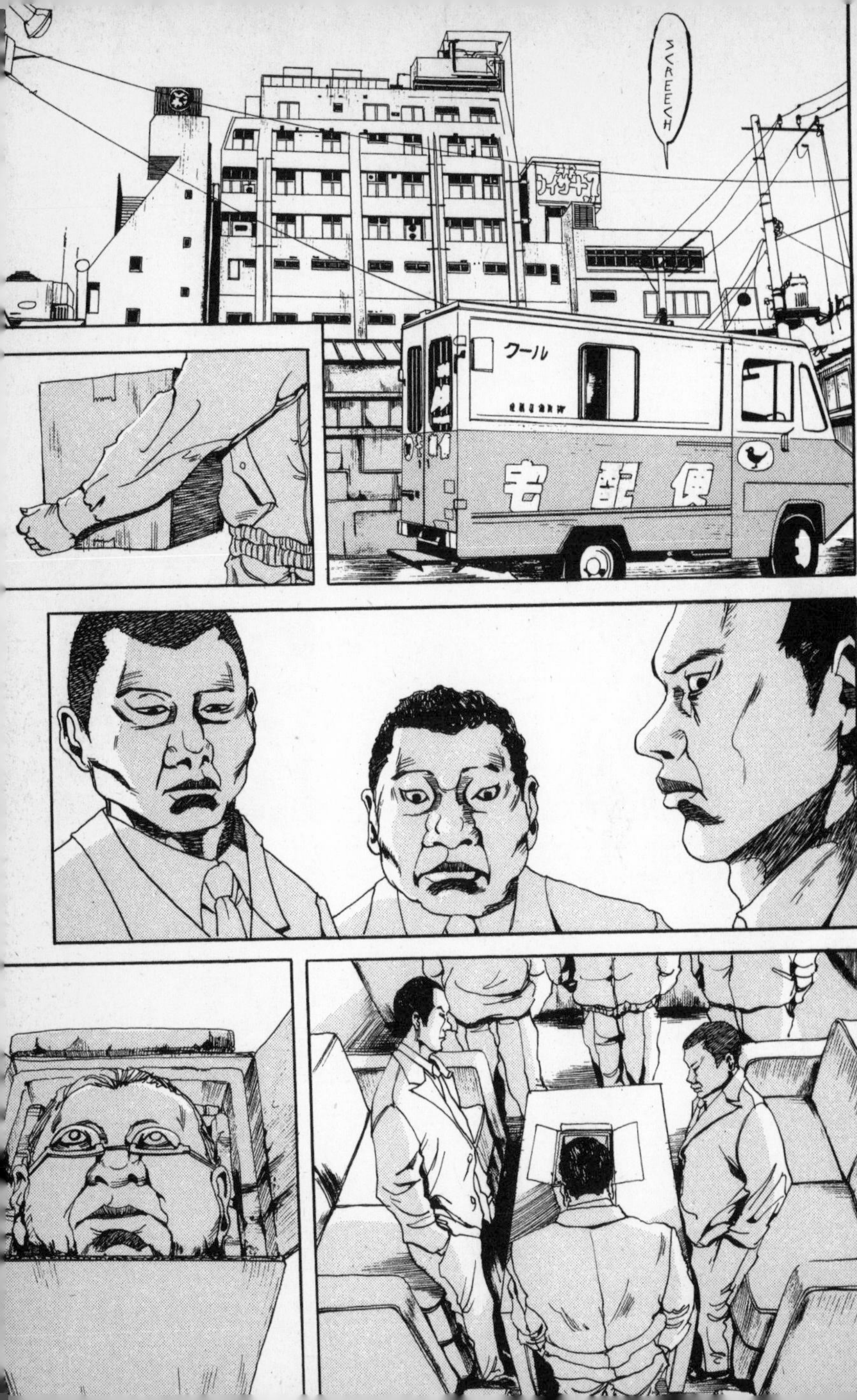
SCREECH
クール
宅配便

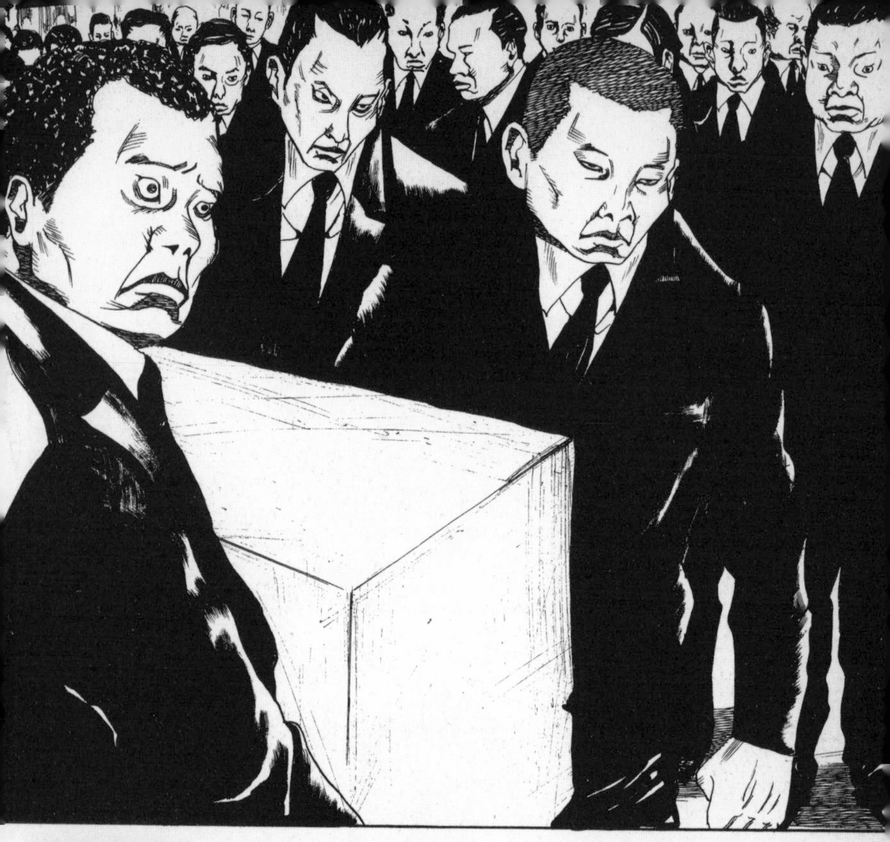
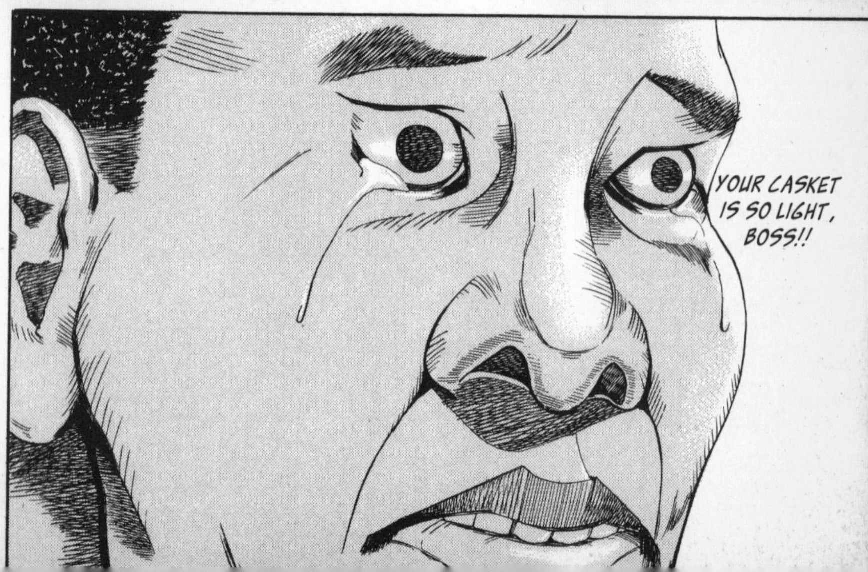
YOUR CASKET IS SO LIGHT, BOSS!!

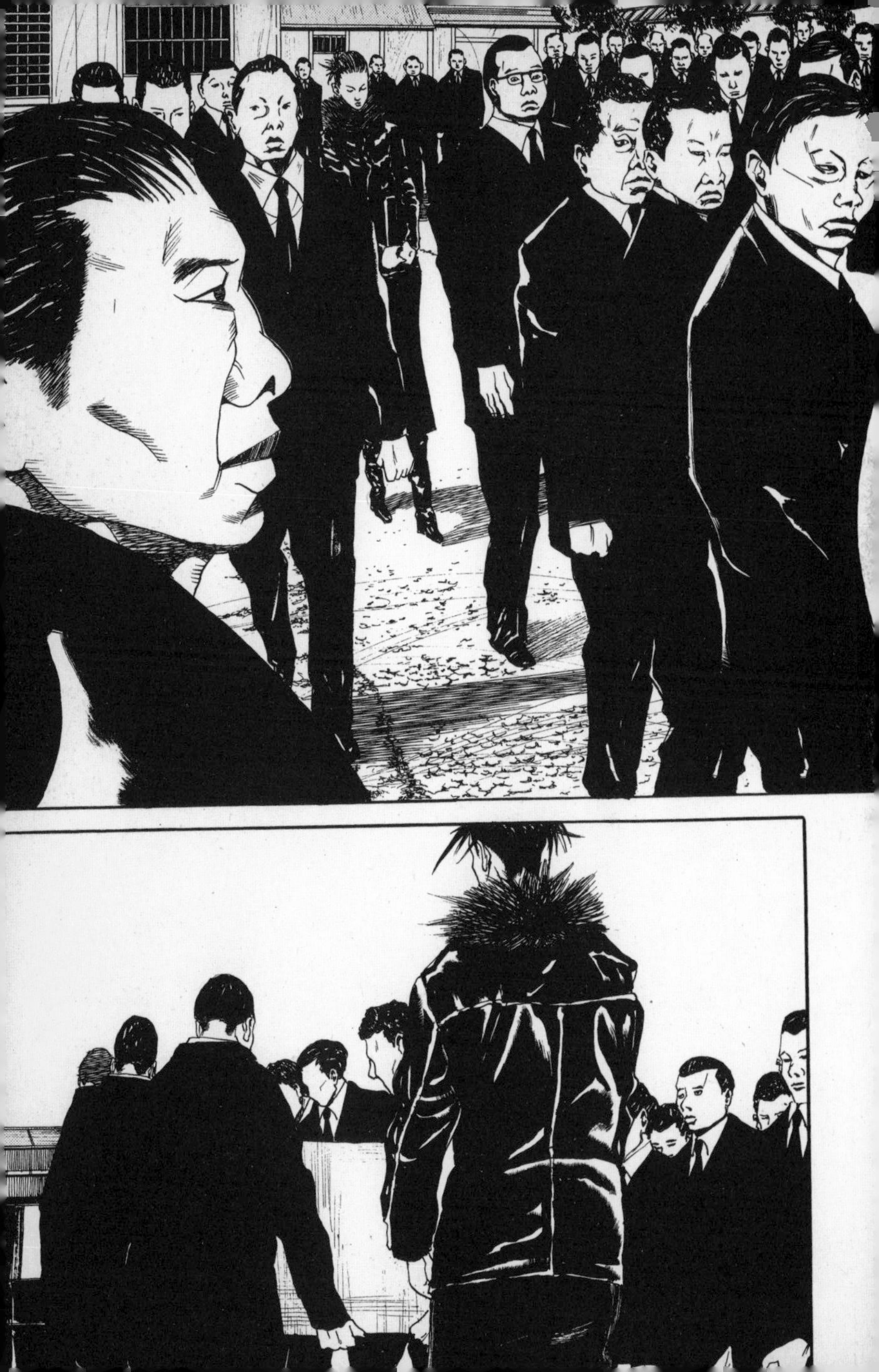

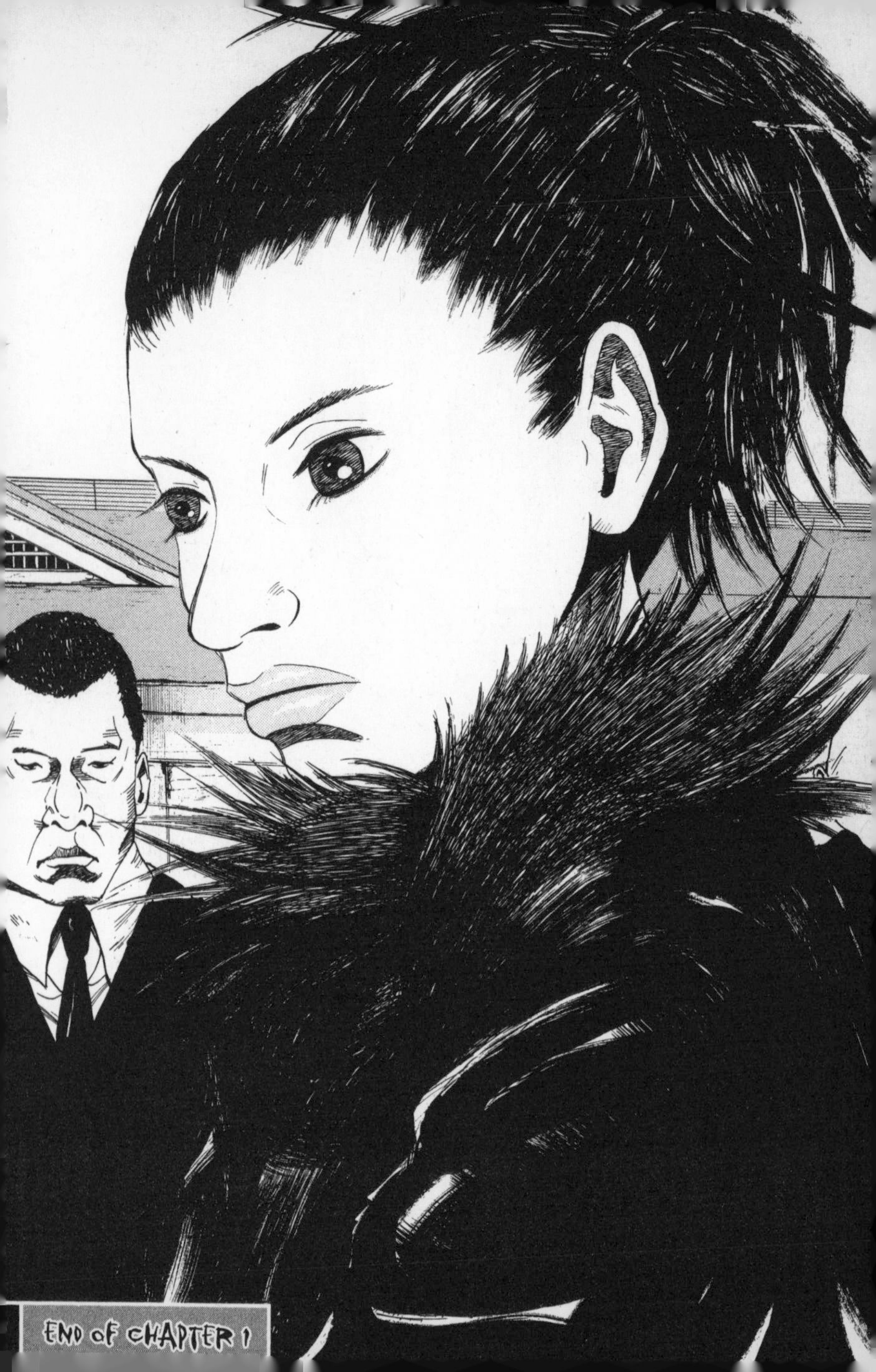
END OF CHAPTER 1

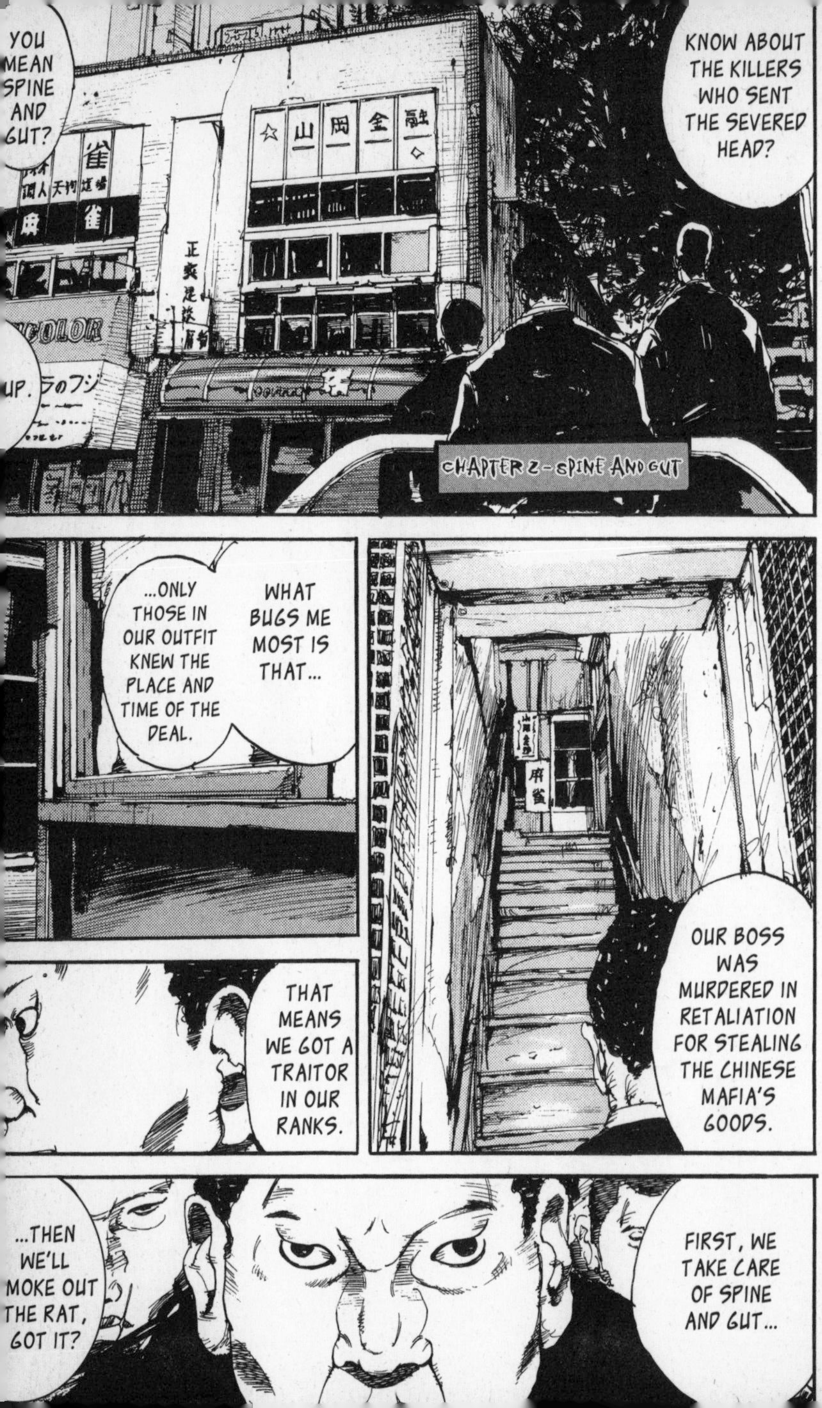
KNOW ABOUT THE KILLERS WHO SENT THE SEVERED HEAD?
YOU MEAN SPINE AND GUT?
UP.
山岡金融
CHAPTER 2 - SPINE AND GUT
OUR BOSS WAS MURDERED IN RETALIATION FOR STEALING THE CHINESE MAFIA'S GOODS.
WHAT BUGS ME MOST IS THAT...
...ONLY THOSE IN OUR OUTFIT KNEW THE PLACE AND TIME OF THE DEAL.
THAT MEANS WE GOT A TRAITOR IN OUR RANKS.
FIRST, WE TAKE CARE OF SPINE AND GUT...
...THEN WE'LL MOKE OUT THE RAT, GOT IT?

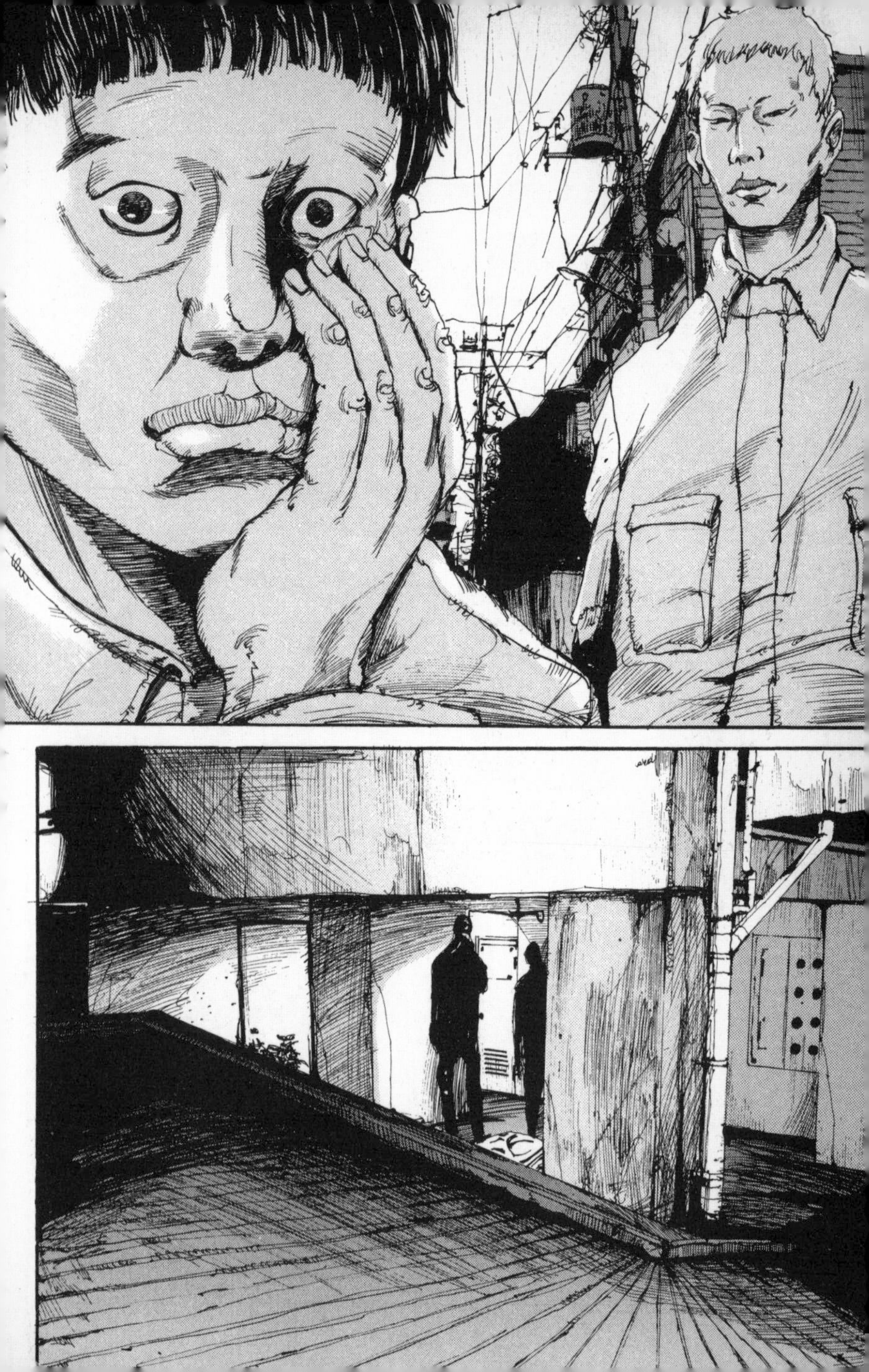

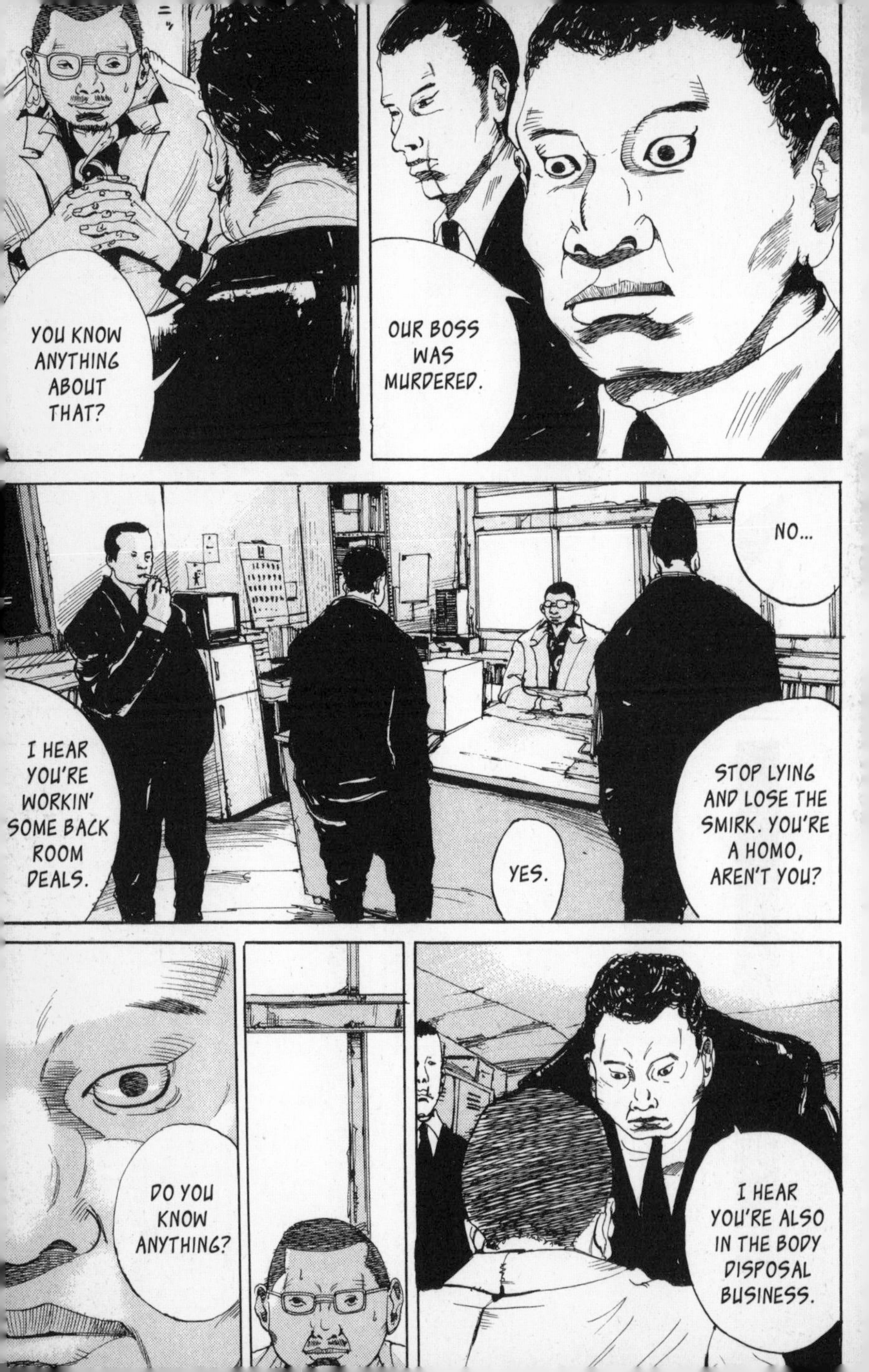
OUR BOSS WAS MURDERED.
ニッ
YOU KNOW ANYTHING ABOUT THAT?
NO...
STOP LYING AND LOSE THE SMIRK. YOU'RE A HOMO, AREN'T YOU?
YES.
I HEAR YOU'RE WORKIN' SOME BACK ROOM DEALS.
I HEAR YOU'RE ALSO IN THE BODY DISPOSAL BUSINESS.
DO YOU KNOW ANYTHING?

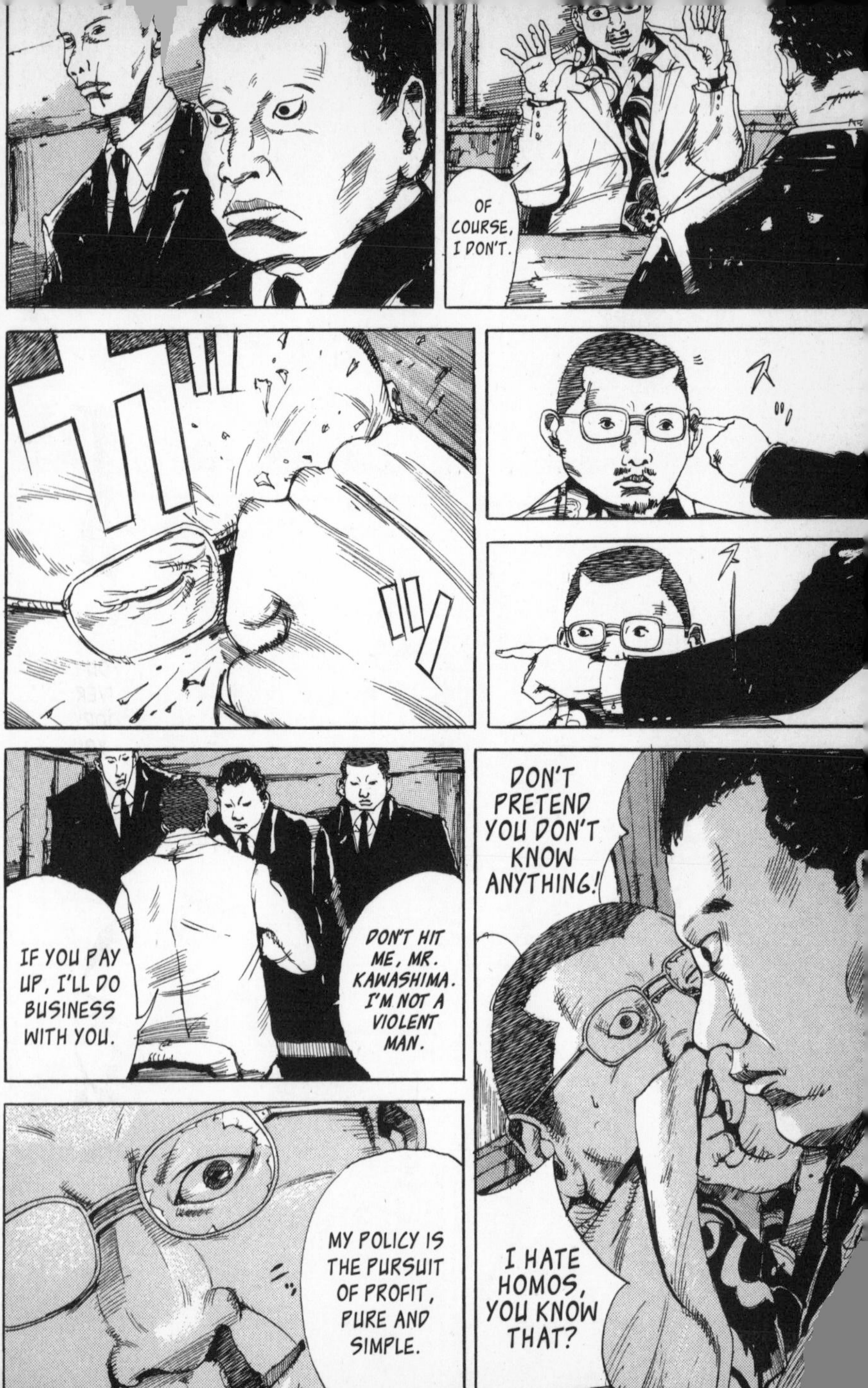
OF COURSE, I DON'T.
DON'T PRETEND YOU DON'T KNOW ANYTHING!
I HATE HOMOS, YOU KNOW THAT?
DON'T HIT ME, MR. KAWASHIMA. I'M NOT A VIOLENT MAN.
IF YOU PAY UP, I'LL DO BUSINESS WITH YOU.
MY POLICY IS THE PURSUIT OF PROFIT, PURE AND SIMPLE.

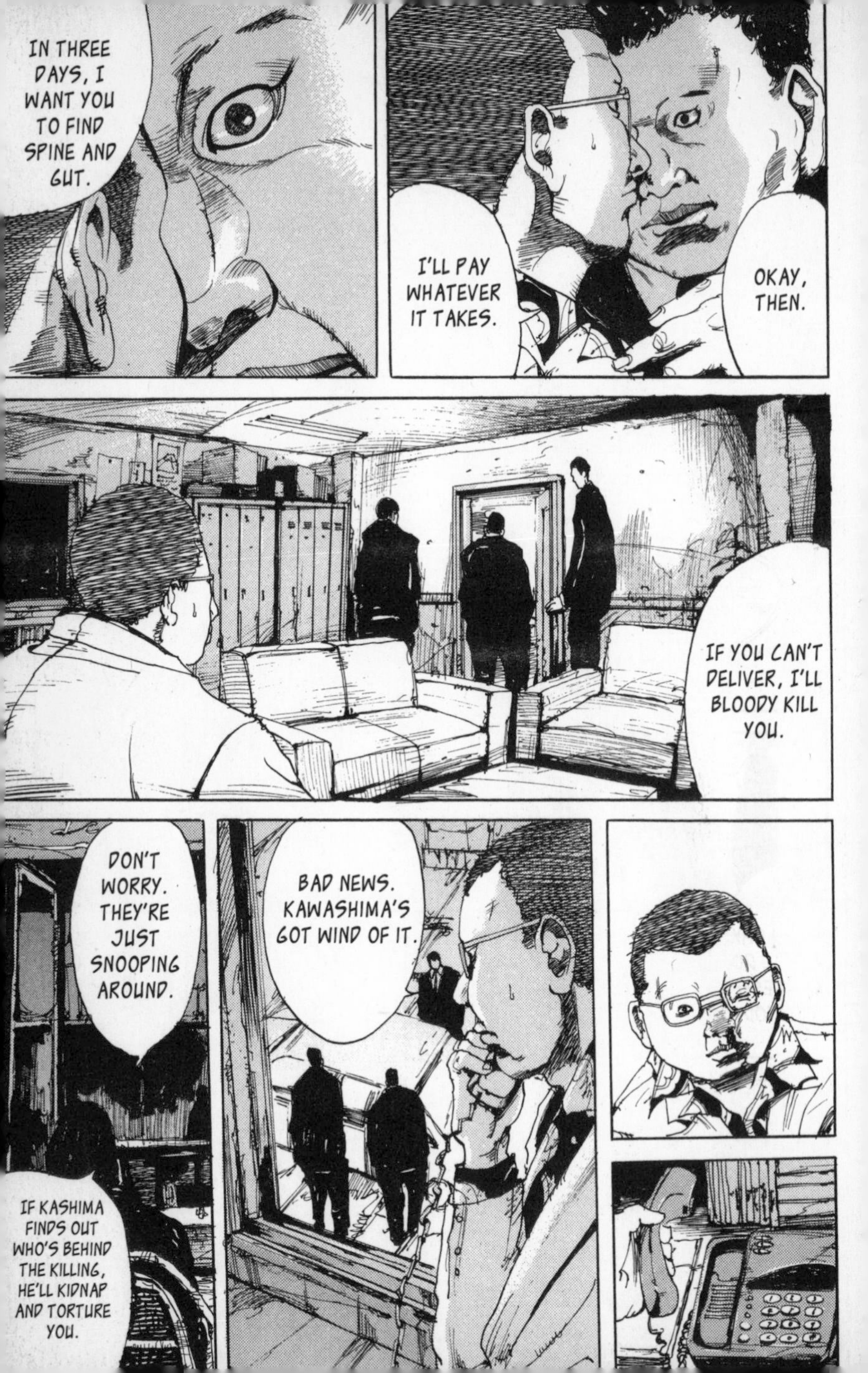
OKAY, THEN.
I'LL PAY WHATEVER IT TAKES.
IN THREE DAYS, I WANT YOU TO FIND SPINE AND GUT.
IF YOU CAN'T DELIVER, I'LL BLOODY KILL YOU.
BAD NEWS. KAWASHIMA'S GOT WIND OF IT.
DON'T WORRY. THEY'RE JUST SNOOPING AROUND.
IF KASHIMA FINDS OUT WHO'S BEHIND THE KILLING, HE'LL KIDNAP AND TORTURE YOU.

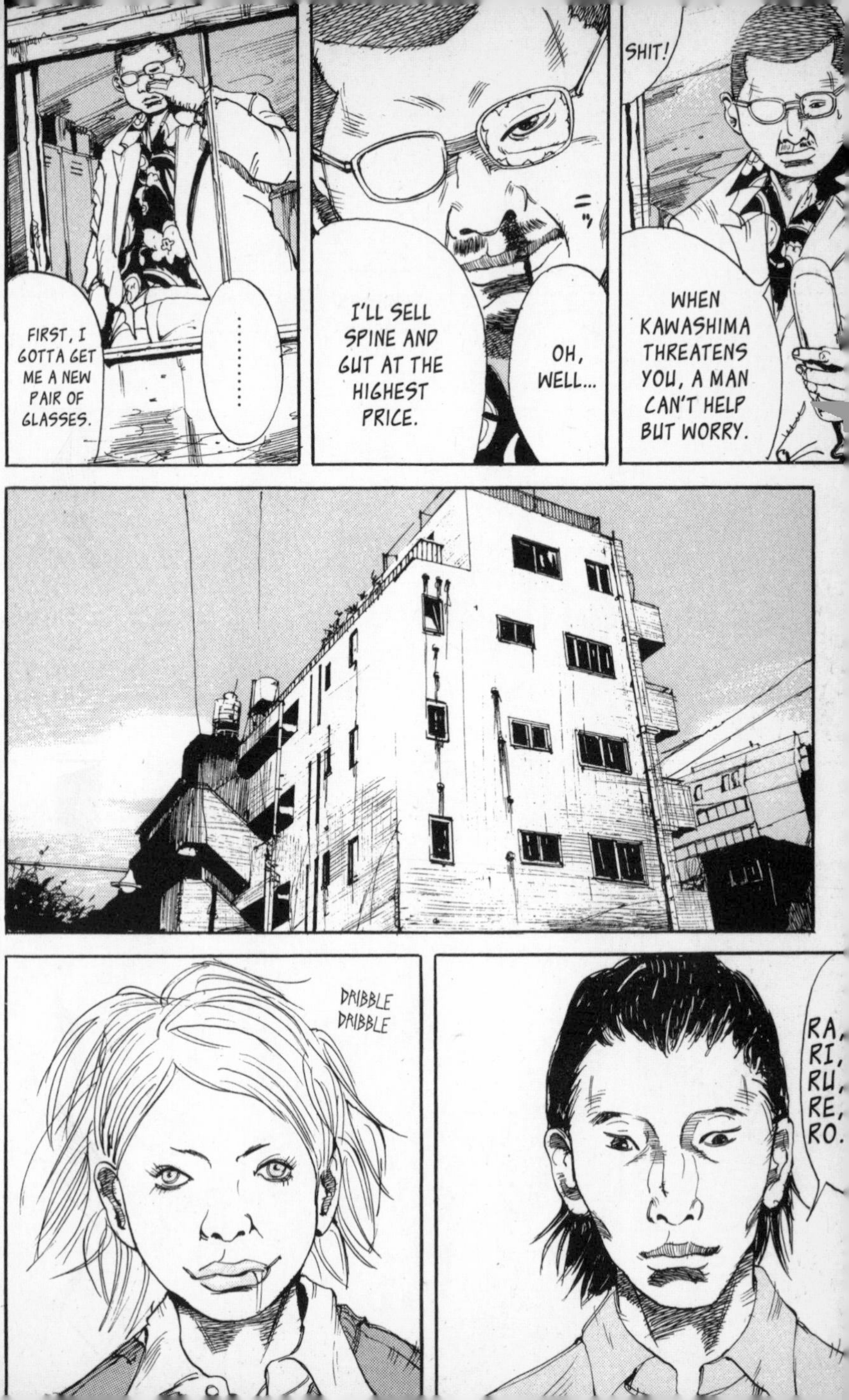
SHIT!
WHEN KAWASHIMA THREATENS YOU, A MAN CAN'T HELP BUT WORRY.
OH, WELL...
I'LL SELL SPINE AND GUT AT THE HIGHEST PRICE.
......
FIRST, I GOTTA GET ME A NEW PAIR OF GLASSES.
RA, RI, RU, RE, RO.
DRIBBLE DRIBBLE

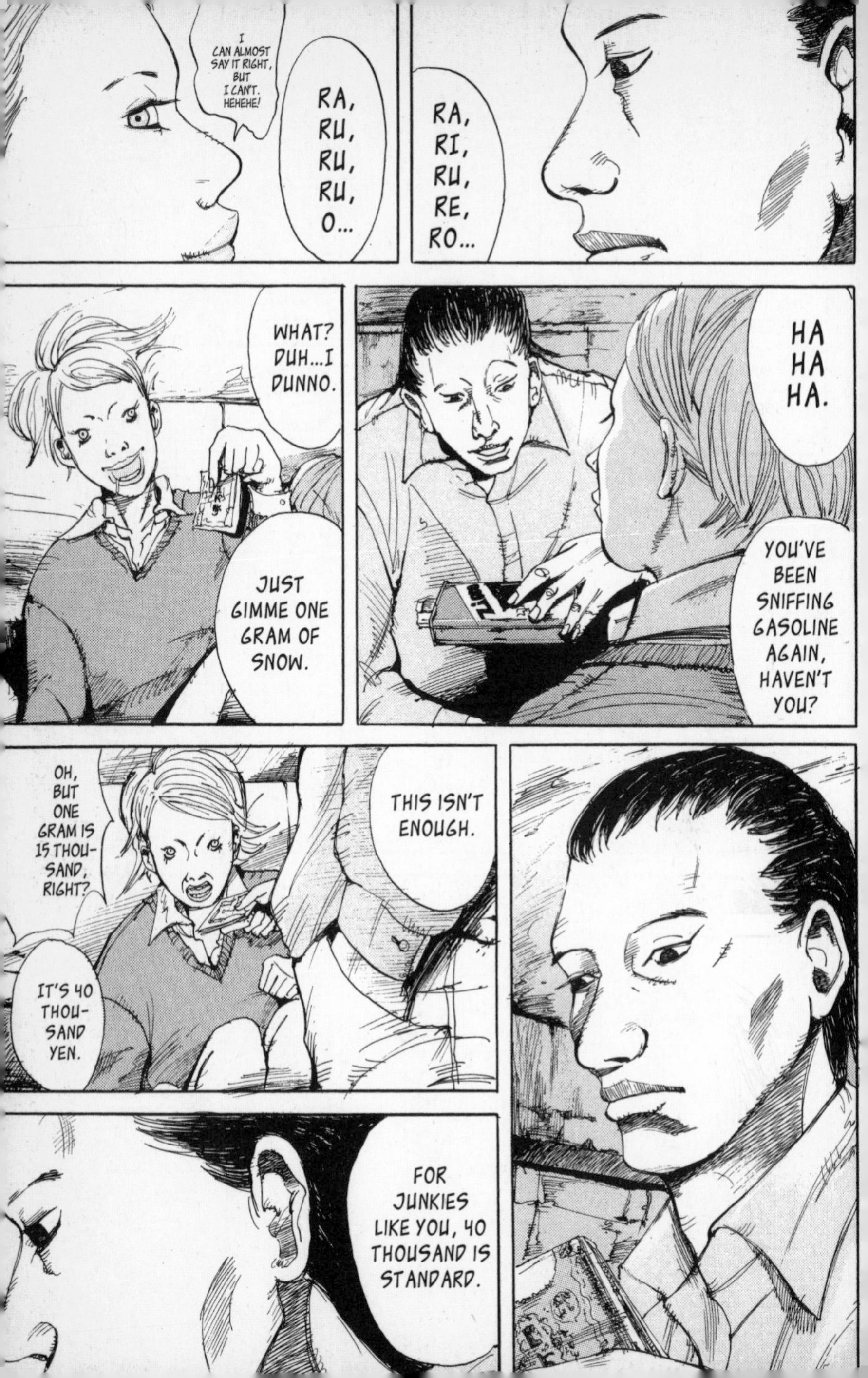
RA, RI, RU, RE, RO...
RA, RU, RU, RU, O...
I CAN ALMOST SAY IT RIGHT, BUT I CAN'T. HEHEHE!
HA HA HA.
YOU'VE BEEN SNIFFING GASOLINE AGAIN, HAVEN'T YOU?
WHAT? DUH...I DUNNO.
JUST GIMME ONE GRAM OF SNOW.
THIS ISN'T ENOUGH.
OH, BUT ONE GRAM IS 15 THOU-SAND, RIGHT?
IT'S 40 THOU-SAND YEN.
FOR JUNKIES LIKE YOU, 40 THOUSAND IS STANDARD.

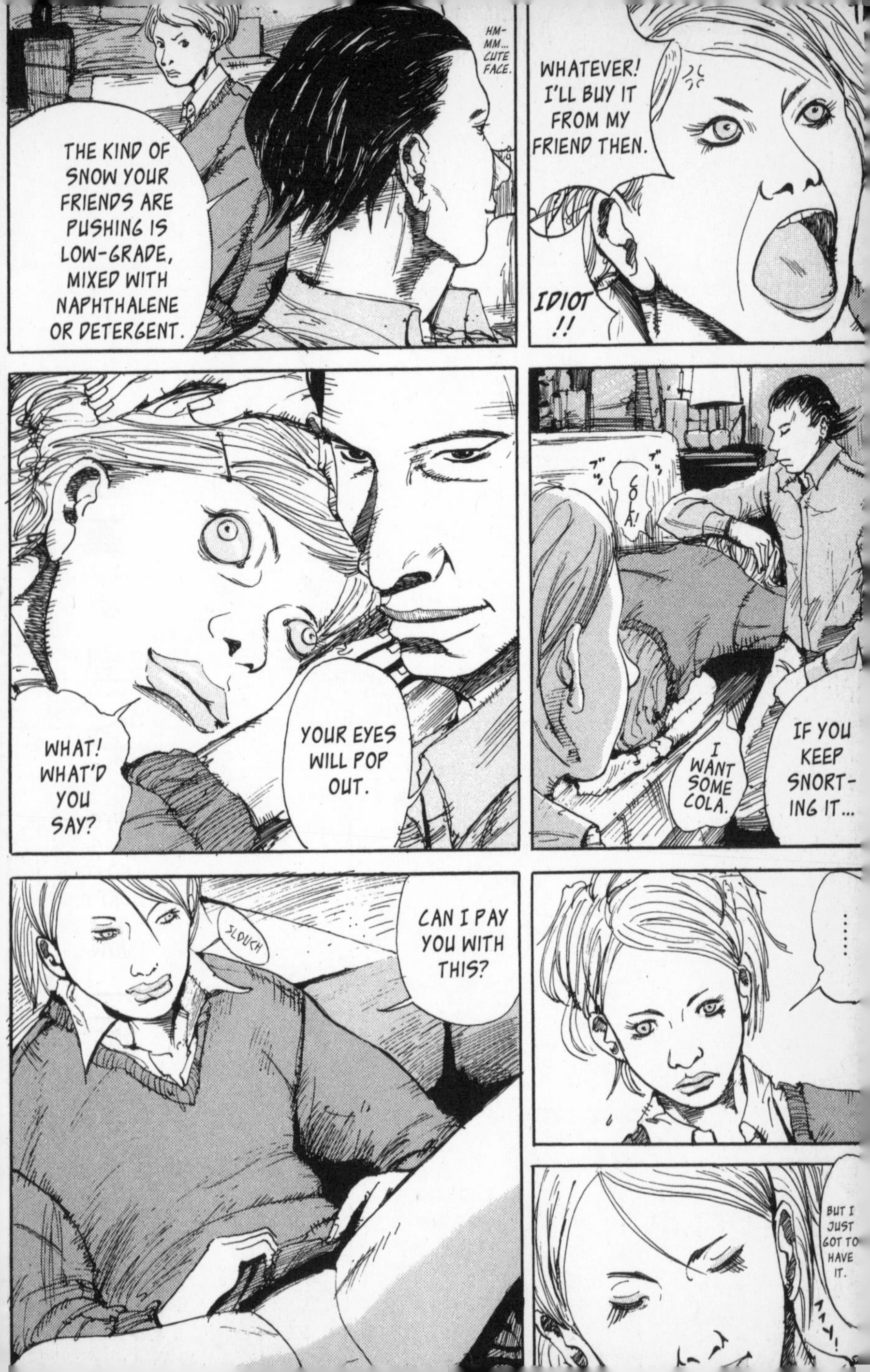
WHATEVER! I'LL BUY IT FROM MY FRIEND THEN.
IDIOT!!
HM-MM... CUTE FACE.
THE KIND OF SNOW YOUR FRIENDS ARE PUSHING IS LOW-GRADE, MIXED WITH NAPHTHALENE OR DETERGENT.
COLA!
IF YOU KEEP SNORT-ING IT...
I WANT SOME COLA.
YOUR EYES WILL POP OUT.
WHAT! WHAT'D YOU SAY?
......
BUT I JUST GOT TO HAVE IT.
CAN I PAY YOU WITH THIS?
SLOUCH

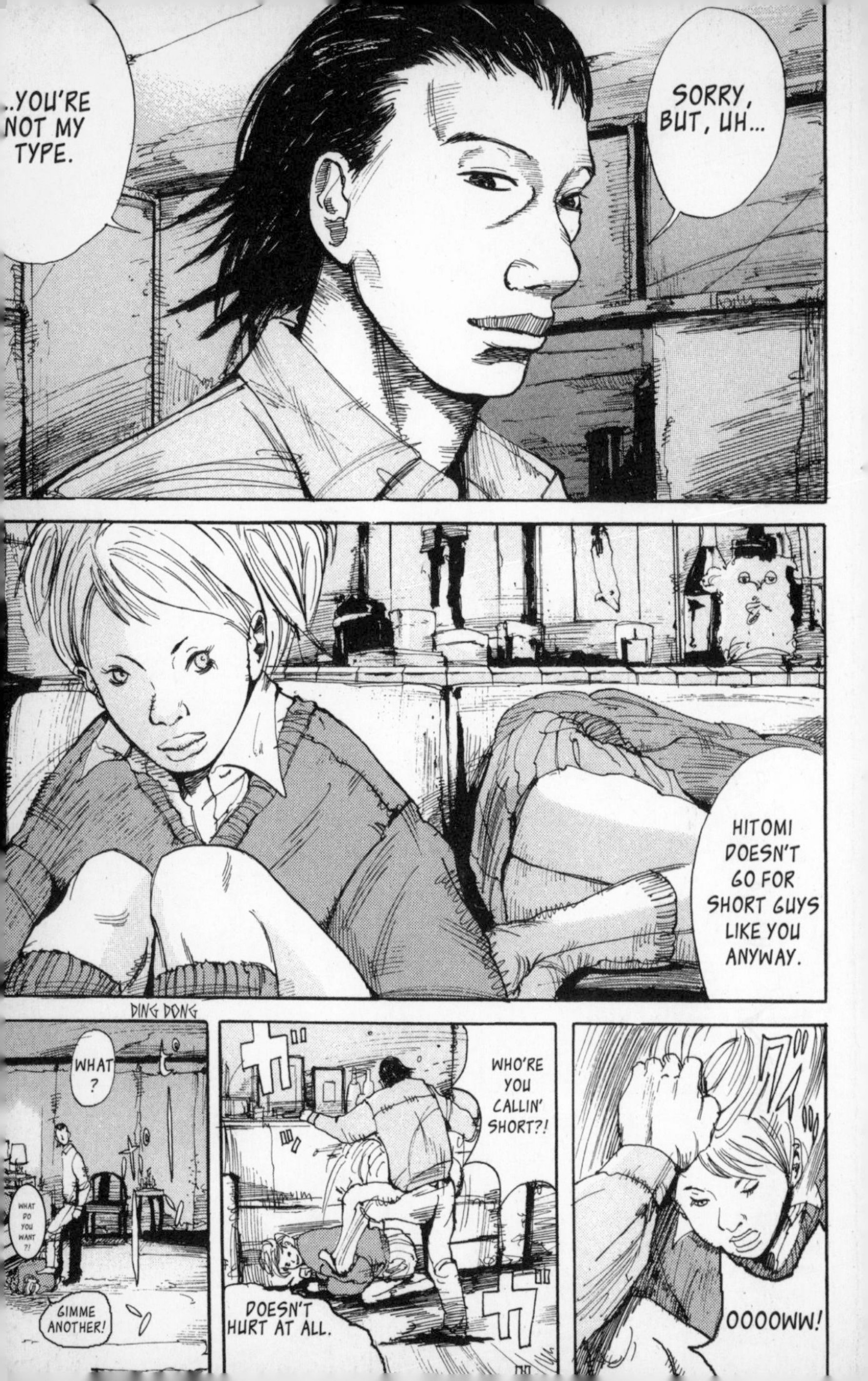
SORRY, BUT, UH...
..YOU'RE NOT MY TYPE.
HITOMI DOESN'T GO FOR SHORT GUYS LIKE YOU ANYWAY.
OOOOWW!
WHO'RE YOU CALLIN' SHORT?!
DOESN'T HURT AT ALL.
DING DONG
WHAT ?
WHAT DO YOU WANT ?!
GIMME ANOTHER!

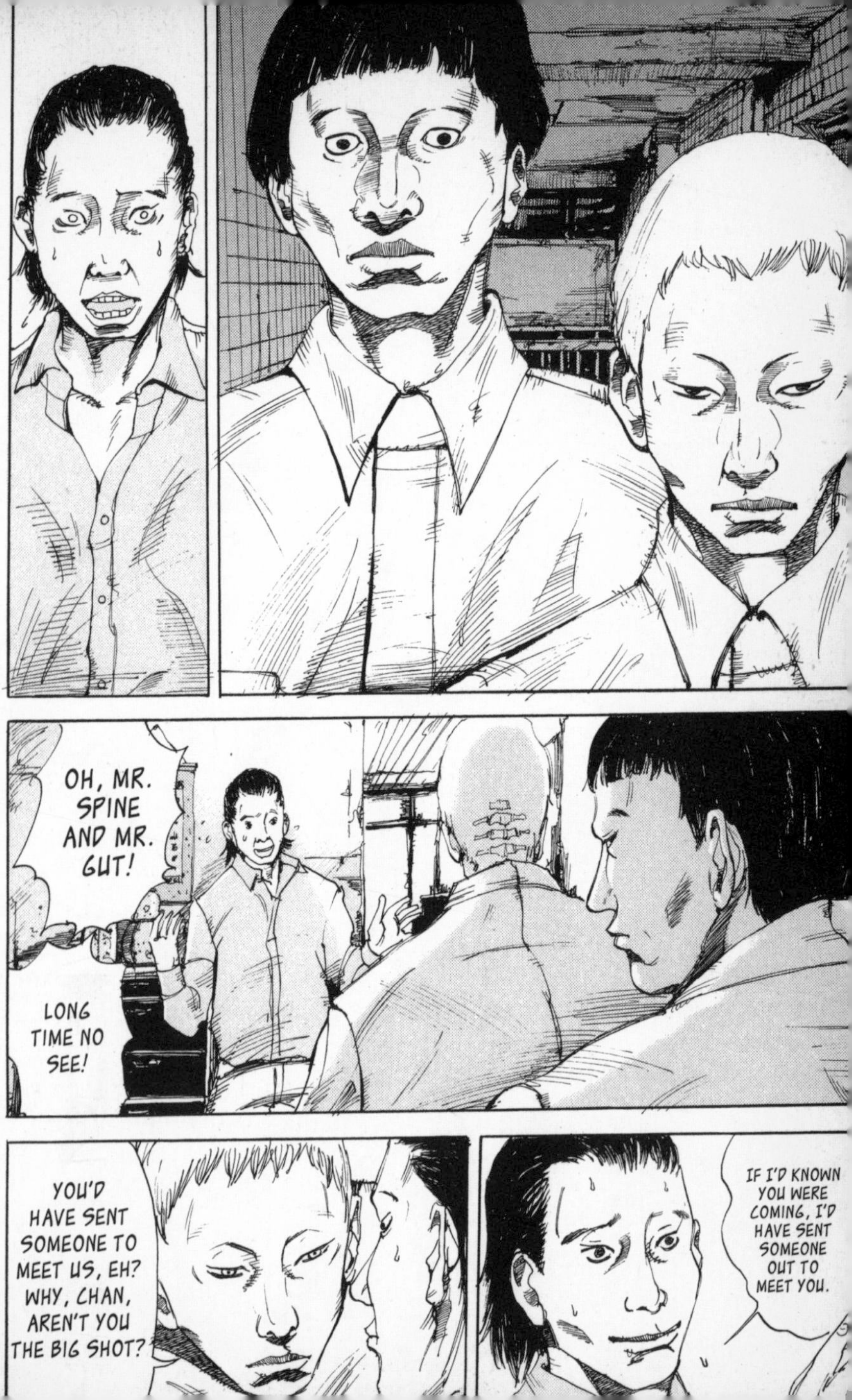
OH, MR. SPINE AND MR. GUT!
LONG TIME NO SEE!
IF I'D KNOWN YOU WERE COMING, I'D HAVE SENT SOMEONE OUT TO MEET YOU.
YOU'D HAVE SENT SOMEONE TO MEET US, EH? WHY, CHAN, AREN'T YOU THE BIG SHOT?

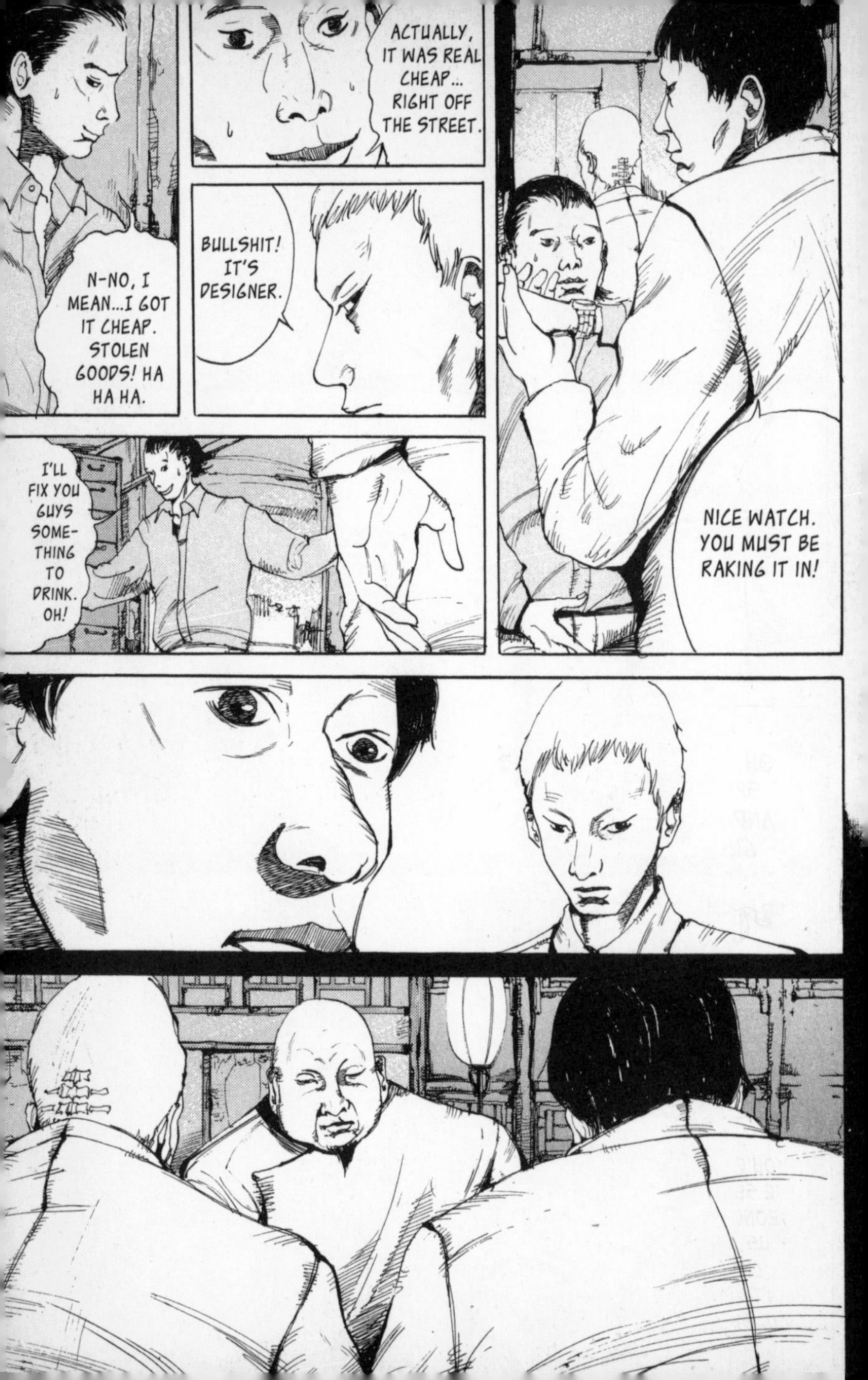
NICE WATCH. YOU MUST BE RAKING IT IN!
ACTUALLY, IT WAS REAL CHEAP... RIGHT OFF THE STREET.
BULLSHIT! IT'S DESIGNER.
N-NO, I MEAN...I GOT IT CHEAP. STOLEN GOODS! HA HA HA.
I'LL FIX YOU GUYS SOME-THING TO DRINK. OH!

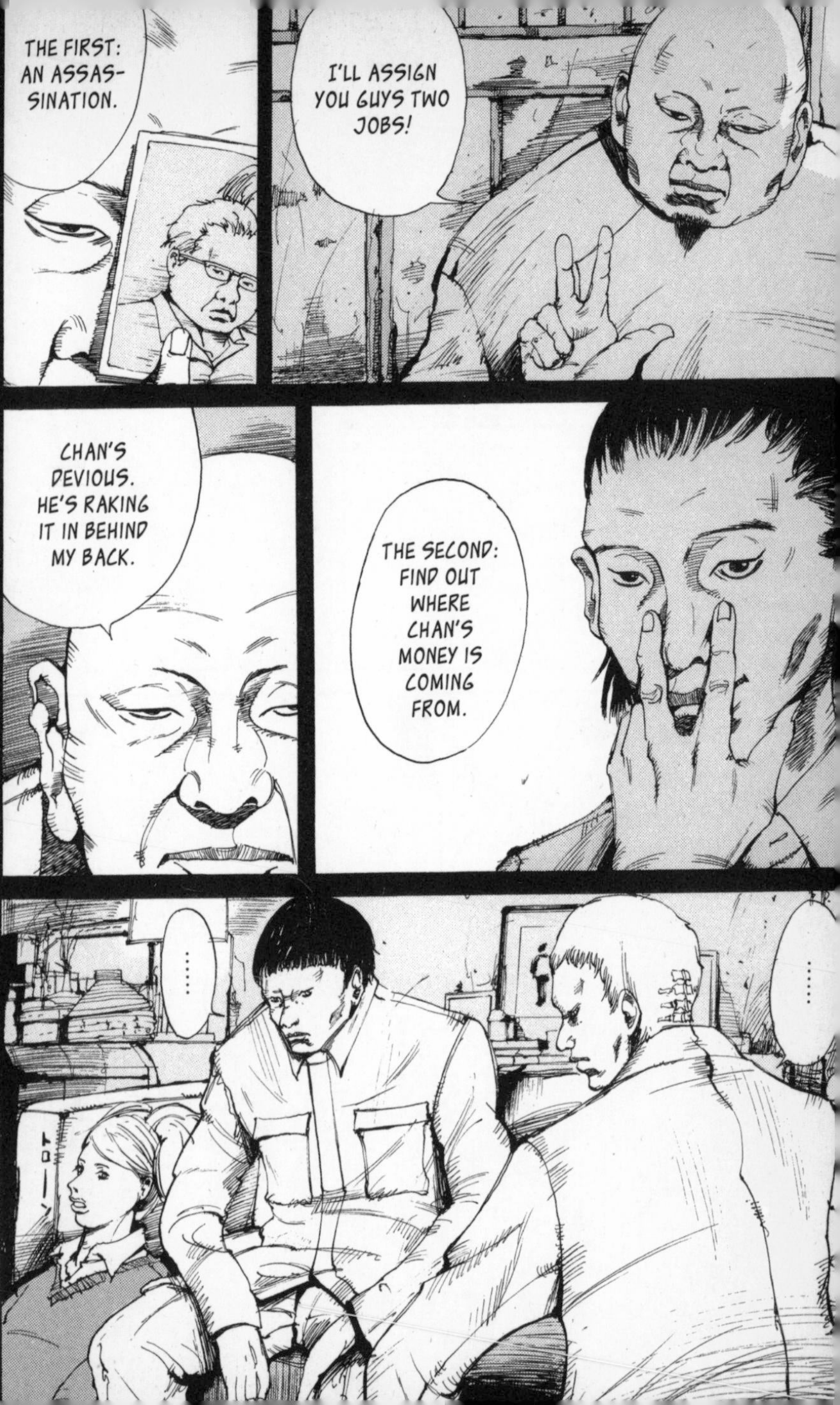
I'LL ASSIGN YOU GUYS TWO JOBS!
THE FIRST: AN ASSASSINATION.
THE SECOND: FIND OUT WHERE CHAN'S MONEY IS COMING FROM.
CHAN'S DEVIOUS. HE'S RAKING IT IN BEHIND MY BACK.
......
......
トローン

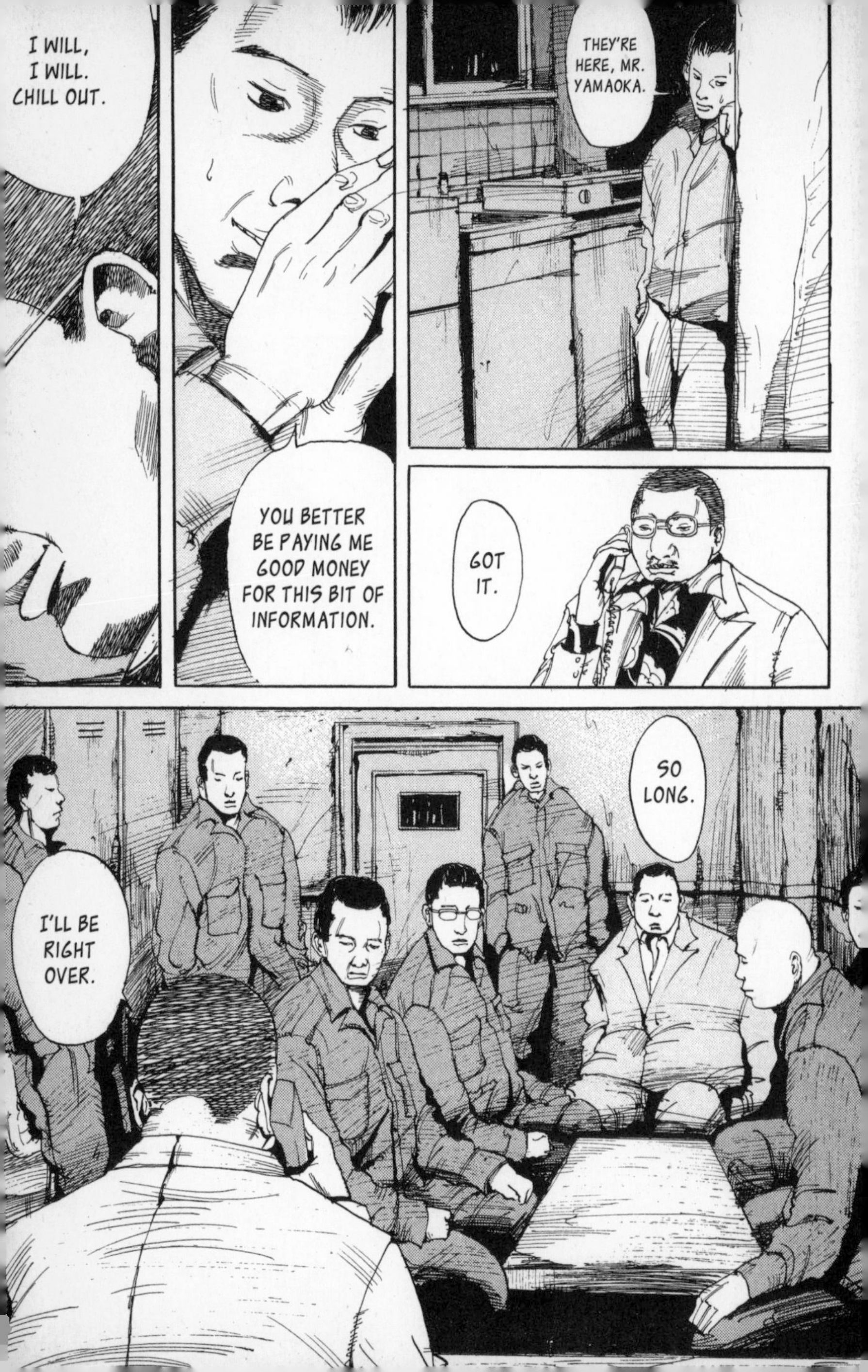
THEY'RE HERE, MR. YAMAOKA.
GOT IT.
YOU BETTER BE PAYING ME GOOD MONEY FOR THIS BIT OF INFORMATION.
I WILL, I WILL. CHILL OUT.
SO LONG.
I'LL BE RIGHT OVER.

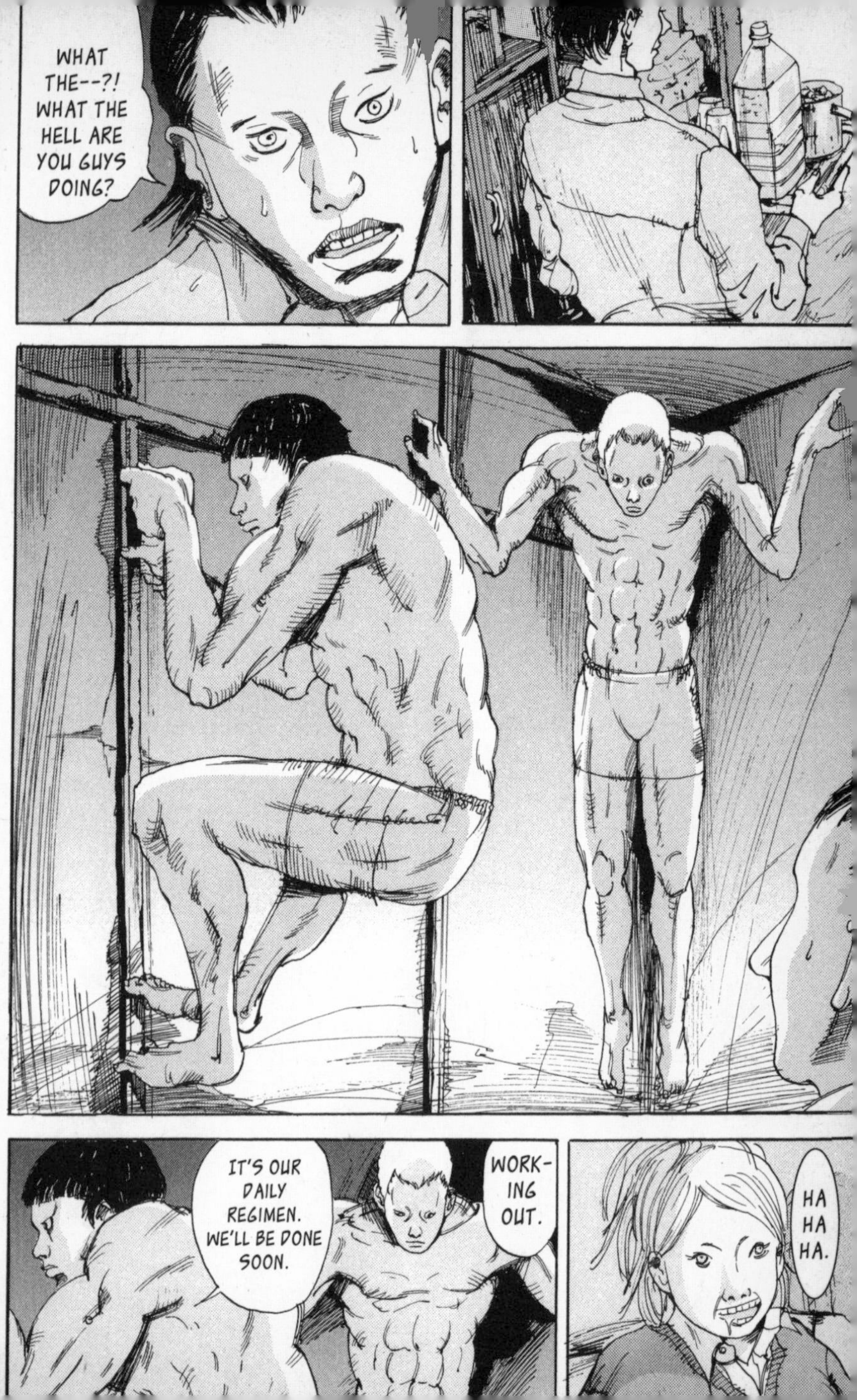
WHAT THE--?! WHAT THE HELL ARE YOU GUYS DOING?
HA HA HA.
WORK-ING OUT.
IT'S OUR DAILY REGIMEN. WE'LL BE DONE SOON.

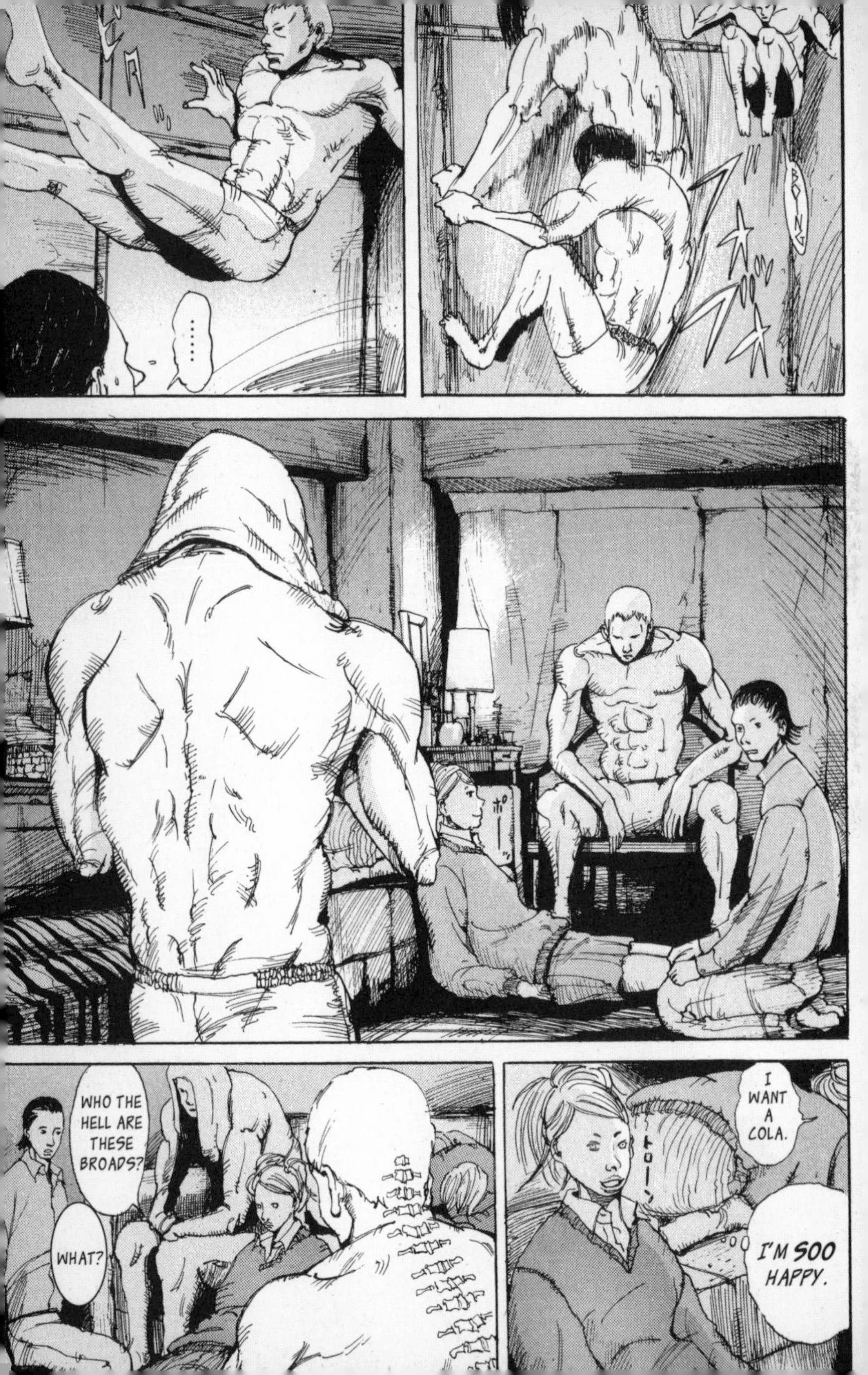
BOYING
......
I WANT A COLA.
I'M SOO HAPPY.
WHO THE HELL ARE THESE BROADS?
WHAT?

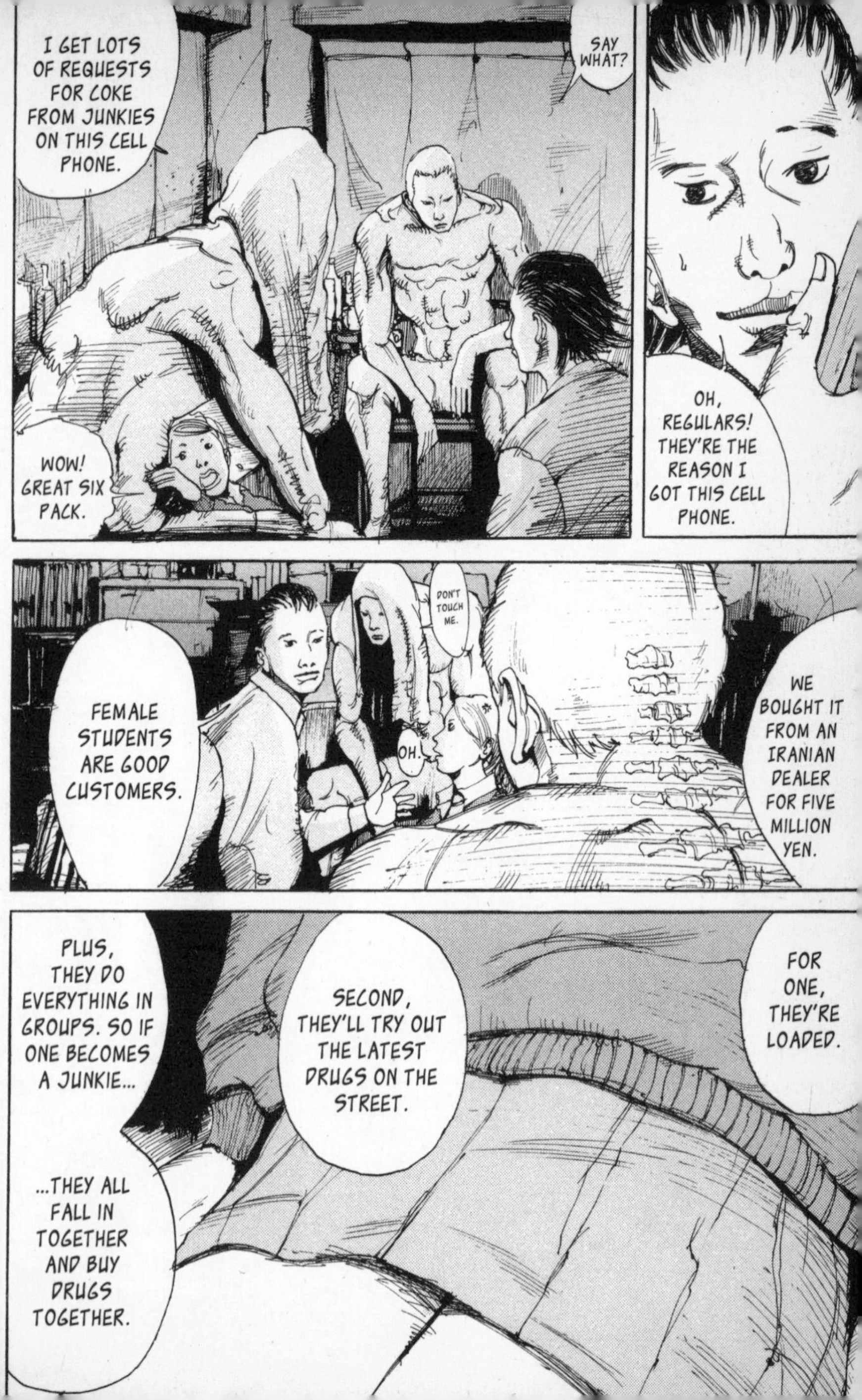
OH, REGULARS! THEY'RE THE REASON I GOT THIS CELL PHONE.
SAY WHAT?
I GET LOTS OF REQUESTS FOR COKE FROM JUNKIES ON THIS CELL PHONE.
WOW! GREAT SIX PACK.
WE BOUGHT IT FROM AN IRANIAN DEALER FOR FIVE MILLION YEN.
DON'T TOUCH ME.
OH.
FEMALE STUDENTS ARE GOOD CUSTOMERS.
FOR ONE, THEY'RE LOADED.
SECOND, THEY'LL TRY OUT THE LATEST DRUGS ON THE STREET.
PLUS, THEY DO EVERYTHING IN GROUPS. SO IF ONE BECOMES A JUNKIE...
...THEY ALL FALL IN TOGETHER AND BUY DRUGS TOGETHER.

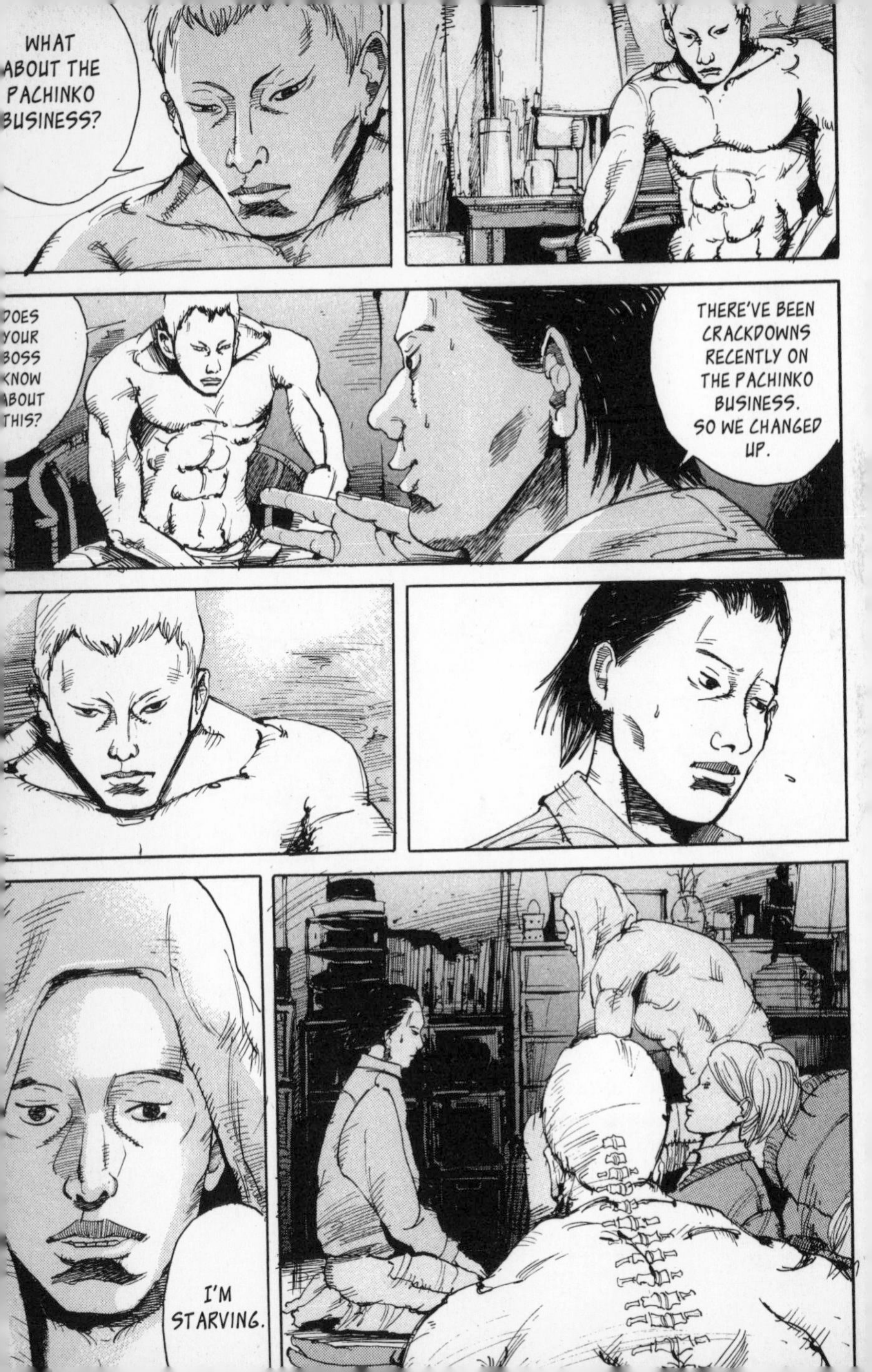
WHAT ABOUT THE PACHINKO BUSINESS?
THERE'VE BEEN CRACKDOWNS RECENTLY ON THE PACHINKO BUSINESS. SO WE CHANGED UP.
DOES YOUR BOSS KNOW ABOUT THIS?
I'M STARVING.

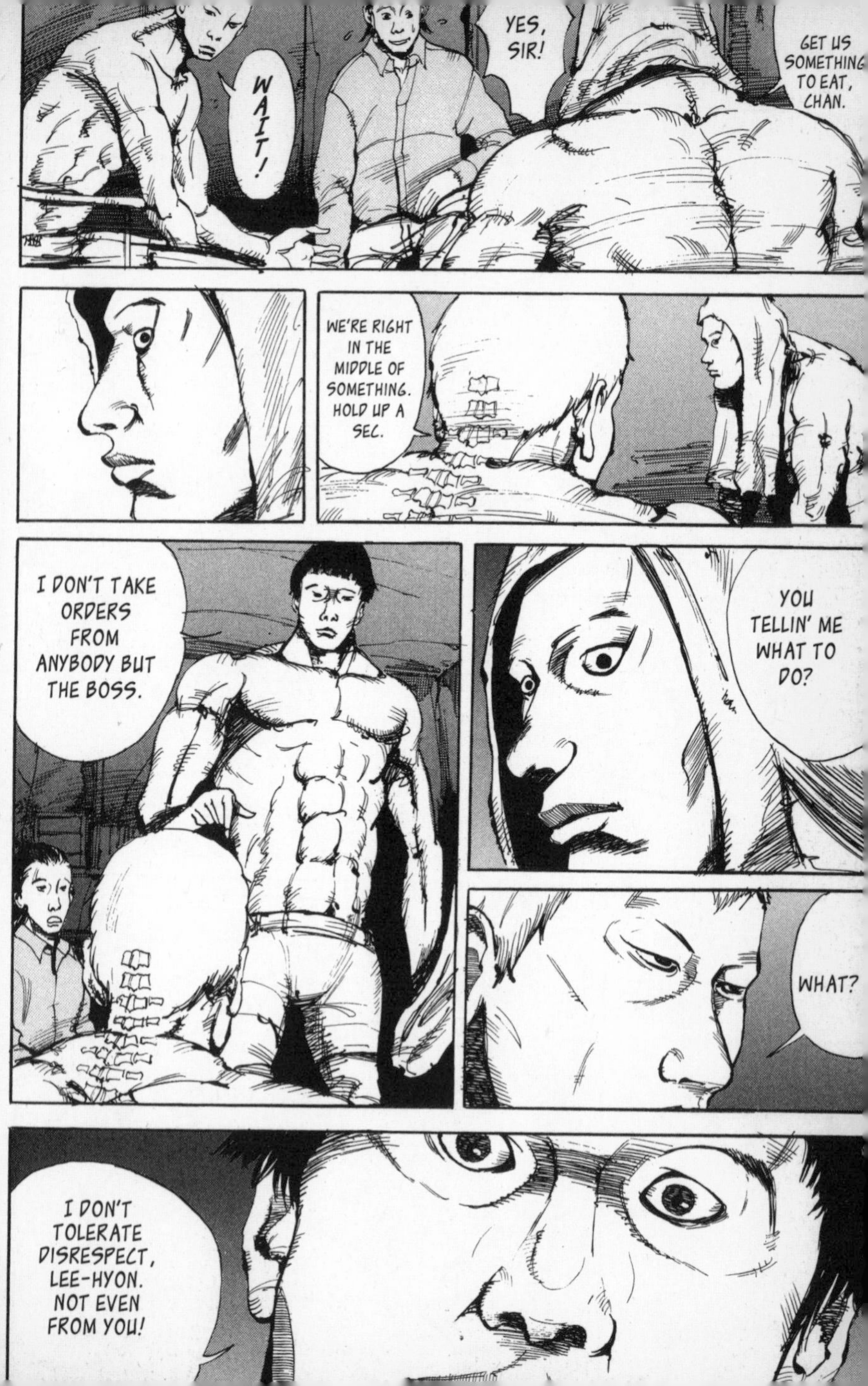
GET US SOMETHING TO EAT, CHAN.
YES, SIR!
WAIT!
WE'RE RIGHT IN THE MIDDLE OF SOMETHING. HOLD UP A SEC.
YOU TELLIN' ME WHAT TO DO?
WHAT?
I DON'T TAKE ORDERS FROM ANYBODY BUT THE BOSS.
I DON'T TOLERATE DISRESPECT, LEE-HYON. NOT EVEN FROM YOU!

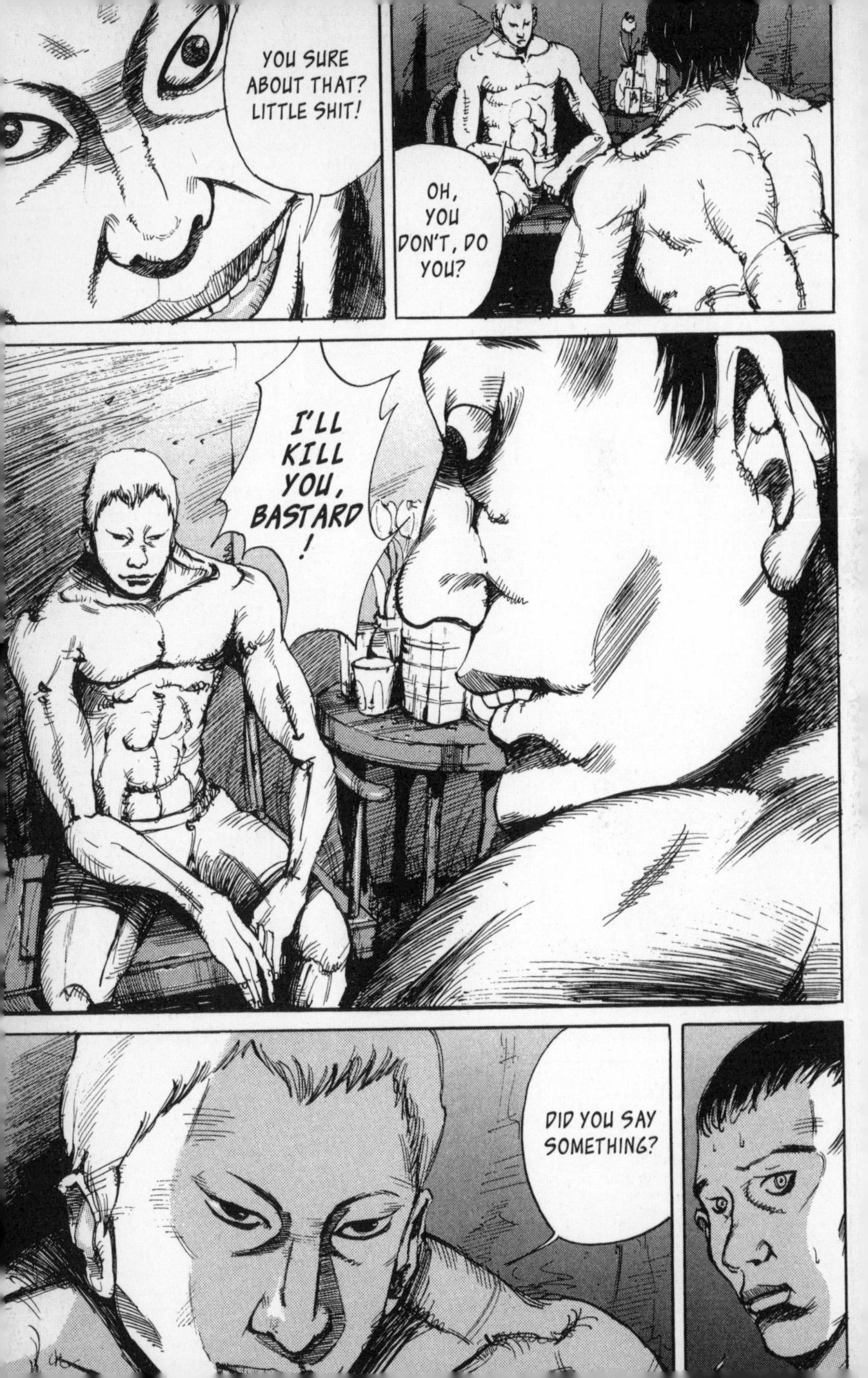
OH, YOU DON'T, DO YOU?
YOU SURE ABOUT THAT? LITTLE SHIT!
I'LL KILL YOU, BASTARD!
DID YOU SAY SOMETHING?

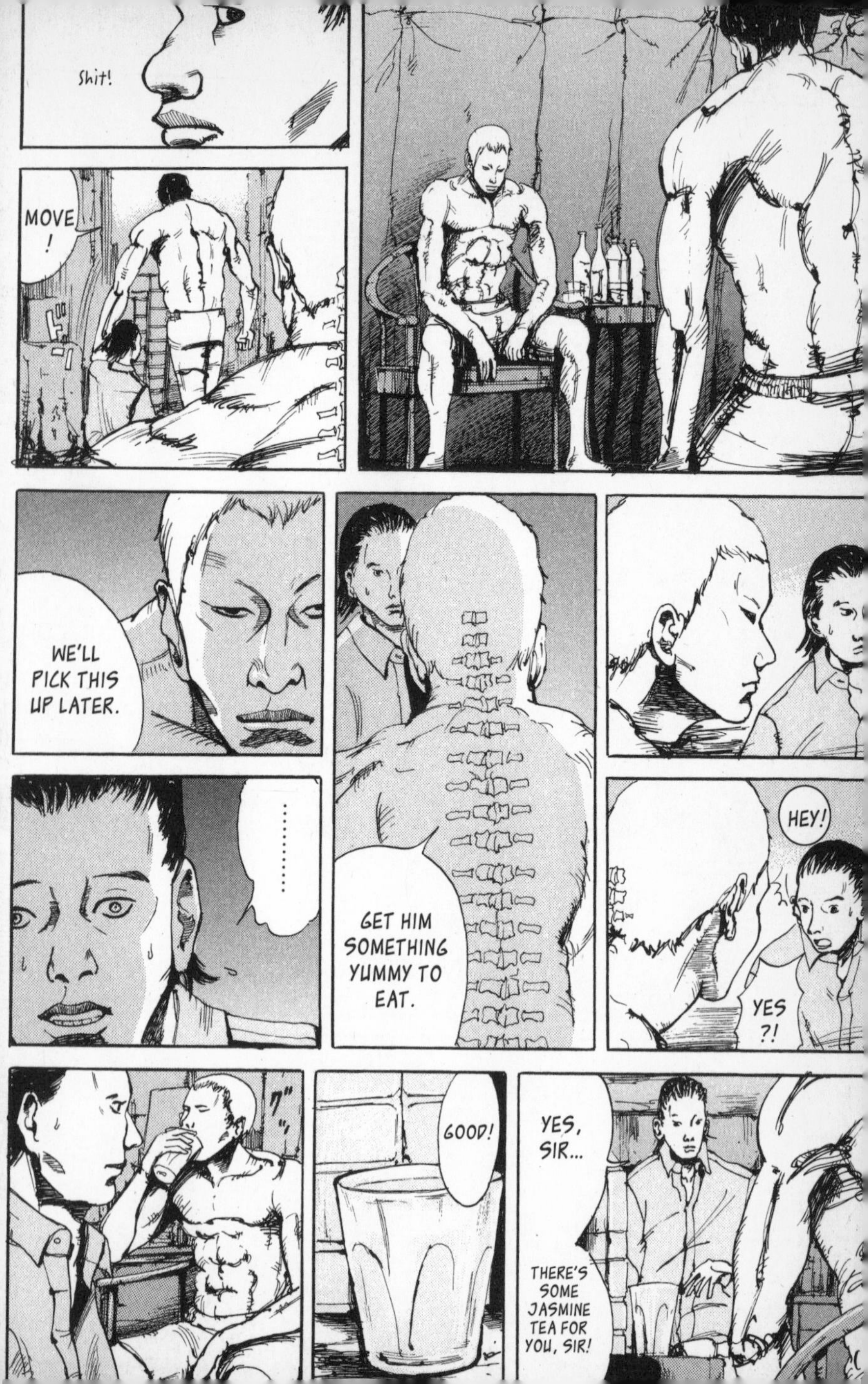

Shit!
MOVE!
HEY!
YES ?!
GET HIM SOMETHING YUMMY TO EAT.
WE'LL PICK THIS UP LATER.
......
YES, SIR...
THERE'S SOME JASMINE TEA FOR YOU, SIR!
GOOD!

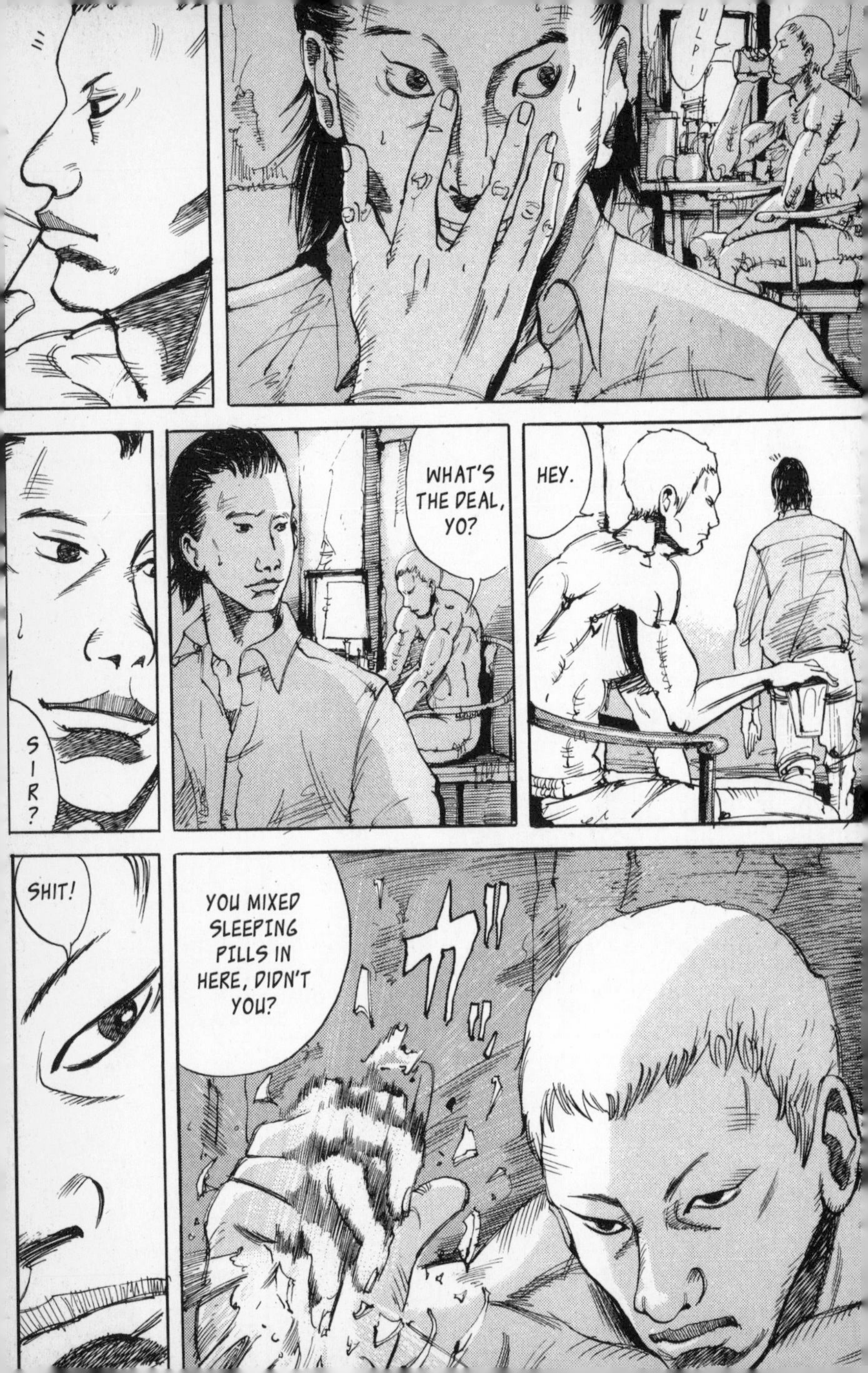
ULP!
HEY.
WHAT'S THE DEAL, YO?
SIR?
YOU MIXED SLEEPING PILLS IN HERE, DIDN'T YOU?
SHIT!

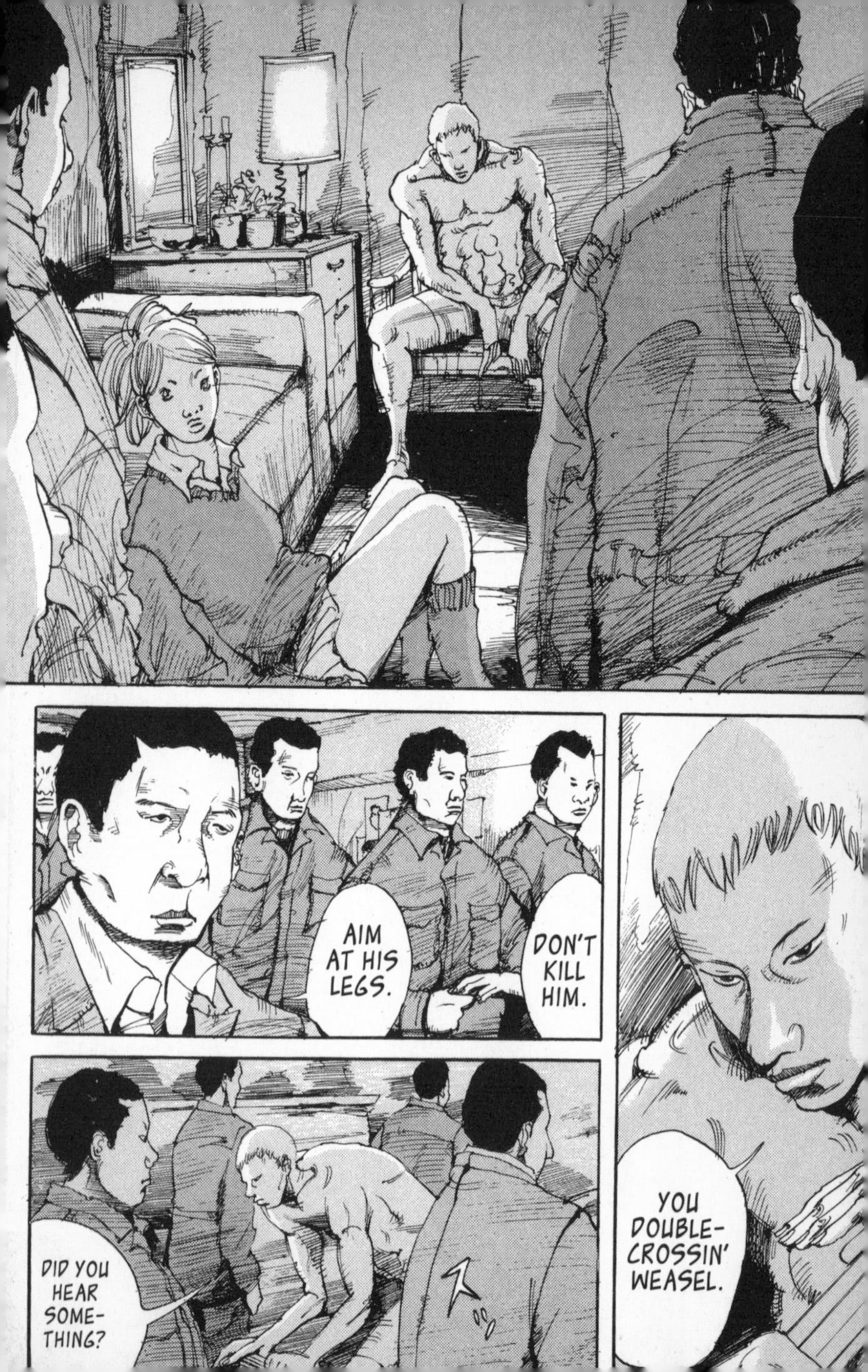
YOU DOUBLE-CROSSIN' WEASEL.
DON'T KILL HIM.
AIM AT HIS LEGS.
DID YOU HEAR SOME-THING?

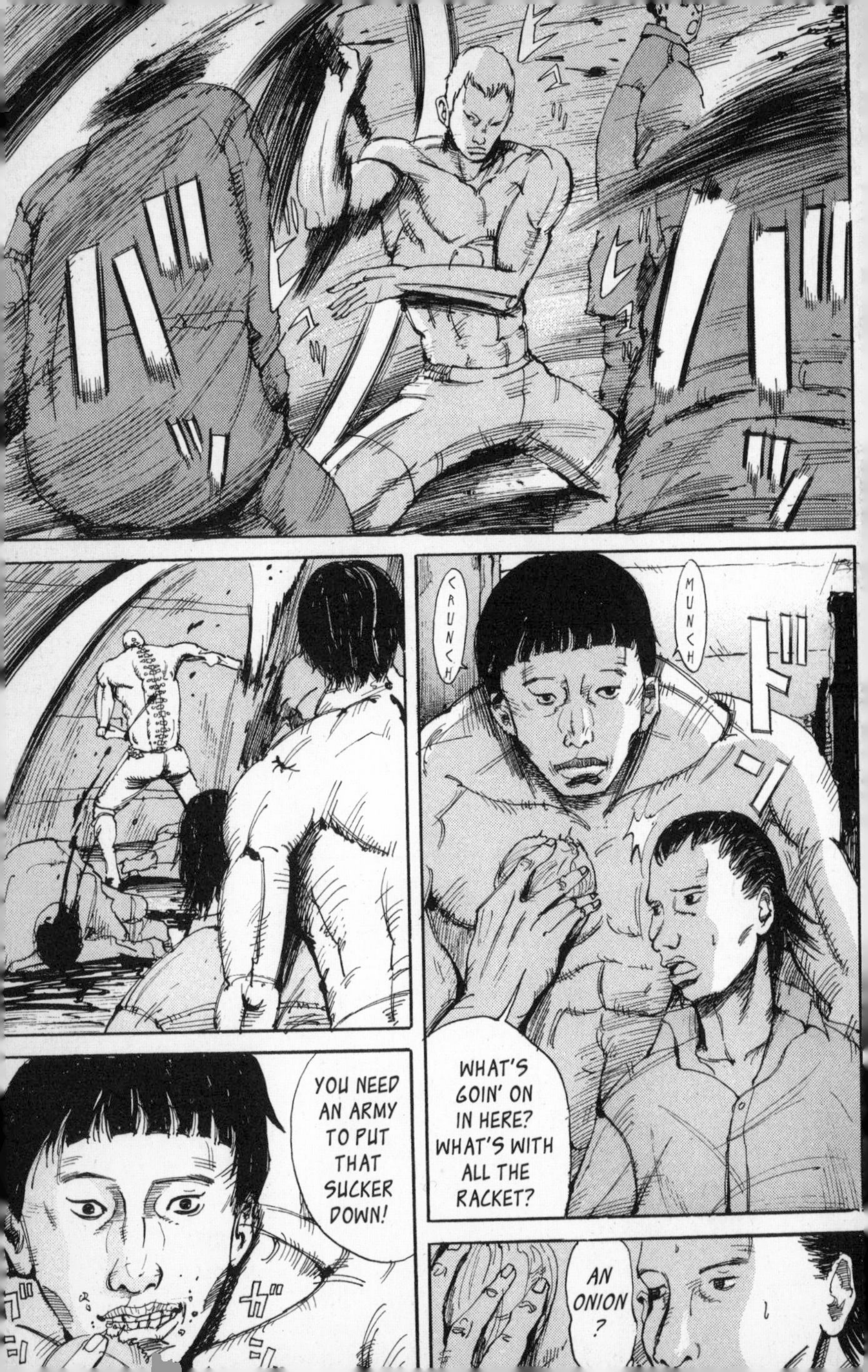
MUNCH
CRUNCH
WHAT'S GOIN' ON IN HERE? WHAT'S WITH ALL THE RACKET?
YOU NEED AN ARMY TO PUT THAT SUCKER DOWN!
AN ONION?

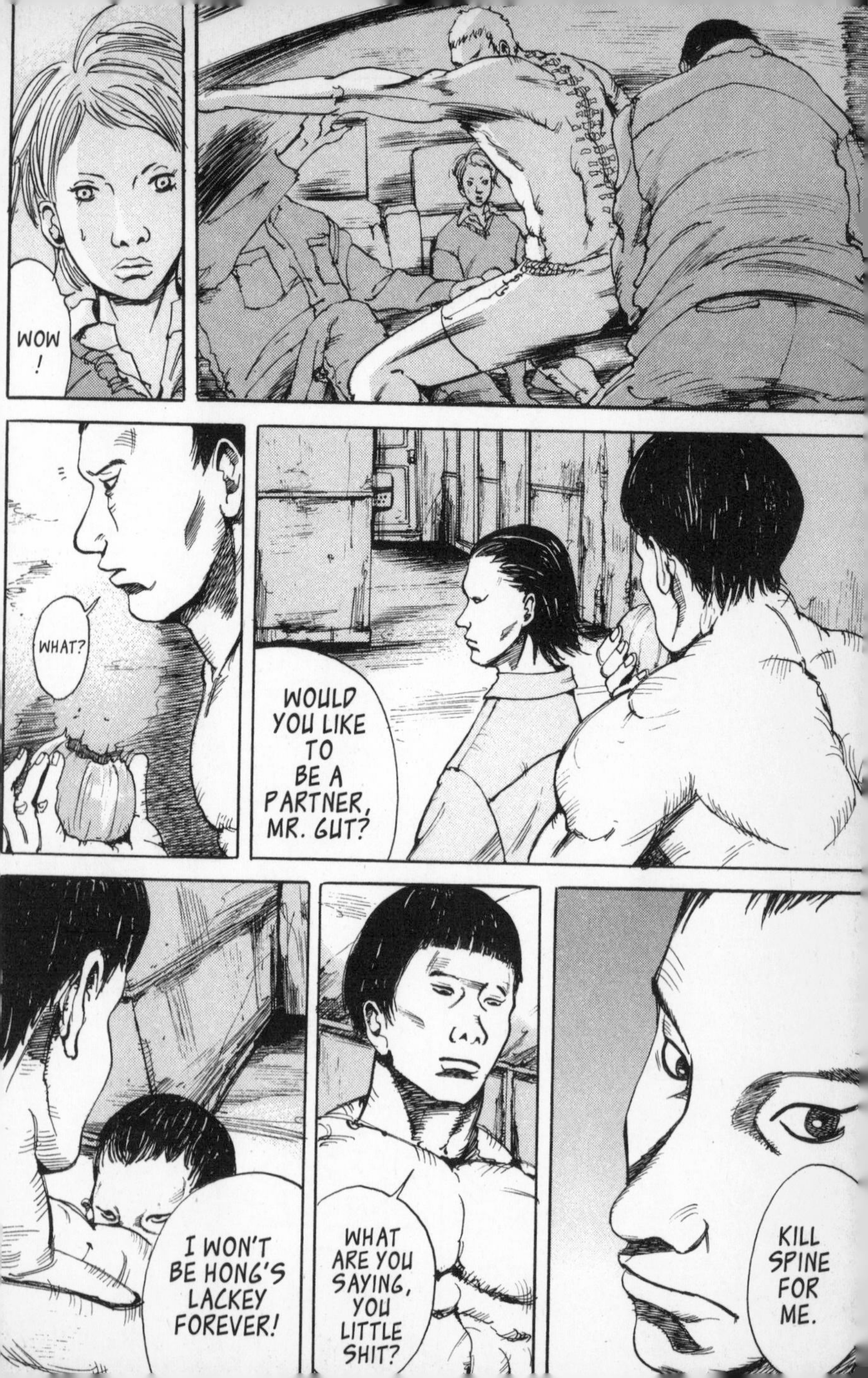
WOW!
WOULD YOU LIKE TO BE A PARTNER, MR. GUT?
WHAT?
KILL SPINE FOR ME.
WHAT ARE YOU SAYING, YOU LITTLE SHIT?
I WON'T BE HONG'S LACKEY FOREVER!

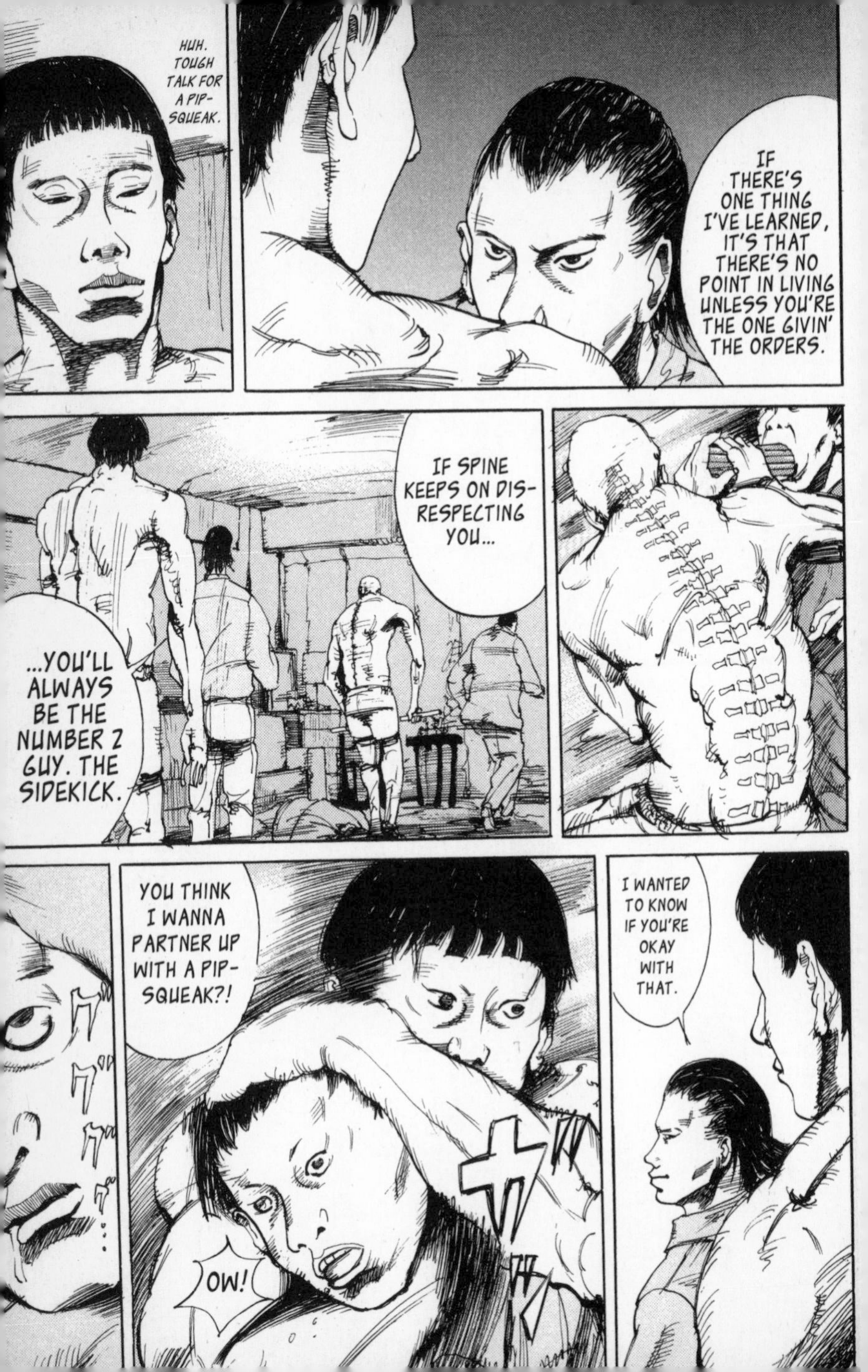
IF THERE'S ONE THING I'VE LEARNED, IT'S THAT THERE'S NO POINT IN LIVING UNLESS YOU'RE THE ONE GIVIN' THE ORDERS.
HUH. TOUGH TALK FOR A PIP-SQUEAK.
IF SPINE KEEPS ON DIS-RESPECTING YOU...
...YOU'LL ALWAYS BE THE NUMBER 2 GUY. THE SIDEKICK.
I WANTED TO KNOW IF YOU'RE OKAY WITH THAT.
YOU THINK I WANNA PARTNER UP WITH A PIP-SQUEAK?!
OW!

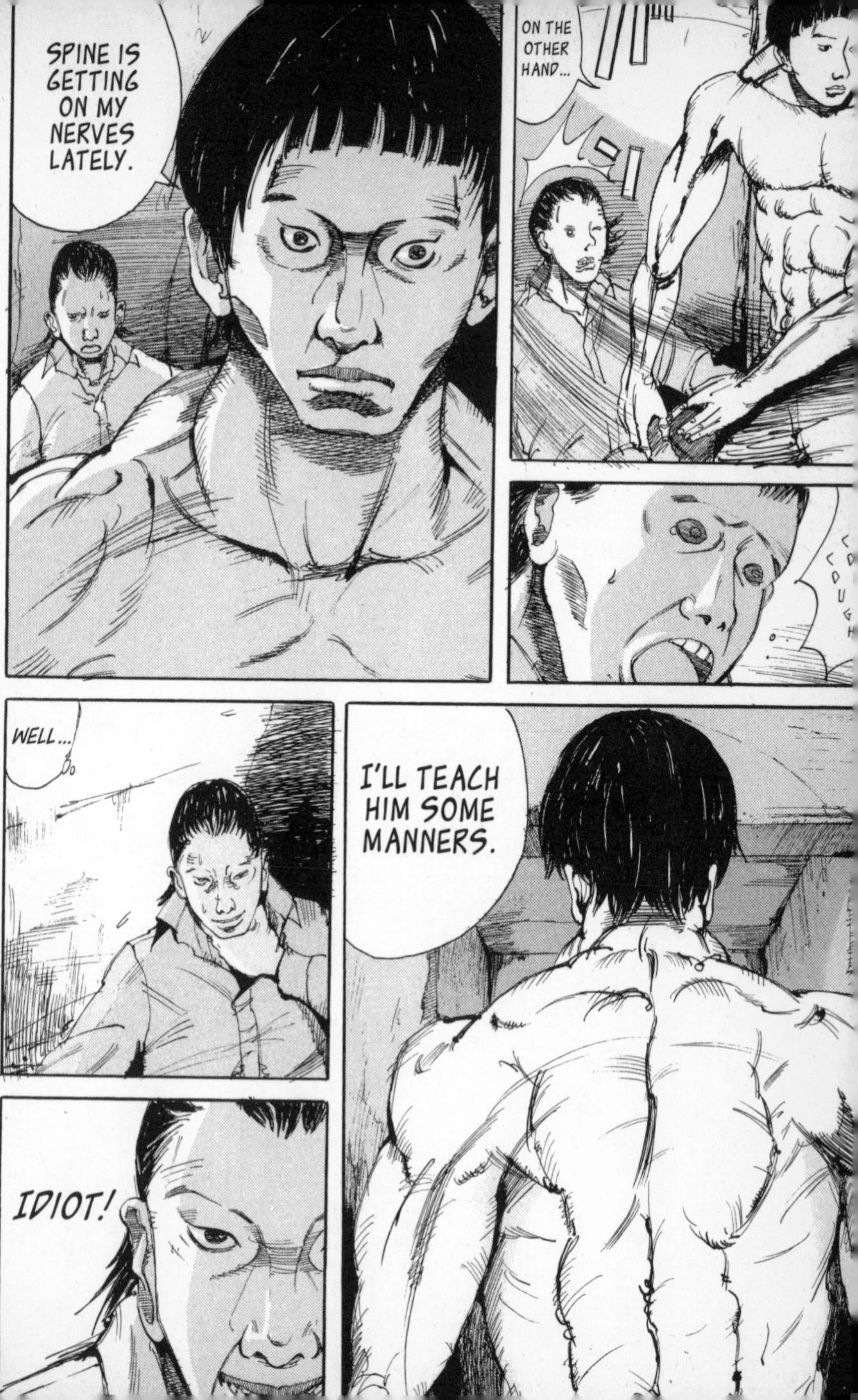
ON THE OTHER HAND...
COUGH
SPINE IS GETTING ON MY NERVES LATELY.
I'LL TEACH HIM SOME MANNERS.
WELL...
IDIOT!

HICK
HICK
SHIT!

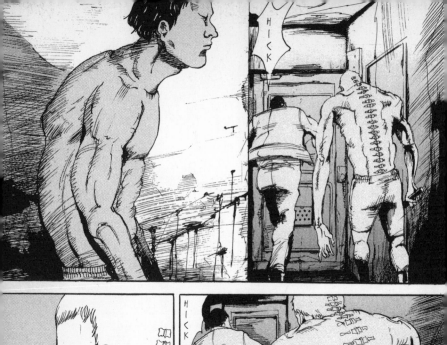

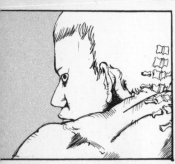

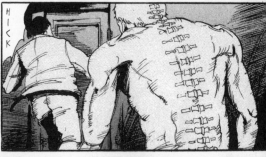

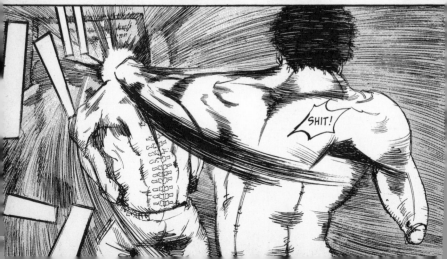

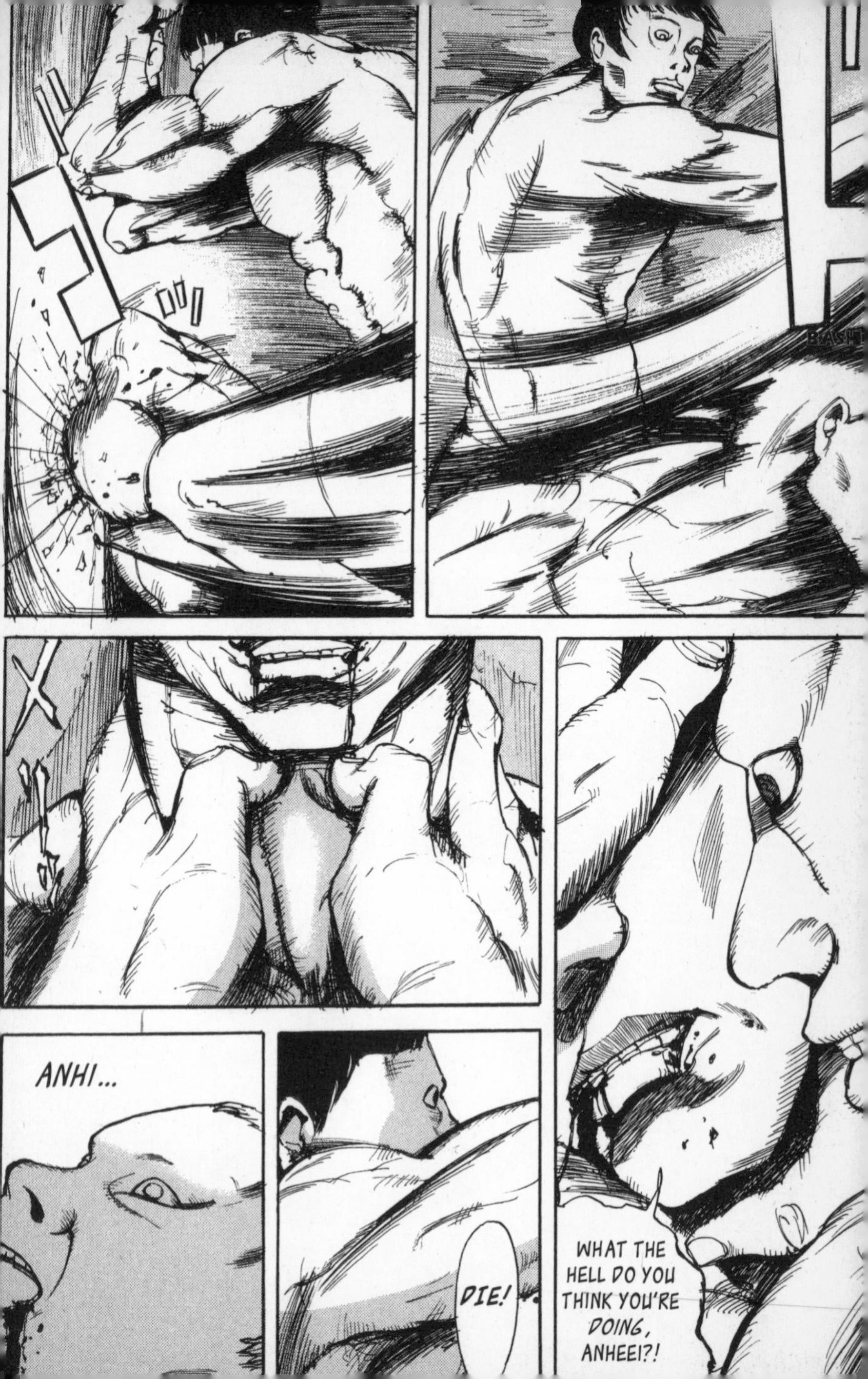
WHAT THE HELL DO YOU THINK YOU'RE DOING, ANHEEI?!
DIE!
ANHI...

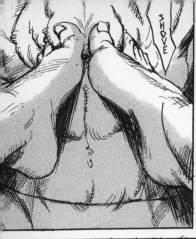

SHOVE

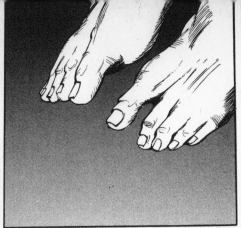

RIP

DIDN'T HURT AT ALL.

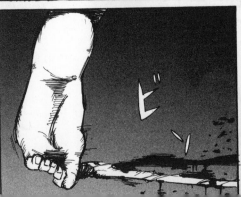

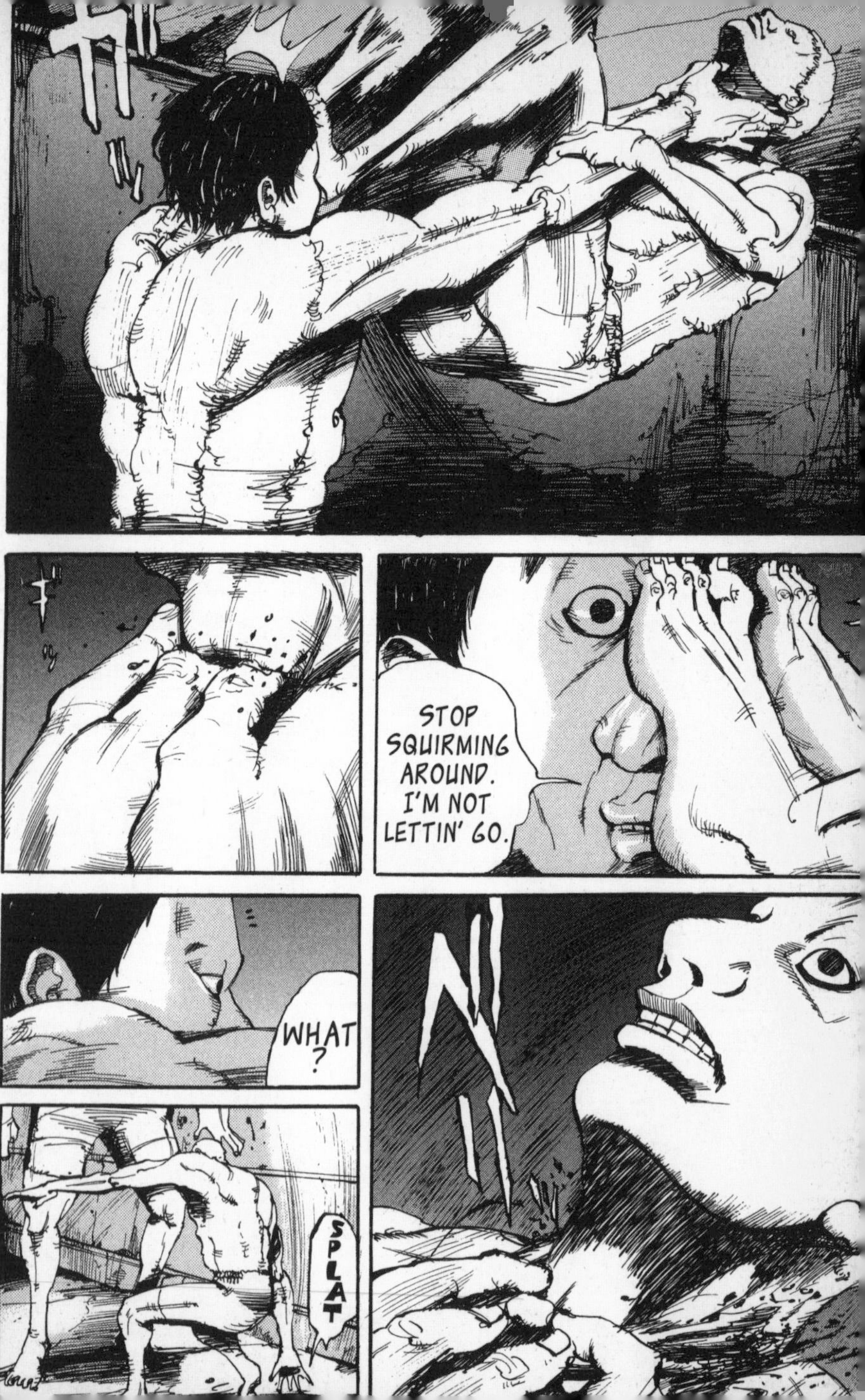
STOP SQUIRMING AROUND. I'M NOT LETTIN' GO.
WHAT?
SPLAT

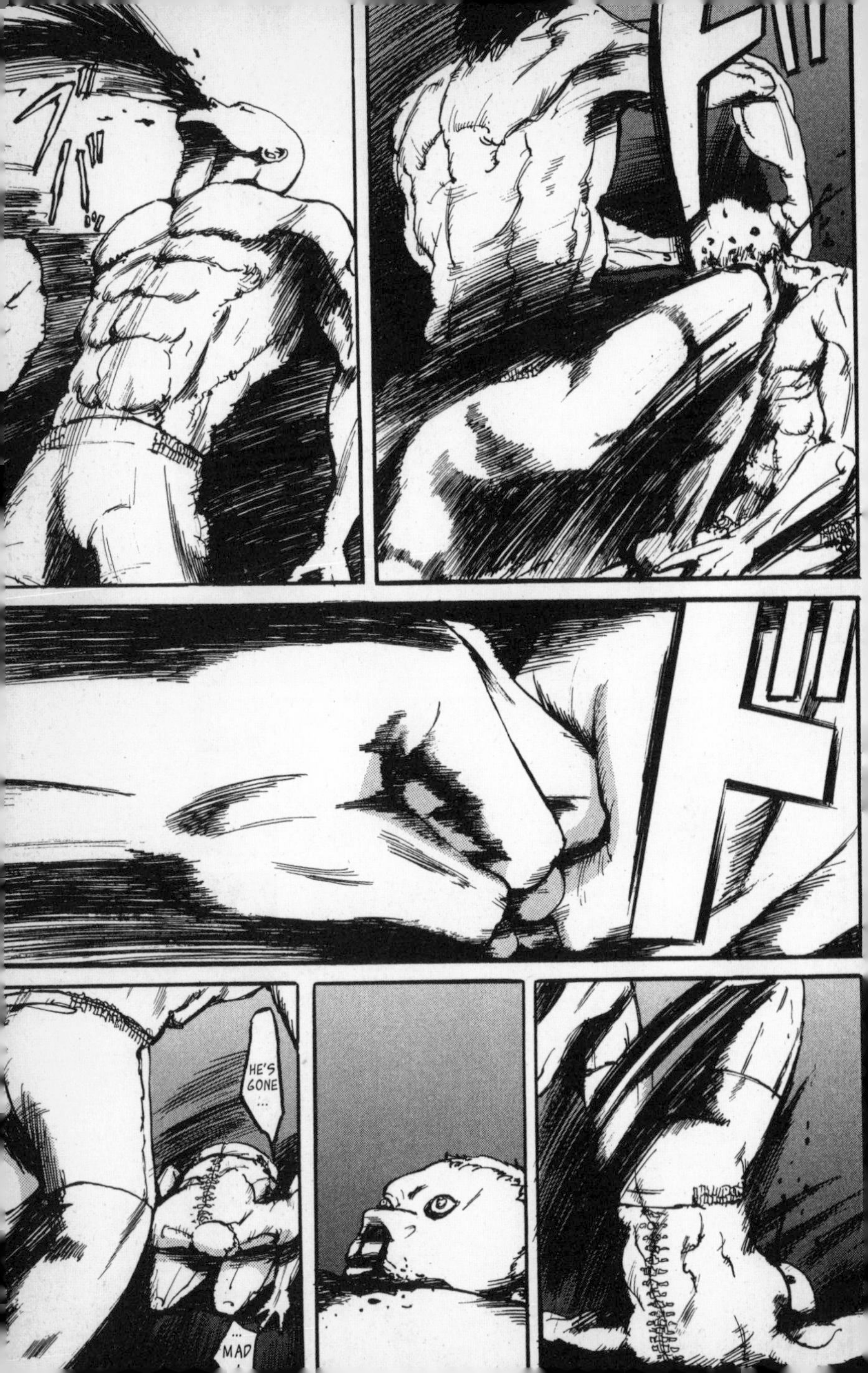
HE'S GONE ...
... MAD

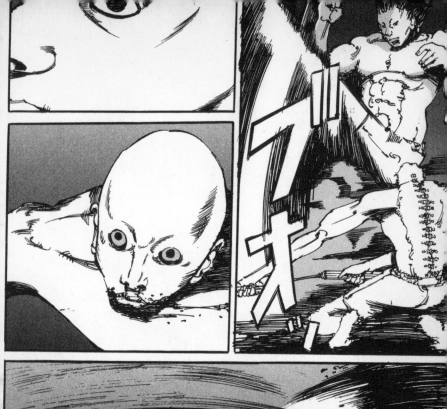
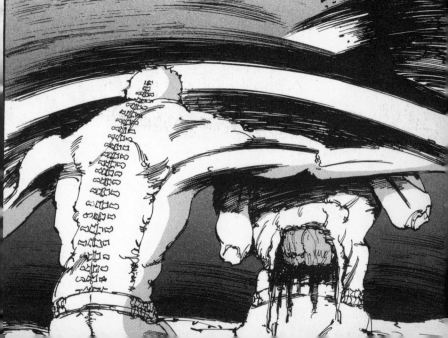

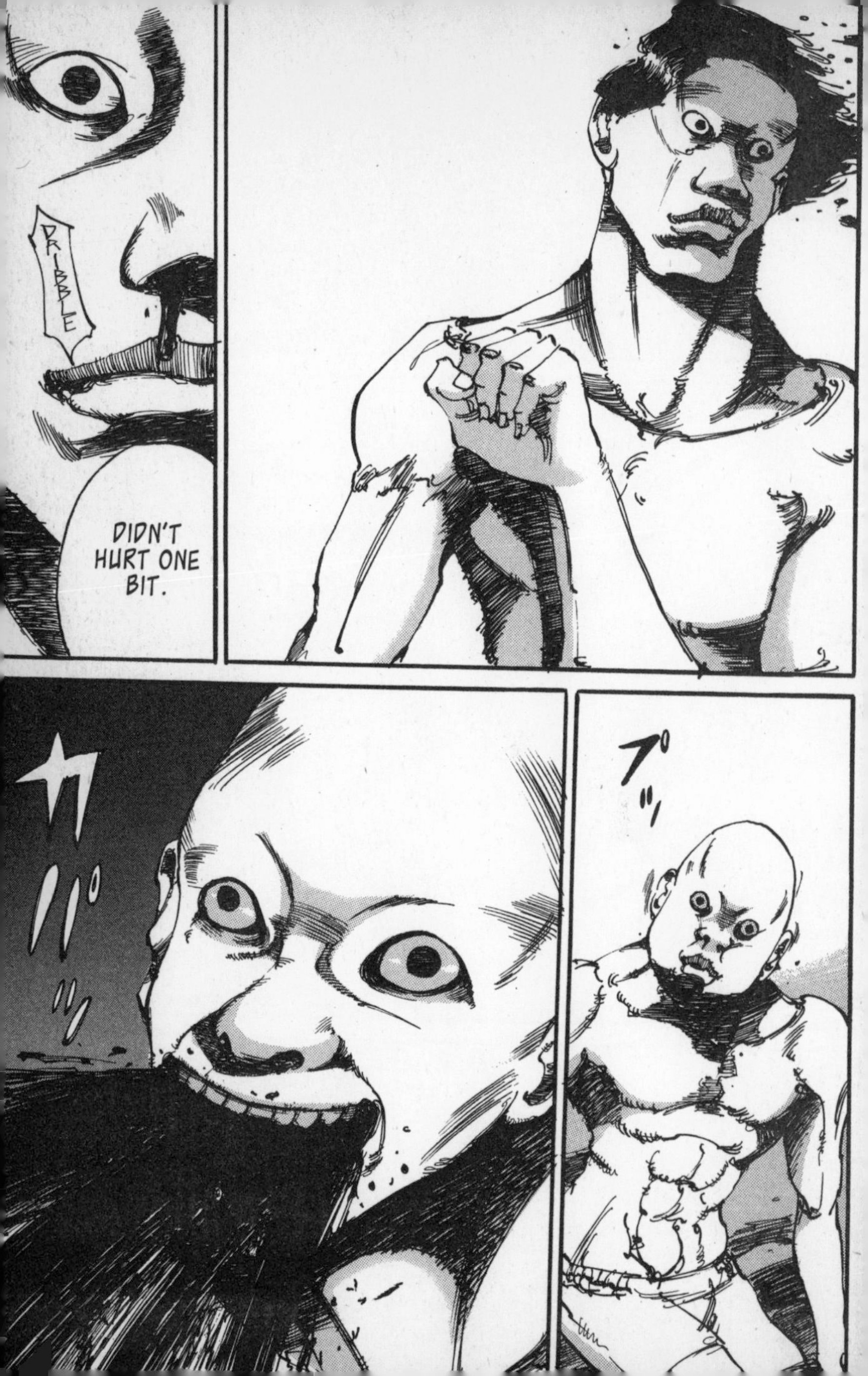
DRIBBLE
DIDN'T HURT ONE BIT.

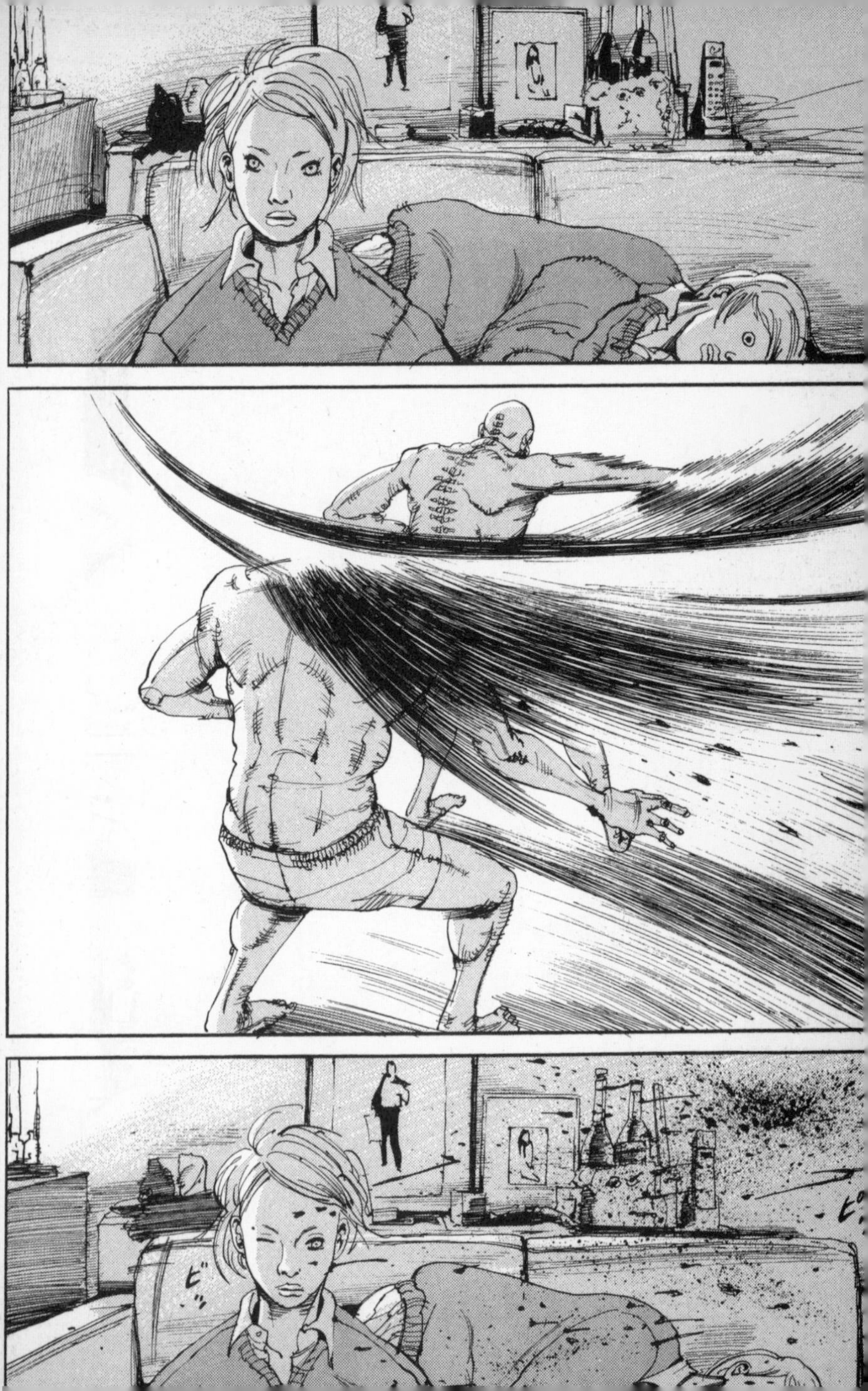
ビッ

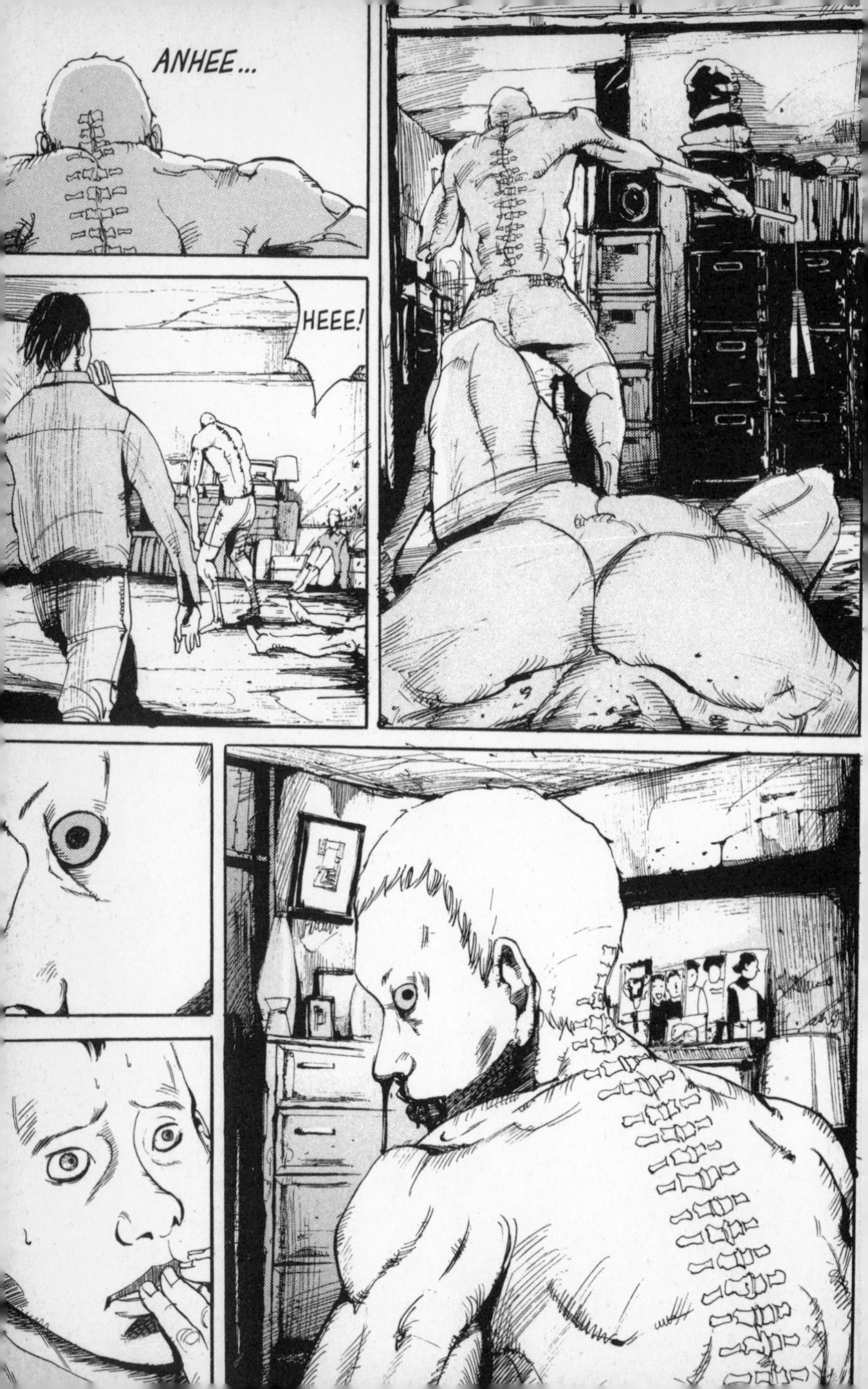
ANHEE...
HEEE!

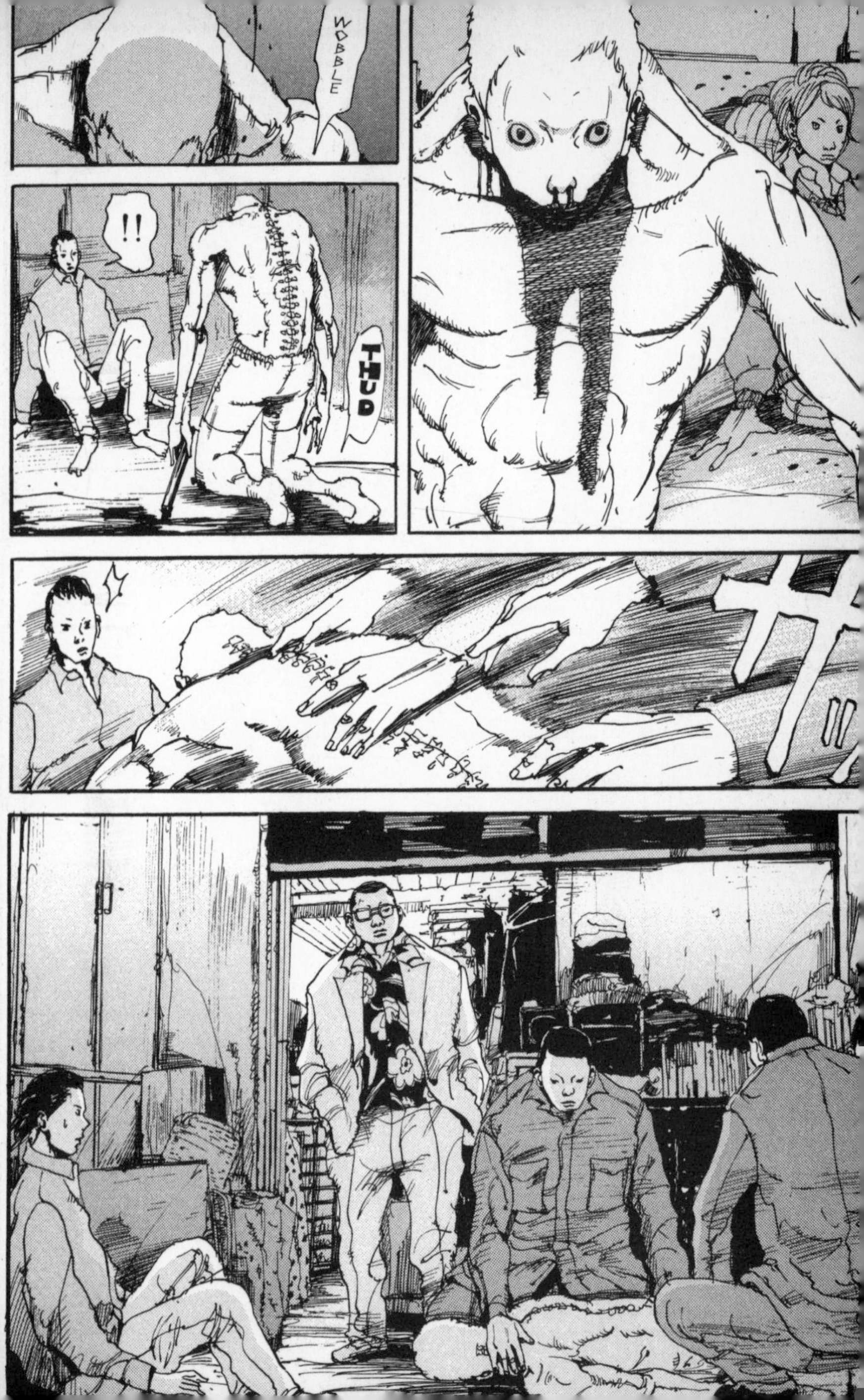
WOBBLE
!!
THUD

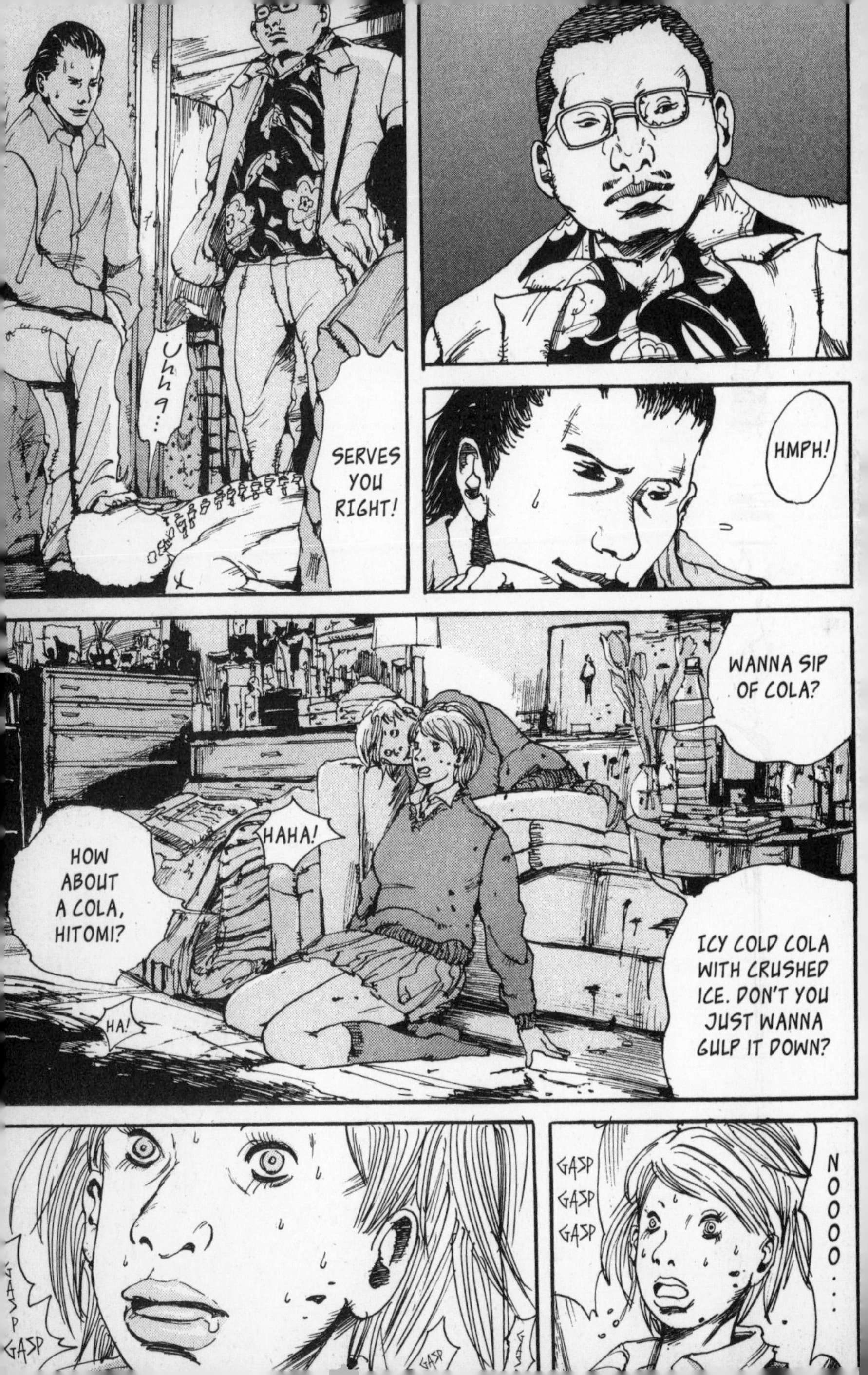
HMPH!
Unng...
SERVES YOU RIGHT!
WANNA SIP OF COLA?
ICY COLD COLA WITH CRUSHED ICE. DON'T YOU JUST WANNA GULP IT DOWN?
HAHA!
HOW ABOUT A COLA, HITOMI?
HA!
NOOOO...
GASP GASP GASP
GASP GASP
GASP

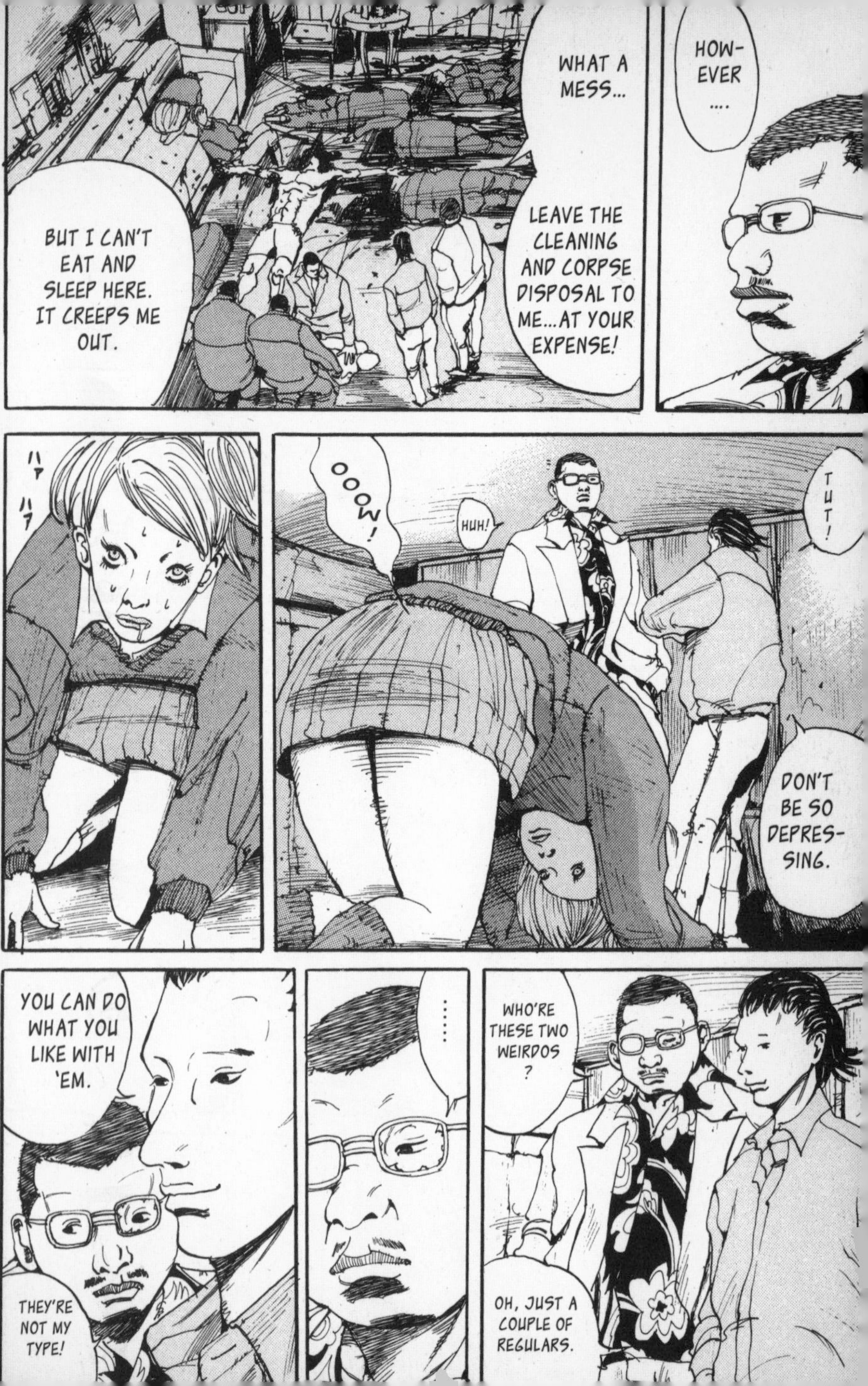
HOW-EVER ....
WHAT A MESS...
LEAVE THE CLEANING AND CORPSE DISPOSAL TO ME...AT YOUR EXPENSE!
BUT I CAN'T EAT AND SLEEP HERE. IT CREEPS ME OUT.
TUT!
OOOW!
HUH!
DON'T BE SO DEPRES-SING.
ハァ ハァ
WHO'RE THESE TWO WEIRDOS ?
OH, JUST A COUPLE OF REGULARS.
......
YOU CAN DO WHAT YOU LIKE WITH 'EM.
THEY'RE NOT MY TYPE!

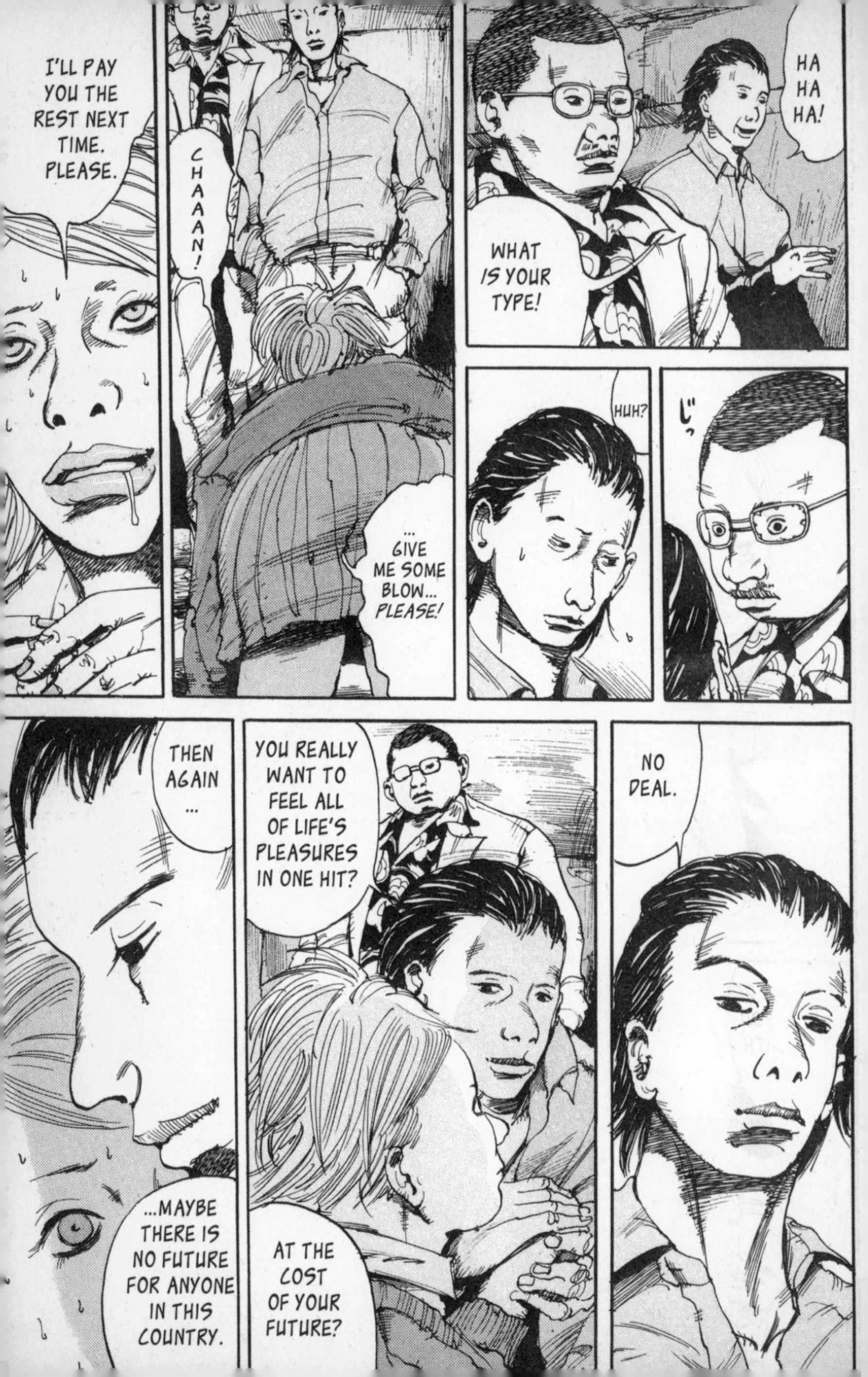
HA HA HA!
WHAT IS YOUR TYPE!
じっ
HUH?
CHAAAAN!
...GIVE ME SOME BLOW... PLEASE!
I'LL PAY YOU THE REST NEXT TIME. PLEASE.
NO DEAL.
YOU REALLY WANT TO FEEL ALL OF LIFE'S PLEASURES IN ONE HIT?
AT THE COST OF YOUR FUTURE?
THEN AGAIN ...
...MAYBE THERE IS NO FUTURE FOR ANYONE IN THIS COUNTRY.

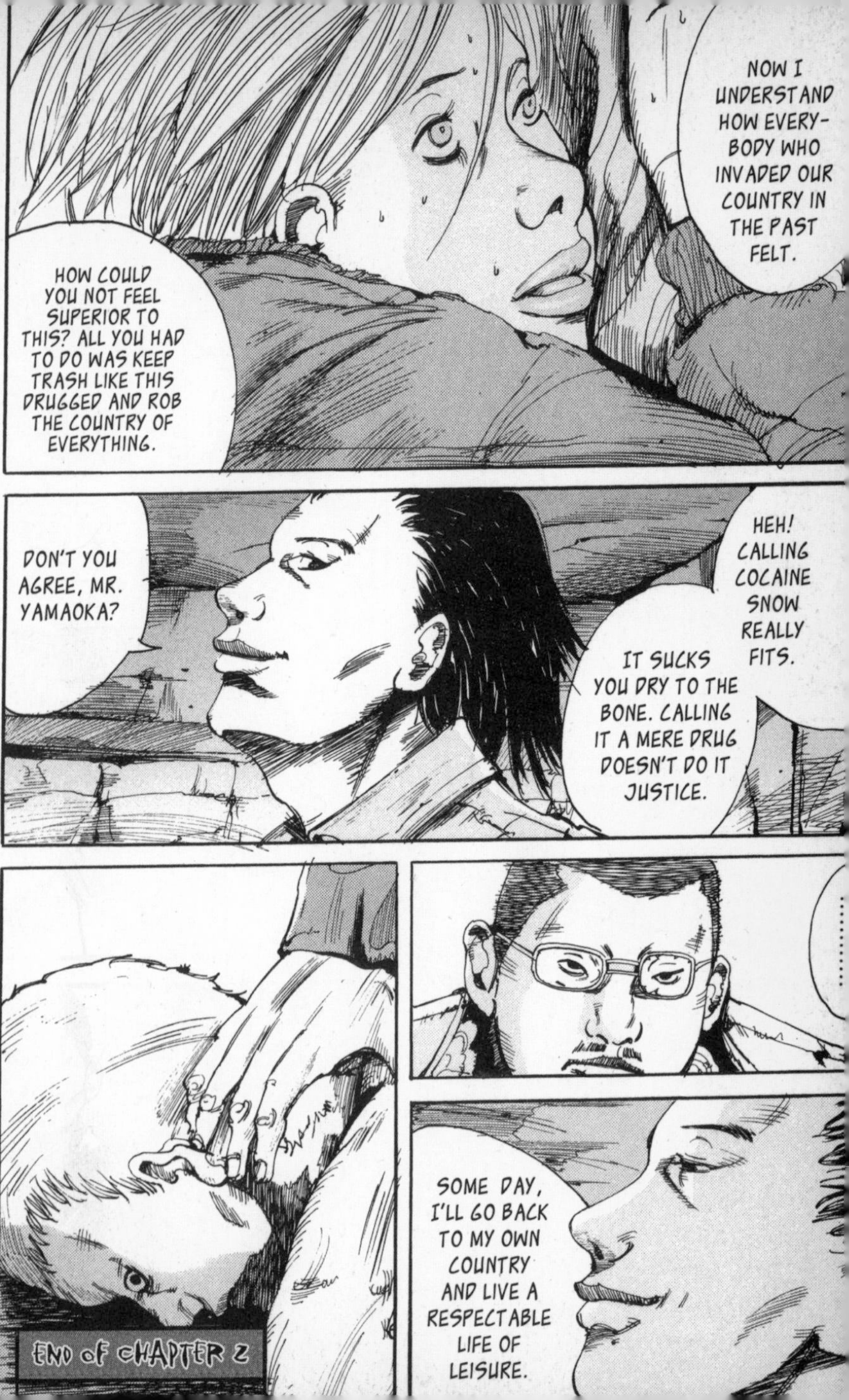
NOW I UNDERSTAND HOW EVERY-BODY WHO INVADED OUR COUNTRY IN THE PAST FELT.
HOW COULD YOU NOT FEEL SUPERIOR TO THIS? ALL YOU HAD TO DO WAS KEEP TRASH LIKE THIS DRUGGED AND ROB THE COUNTRY OF EVERYTHING.
HEH! CALLING COCAINE SNOW REALLY FITS.
IT SUCKS YOU DRY TO THE BONE. CALLING IT A MERE DRUG DOESN'T DO IT JUSTICE.
DON'T YOU AGREE, MR. YAMAOKA?
SOME DAY, I'LL GO BACK TO MY OWN COUNTRY AND LIVE A RESPECTABLE LIFE OF LEISURE.
END OF CHAPTER 2

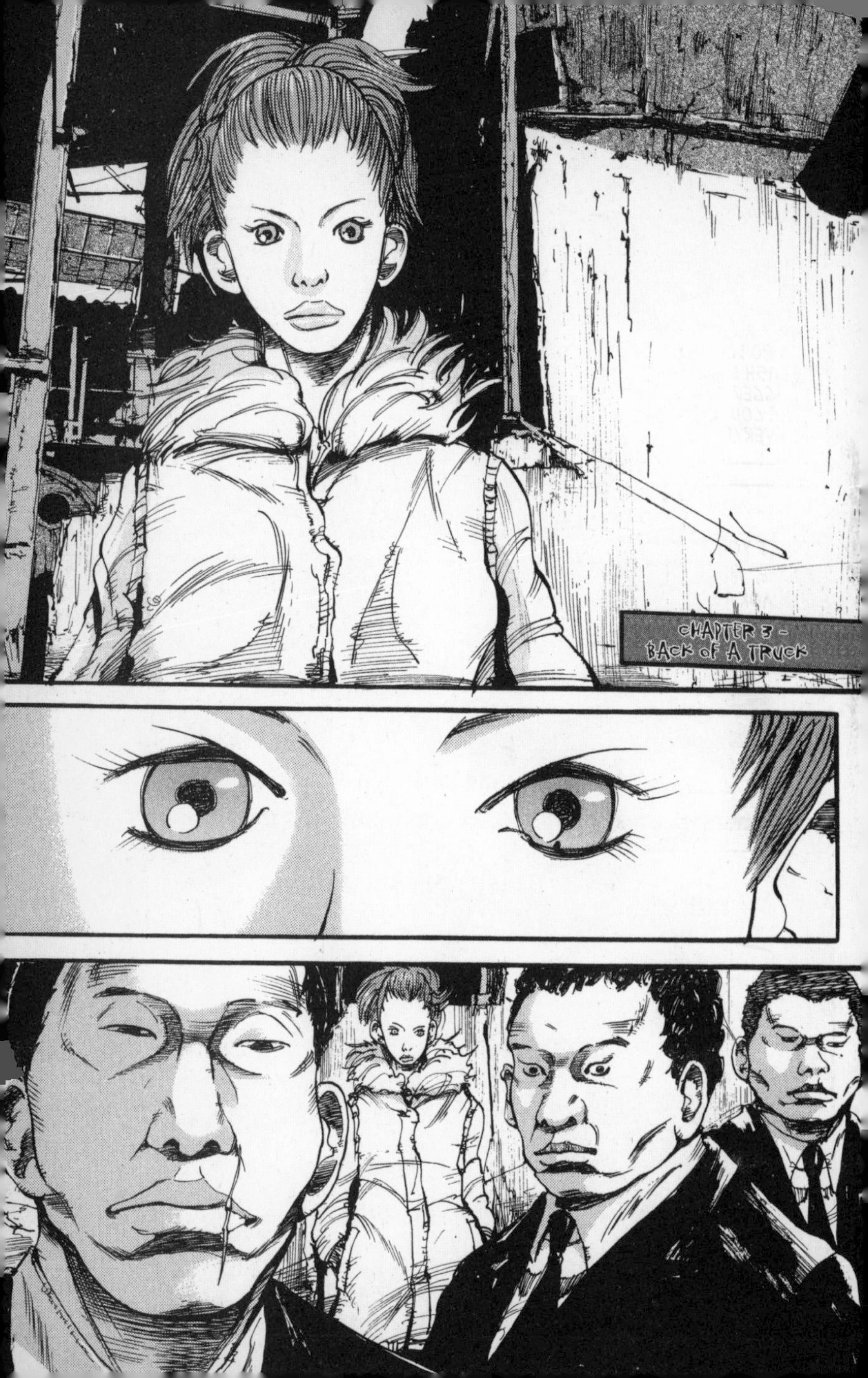
CHAPTER 3 -
BACK OF A TRUCK

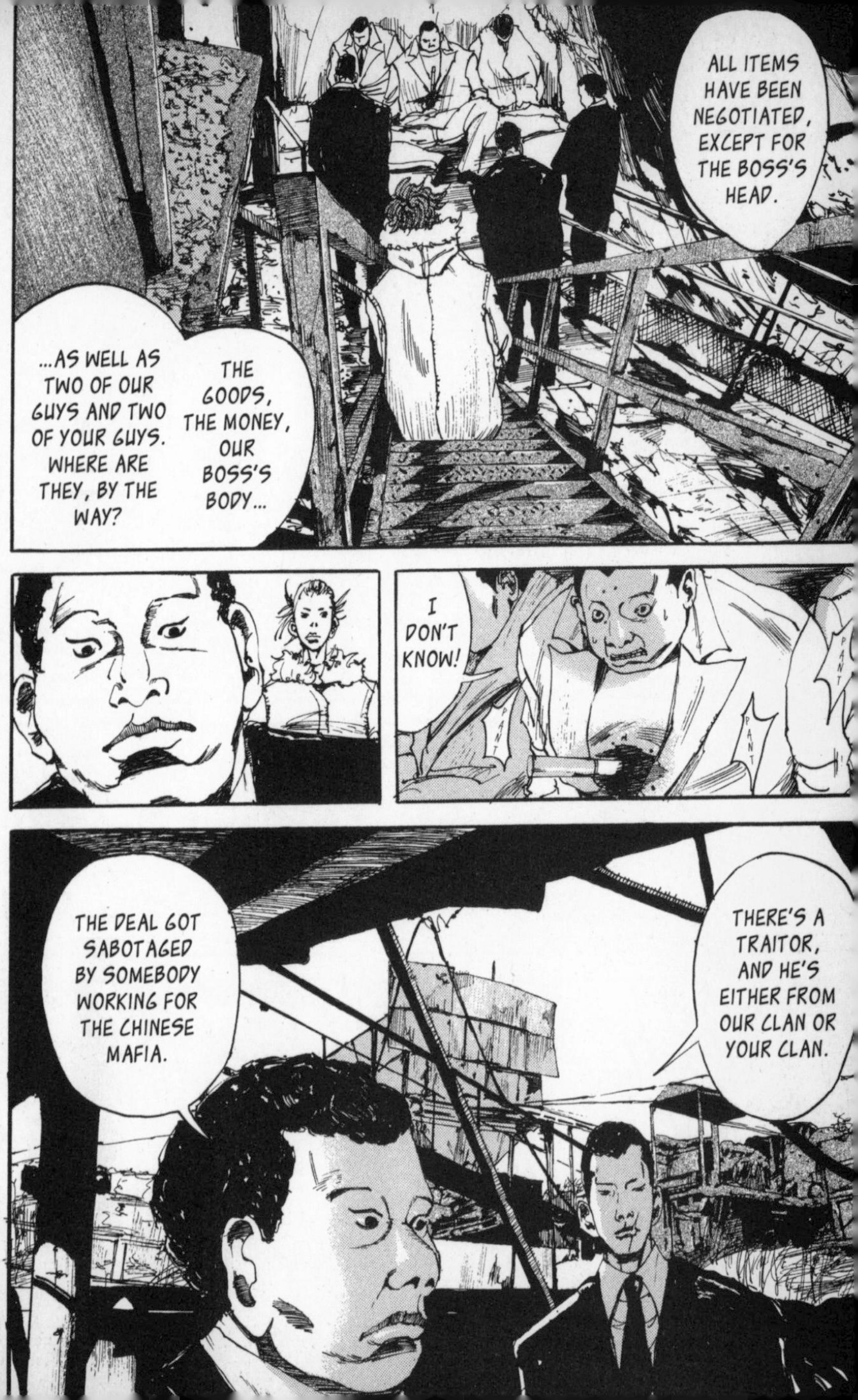
ALL ITEMS HAVE BEEN NEGOTIATED, EXCEPT FOR THE BOSS'S HEAD.
THE GOODS, THE MONEY, OUR BOSS'S BODY...
...AS WELL AS TWO OF OUR GUYS AND TWO OF YOUR GUYS. WHERE ARE THEY, BY THE WAY?
PANT
I DON'T KNOW!
PANT
PANT
THERE'S A TRAITOR, AND HE'S EITHER FROM OUR CLAN OR YOUR CLAN.
THE DEAL GOT SABOTAGED BY SOMEBODY WORKING FOR THE CHINESE MAFIA.

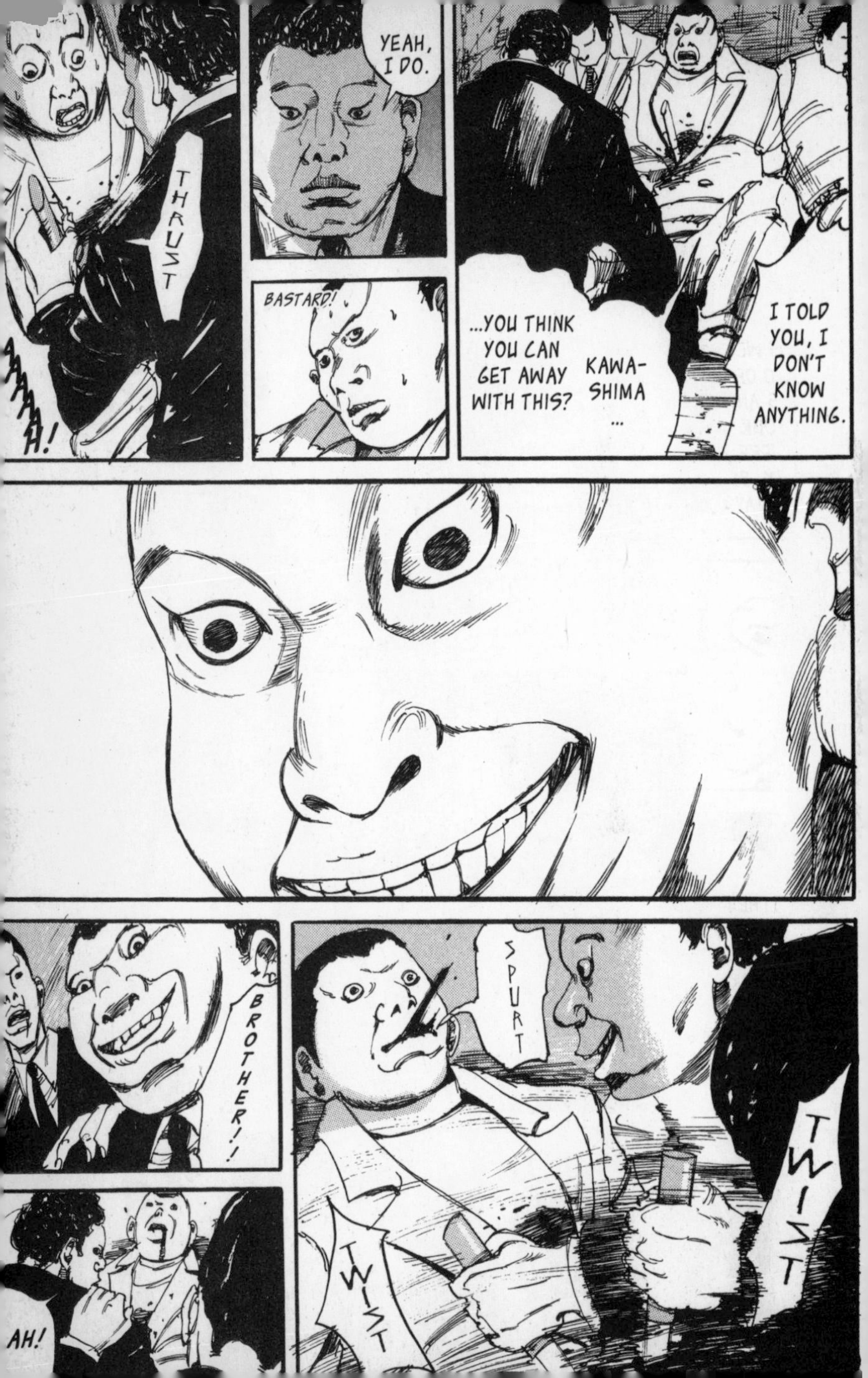
I TOLD YOU, I DON'T KNOW ANYTHING.
KAWA-SHIMA ...
...YOU THINK YOU CAN GET AWAY WITH THIS?
YEAH, I DO.
BASTARD!
THRUST
AAAAAAH!
SPURT
TWIST
TWIST
BROTHER!!
AH!

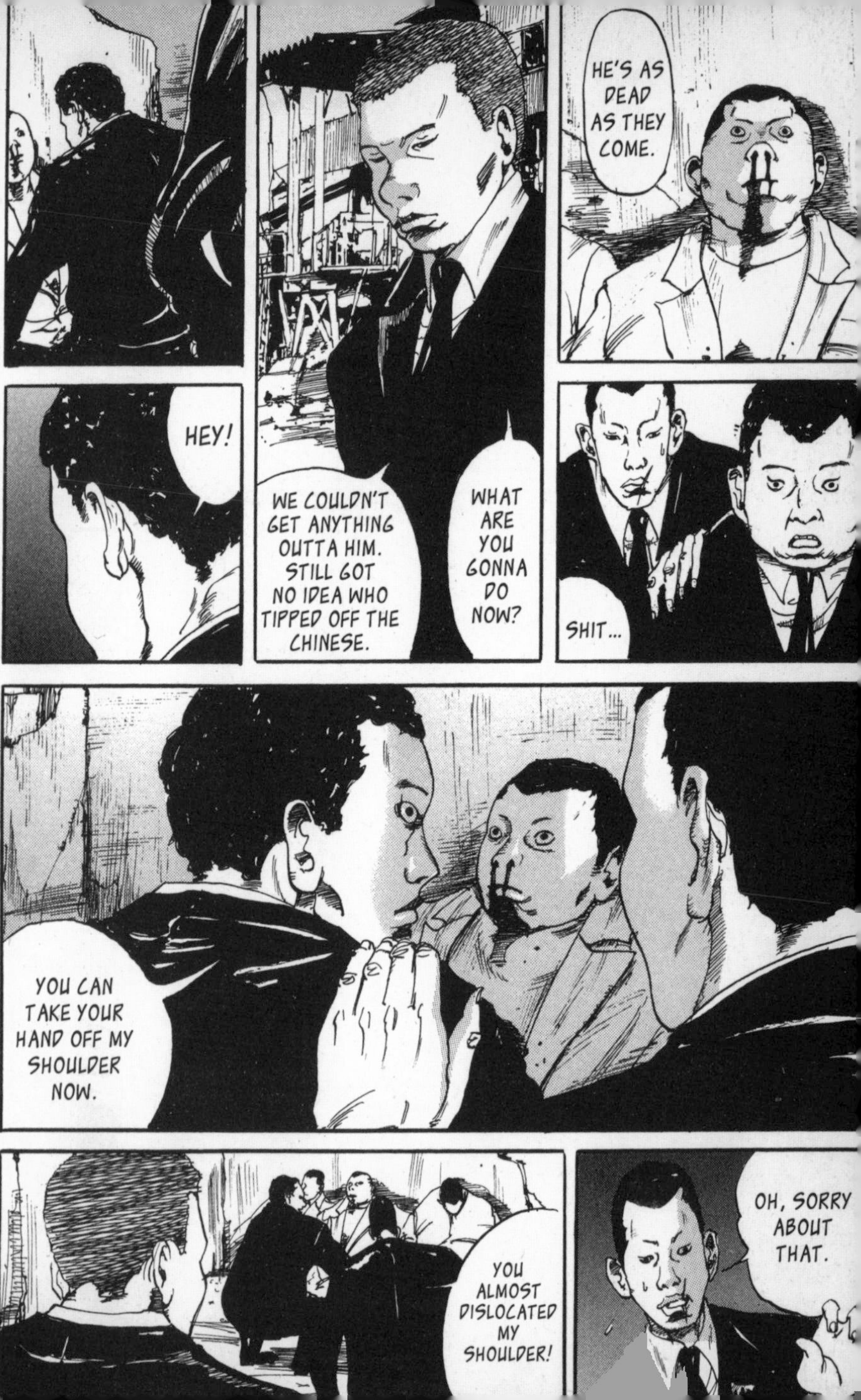
HE'S AS DEAD AS THEY COME.
SHIT...
WHAT ARE YOU GONNA DO NOW?
WE COULDN'T GET ANYTHING OUTTA HIM. STILL GOT NO IDEA WHO TIPPED OFF THE CHINESE.
HEY!
YOU CAN TAKE YOUR HAND OFF MY SHOULDER NOW.
OH, SORRY ABOUT THAT.
YOU ALMOST DISLOCATED MY SHOULDER!

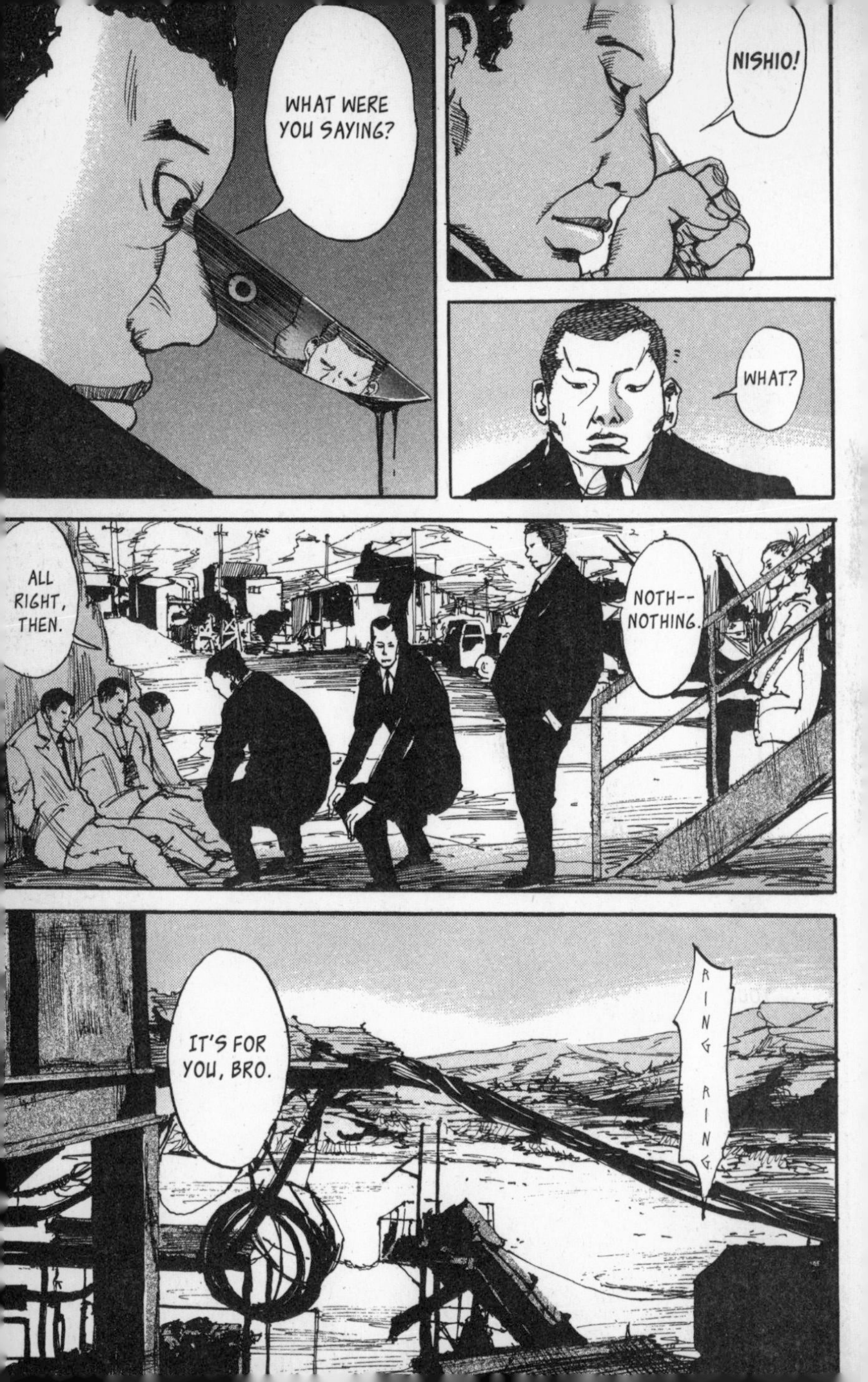
NISHIO!
WHAT?
WHAT WERE YOU SAYING?
NOTH--NOTHING.
ALL RIGHT, THEN.
RING RING
IT'S FOR YOU, BRO.

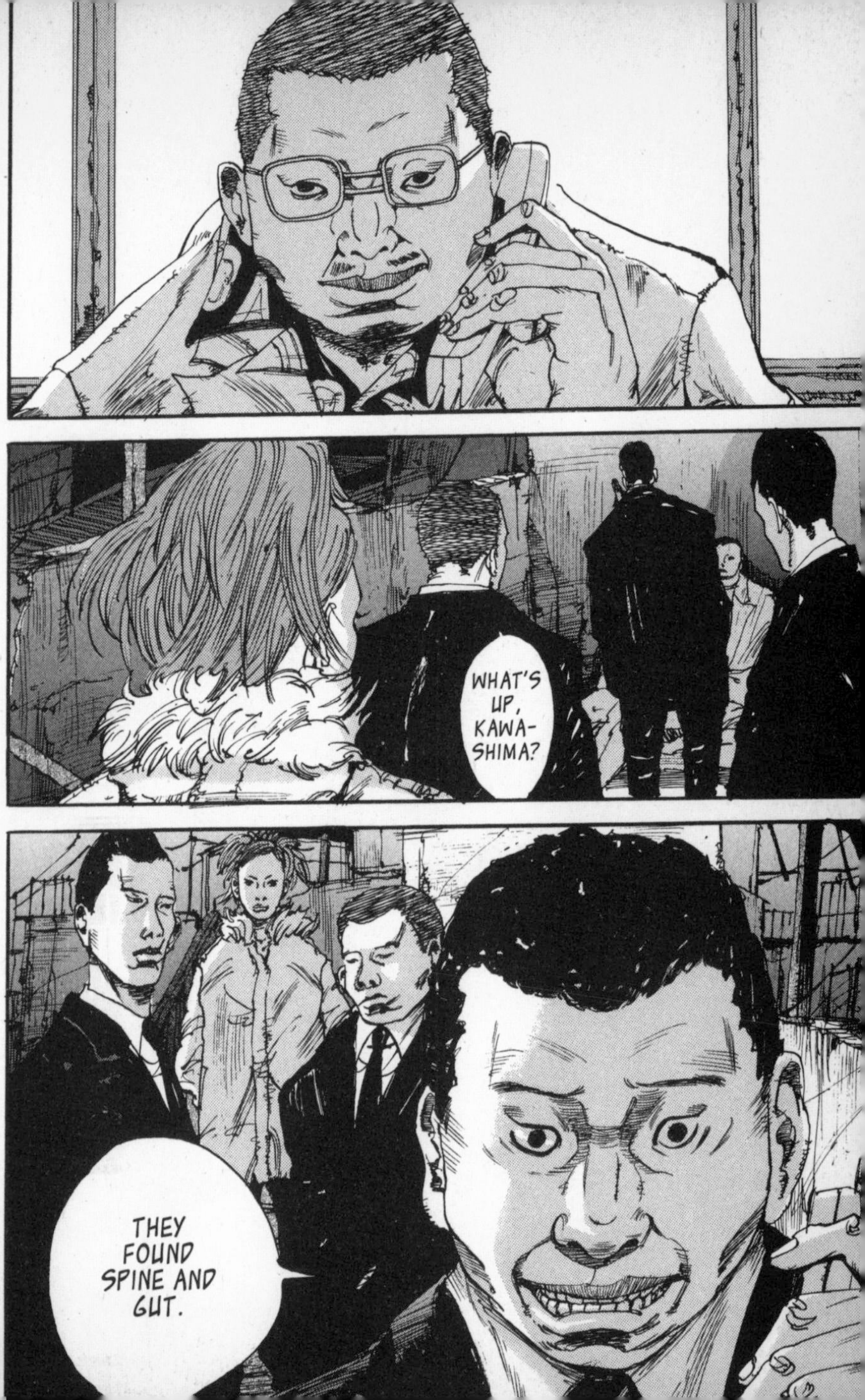
WHAT'S UP, KAWA-SHIMA?
THEY FOUND SPINE AND GUT.

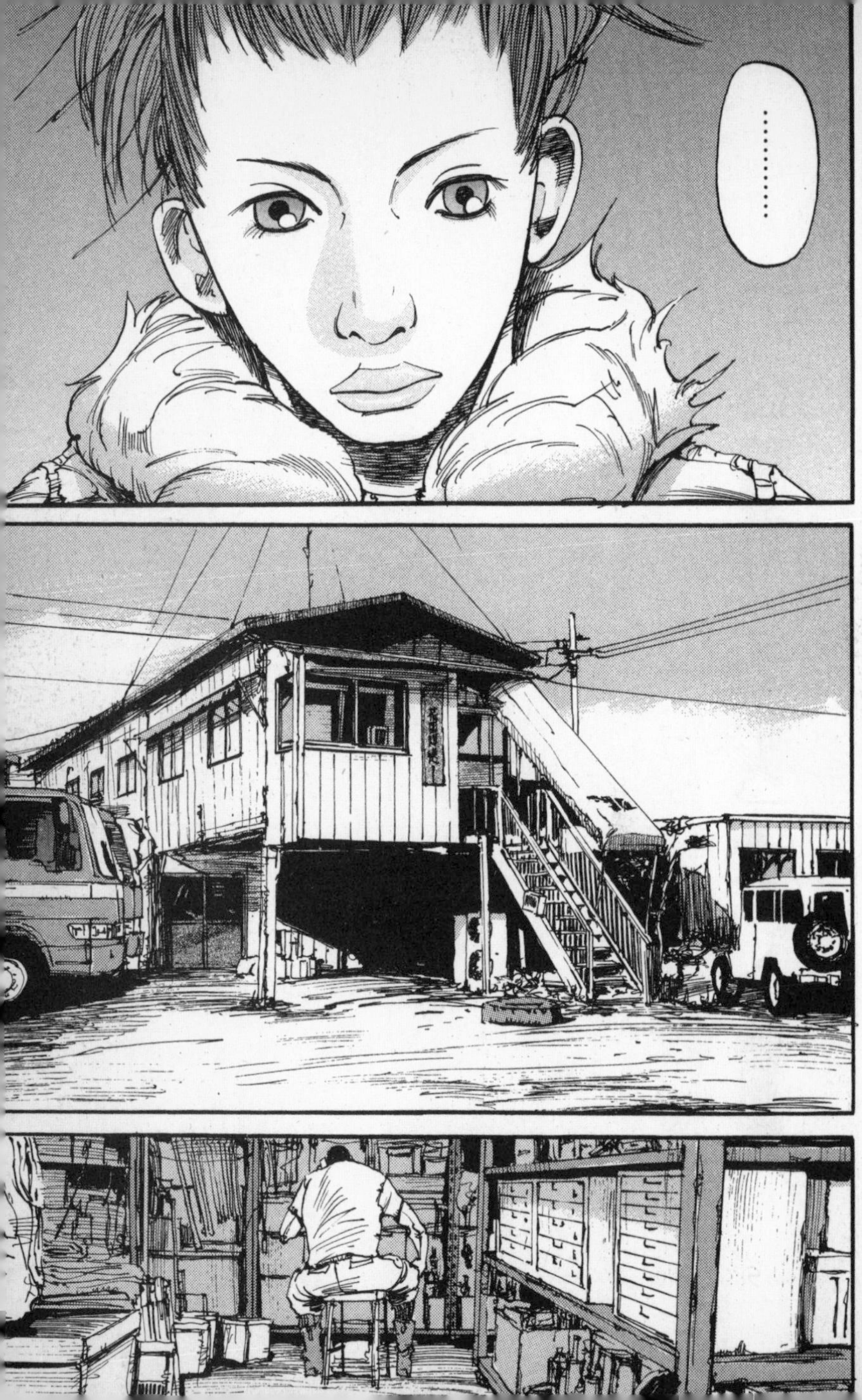
……

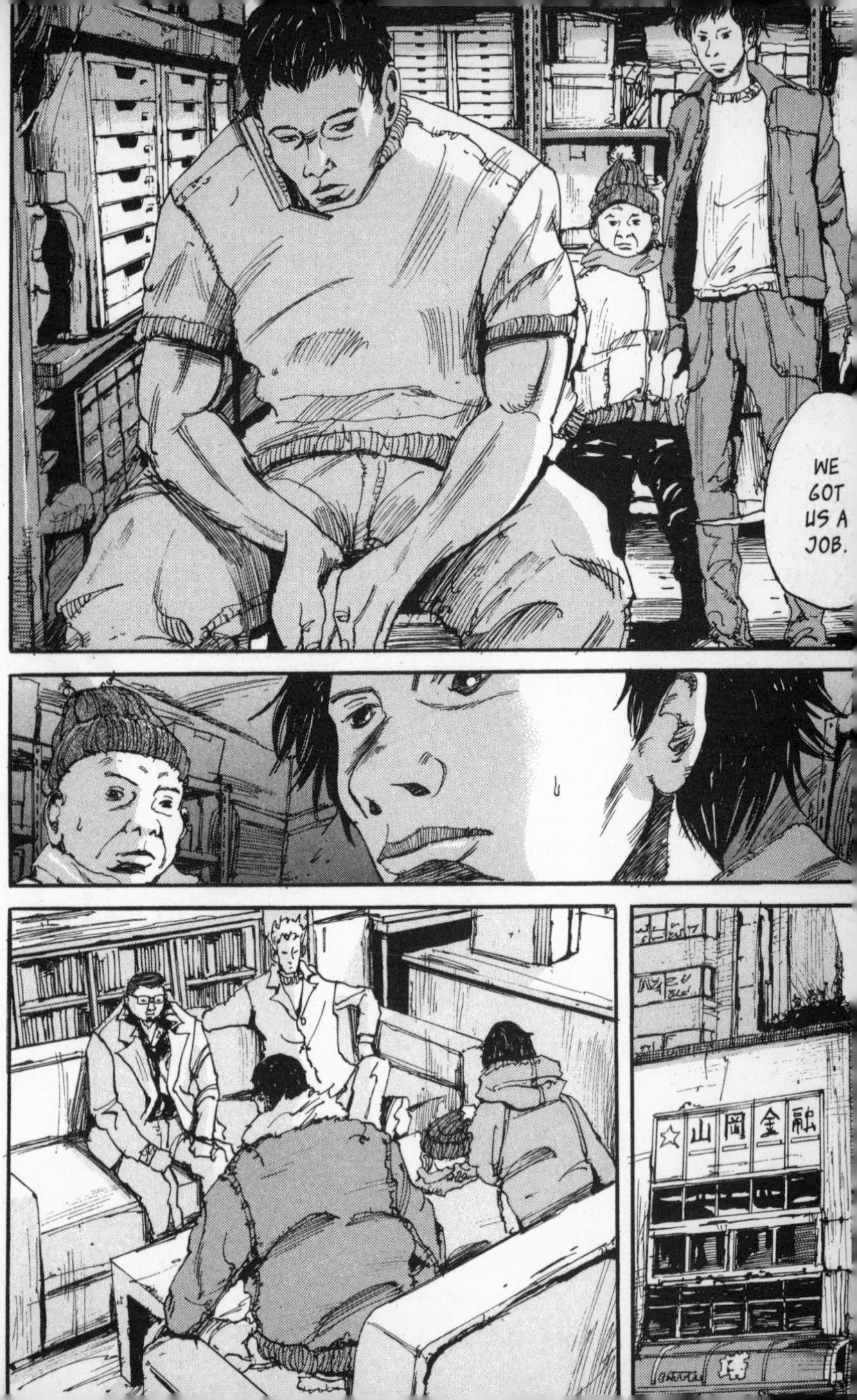
WE GOT US A JOB.
山岡金融

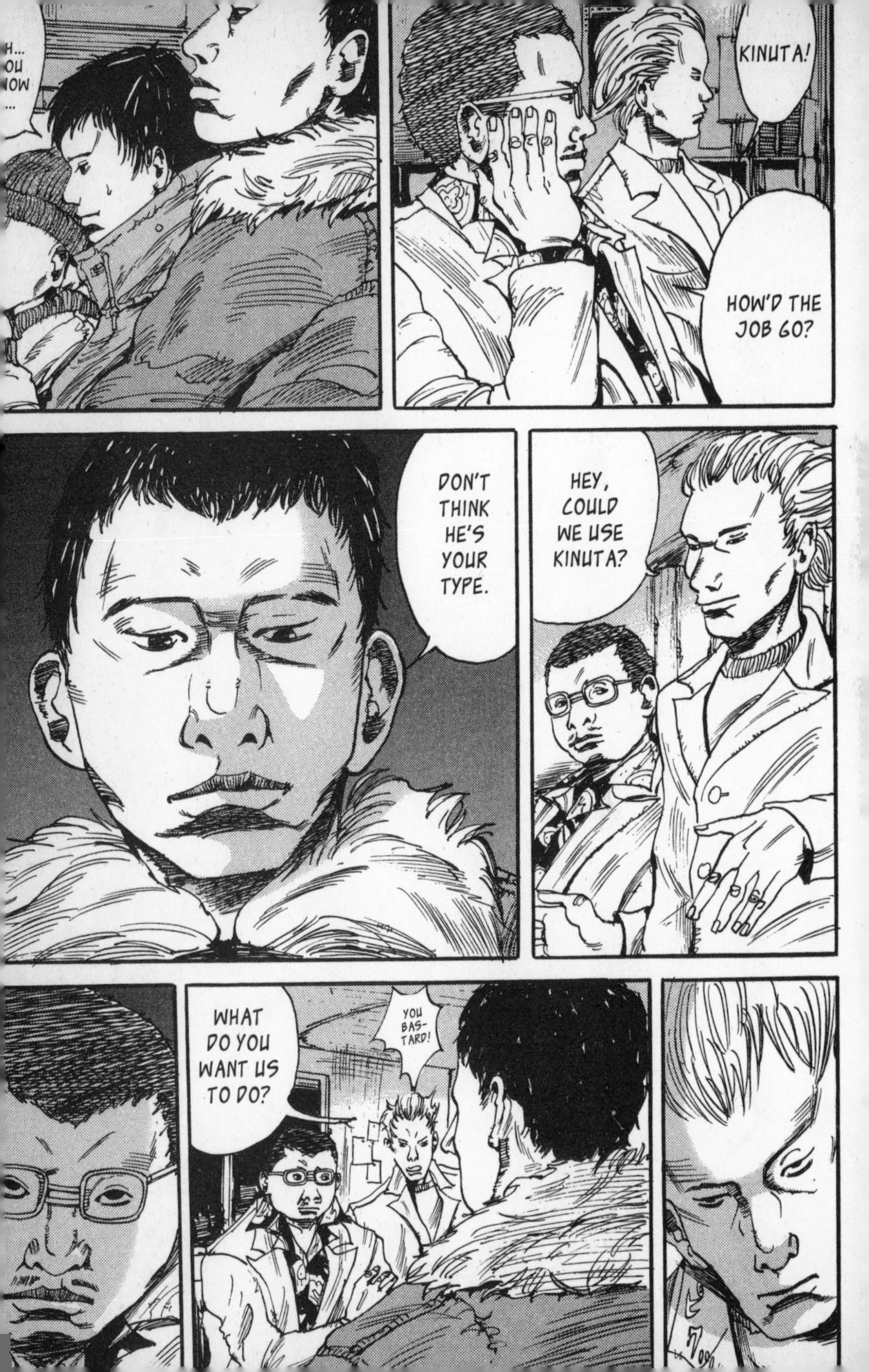
KINUTA!
HOW'D THE JOB GO?
HEY, COULD WE USE KINUTA?
DON'T THINK HE'S YOUR TYPE.
WHAT DO YOU WANT US TO DO?
YOU BAS-TARD!

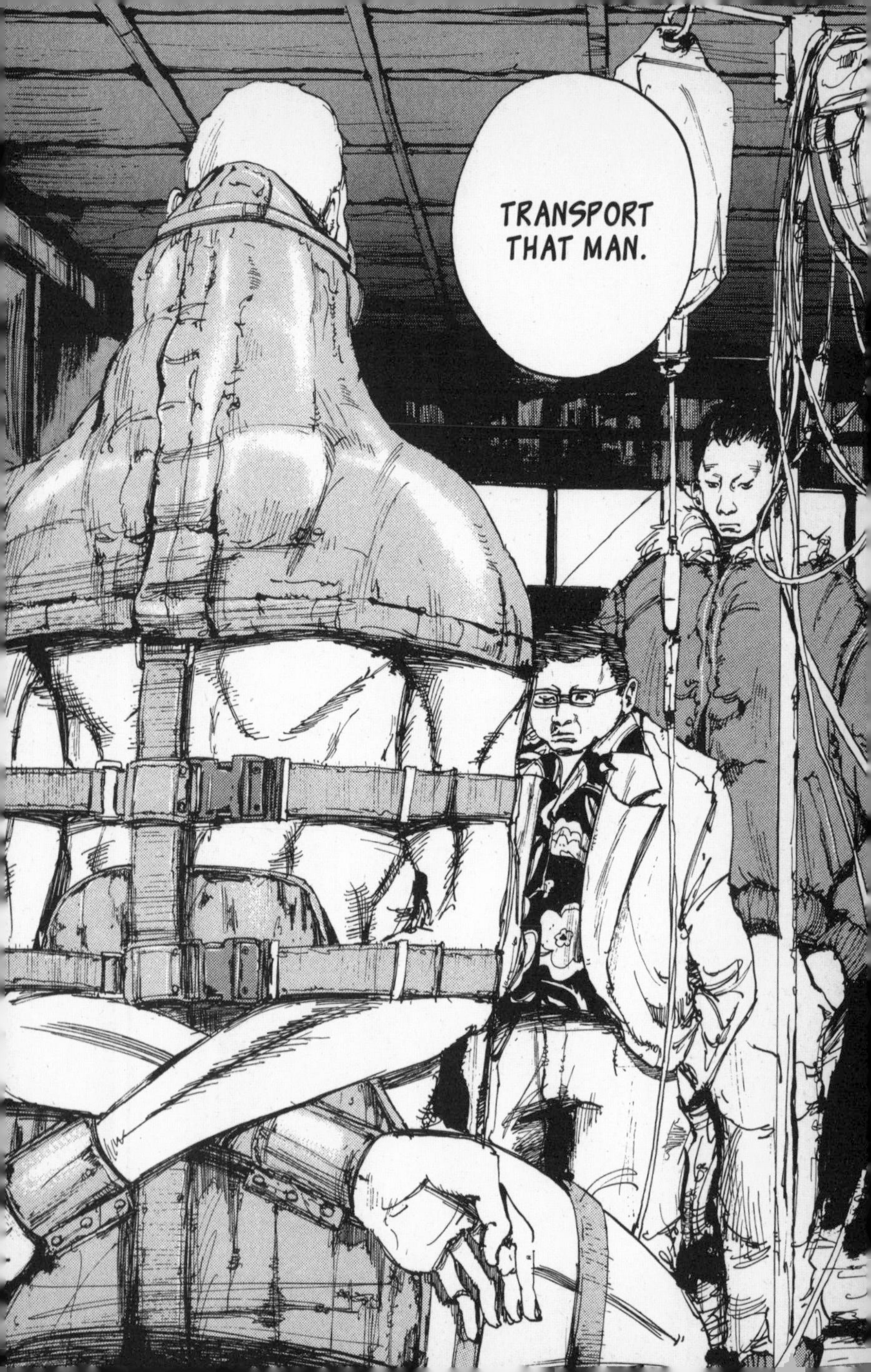
TRANSPORT THAT MAN.

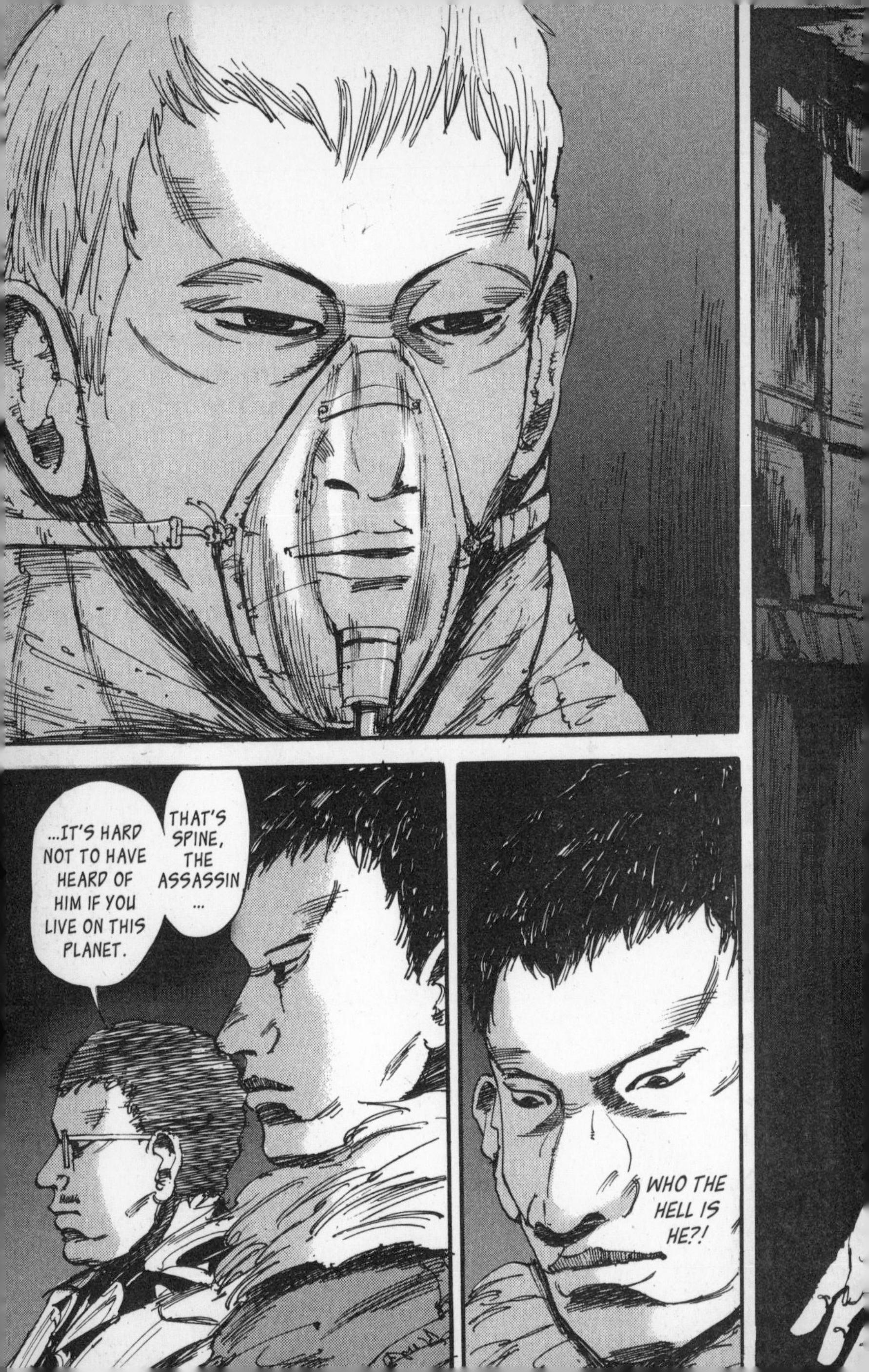
WHO THE HELL IS HE?!
THAT'S SPINE, THE ASSASSIN ...
...IT'S HARD NOT TO HAVE HEARD OF HIM IF YOU LIVE ON THIS PLANET.

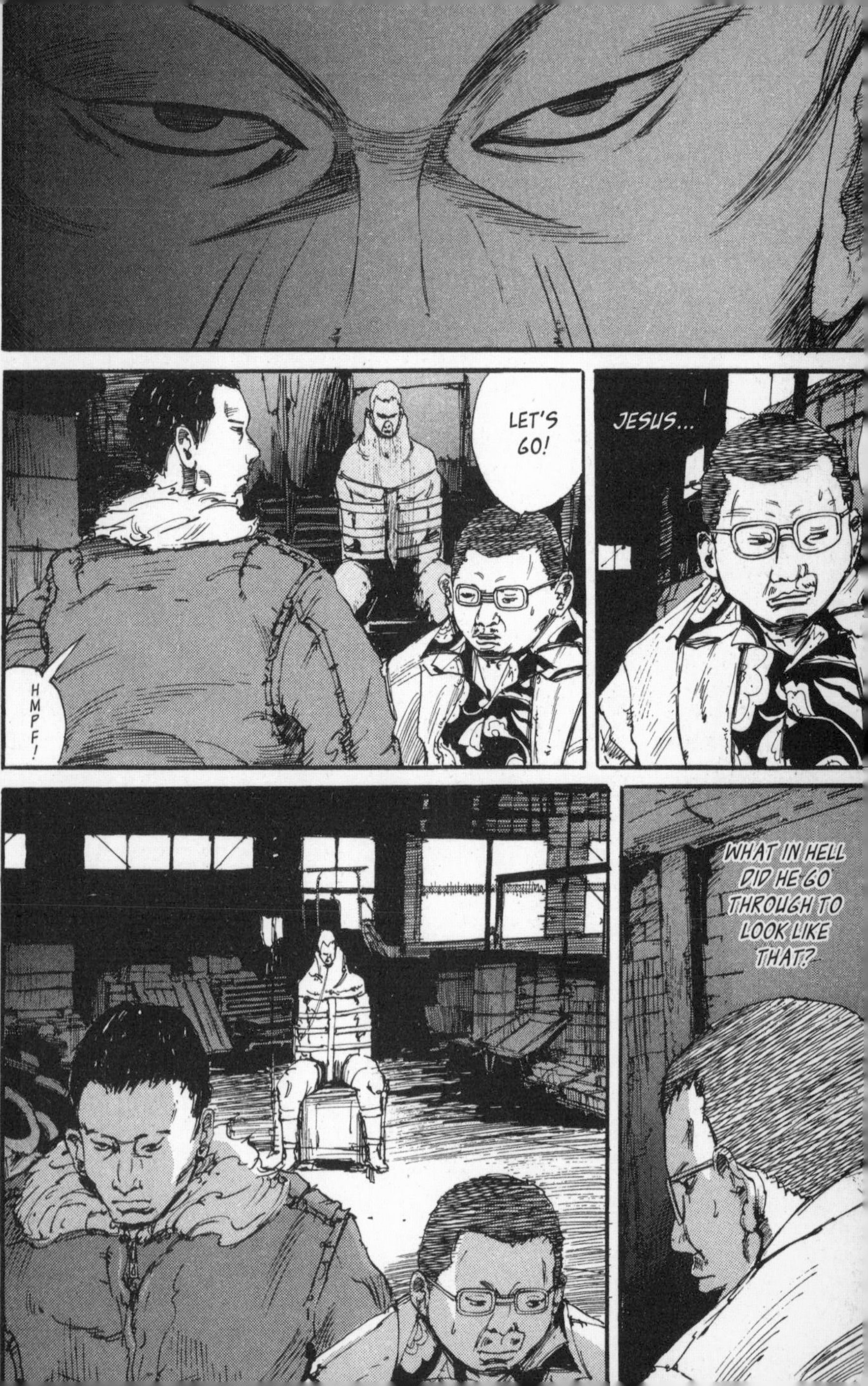
JESUS...
LET'S GO!
HMPF!
WHAT IN HELL DID HE GO THROUGH TO LOOK LIKE THAT?

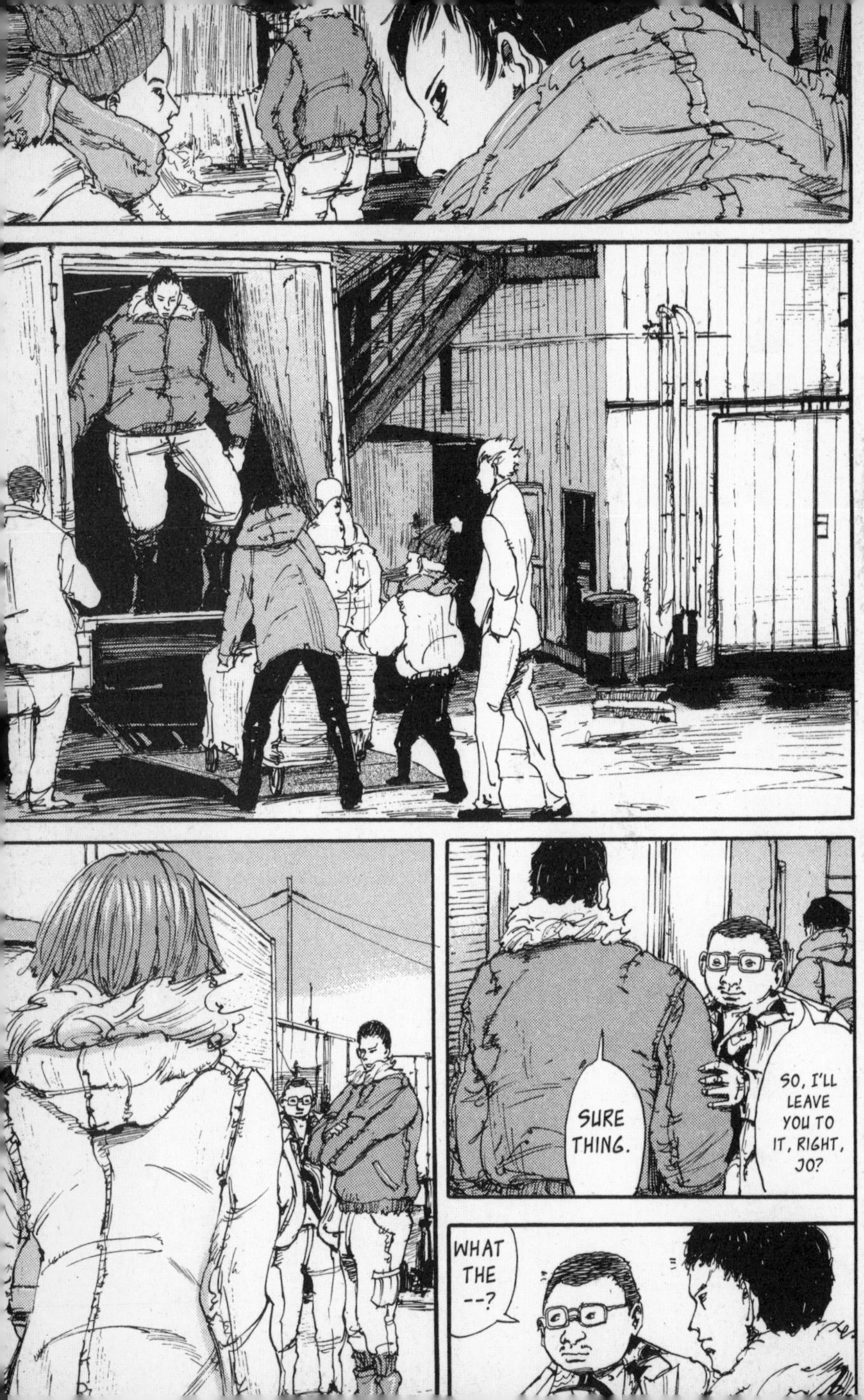
SO, I'LL LEAVE YOU TO IT, RIGHT, JO?
SURE THING.
WHAT THE --?

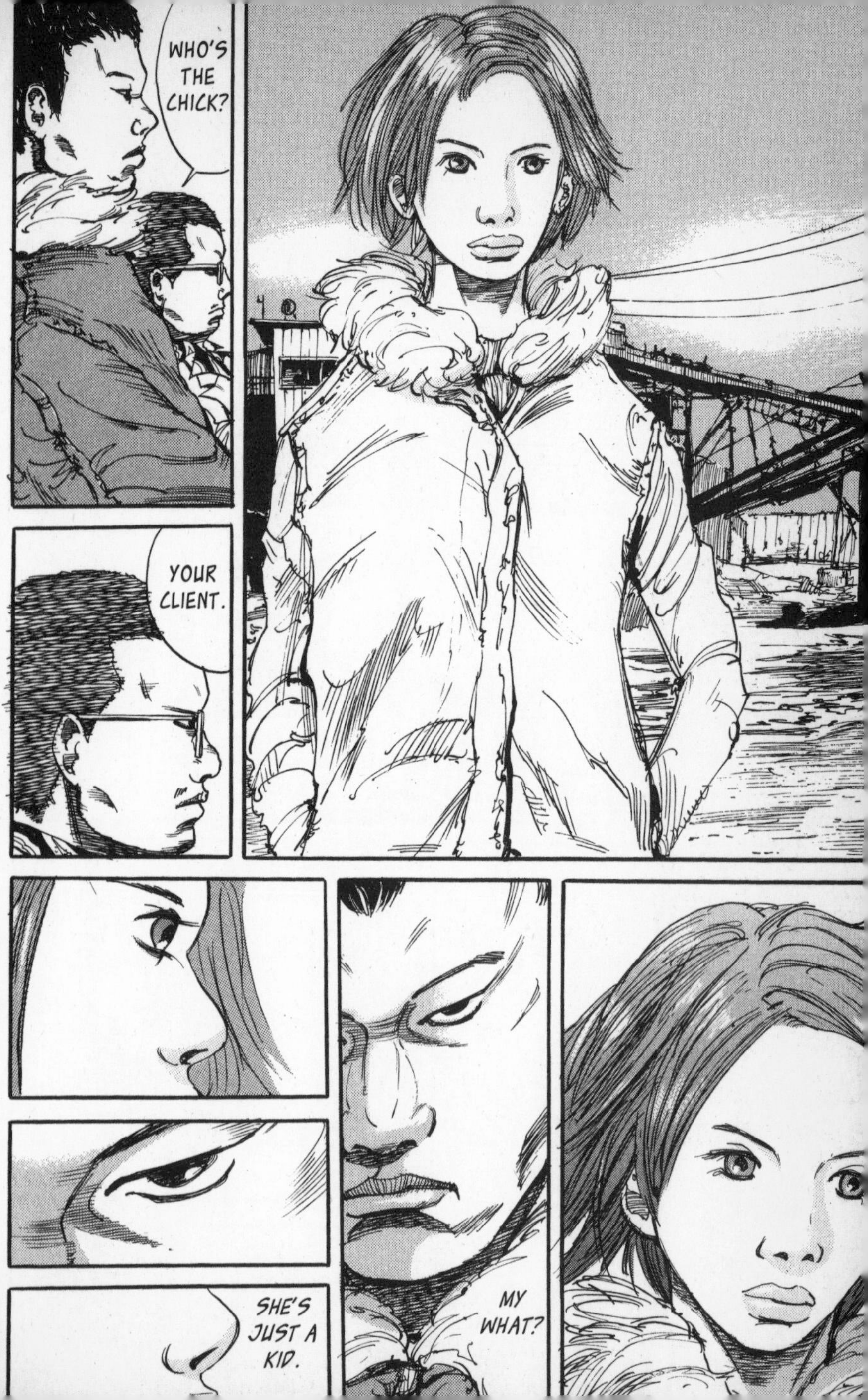
WHO'S THE CHICK?
YOUR CLIENT.
MY WHAT?
SHE'S JUST A KID.

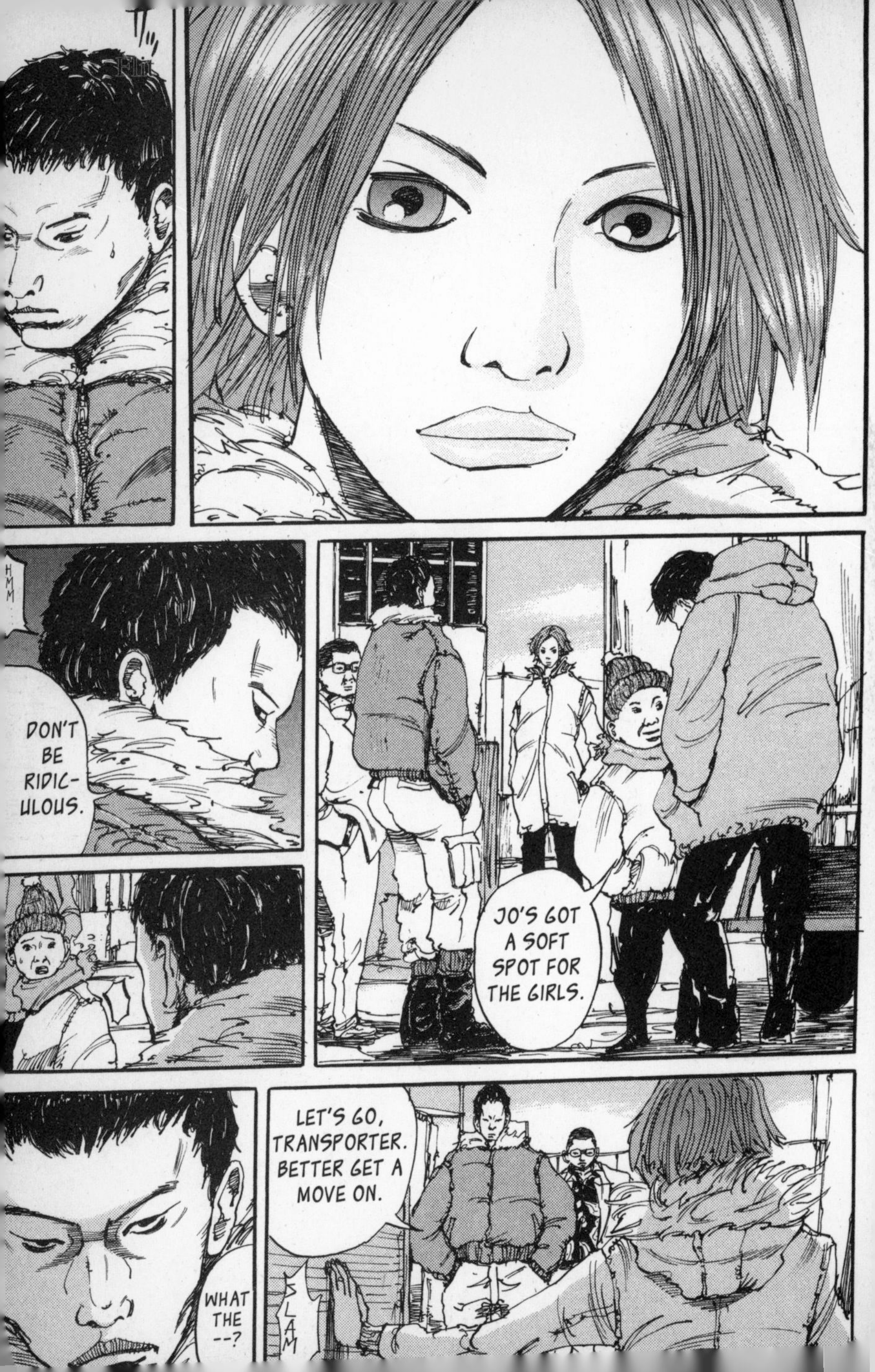
JO'S GOT A SOFT SPOT FOR THE GIRLS.
HMM
DON'T BE RIDIC-ULOUS.
LET'S GO, TRANSPORTER. BETTER GET A MOVE ON.
SLAM
WHAT THE --?

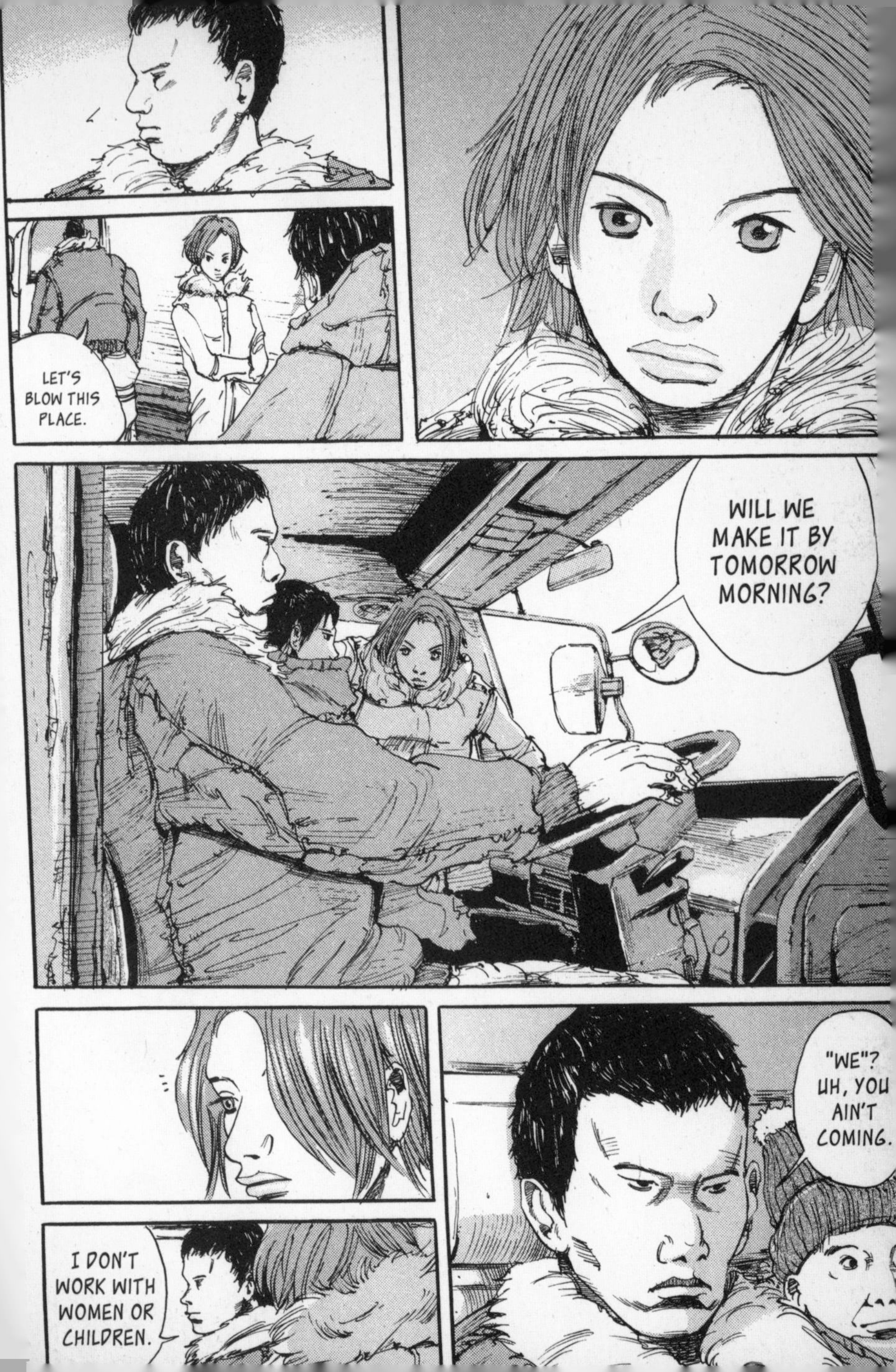
LET'S BLOW THIS PLACE.
WILL WE MAKE IT BY TOMORROW MORNING?
"WE"? UH, YOU AIN'T COMING.
I DON'T WORK WITH WOMEN OR CHILDREN.

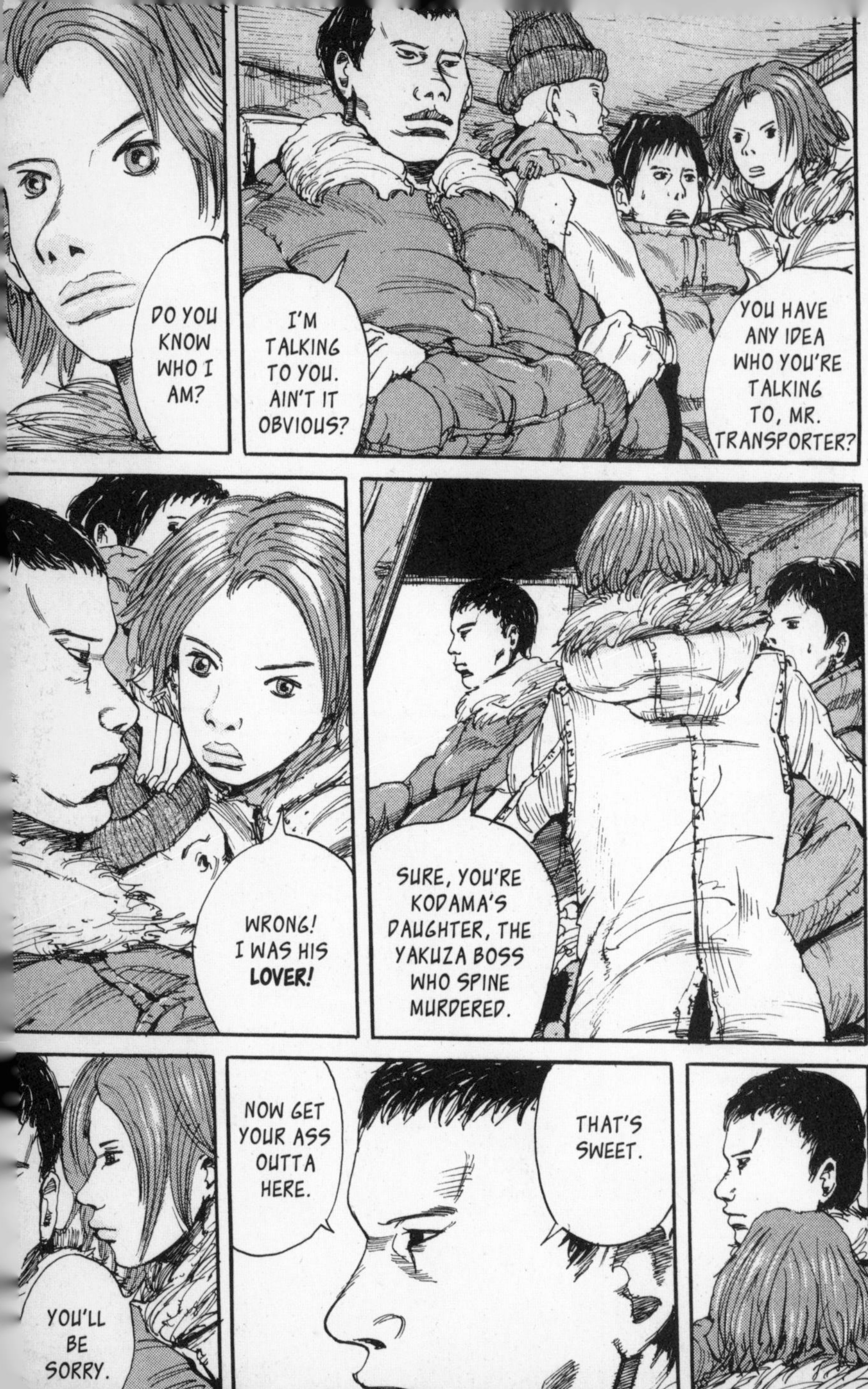
YOU HAVE ANY IDEA WHO YOU'RE TALKING TO, MR. TRANSPORTER?
I'M TALKING TO YOU. AIN'T IT OBVIOUS?
DO YOU KNOW WHO I AM?
SURE, YOU'RE KODAMA'S DAUGHTER, THE YAKUZA BOSS WHO SPINE MURDERED.
WRONG! I WAS HIS **LOVER!**
THAT'S SWEET.
NOW GET YOUR ASS OUTTA HERE.
YOU'LL BE SORRY.

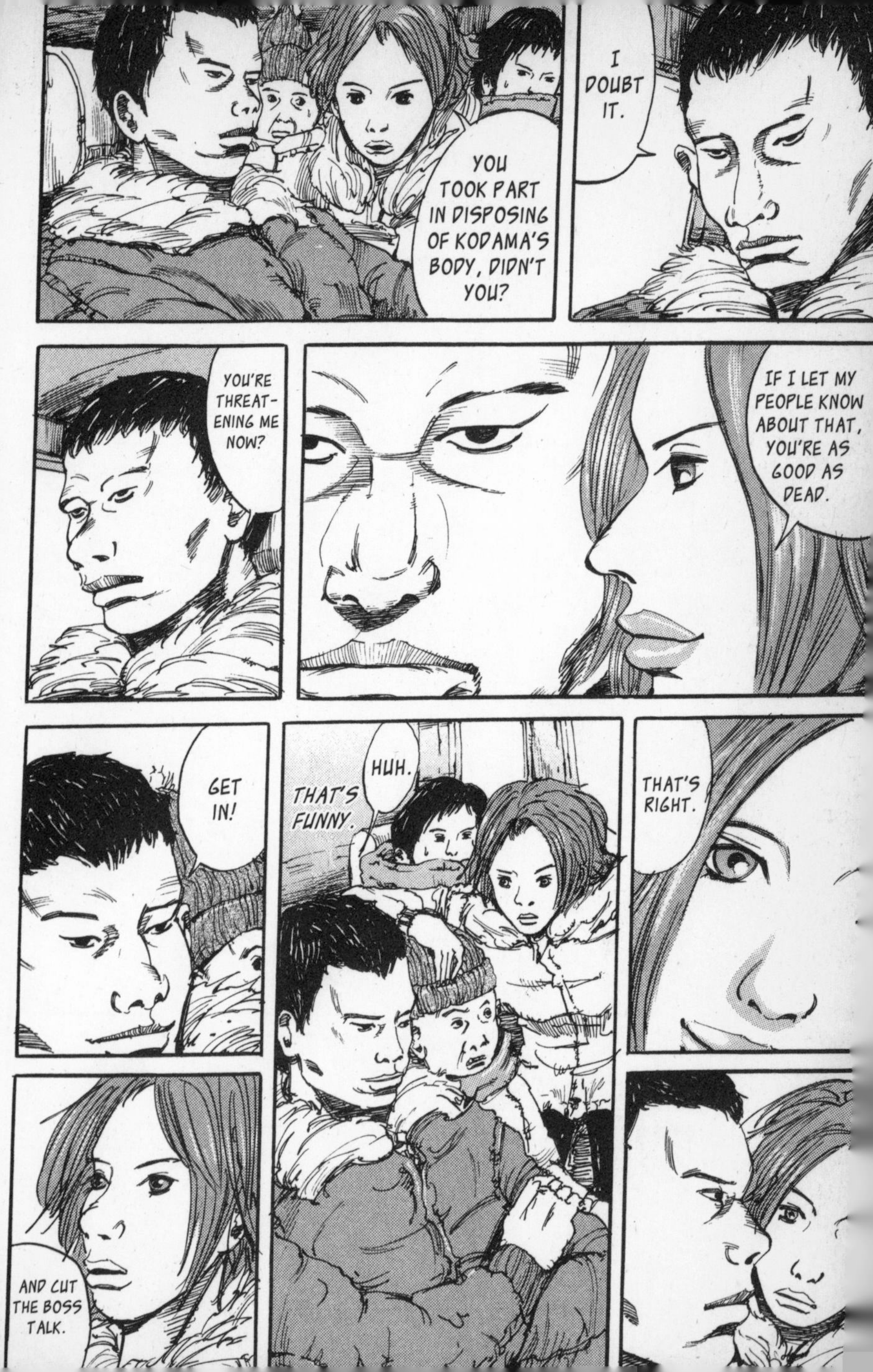
I DOUBT IT.
YOU TOOK PART IN DISPOSING OF KODAMA'S BODY, DIDN'T YOU?
IF I LET MY PEOPLE KNOW ABOUT THAT, YOU'RE AS GOOD AS DEAD.
YOU'RE THREAT-ENING ME NOW?
THAT'S RIGHT.
HUH.
THAT'S FUNNY.
GET IN!
AND CUT THE BOSS TALK.

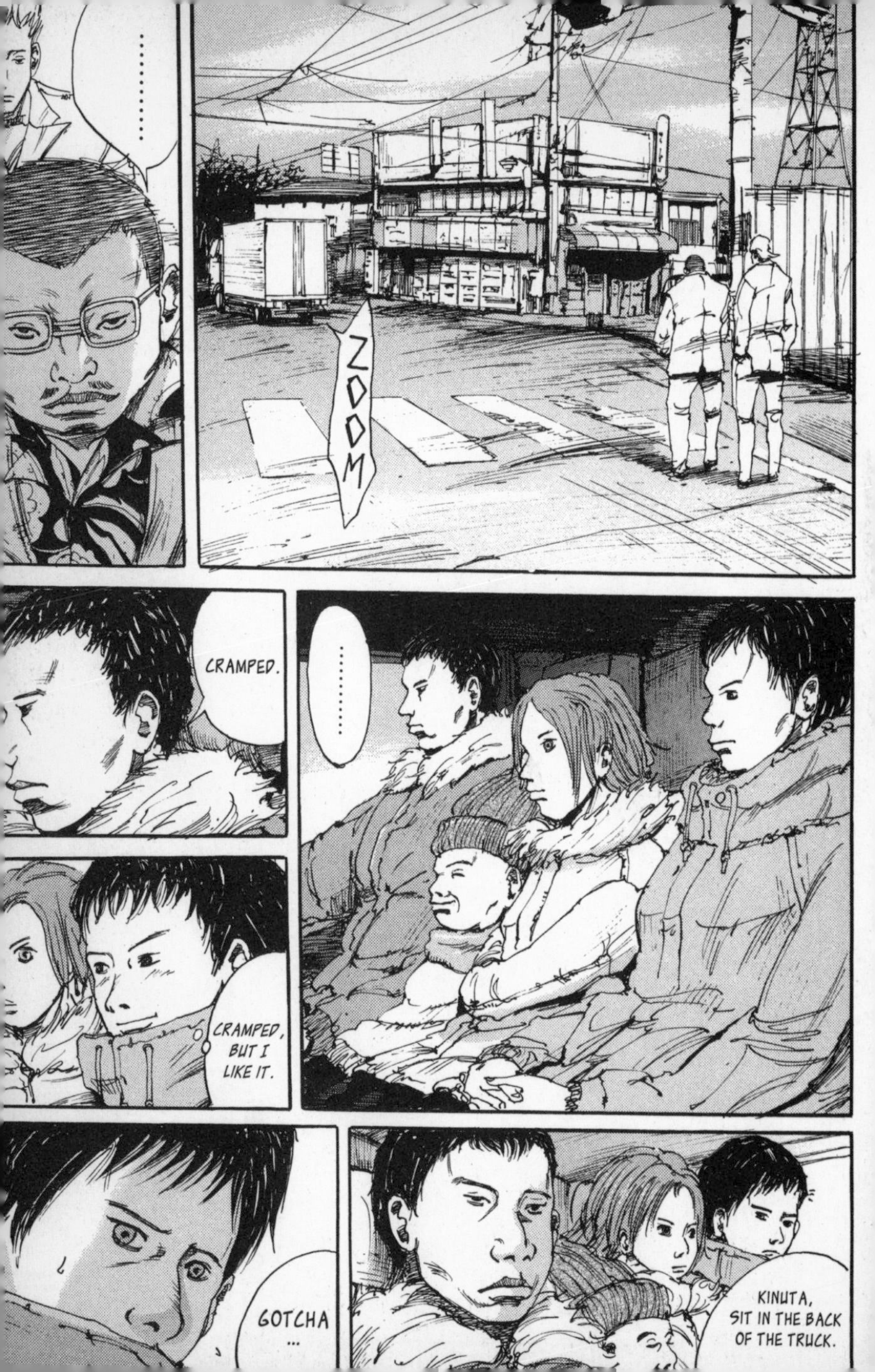
ZOOM
……
……
CRAMPED.
CRAMPED, BUT I LIKE IT.
KINUTA, SIT IN THE BACK OF THE TRUCK.
GOTCHA …

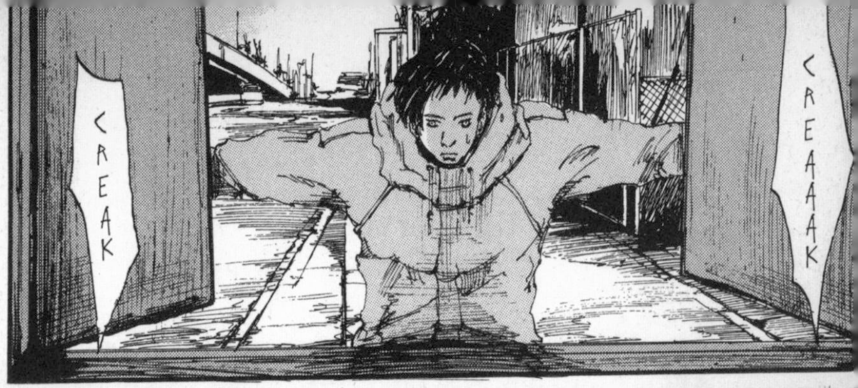
CREAAAK
CREAK

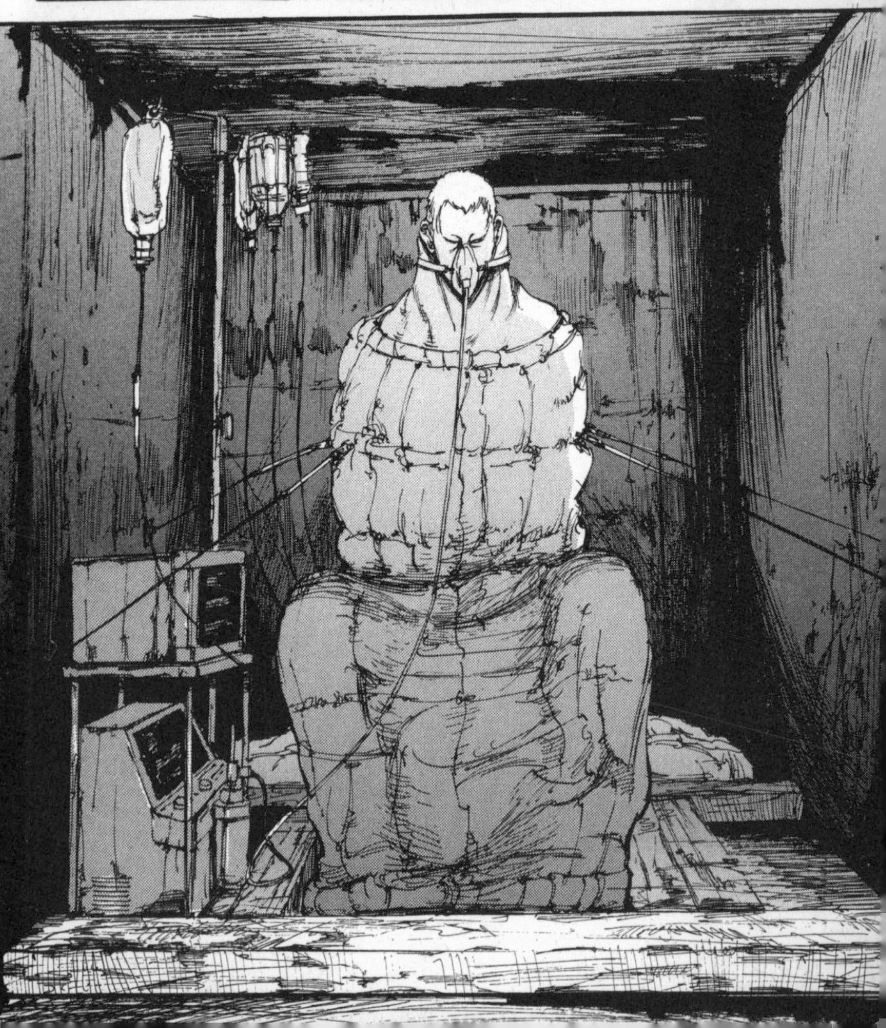

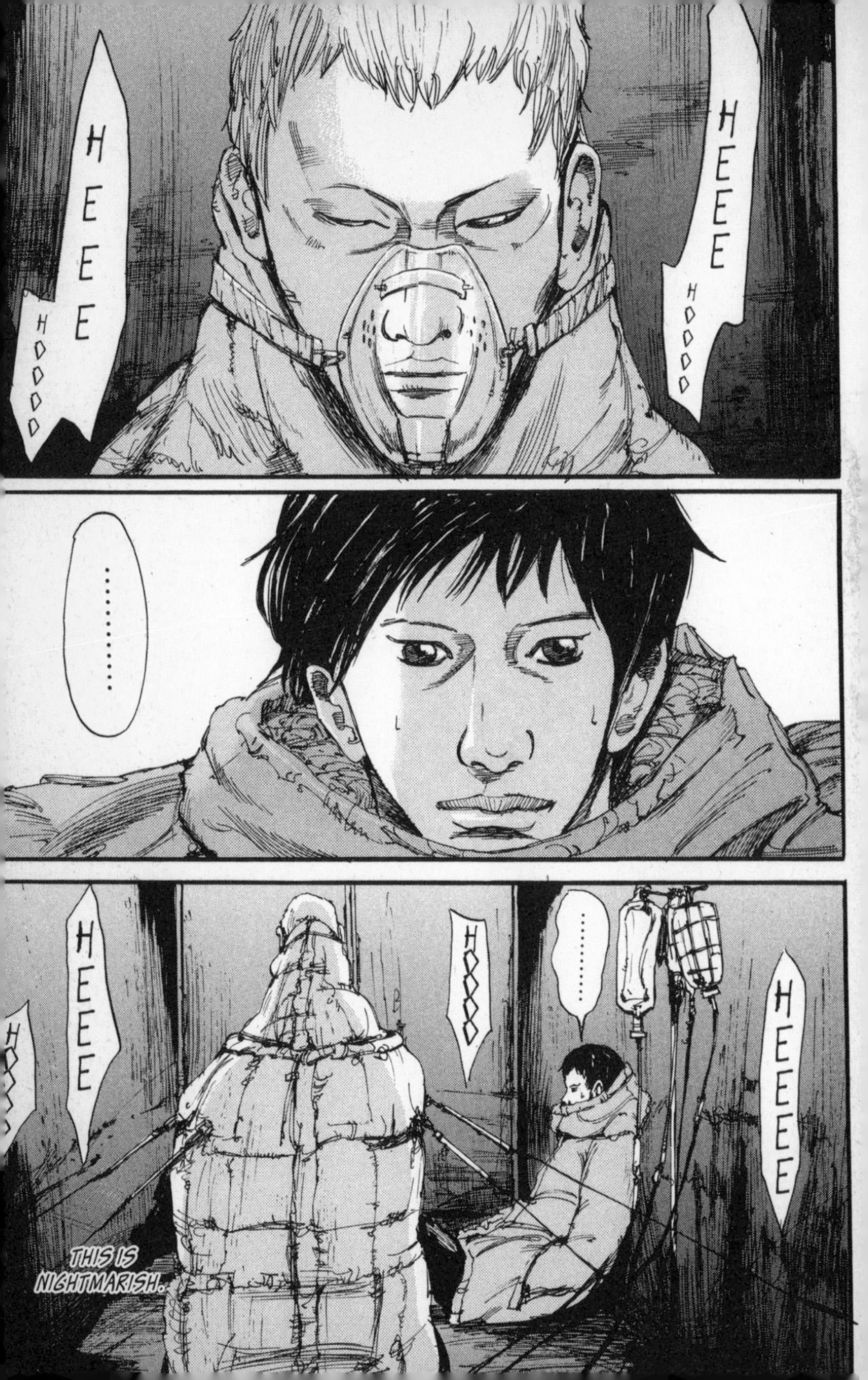
HEEE HOOOO
HEEE HOOOO
……
HEEEE
……
HOOOO
HEEE
THIS IS NIGHTMARISH.

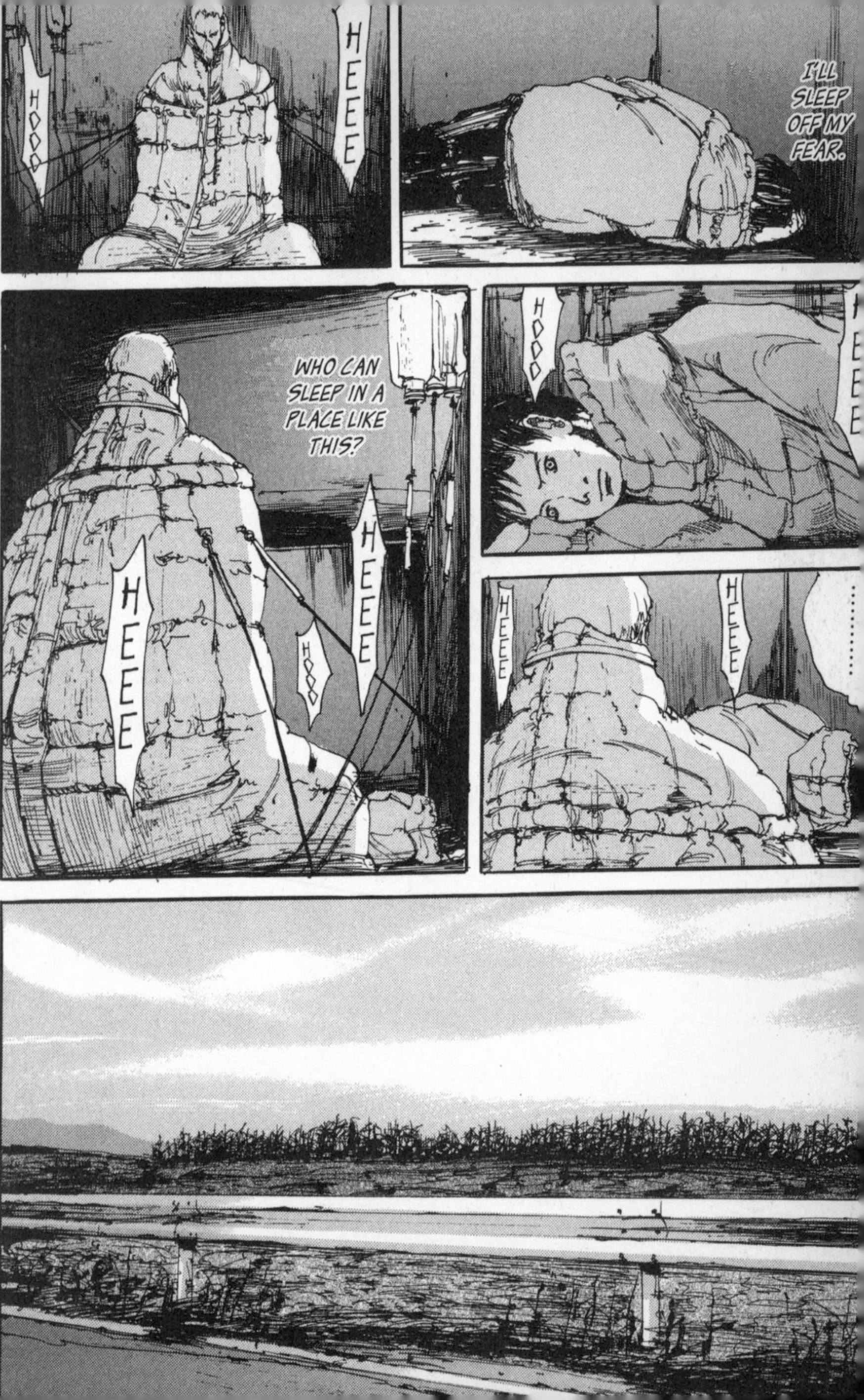
I'LL SLEEP OFF MY FEAR.
HEEE
HOOO
HEEE
HOOO
......
HEEE
HEEE
WHO CAN SLEEP IN A PLACE LIKE THIS?
HEEE
HOOO
HEEE

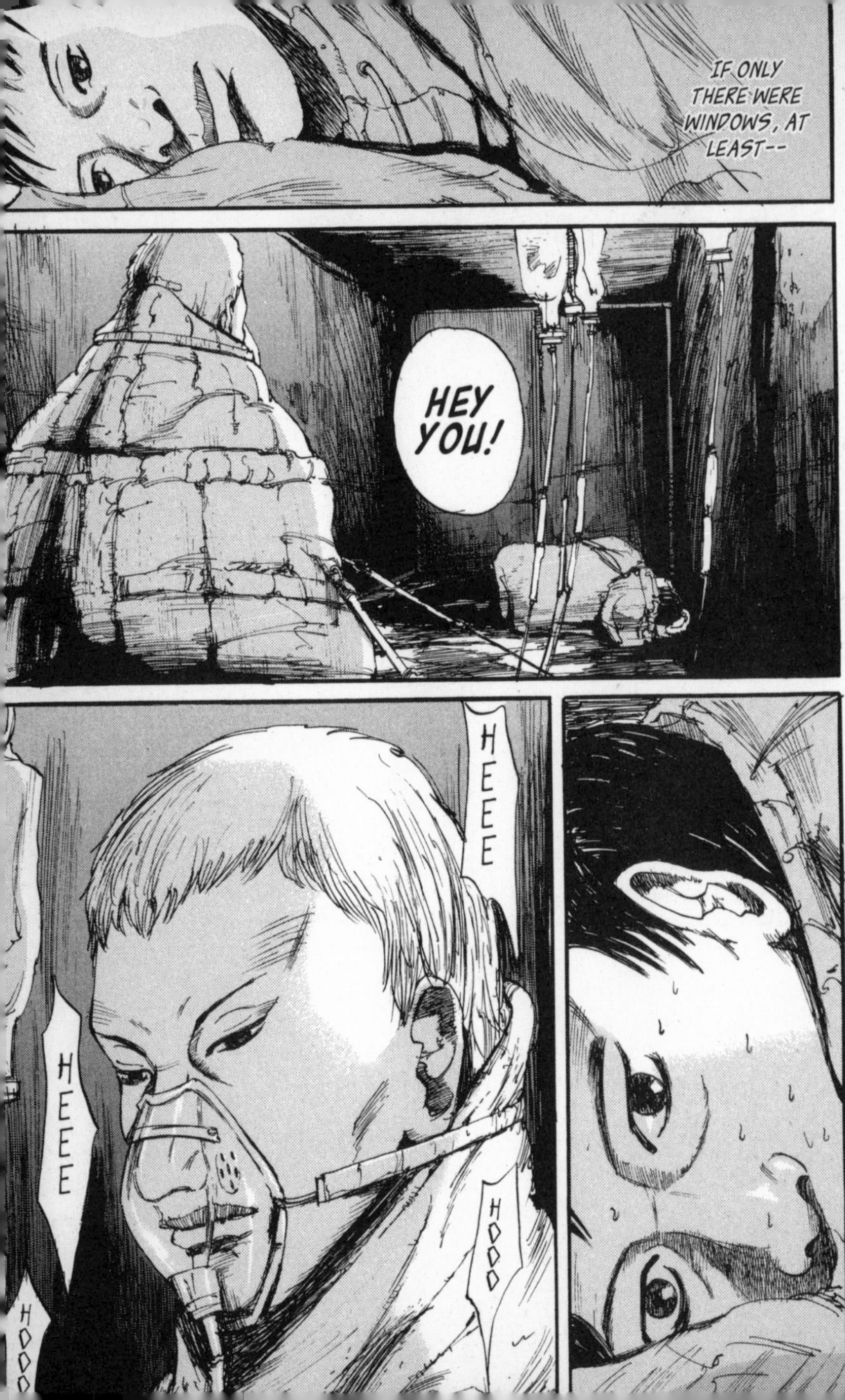
IF ONLY THERE WERE WINDOWS, AT LEAST--
HEY YOU!
HEEE
HOOO
HEEE
HOOO

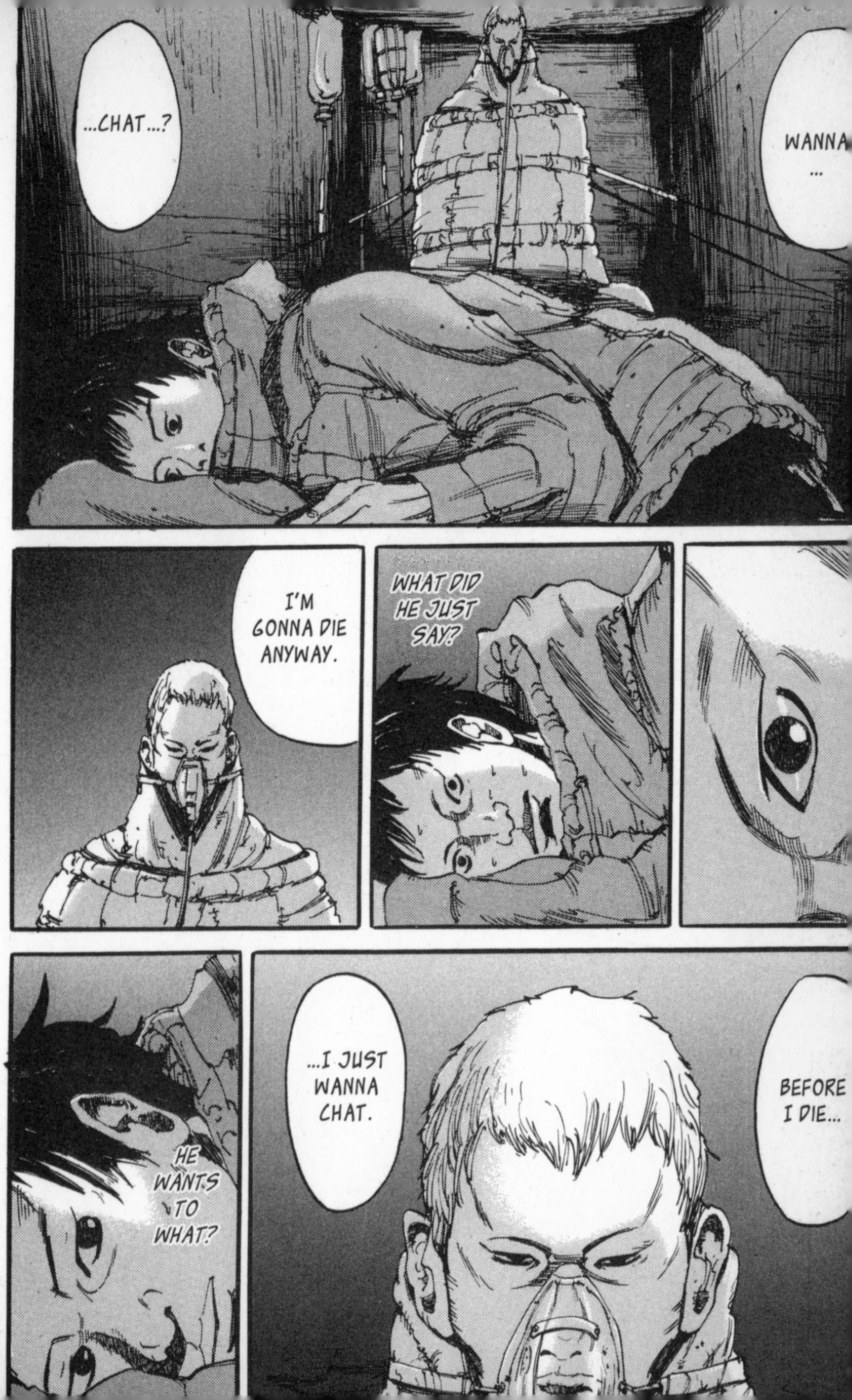
WANNA ...
...CHAT...?
WHAT DID HE JUST SAY?
I'M GONNA DIE ANYWAY.
BEFORE I DIE...
...I JUST WANNA CHAT.
HE WANTS TO WHAT?

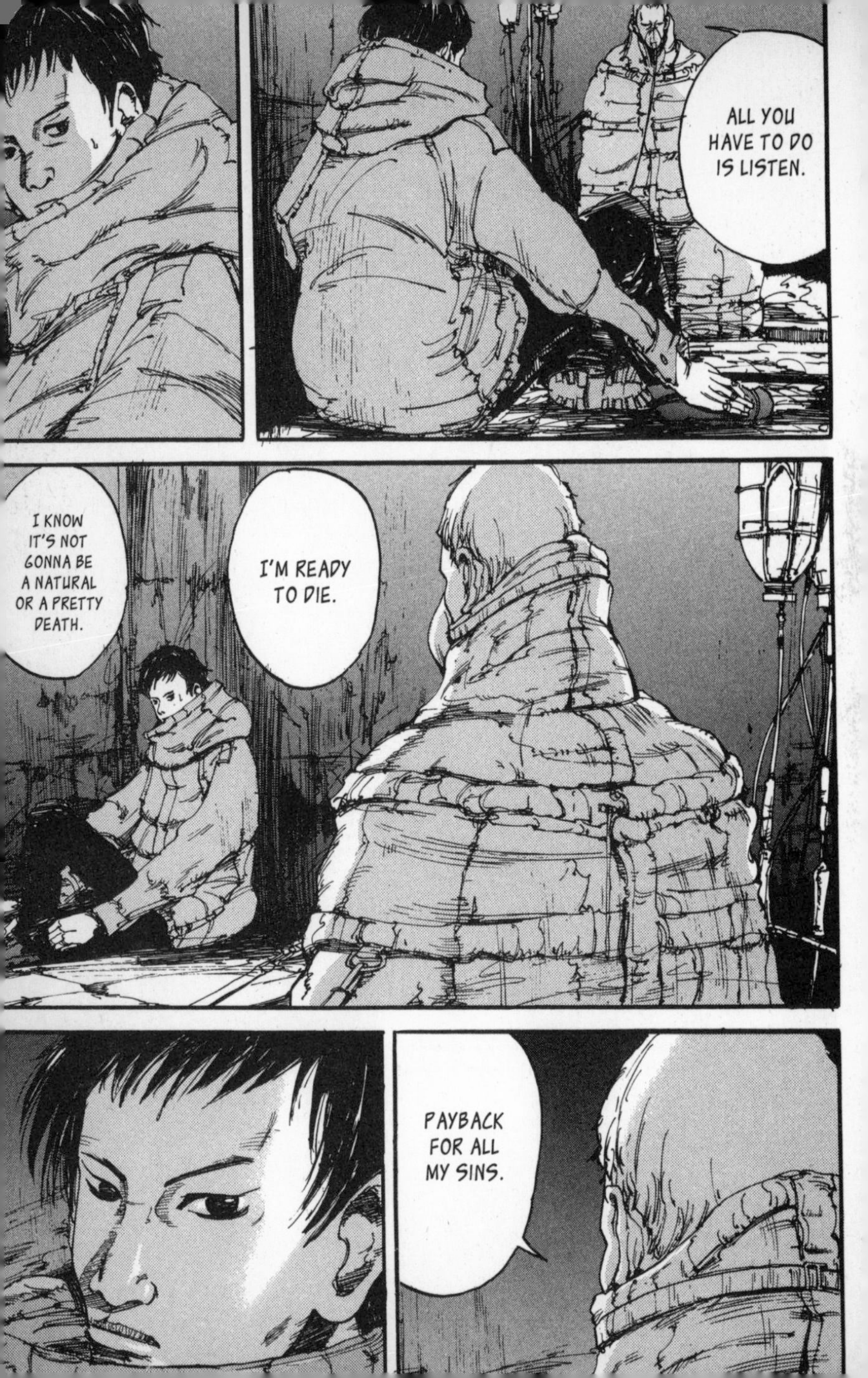
ALL YOU HAVE TO DO IS LISTEN.
I'M READY TO DIE.
I KNOW IT'S NOT GONNA BE A NATURAL OR A PRETTY DEATH.
PAYBACK FOR ALL MY SINS.

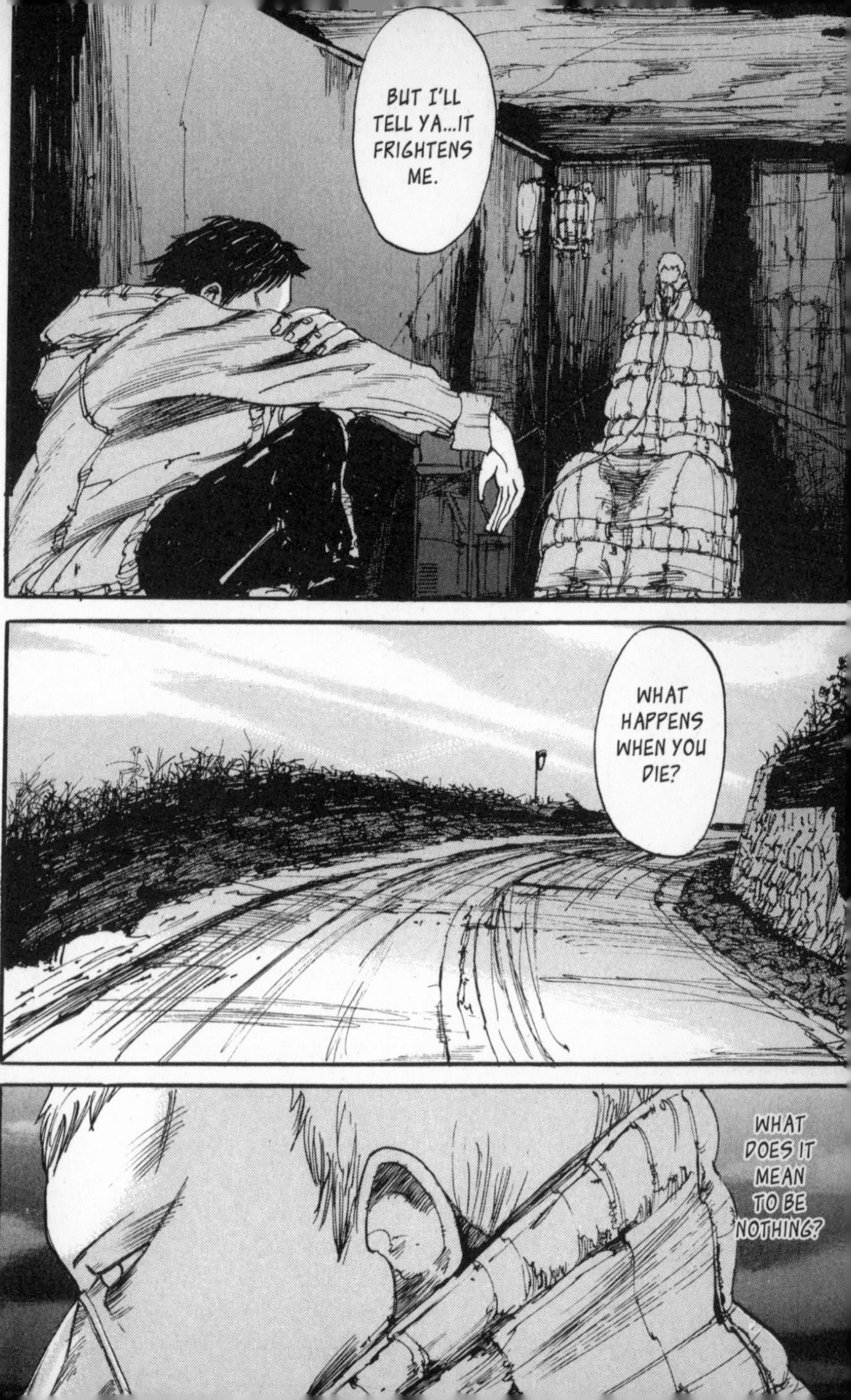
BUT I'LL TELL YA...IT FRIGHTENS ME.
WHAT HAPPENS WHEN YOU DIE?
WHAT DOES IT MEAN TO BE NOTHING?

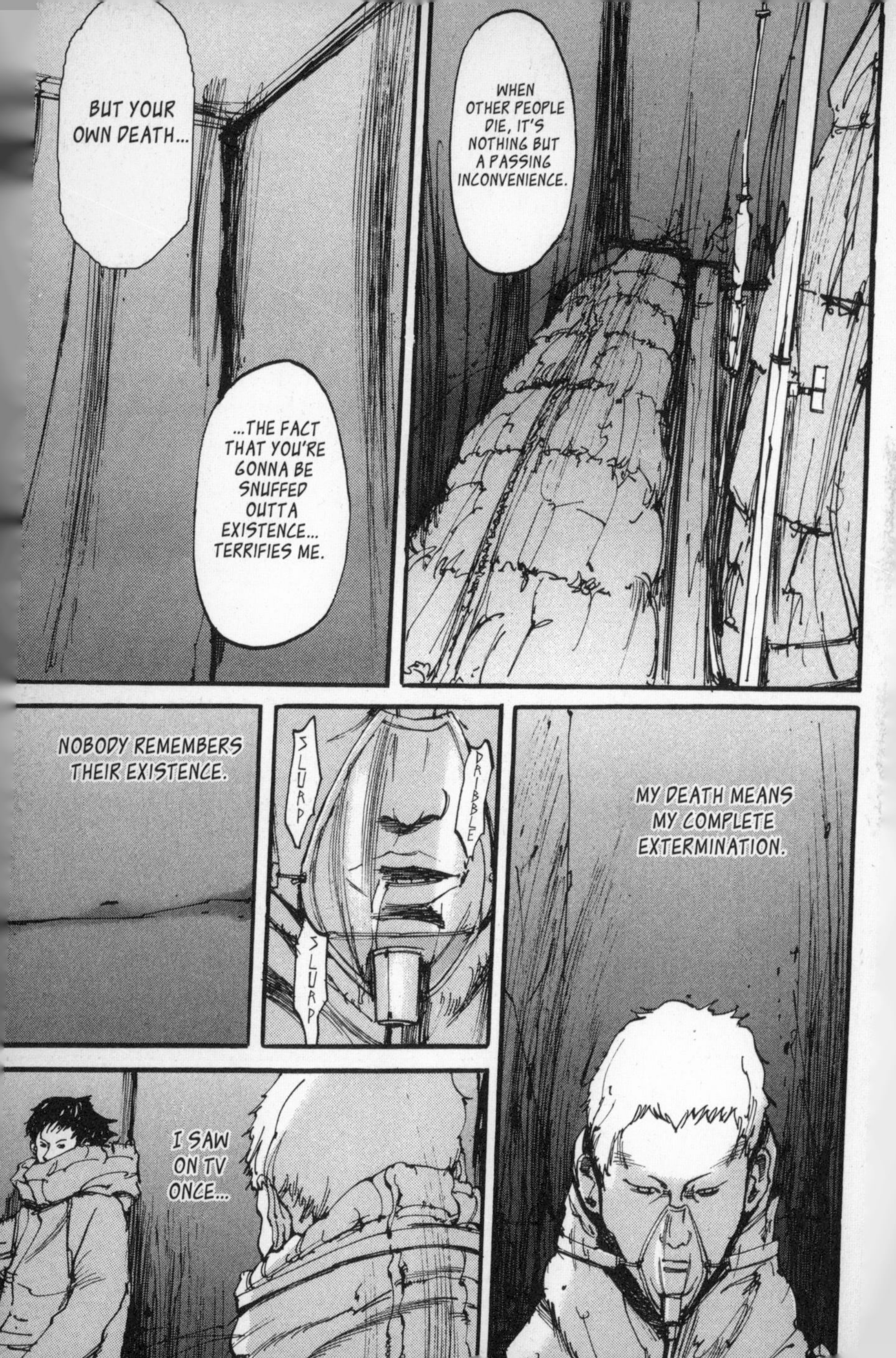
WHEN OTHER PEOPLE DIE, IT'S NOTHING BUT A PASSING INCONVENIENCE.
BUT YOUR OWN DEATH...
...THE FACT THAT YOU'RE GONNA BE SNUFFED OUTTA EXISTENCE... TERRIFIES ME.
MY DEATH MEANS MY COMPLETE EXTERMINATION.
DRIBBLE
SLURP
SLURP
NOBODY REMEMBERS THEIR EXISTENCE.
I SAW ON TV ONCE...

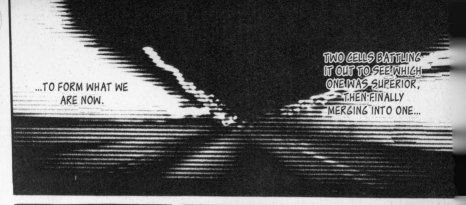

TWO CELLS BATTLING IT OUT TO SEE WHICH ONE WAS SUPERIOR, THEN FINALLY MERGING INTO ONE...
...TO FORM WHAT WE ARE NOW.
ALL EXISTENCE HAS PURPOSE.
EVEN A SINGLE CELL HAS A PURPOSE.
SPIT
SLURP
SLURP
I SPENT MY LIFE TENDING TO MY BOSSES' SELFISH DESIRES.
SPEW
GROSS.
DID MY LIFE HAVE ANY MEANING AT ALL?

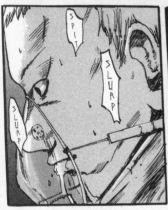

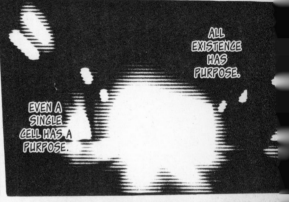

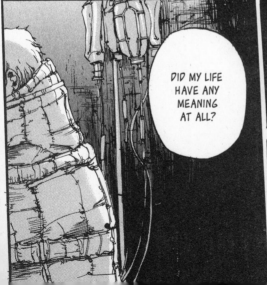

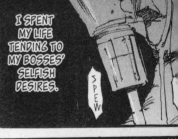

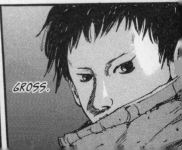

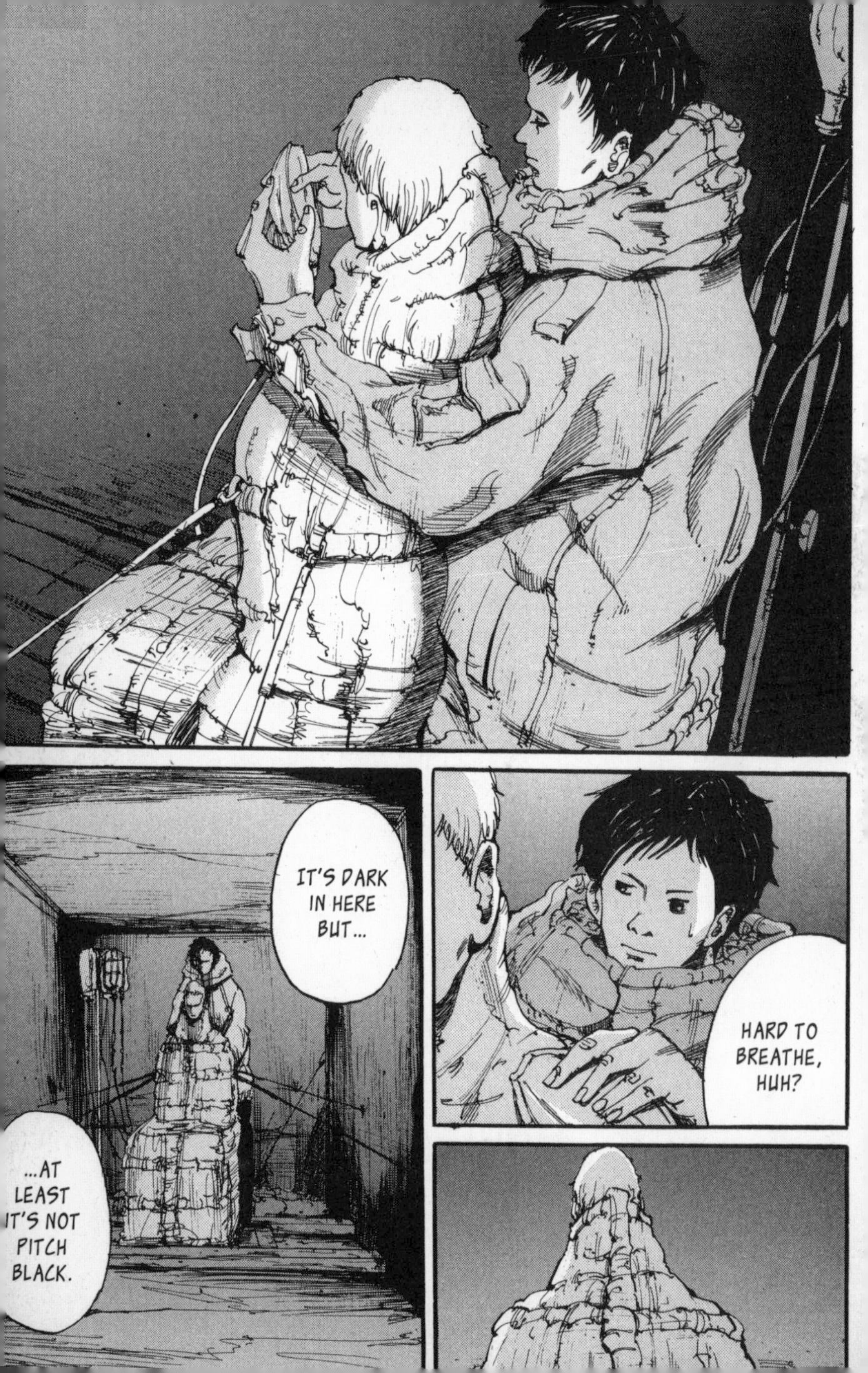
HARD TO BREATHE, HUH?
IT'S DARK IN HERE BUT...
...AT LEAST IT'S NOT PITCH BLACK.

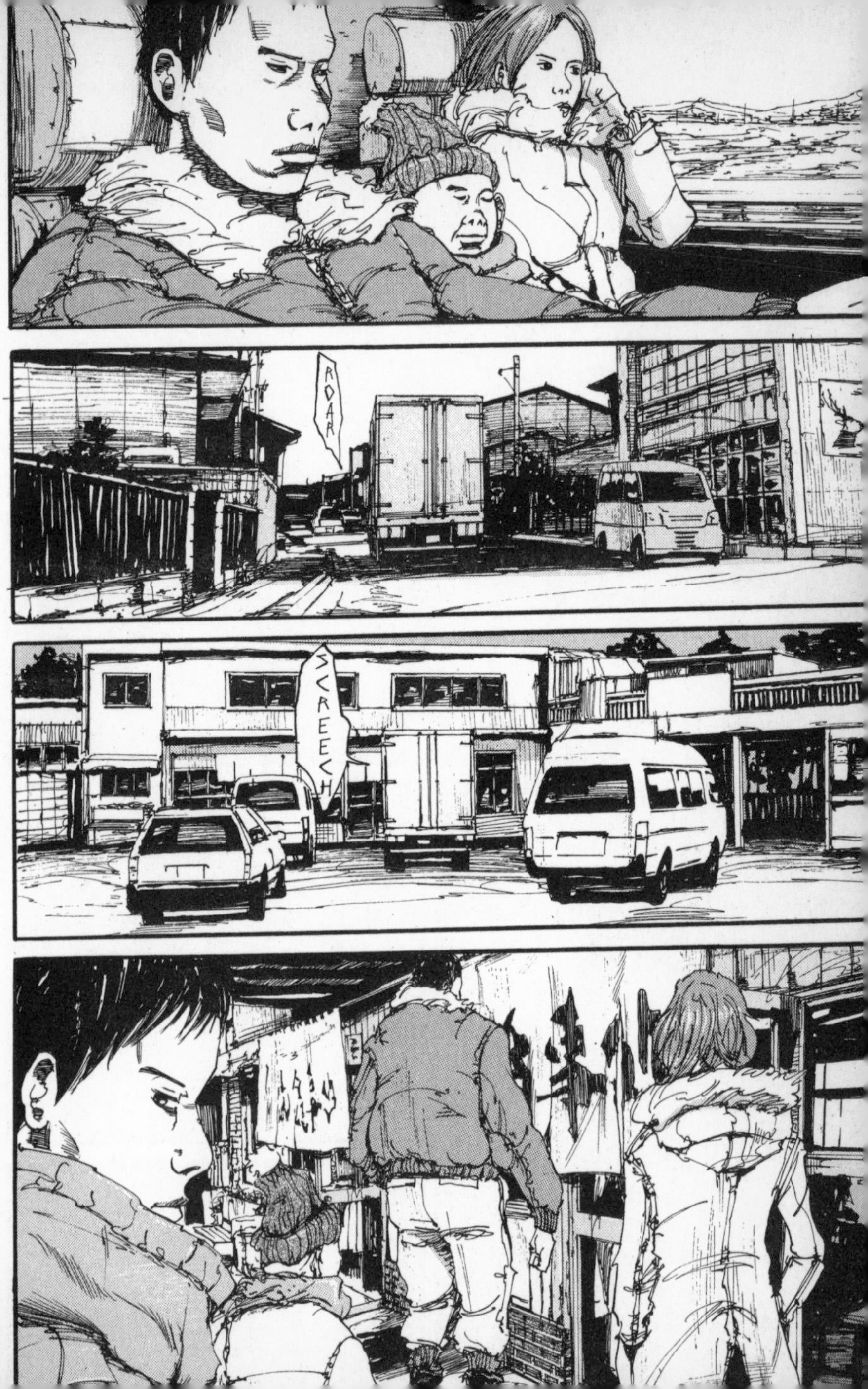
ROAR
SCREECH

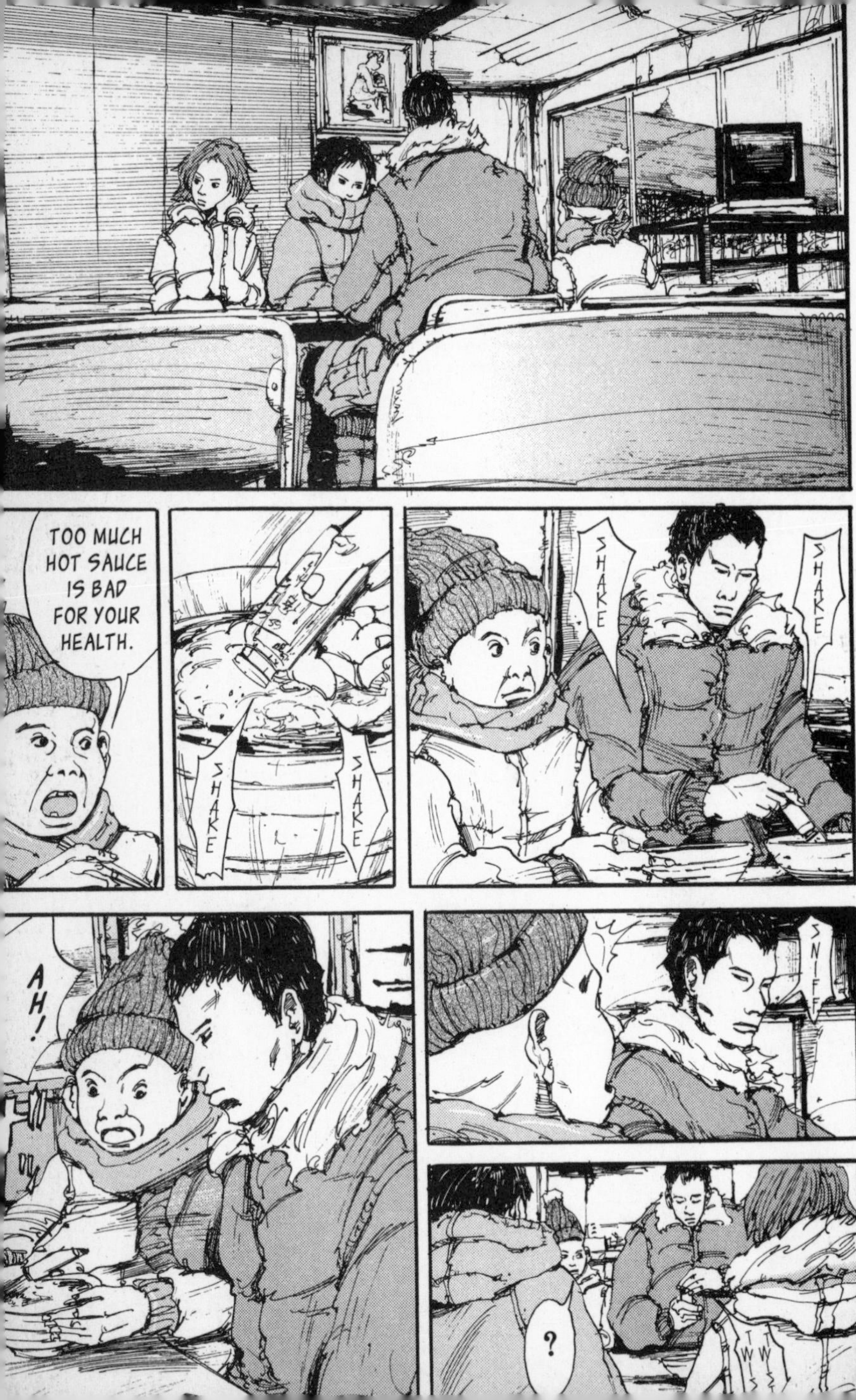
SHAKE
SHAKE
SHAKE
SHAKE
TOO MUCH HOT SAUCE IS BAD FOR YOUR HEALTH.
SNIFF
?
TWIST
TWIST
AH!

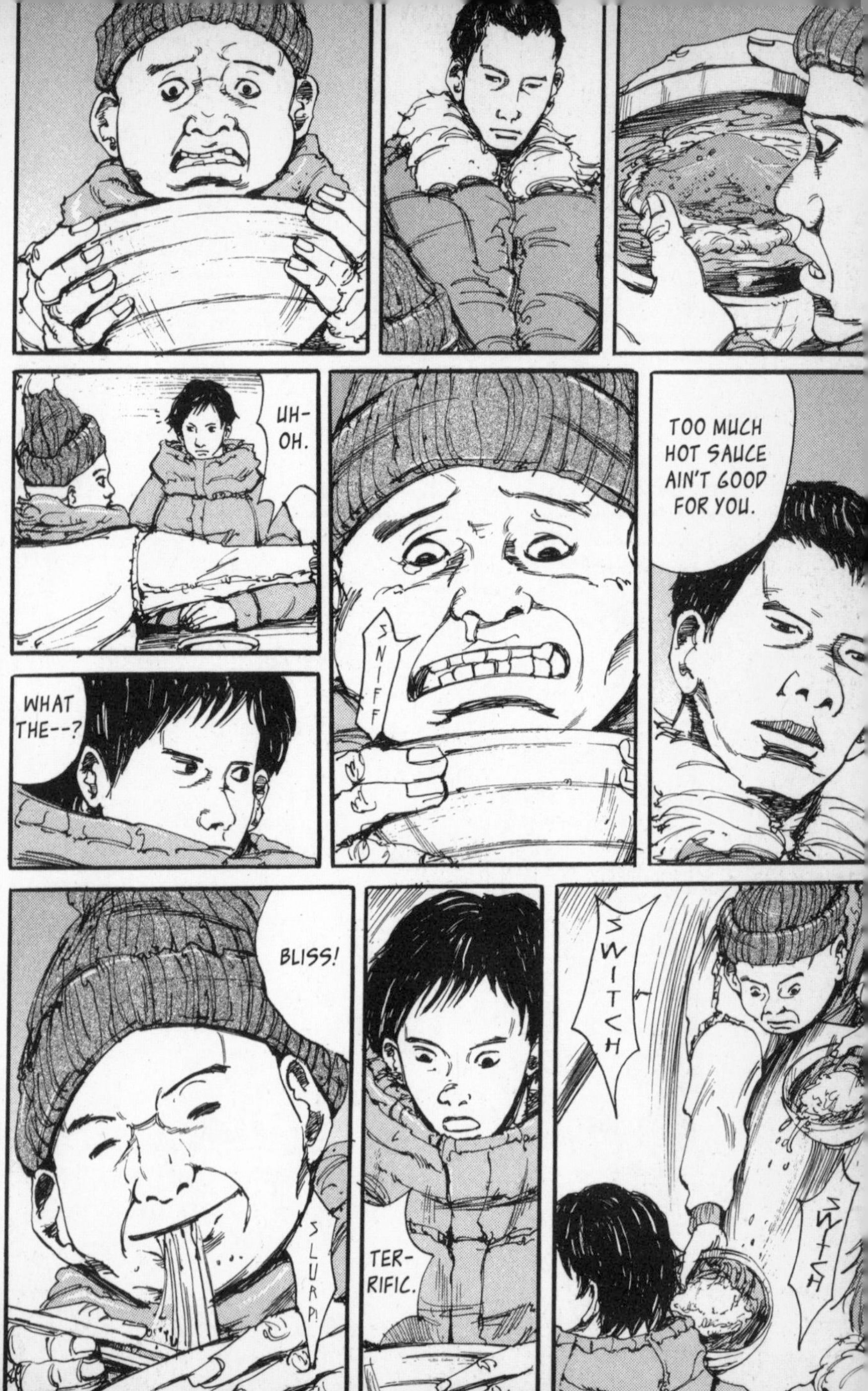
TOO MUCH HOT SAUCE AIN'T GOOD FOR YOU.
SNIFF
UH-OH.
WHAT THE--?
SWITCH
SWITCH
TER-RIFIC.
BLISS!
SLURP!

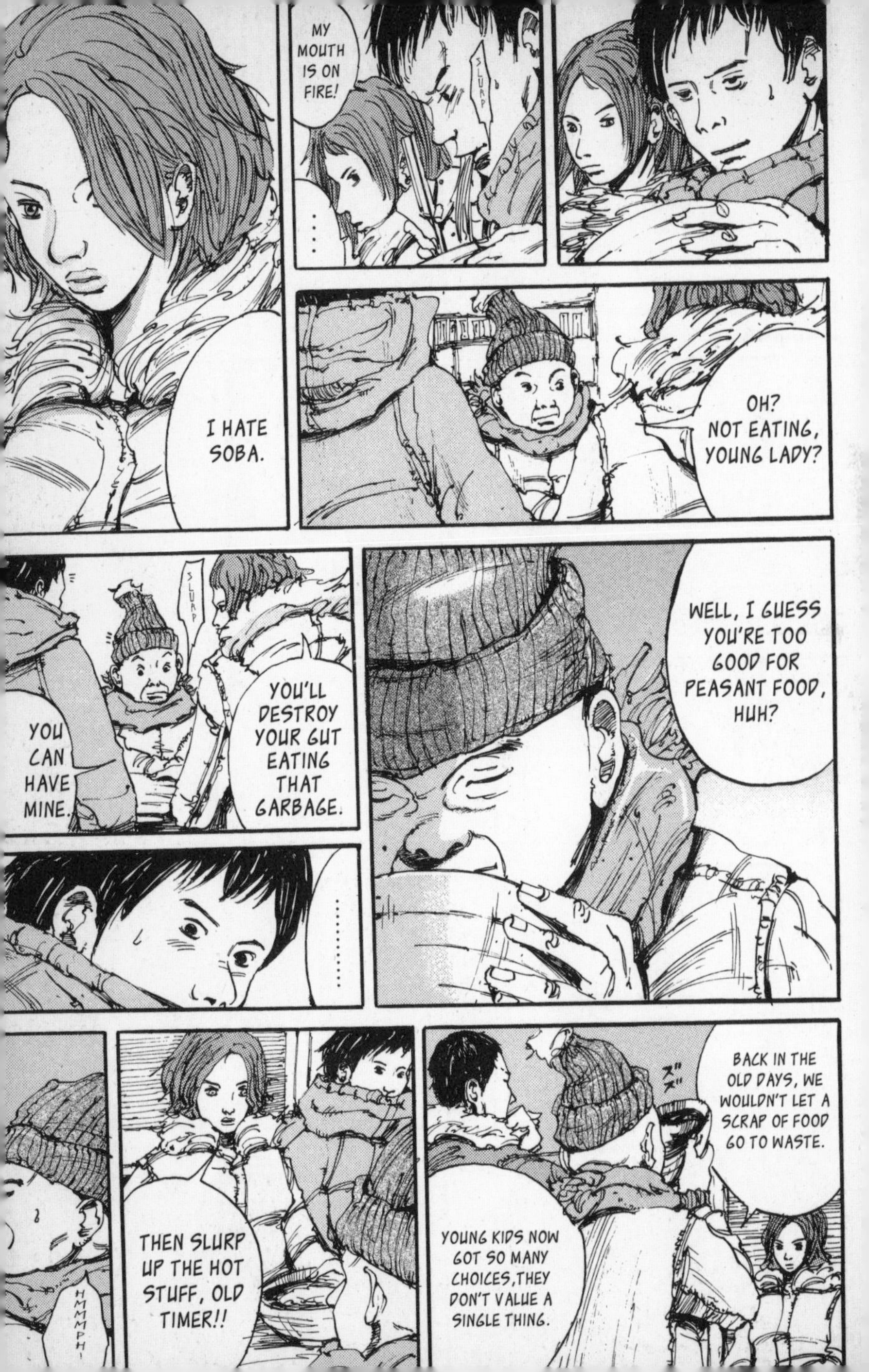
MY MOUTH IS ON FIRE!
SLURP
....
OH? NOT EATING, YOUNG LADY?
I HATE SOBA.
WELL, I GUESS YOU'RE TOO GOOD FOR PEASANT FOOD, HUH?
SLURP
YOU'LL DESTROY YOUR GUT EATING THAT GARBAGE.
YOU CAN HAVE MINE.
....
ズズ
BACK IN THE OLD DAYS, WE WOULDN'T LET A SCRAP OF FOOD GO TO WASTE.
YOUNG KIDS NOW GOT SO MANY CHOICES, THEY DON'T VALUE A SINGLE THING.
THEN SLURP UP THE HOT STUFF, OLD TIMER!!
HMMMPH!

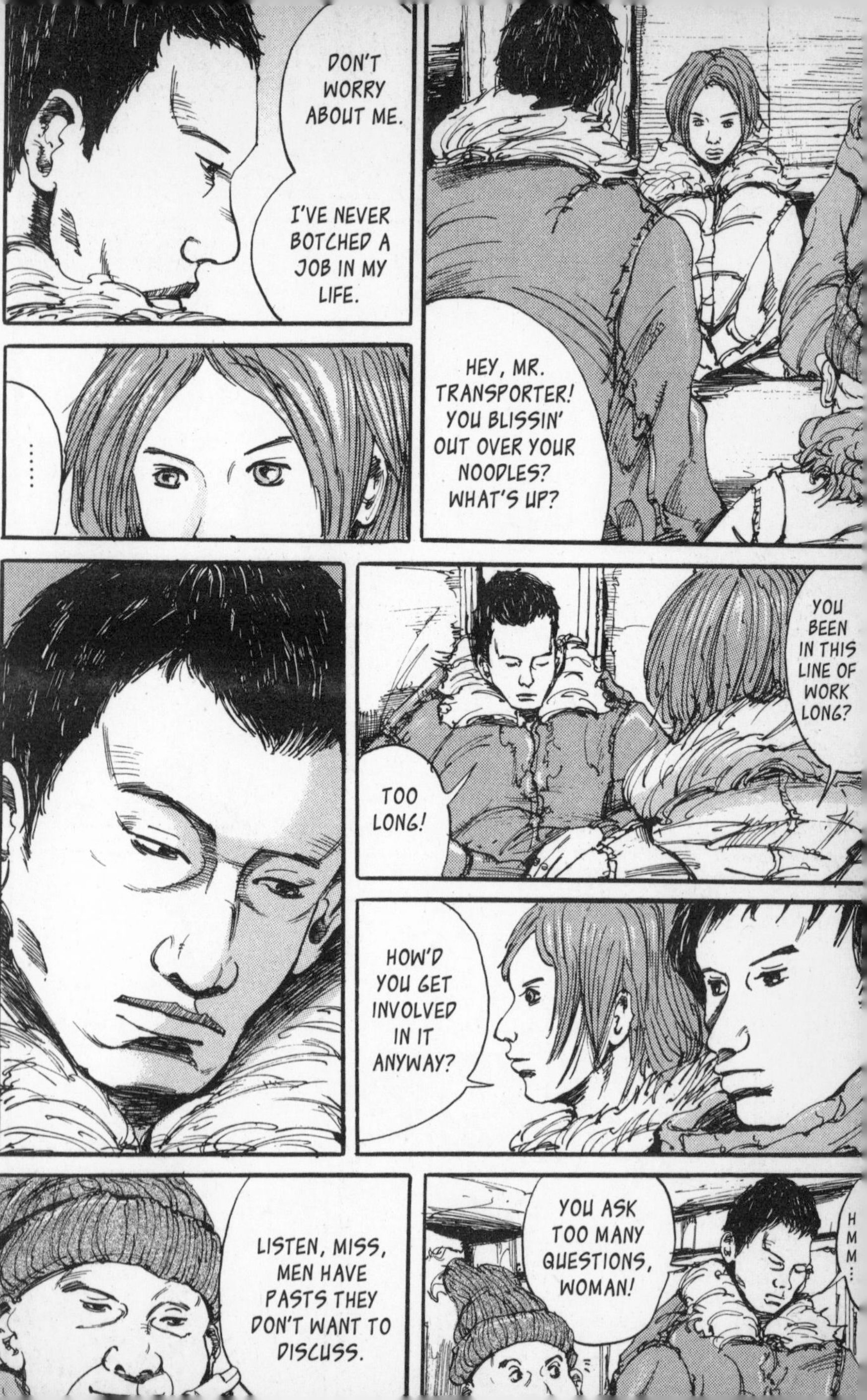
HEY, MR. TRANSPORTER! YOU BLISSIN' OUT OVER YOUR NOODLES? WHAT'S UP?
DON'T WORRY ABOUT ME.
I'VE NEVER BOTCHED A JOB IN MY LIFE.
......
YOU BEEN IN THIS LINE OF WORK LONG?
TOO LONG!
HOW'D YOU GET INVOLVED IN IT ANYWAY?
HMM...
YOU ASK TOO MANY QUESTIONS, WOMAN!
LISTEN, MISS, MEN HAVE PASTS THEY DON'T WANT TO DISCUSS.

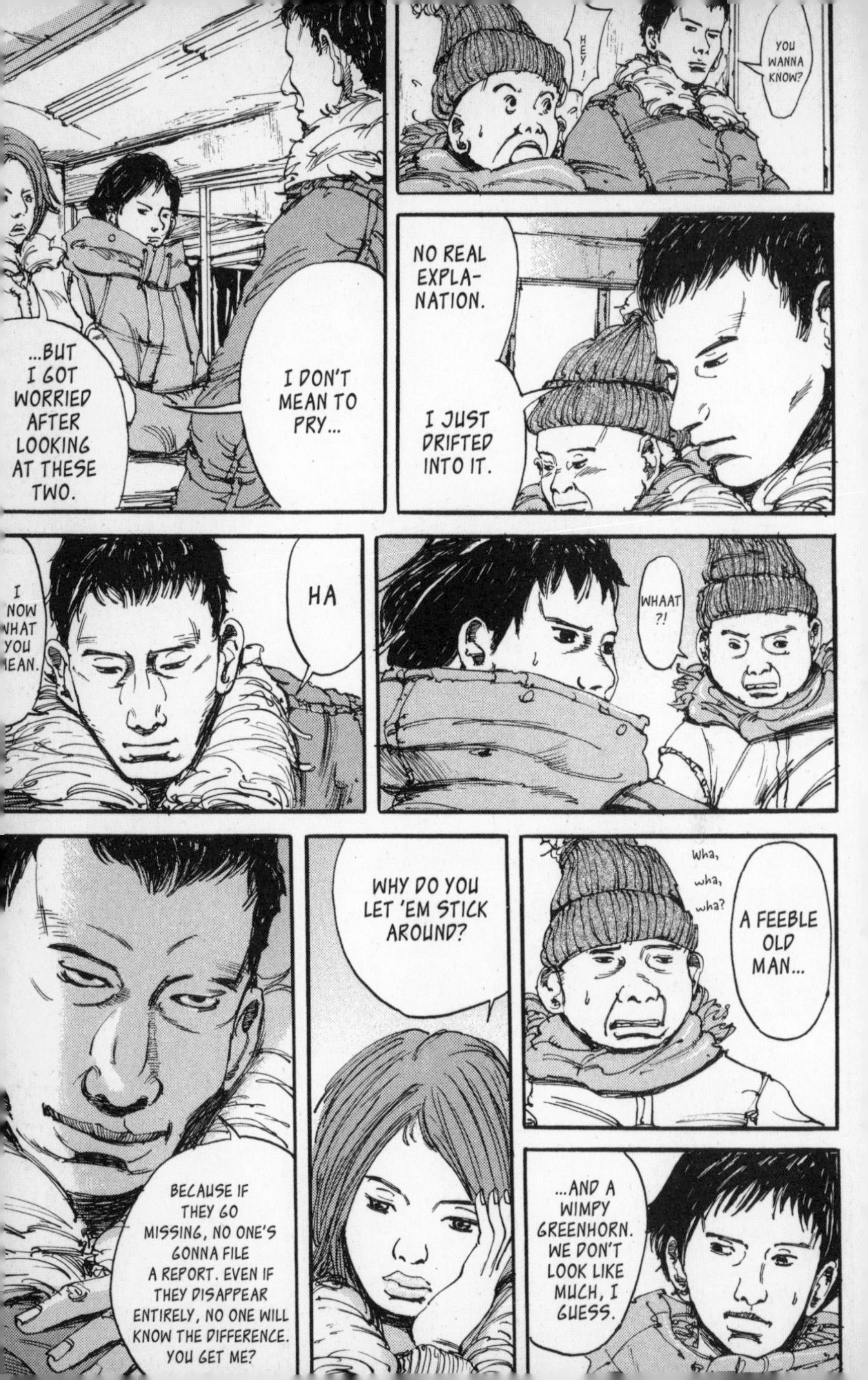
I DON'T MEAN TO PRY...
...BUT I GOT WORRIED AFTER LOOKING AT THESE TWO.
HEY!
YOU WANNA KNOW?
NO REAL EXPLANATION.
I JUST DRIFTED INTO IT.
I NOW WHAT YOU EAN.
HA
WHAAT?!
WHY DO YOU LET 'EM STICK AROUND?
BECAUSE IF THEY GO MISSING, NO ONE'S GONNA FILE A REPORT. EVEN IF THEY DISAPPEAR ENTIRELY, NO ONE WILL KNOW THE DIFFERENCE. YOU GET ME?
wha, wha, wha?
A FEEBLE OLD MAN...
...AND A WIMPY GREENHORN. WE DON'T LOOK LIKE MUCH, I GUESS.

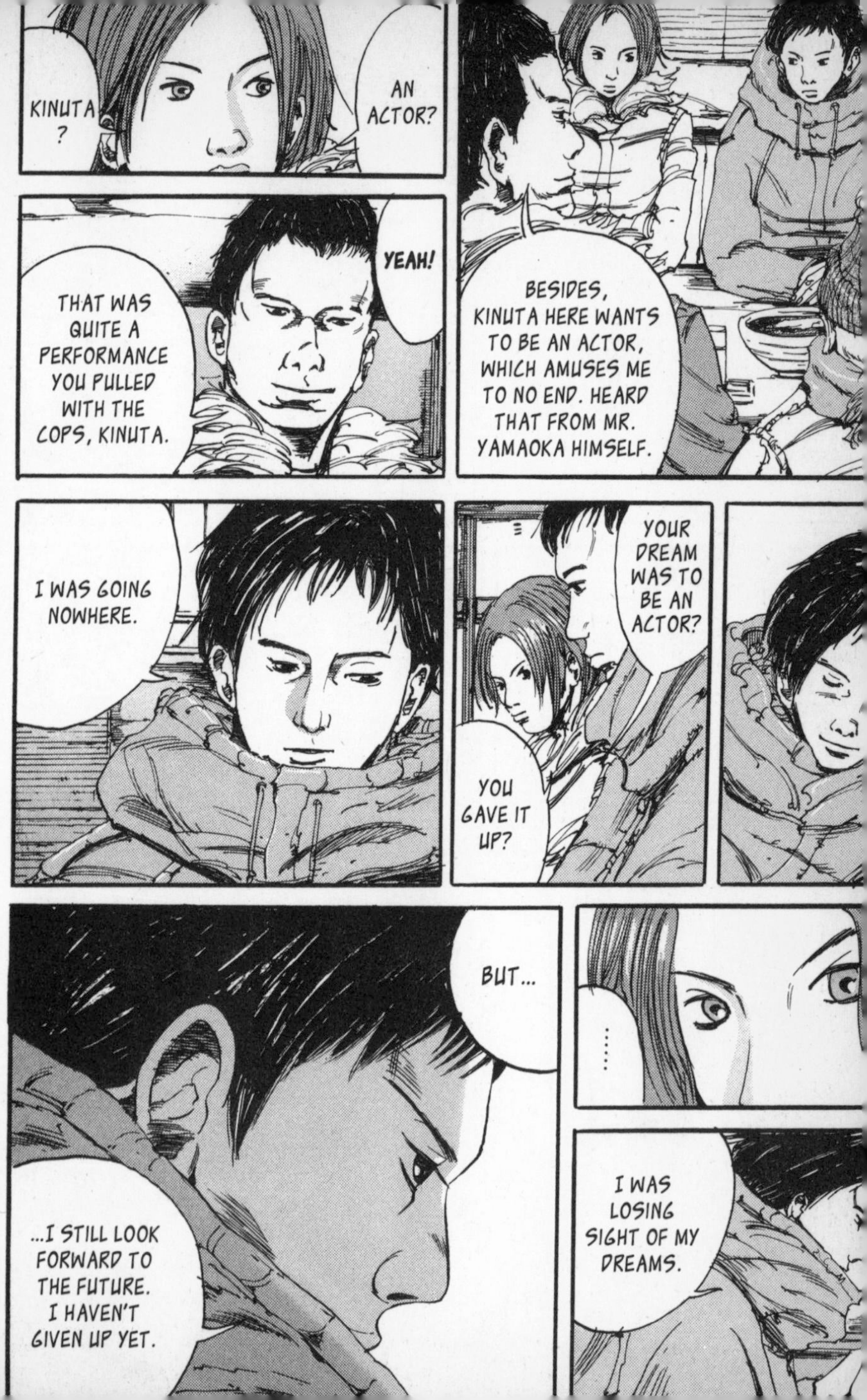
BESIDES, KINUTA HERE WANTS TO BE AN ACTOR, WHICH AMUSES ME TO NO END. HEARD THAT FROM MR. YAMAOKA HIMSELF.
AN ACTOR?
KINUTA ?
YEAH!
THAT WAS QUITE A PERFORMANCE YOU PULLED WITH THE COPS, KINUTA.
YOUR DREAM WAS TO BE AN ACTOR?
YOU GAVE IT UP?
I WAS GOING NOWHERE.
......
I WAS LOSING SIGHT OF MY DREAMS.
BUT...
...I STILL LOOK FORWARD TO THE FUTURE. I HAVEN'T GIVEN UP YET.

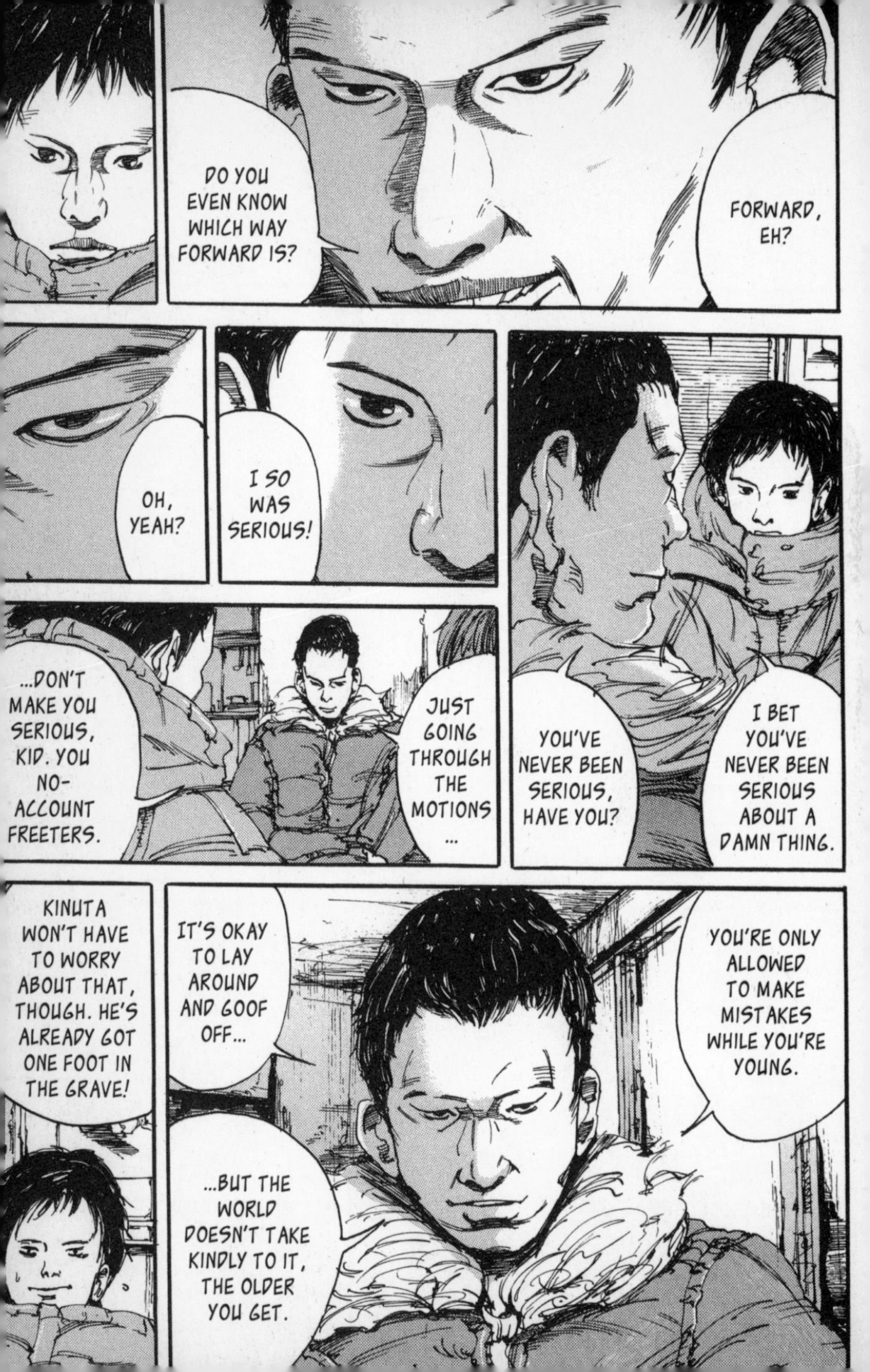
FORWARD, EH?
DO YOU EVEN KNOW WHICH WAY FORWARD IS?
I BET YOU'VE NEVER BEEN SERIOUS ABOUT A DAMN THING.
YOU'VE NEVER BEEN SERIOUS, HAVE YOU?
I SO WAS SERIOUS!
OH, YEAH?
JUST GOING THROUGH THE MOTIONS ...
...DON'T MAKE YOU SERIOUS, KID. YOU NO-ACCOUNT FREETERS.
YOU'RE ONLY ALLOWED TO MAKE MISTAKES WHILE YOU'RE YOUNG.
IT'S OKAY TO LAY AROUND AND GOOF OFF...
...BUT THE WORLD DOESN'T TAKE KINDLY TO IT, THE OLDER YOU GET.
KINUTA WON'T HAVE TO WORRY ABOUT THAT, THOUGH. HE'S ALREADY GOT ONE FOOT IN THE GRAVE!

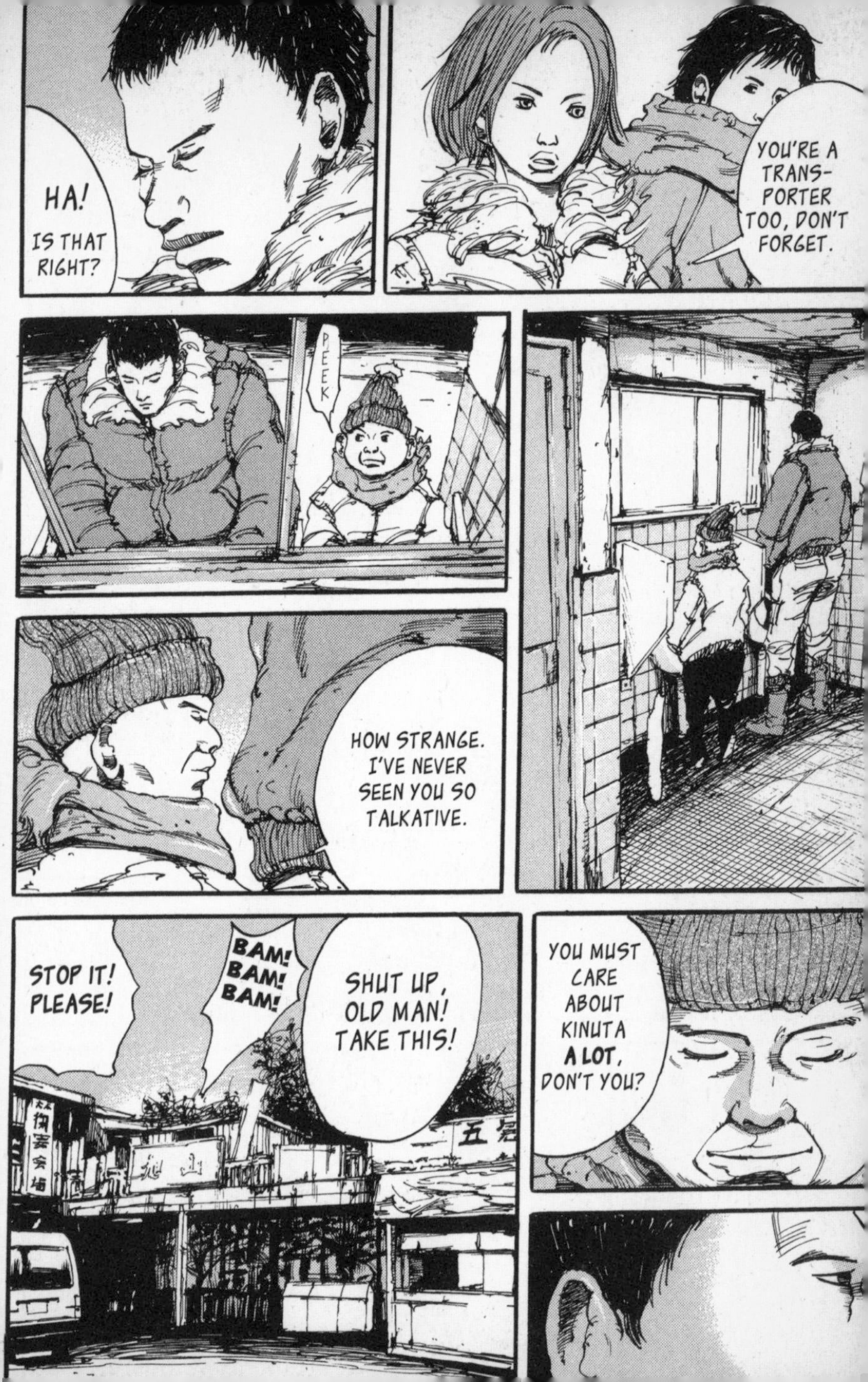
YOU'RE A TRANS-PORTER TOO, DON'T FORGET.
HA!
IS THAT RIGHT?
PEEK
HOW STRANGE. I'VE NEVER SEEN YOU SO TALKATIVE.
YOU MUST CARE ABOUT KINUTA **A LOT**, DON'T YOU?
SHUT UP, OLD MAN! TAKE THIS!
BAM! BAM! BAM!
STOP IT! PLEASE!

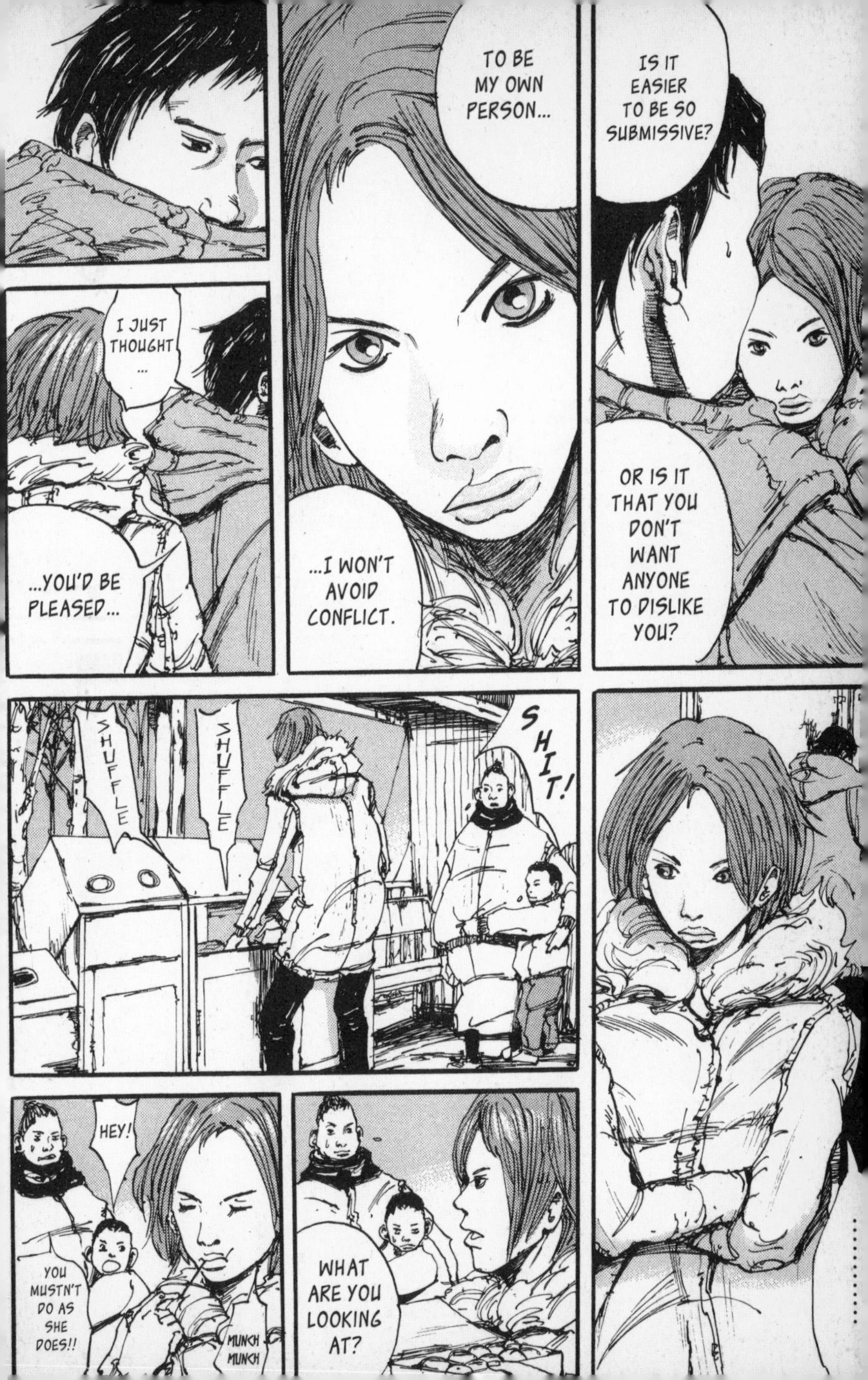
IS IT EASIER TO BE SO SUBMISSIVE?
OR IS IT THAT YOU DON'T WANT ANYONE TO DISLIKE YOU?
TO BE MY OWN PERSON...
...I WON'T AVOID CONFLICT.
I JUST THOUGHT...
...YOU'D BE PLEASED...
SHIT!
SHUFFLE
SHUFFLE
WHAT ARE YOU LOOKING AT?
HEY!
YOU MUSTN'T DO AS SHE DOES!!
MUNCH MUNCH

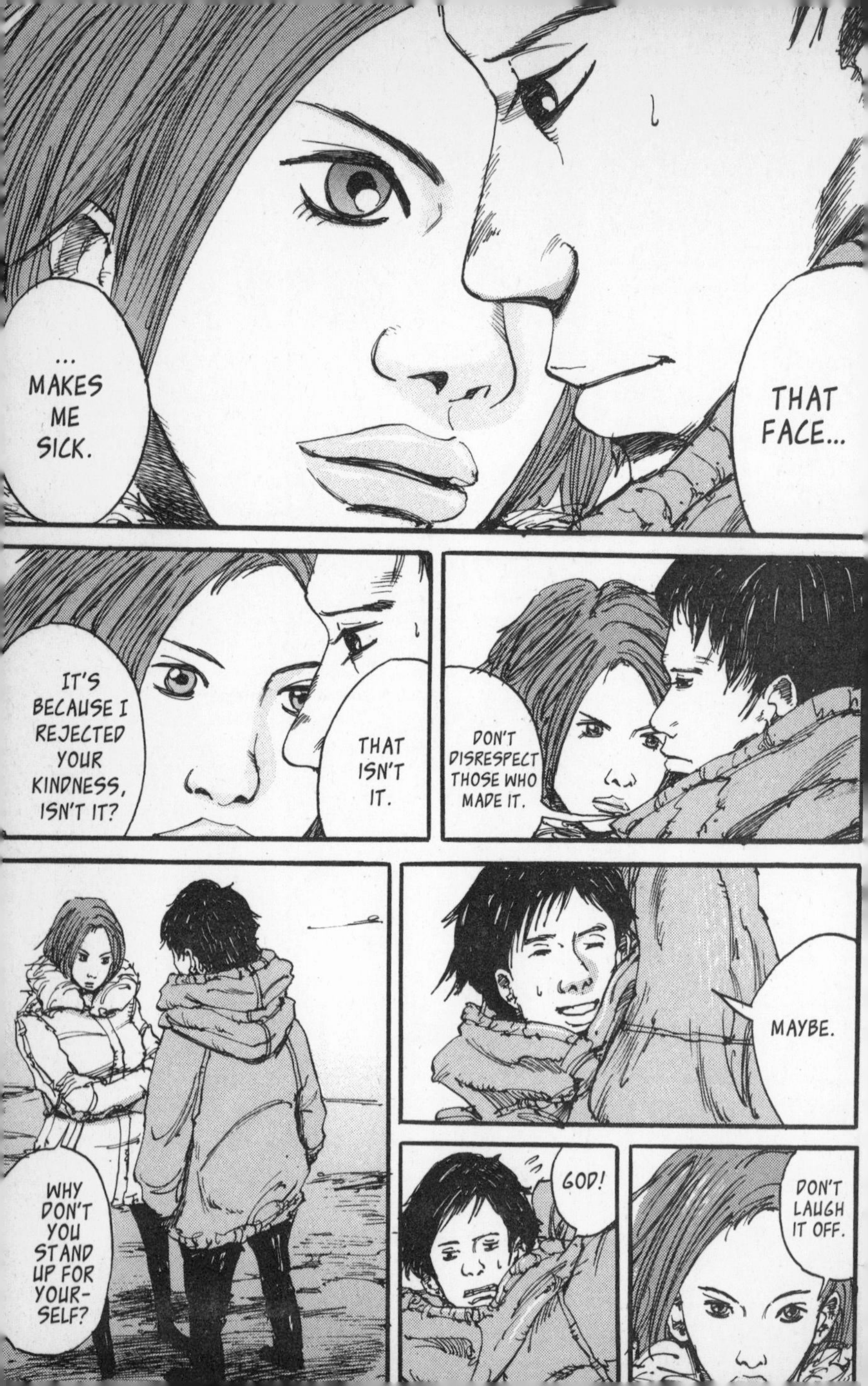
THAT FACE...
...MAKES ME SICK.
DON'T DISRESPECT THOSE WHO MADE IT.
THAT ISN'T IT.
IT'S BECAUSE I REJECTED YOUR KINDNESS, ISN'T IT?
MAYBE.
DON'T LAUGH IT OFF.
GOD!
WHY DON'T YOU STAND UP FOR YOUR-SELF?

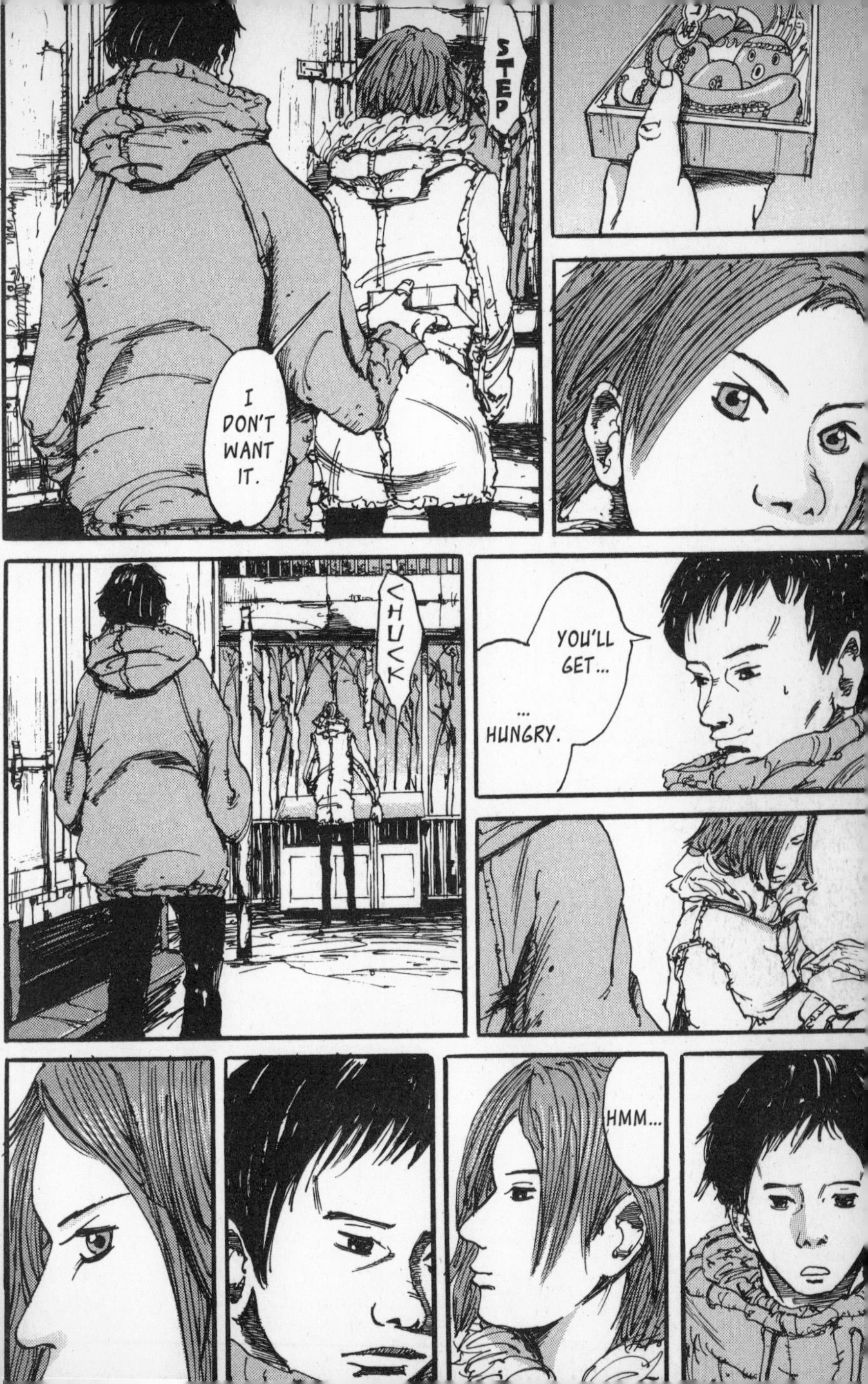
STEP
I DON'T WANT IT.
YOU'LL GET...
... HUNGRY.
CHUCK
HMM...

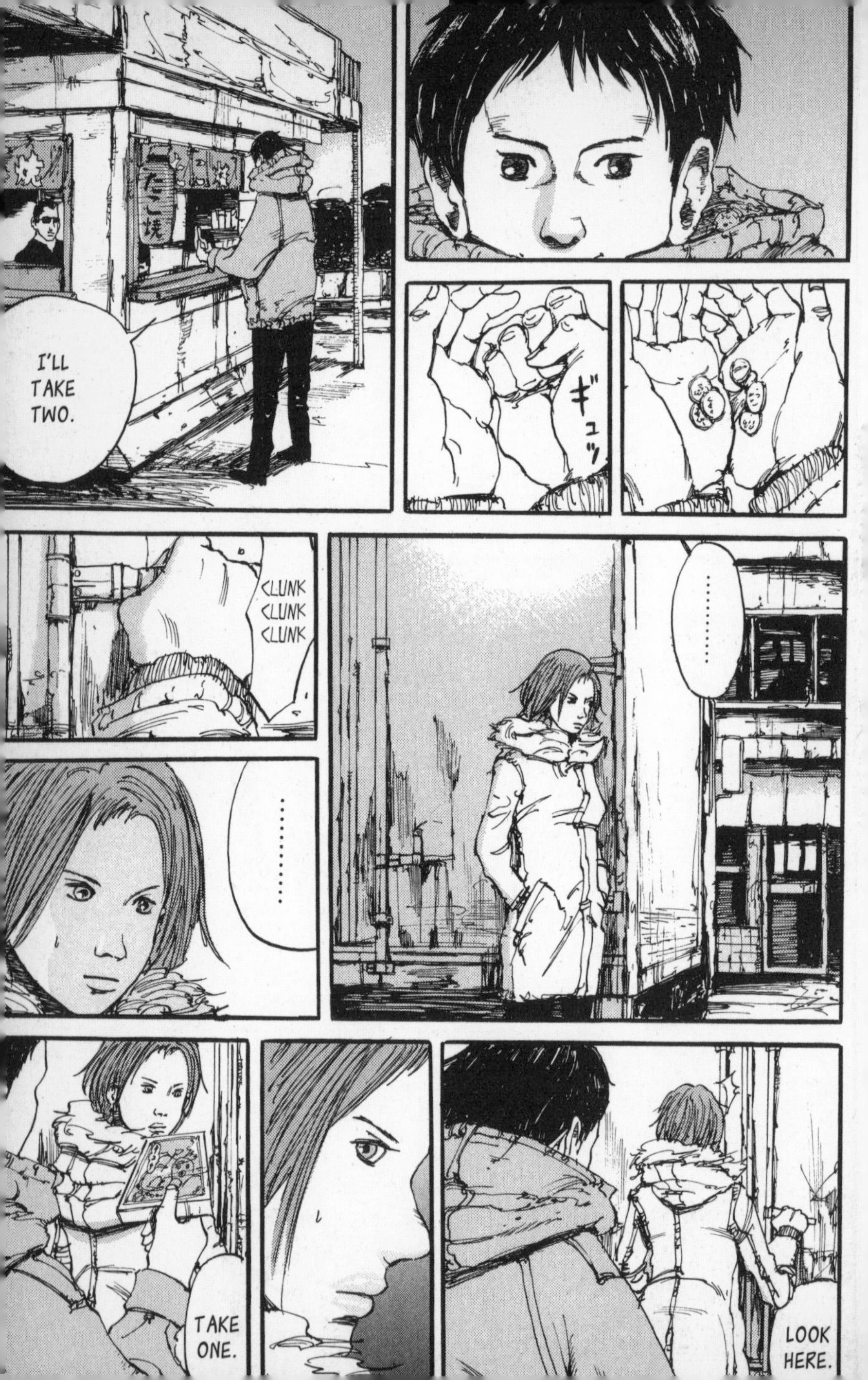
ギュッ
たこ焼
I'LL TAKE TWO.
......
CLUNK CLUNK CLUNK
......
LOOK HERE.
TAKE ONE.

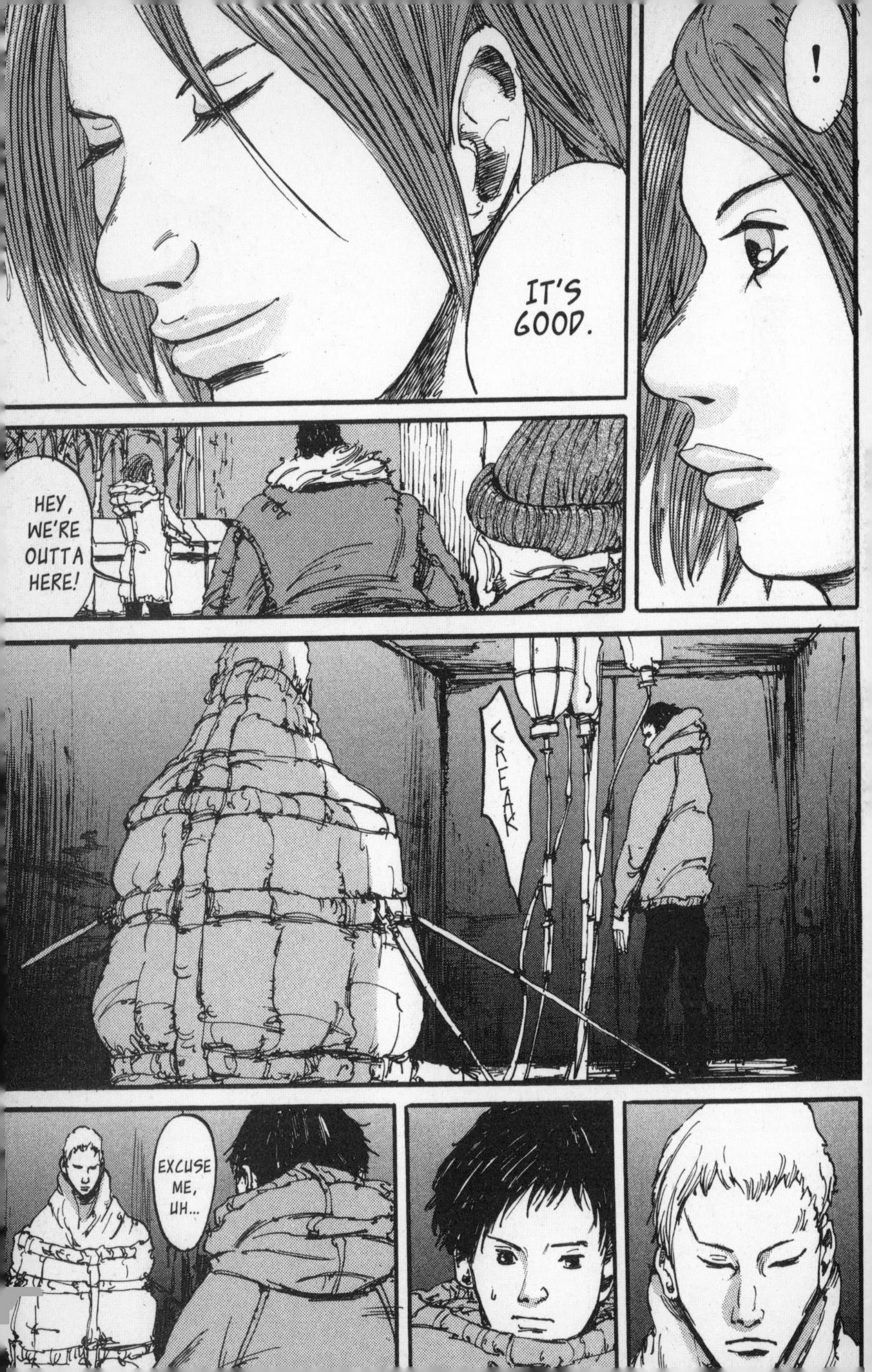
!
IT'S GOOD.
HEY, WE'RE OUTTA HERE!
CREAK
EXCUSE ME, UH...

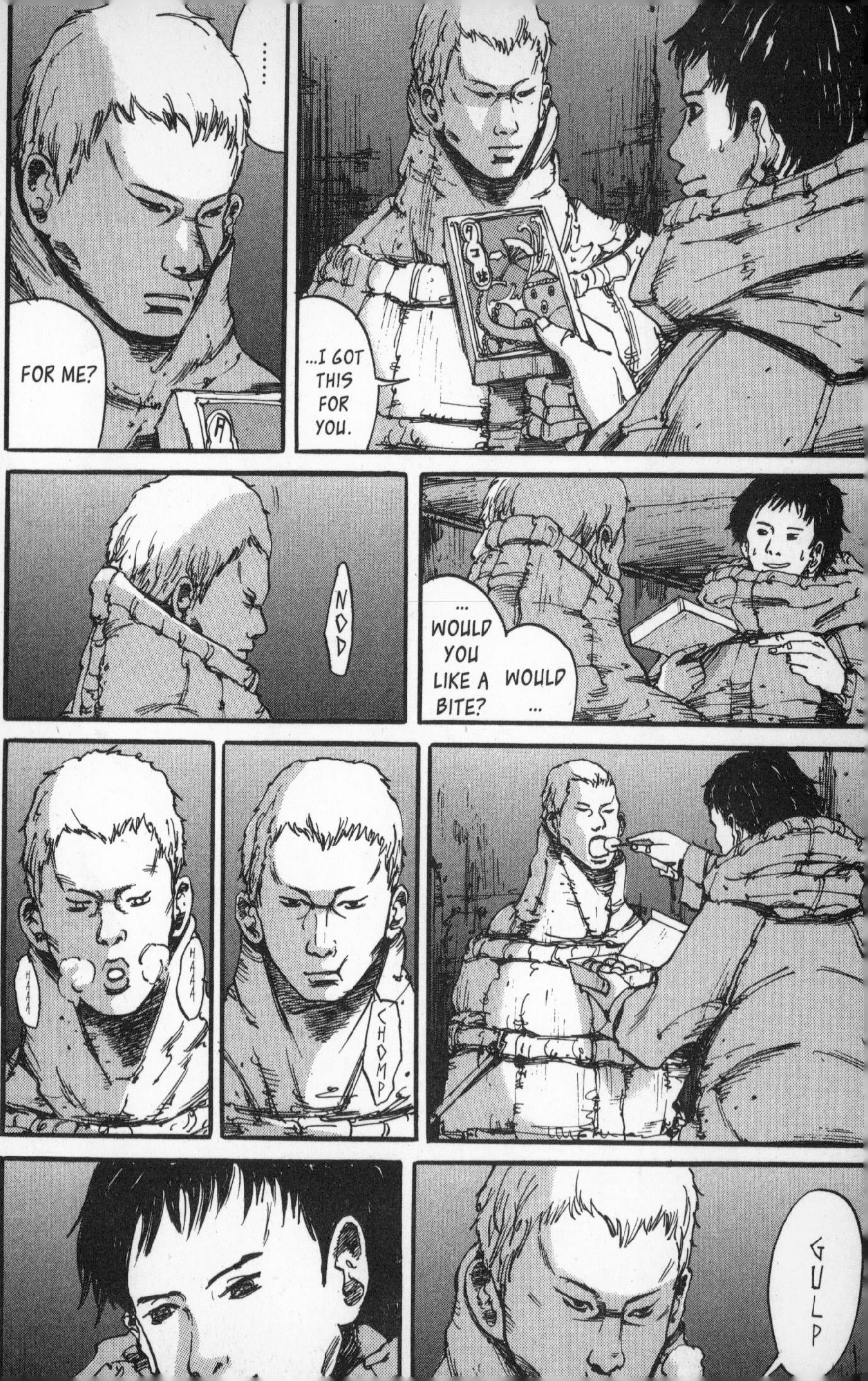
...I GOT THIS FOR YOU.
......
FOR ME?
WOULD ...
... WOULD YOU LIKE A BITE?
NOD
CHOMP
HAAA
HAAA
GULP

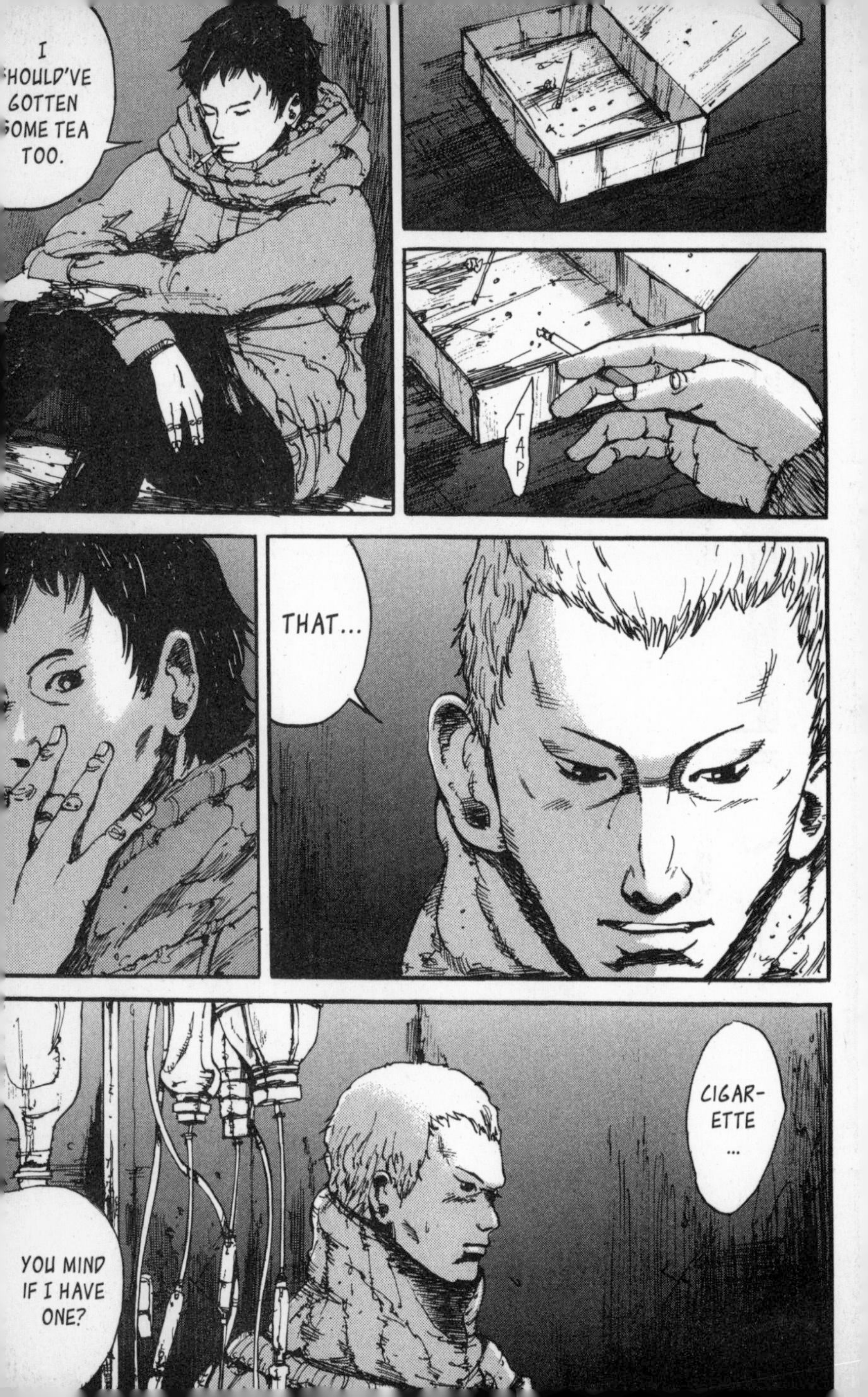
TAP
I SHOULD'VE GOTTEN SOME TEA TOO.
THAT...
CIGARETTE...
YOU MIND IF I HAVE ONE?

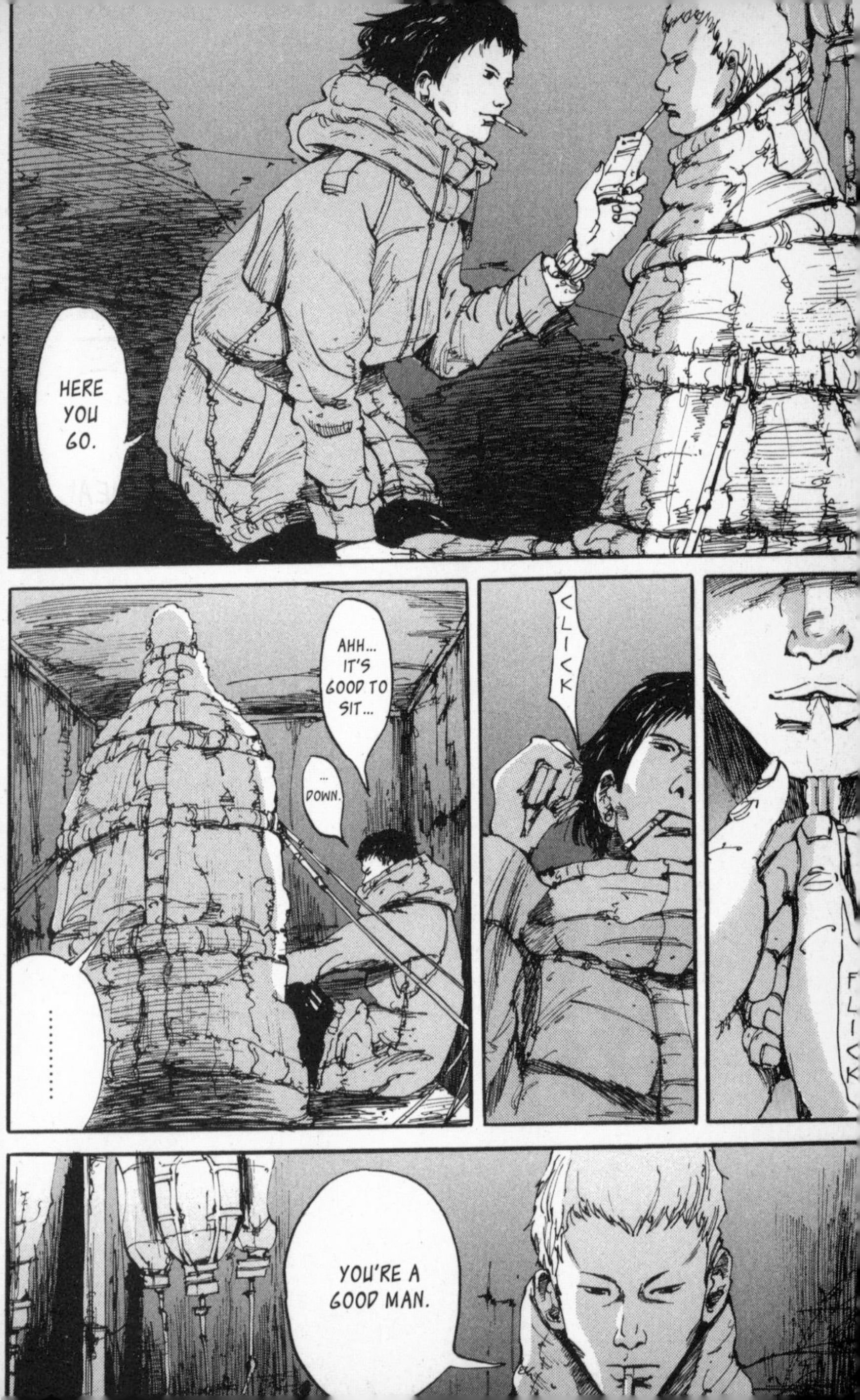
HERE YOU GO.
FLICK
CLICK
AHH... IT'S GOOD TO SIT...
... DOWN.
......
YOU'RE A GOOD MAN.

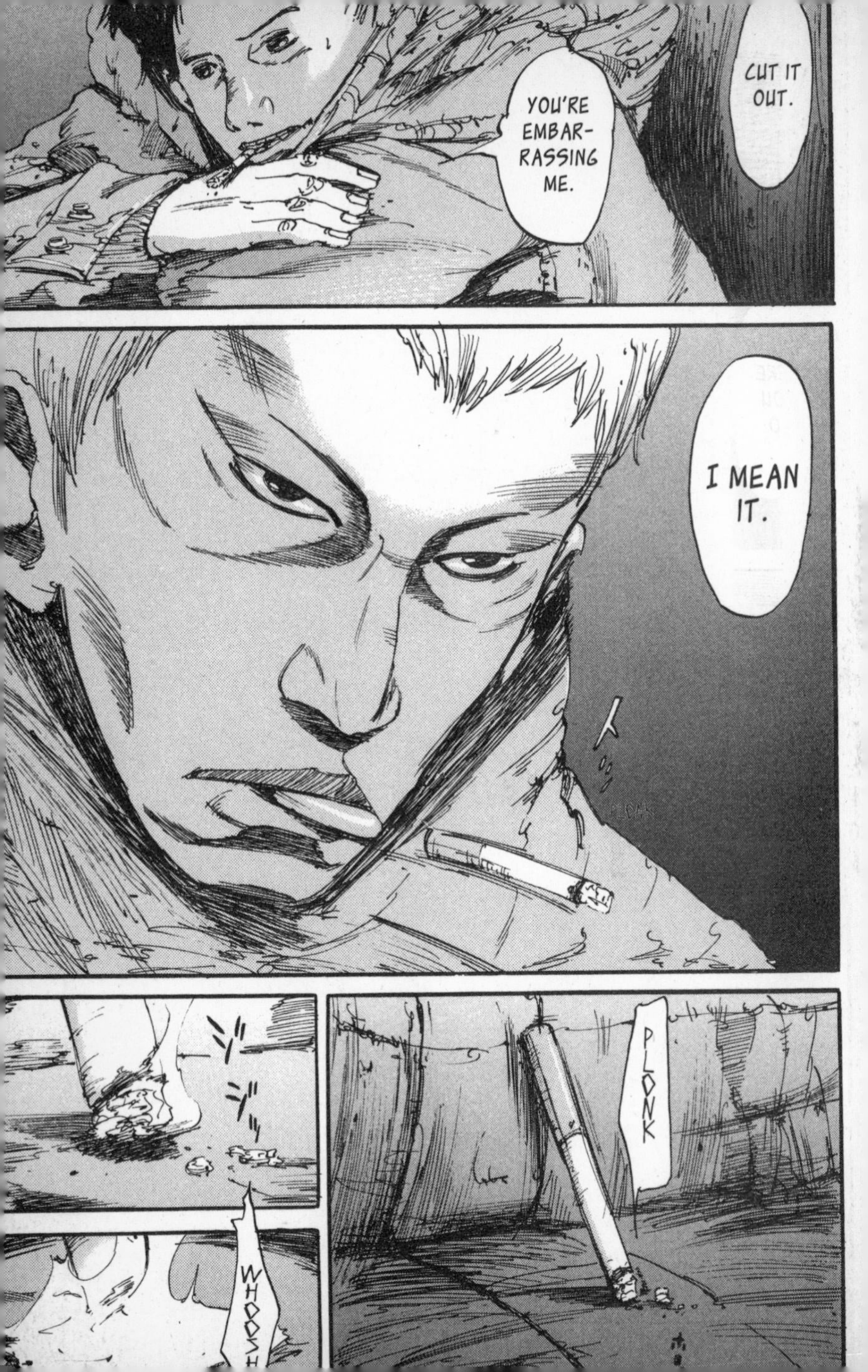
CUT IT OUT.
YOU'RE EMBAR-RASSING ME.
I MEAN IT.
PLONK
WHOOSH

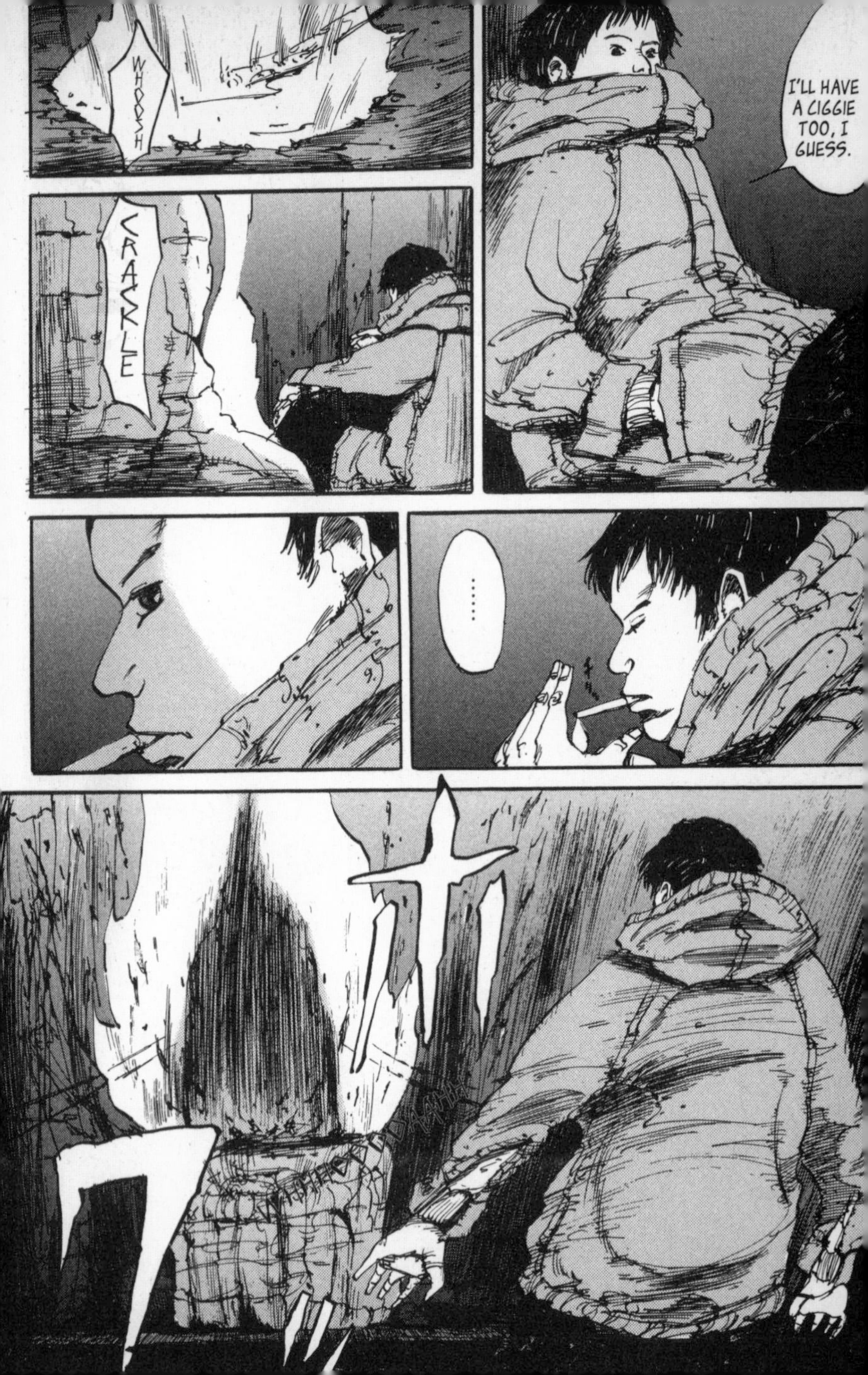
I'LL HAVE A CIGGIE TOO, I GUESS.
WHOOSH
CRACKLE
......

GUSH

GRAB

YIKES!

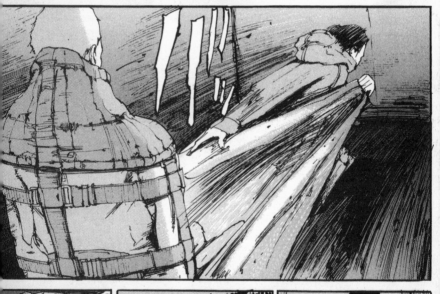

THUMP

THUMP

THUMP

THUMP

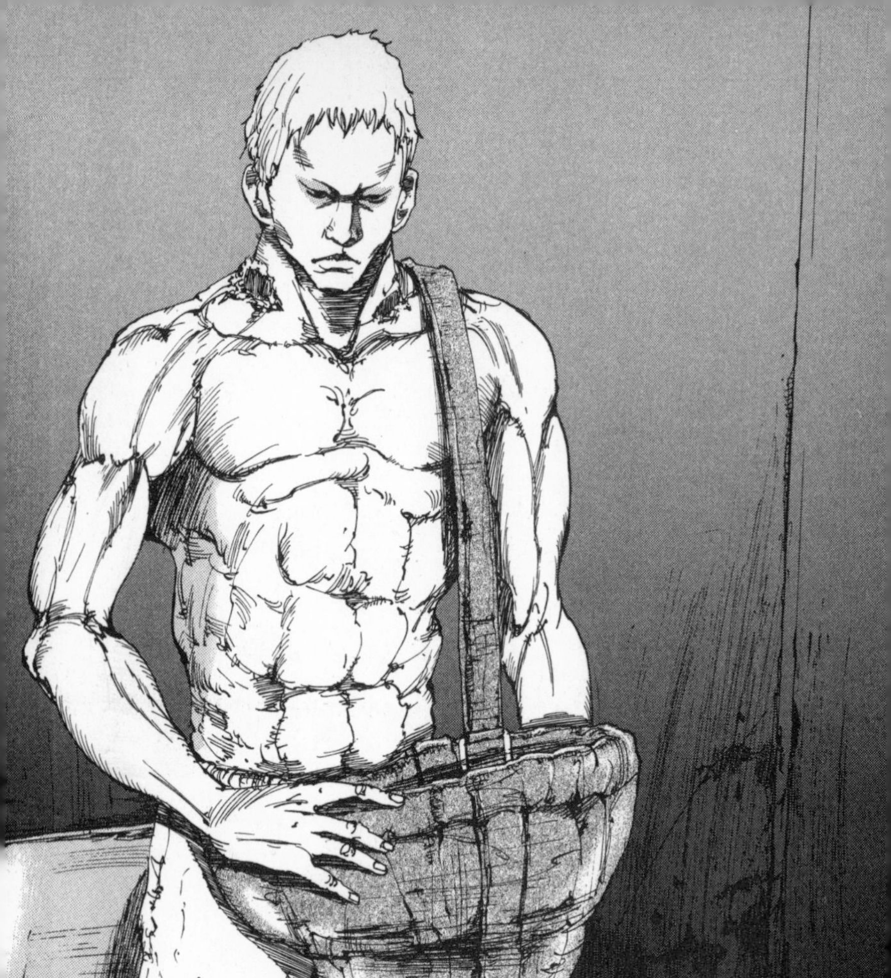

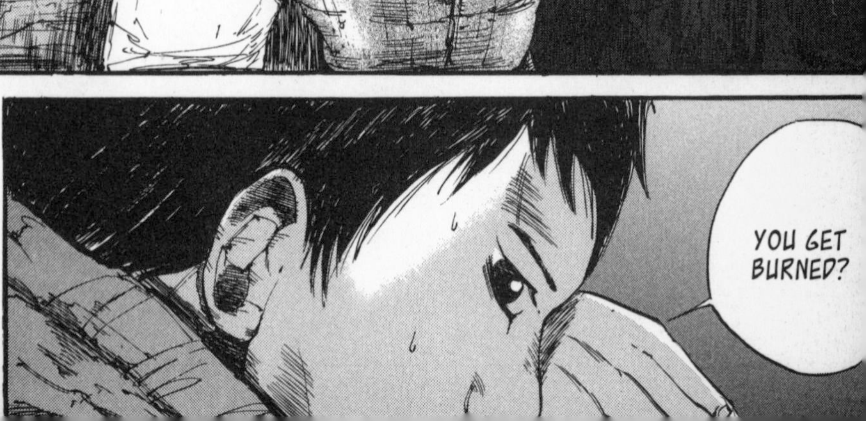
YOU GET BURNED?

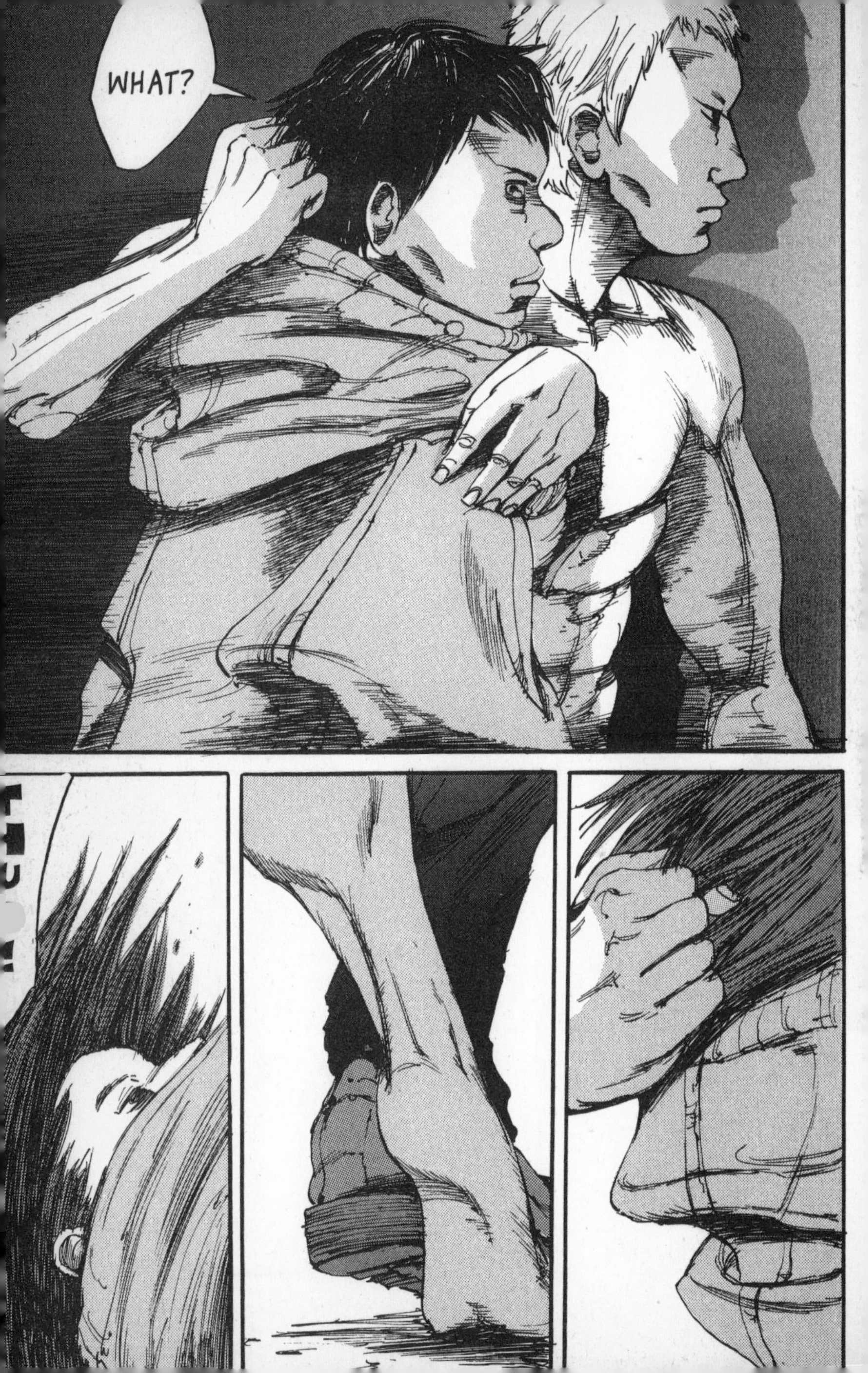
WHAT?

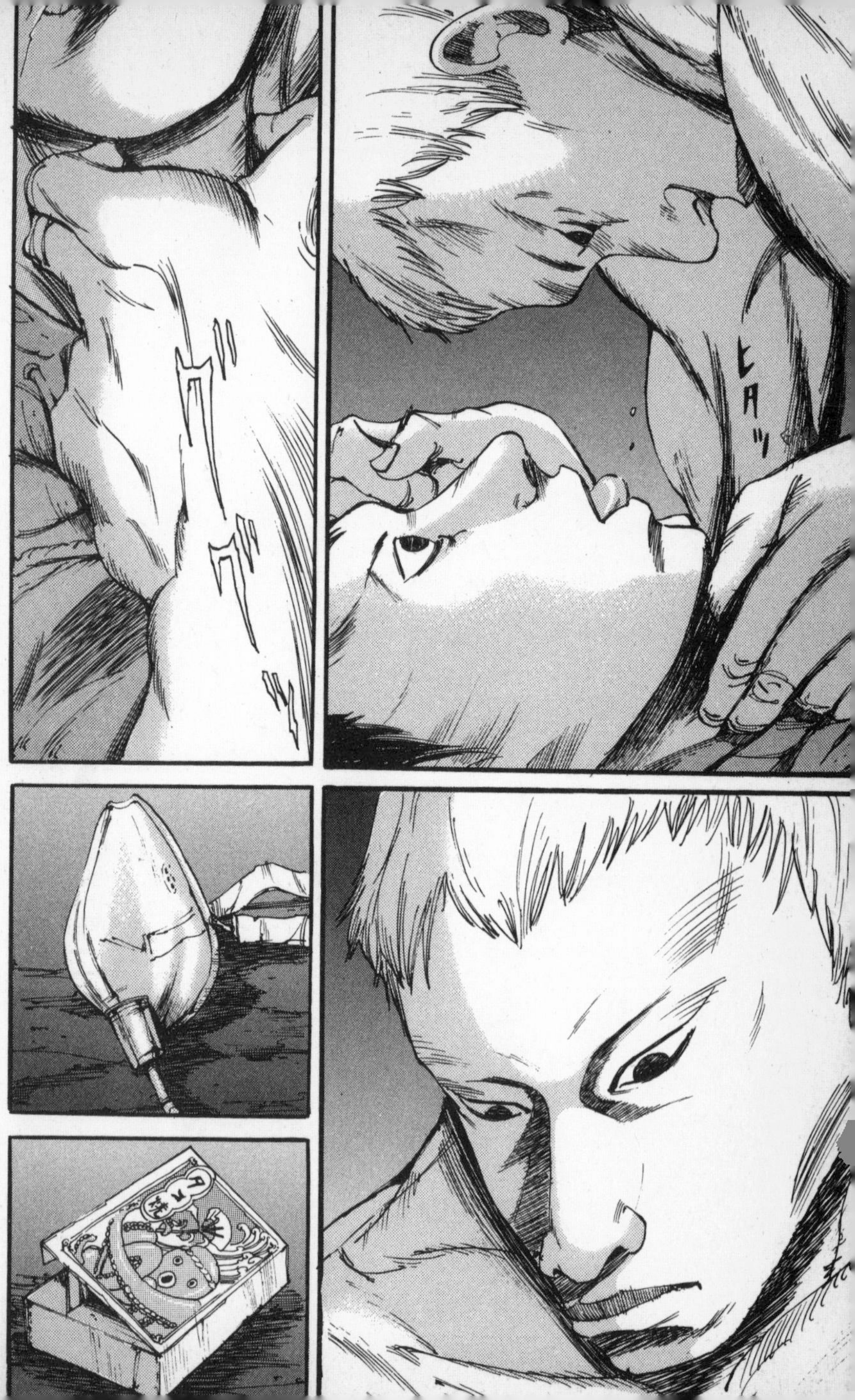

ヒクッ
ガガッ

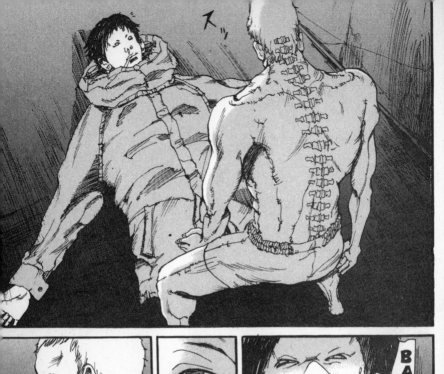

BANG

THUMP!

THUMP!

THUMP!

THUMP!

THUMP!

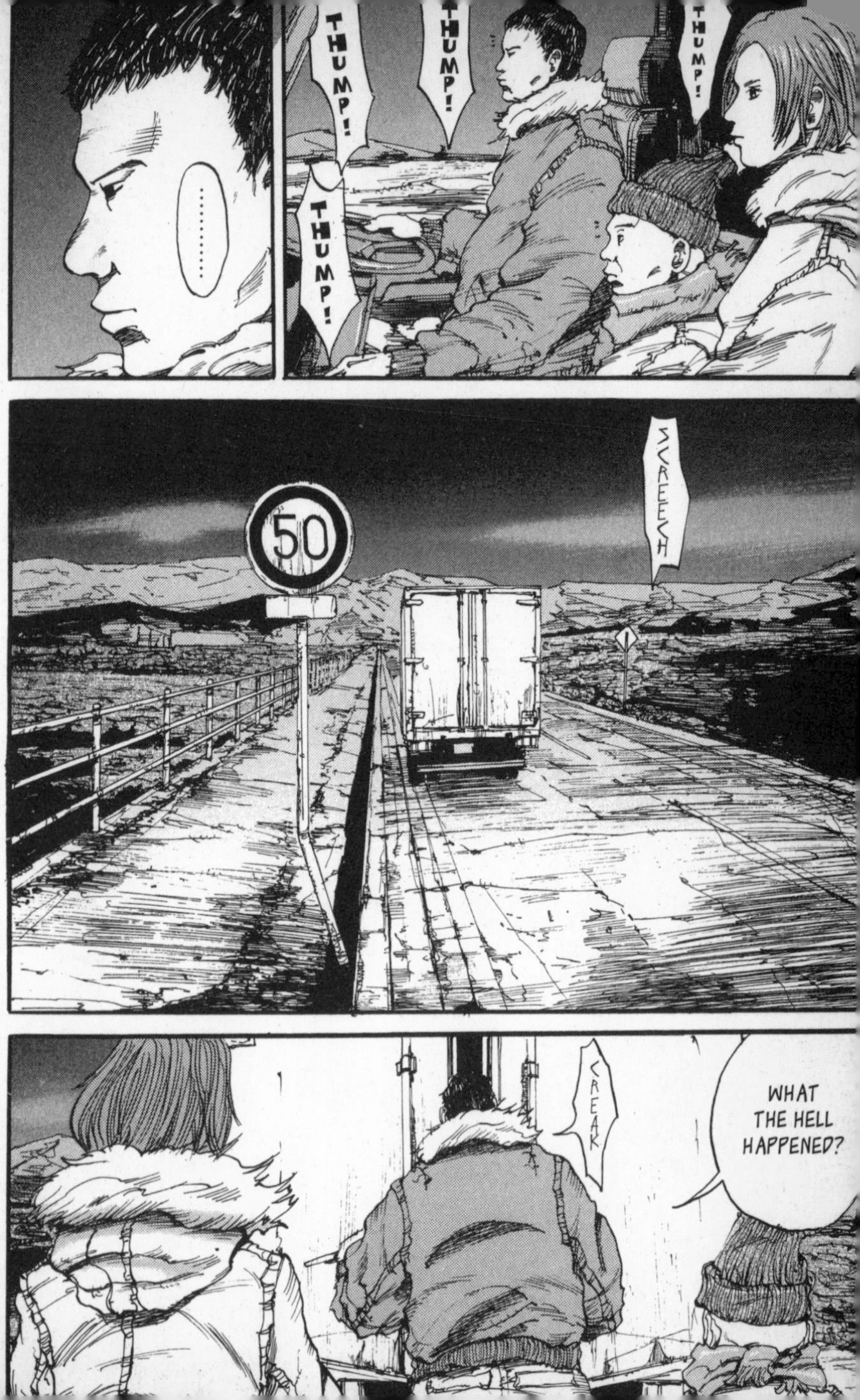
THUMP!
THUMP!
THUMP!
THUMP!
......
SCREECH
WHAT THE HELL HAPPENED?
CREAK

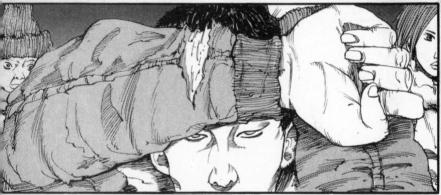

HUH?!

WHAT THE--
?!

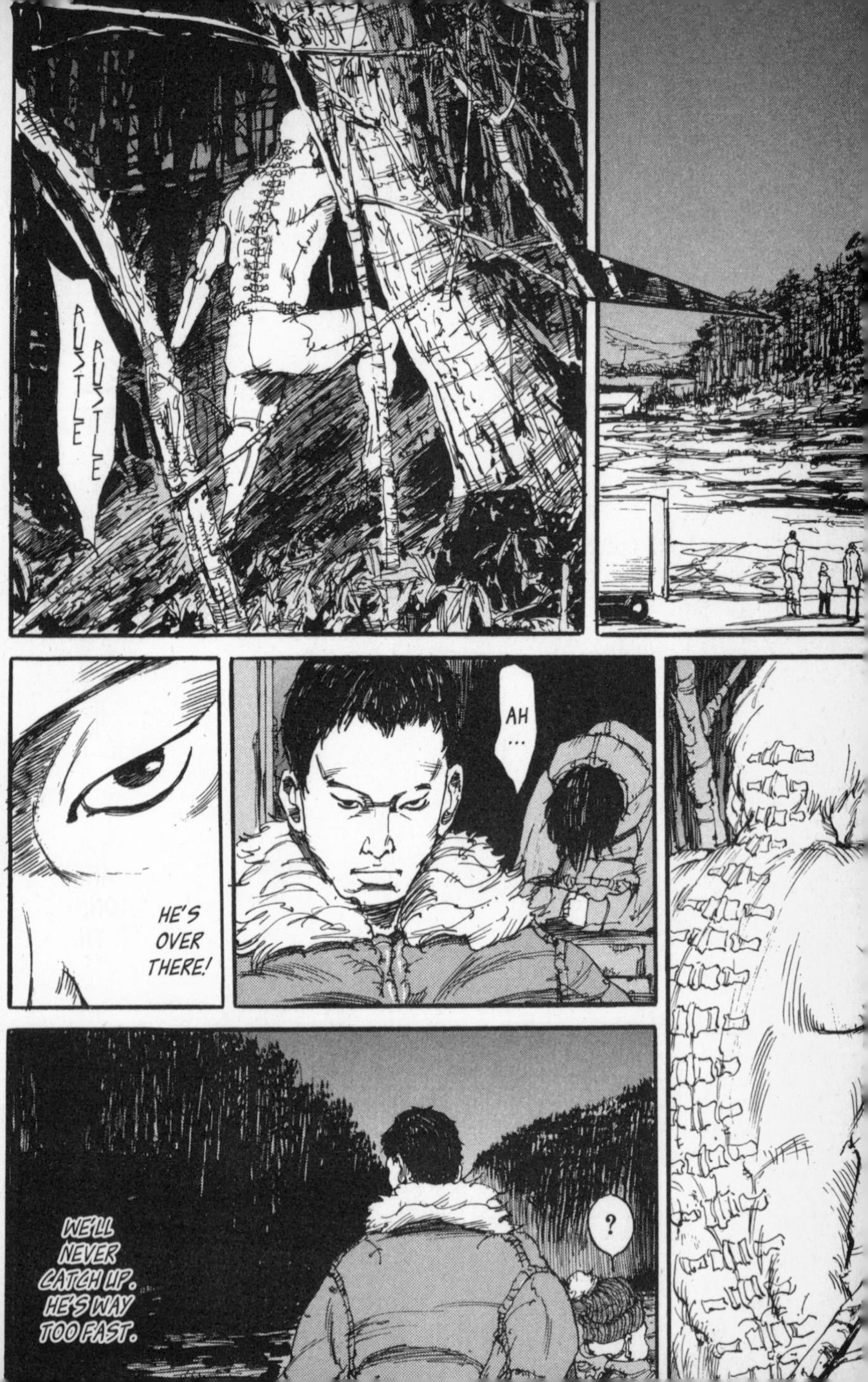
RUSTLE RUSTLE
AH ...
HE'S OVER THERE!
?
WE'LL NEVER CATCH UP. HE'S WAY TOO FAST.

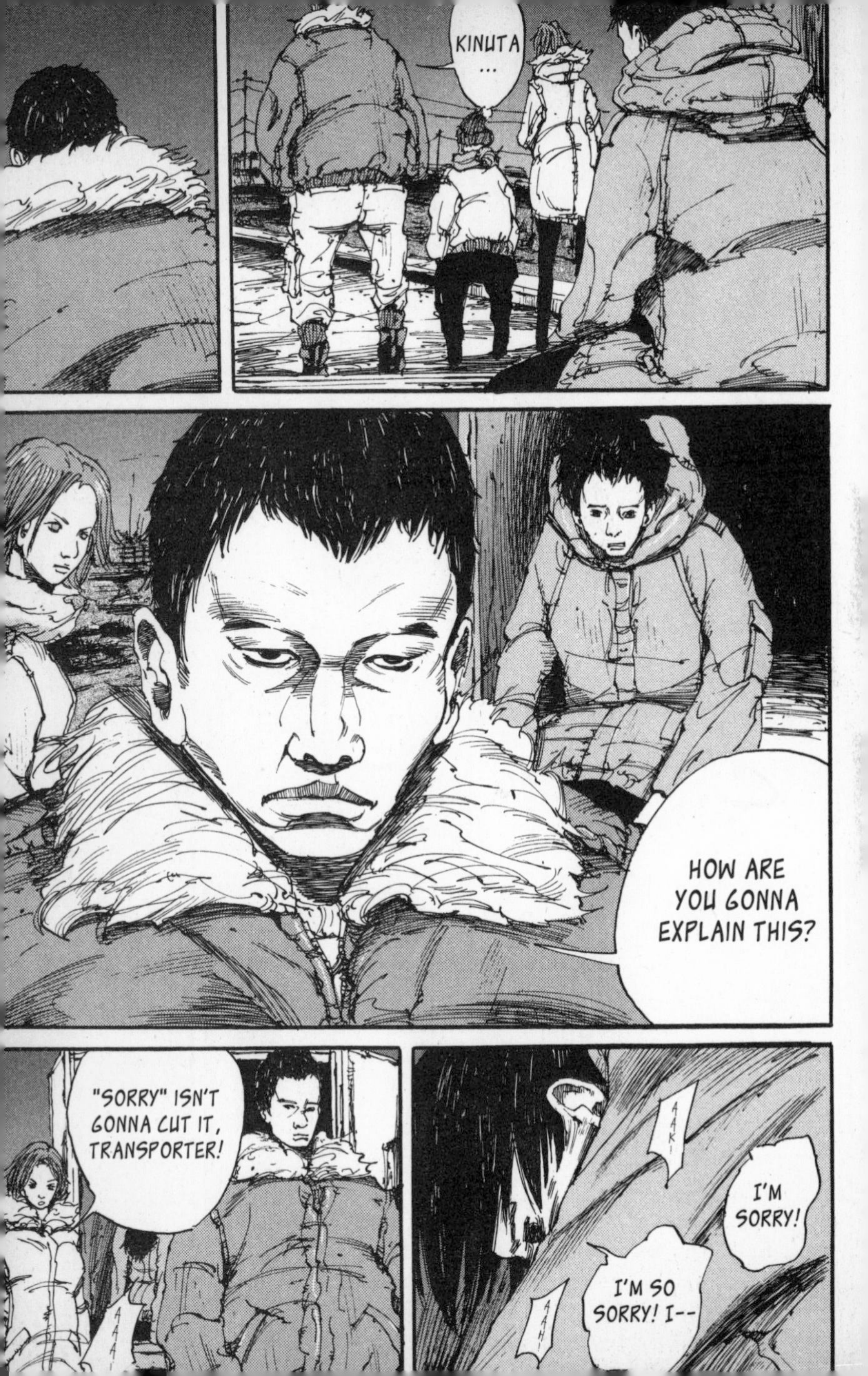
KINUTA ...
HOW ARE YOU GONNA EXPLAIN THIS?
I'M SORRY!
I'M SO SORRY! I--
"SORRY" ISN'T GONNA CUT IT, TRANSPORTER!

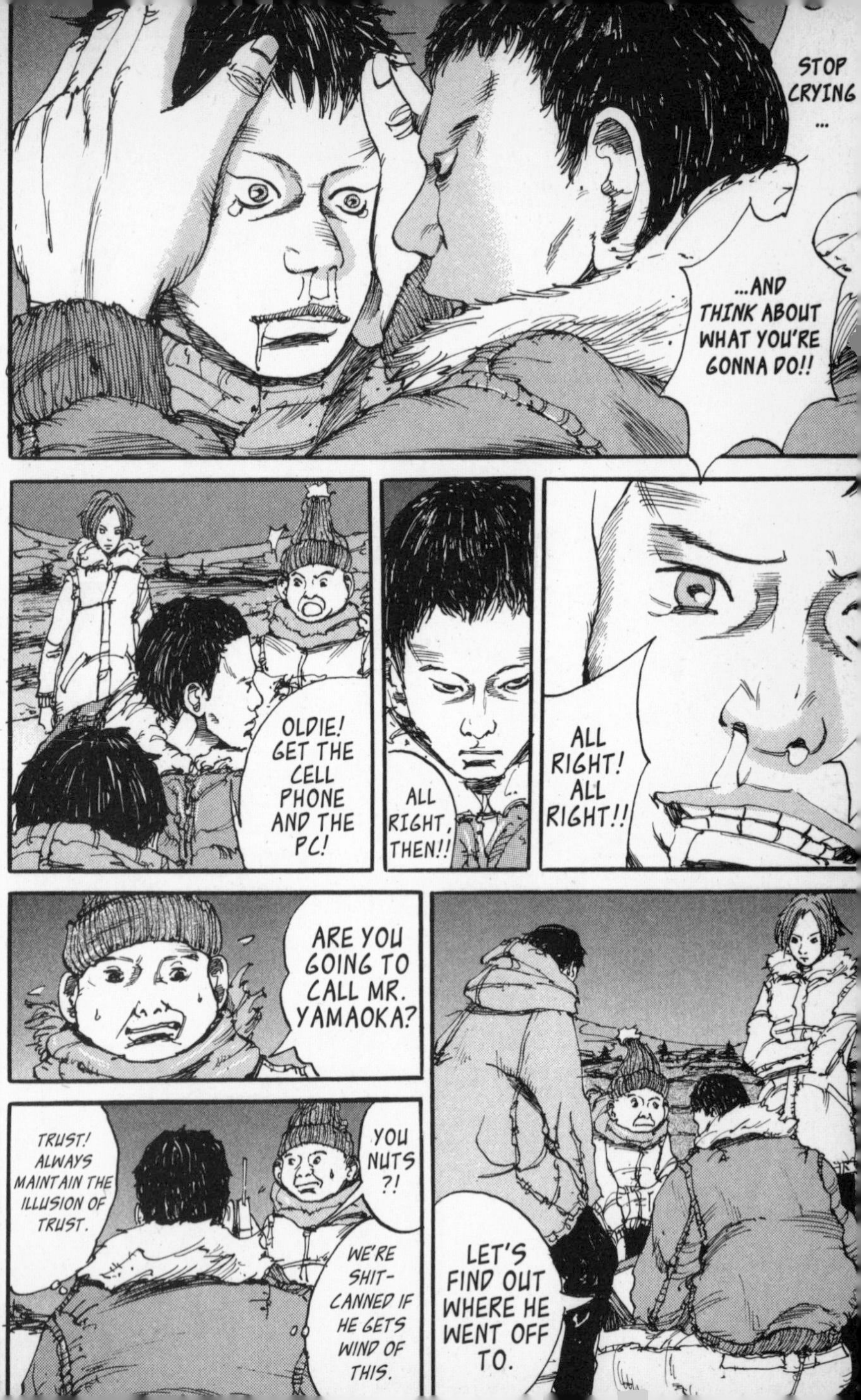
STOP CRYING ...
...AND THINK ABOUT WHAT YOU'RE GONNA DO!!
ALL RIGHT! ALL RIGHT!!
ALL RIGHT, THEN!!
OLDIE! GET THE CELL PHONE AND THE PC!
LET'S FIND OUT WHERE HE WENT OFF TO.
ARE YOU GOING TO CALL MR. YAMAOKA?
YOU NUTS?!
WE'RE SHIT-CANNED IF HE GETS WIND OF THIS.
TRUST! ALWAYS MAINTAIN THE ILLUSION OF TRUST.

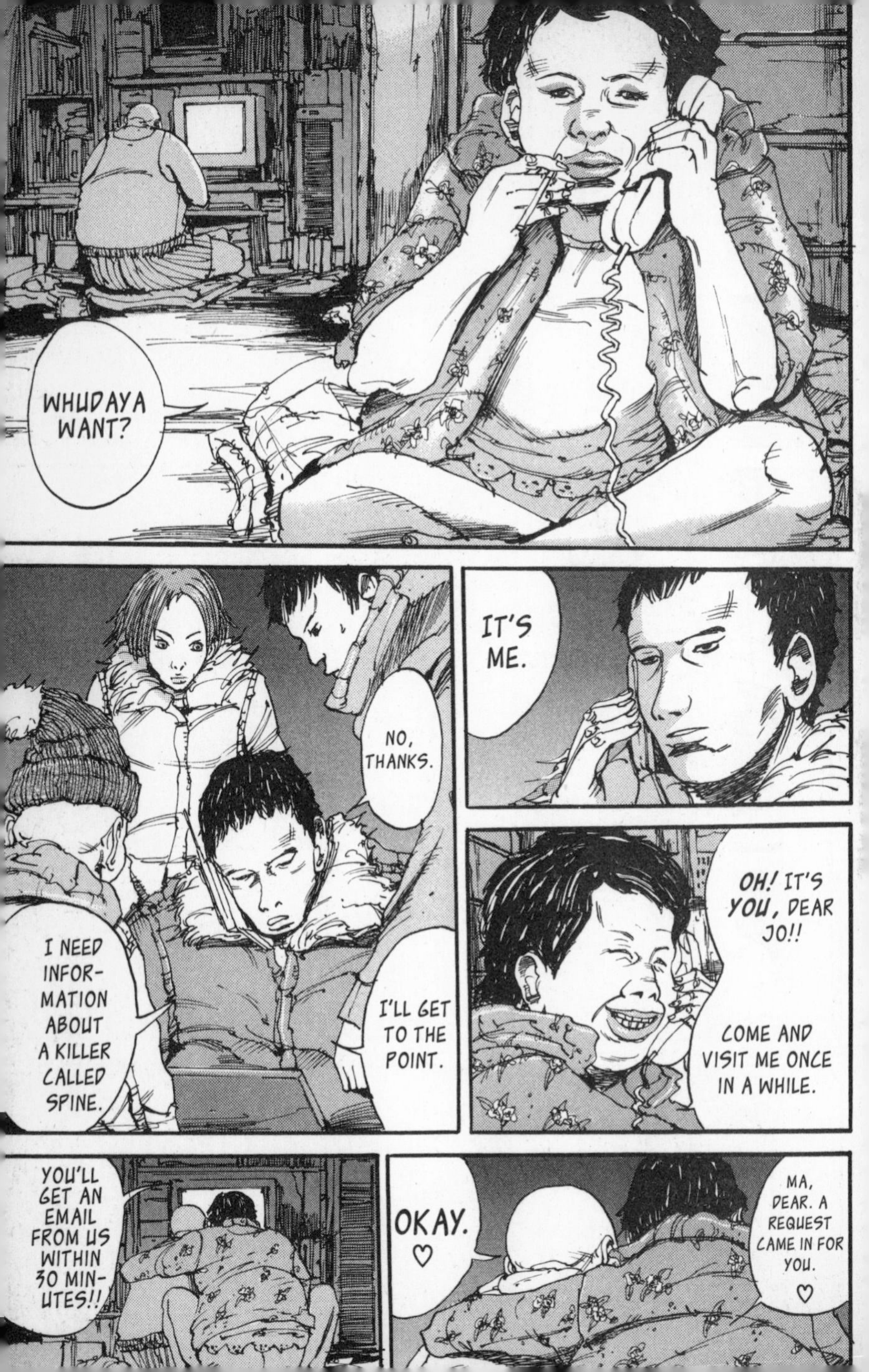
WHUDAYA WANT?
IT'S ME.
OH! IT'S YOU, DEAR JO!!
COME AND VISIT ME ONCE IN A WHILE.
NO, THANKS.
I'LL GET TO THE POINT.
I NEED INFORMATION ABOUT A KILLER CALLED SPINE.
MA, DEAR. A REQUEST CAME IN FOR YOU. ♡
OKAY. ♡
YOU'LL GET AN EMAIL FROM US WITHIN 30 MINUTES!!

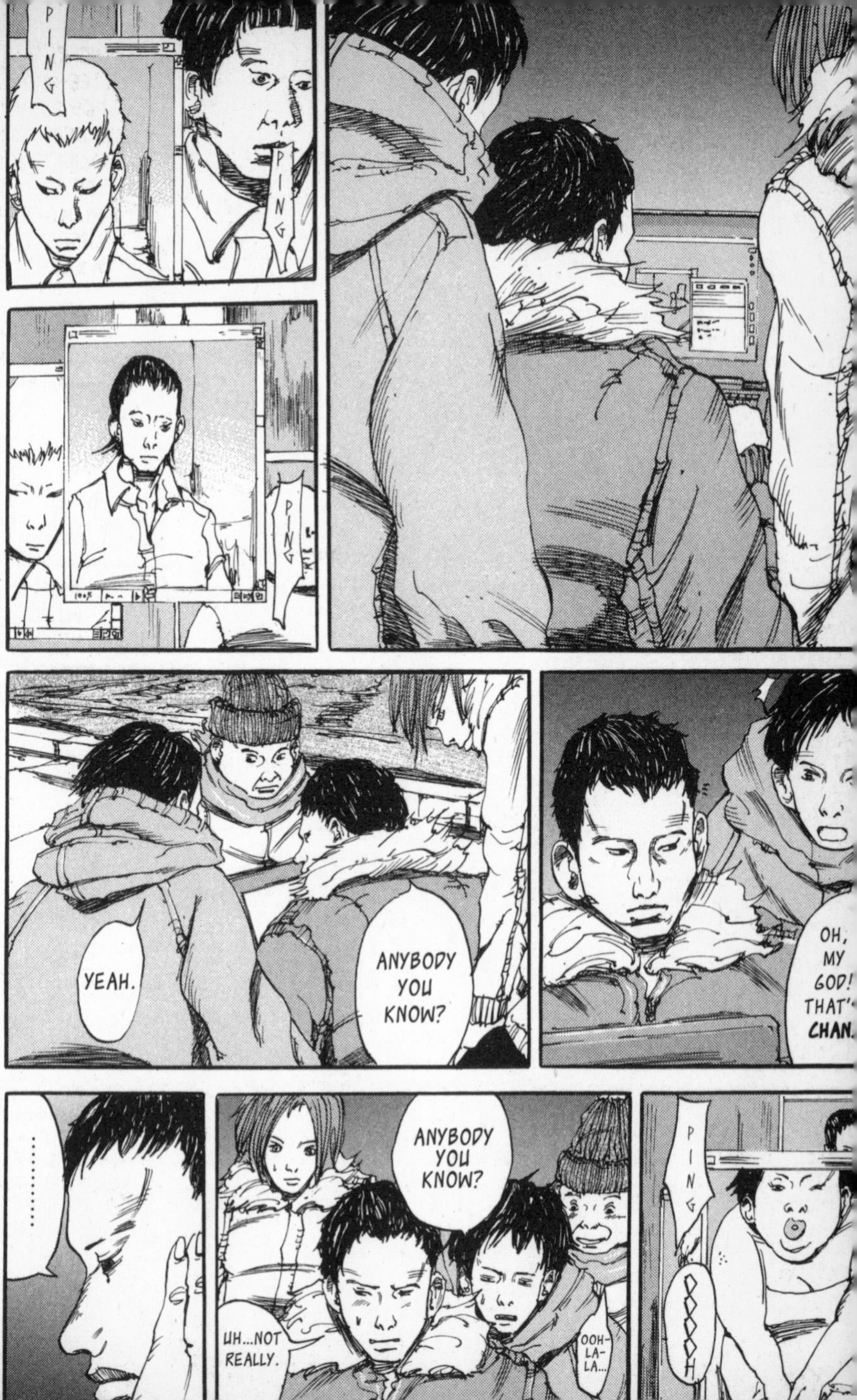
PING
PING
PING
OH, MY GOD! THAT' CHAN.
ANYBODY YOU KNOW?
YEAH.
PING
OOOOH
ANYBODY YOU KNOW?
OOH-LA-LA...
UH...NOT REALLY.
....

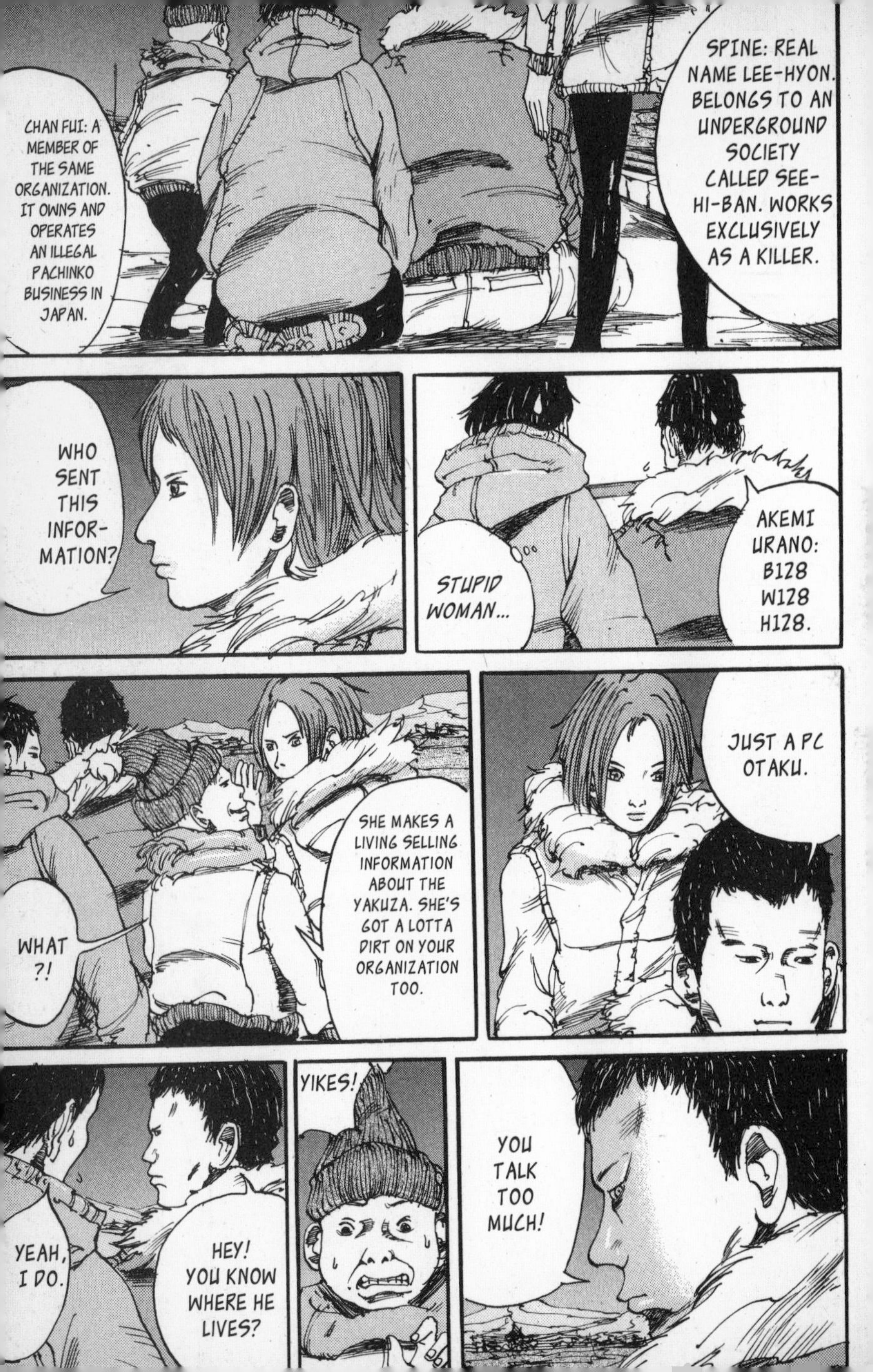
SPINE: REAL NAME LEE-HYON. BELONGS TO AN UNDERGROUND SOCIETY CALLED SEE-HI-BAN. WORKS EXCLUSIVELY AS A KILLER.
CHAN FUI: A MEMBER OF THE SAME ORGANIZATION. IT OWNS AND OPERATES AN ILLEGAL PACHINKO BUSINESS IN JAPAN.
AKEMI URANO: B128 W128 H128.
STUPID WOMAN...
WHO SENT THIS INFOR-MATION?
JUST A PC OTAKU.
SHE MAKES A LIVING SELLING INFORMATION ABOUT THE YAKUZA. SHE'S GOT A LOTTA DIRT ON YOUR ORGANIZATION TOO.
WHAT?!
YOU TALK TOO MUCH!
YIKES!
HEY! YOU KNOW WHERE HE LIVES?
YEAH, I DO.

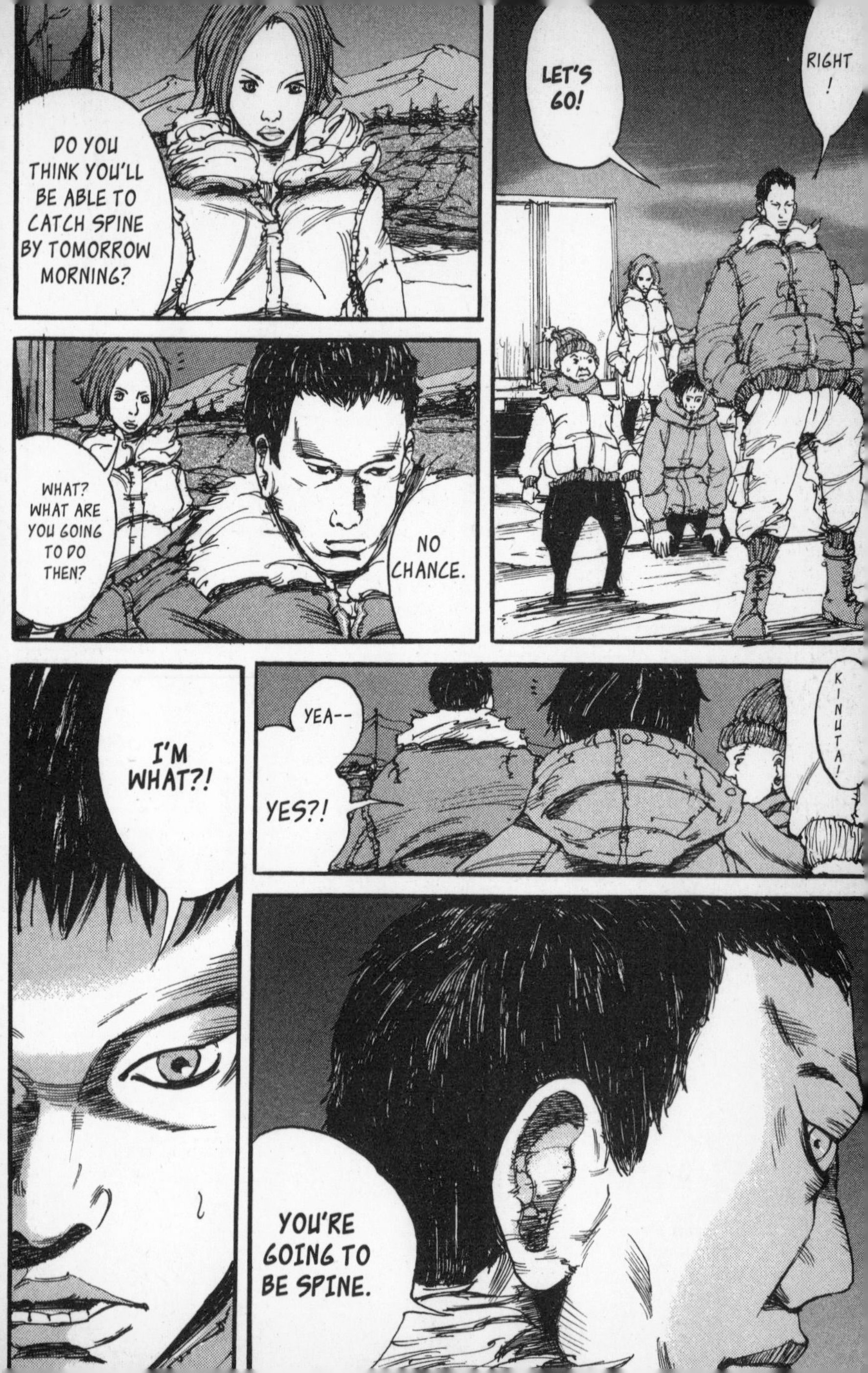
RIGHT!
LET'S GO!
DO YOU THINK YOU'LL BE ABLE TO CATCH SPINE BY TOMORROW MORNING?
NO CHANCE.
WHAT? WHAT ARE YOU GOING TO DO THEN?
KINUTA!
YEA--
YES?!
YOU'RE GOING TO BE SPINE.
I'M WHAT?!

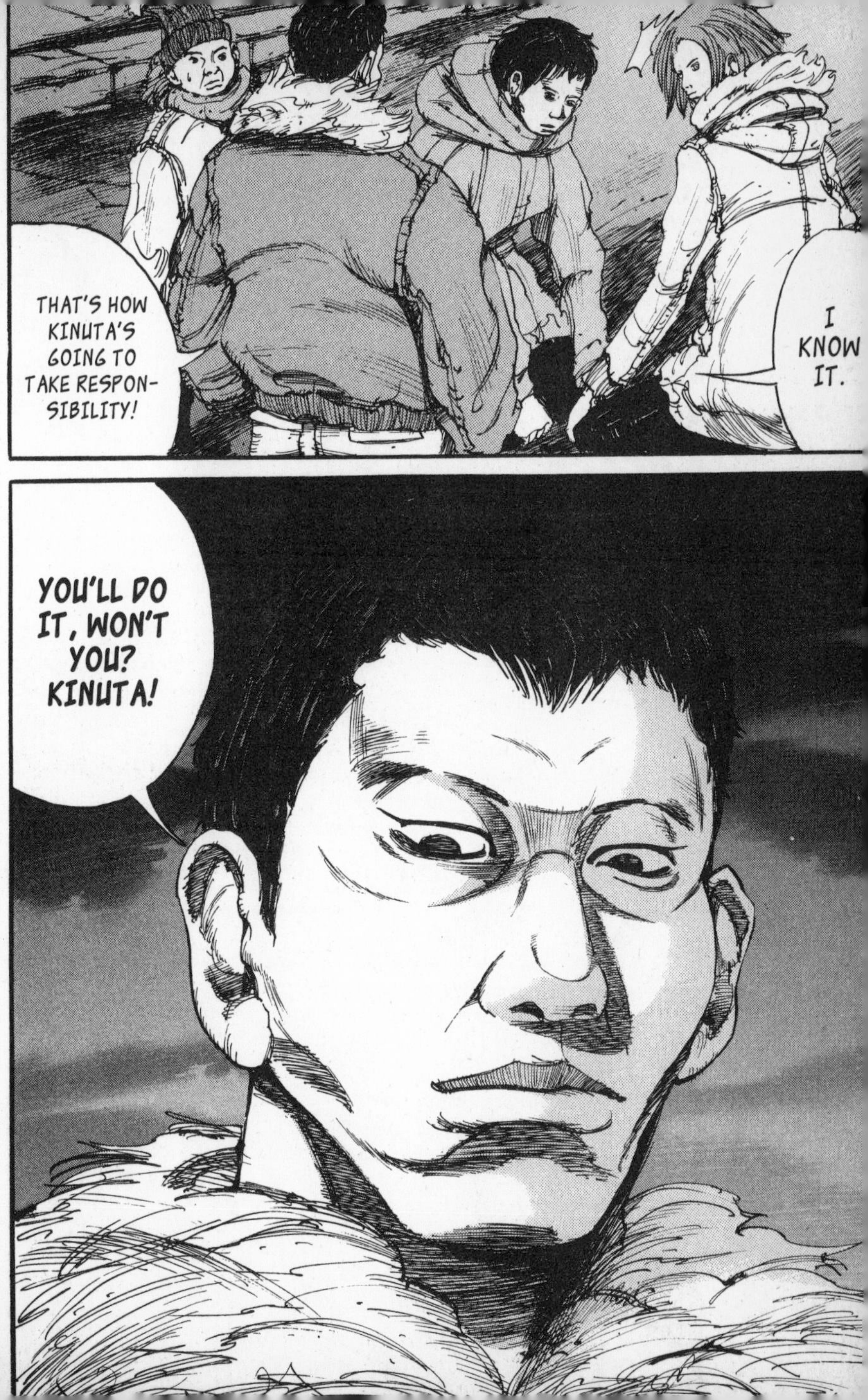
THAT'S HOW KINUTA'S GOING TO TAKE RESPON-SIBILITY!
I KNOW IT.
YOU'LL DO IT, WON'T YOU? KINUTA!

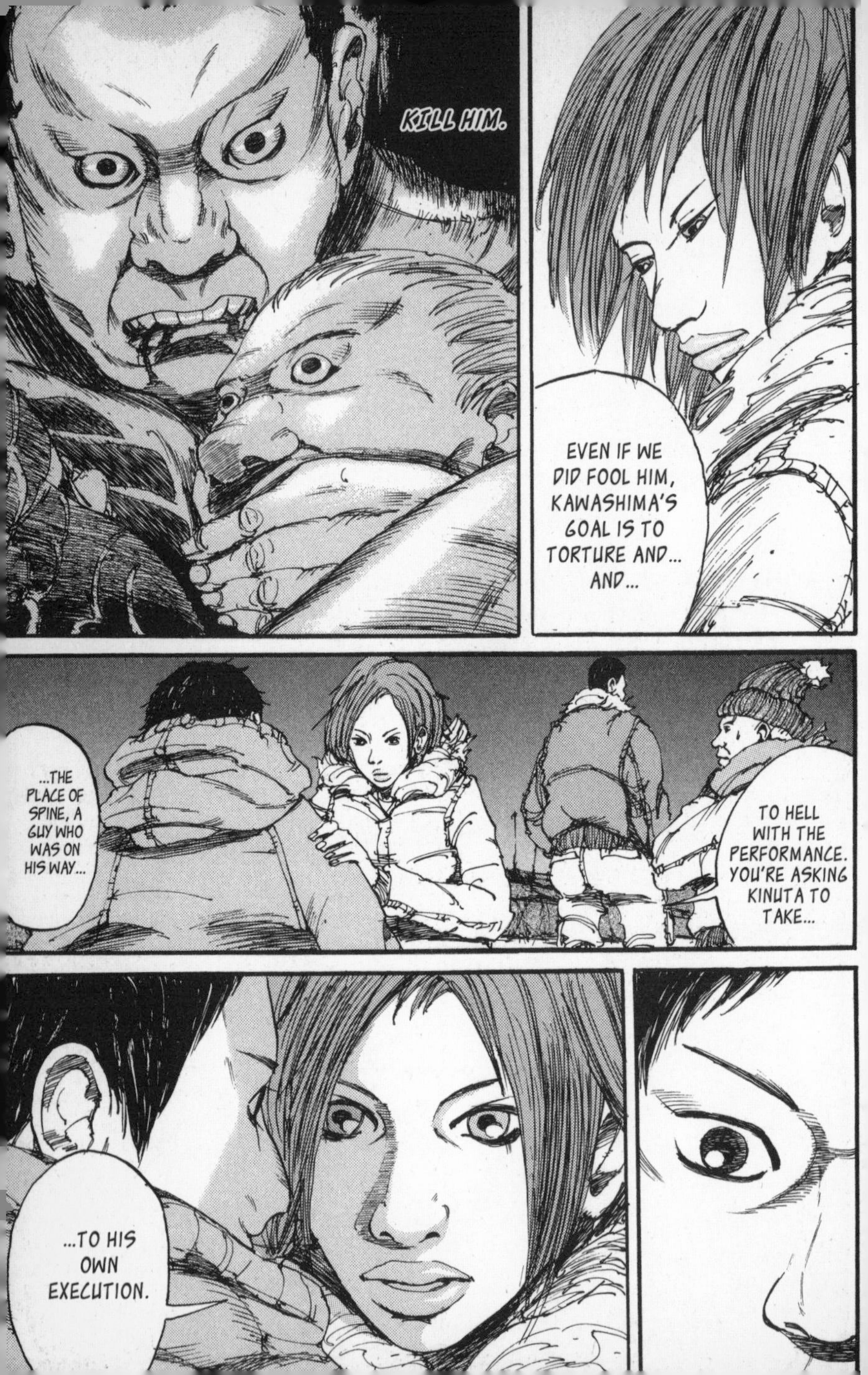
EVEN IF WE DID FOOL HIM, KAWASHIMA'S GOAL IS TO TORTURE AND... AND...
KILL HIM.
TO HELL WITH THE PERFORMANCE. YOU'RE ASKING KINUTA TO TAKE...
...THE PLACE OF SPINE, A GUY WHO WAS ON HIS WAY...
...TO HIS OWN EXECUTION.

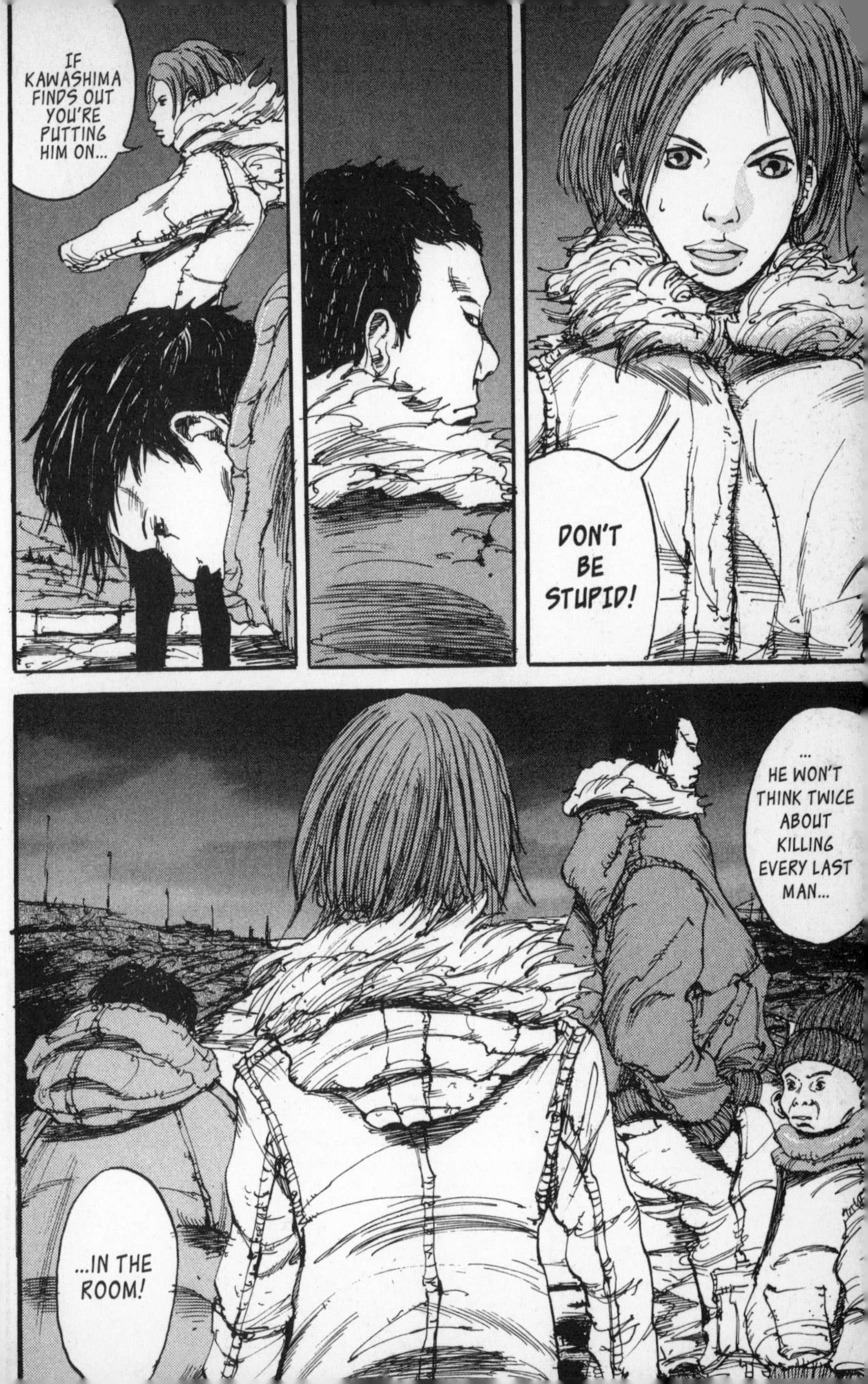
DON'T BE STUPID!
IF KAWASHIMA FINDS OUT YOU'RE PUTTING HIM ON...
...HE WON'T THINK TWICE ABOUT KILLING EVERY LAST MAN...
...IN THE ROOM!

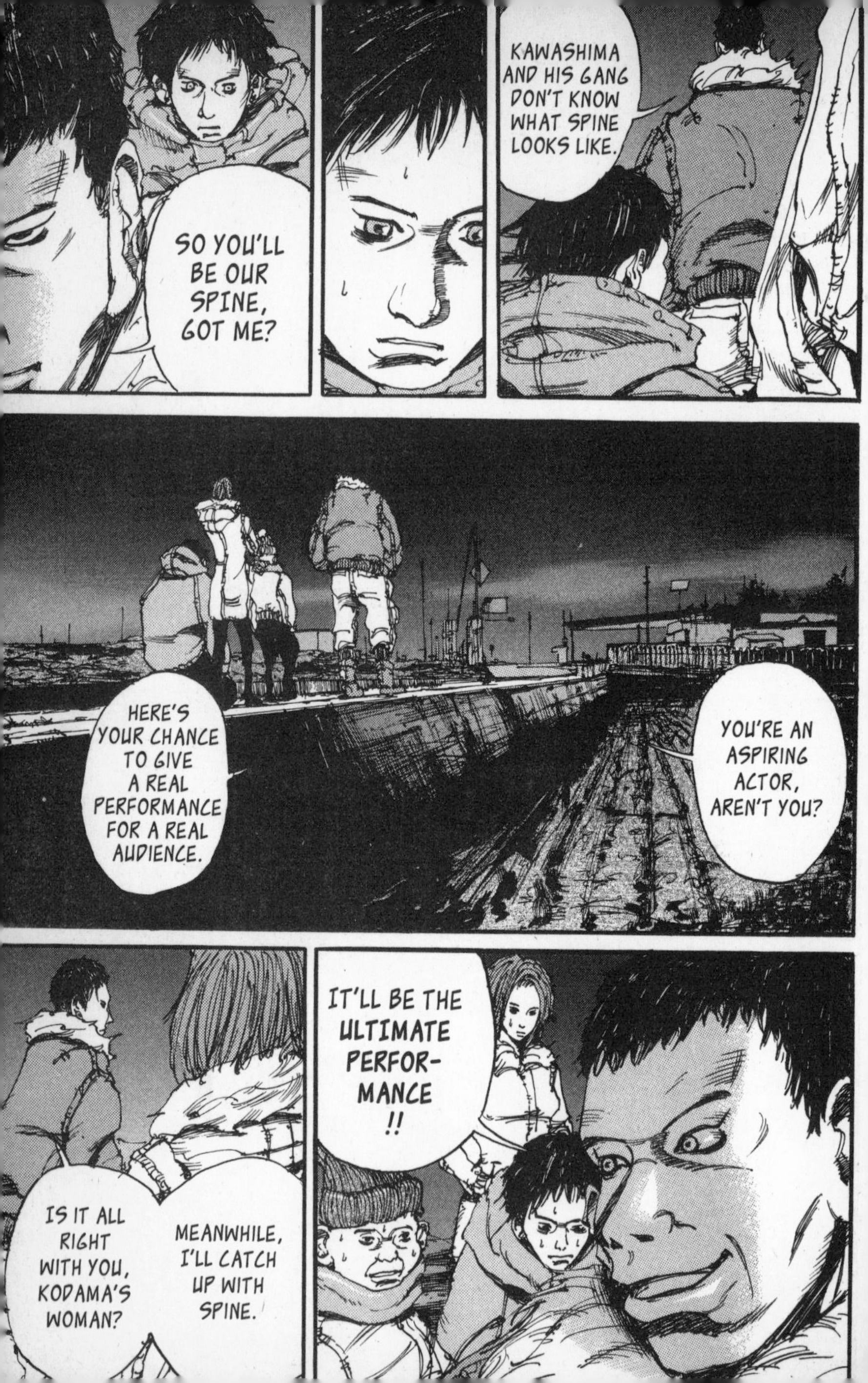
KAWASHIMA AND HIS GANG DON'T KNOW WHAT SPINE LOOKS LIKE.
SO YOU'LL BE OUR SPINE, GOT ME?
YOU'RE AN ASPIRING ACTOR, AREN'T YOU?
HERE'S YOUR CHANCE TO GIVE A REAL PERFORMANCE FOR A REAL AUDIENCE.
IT'LL BE THE **ULTIMATE PERFORMANCE**!!
MEANWHILE, I'LL CATCH UP WITH SPINE.
IS IT ALL RIGHT WITH YOU, KODAMA'S WOMAN?

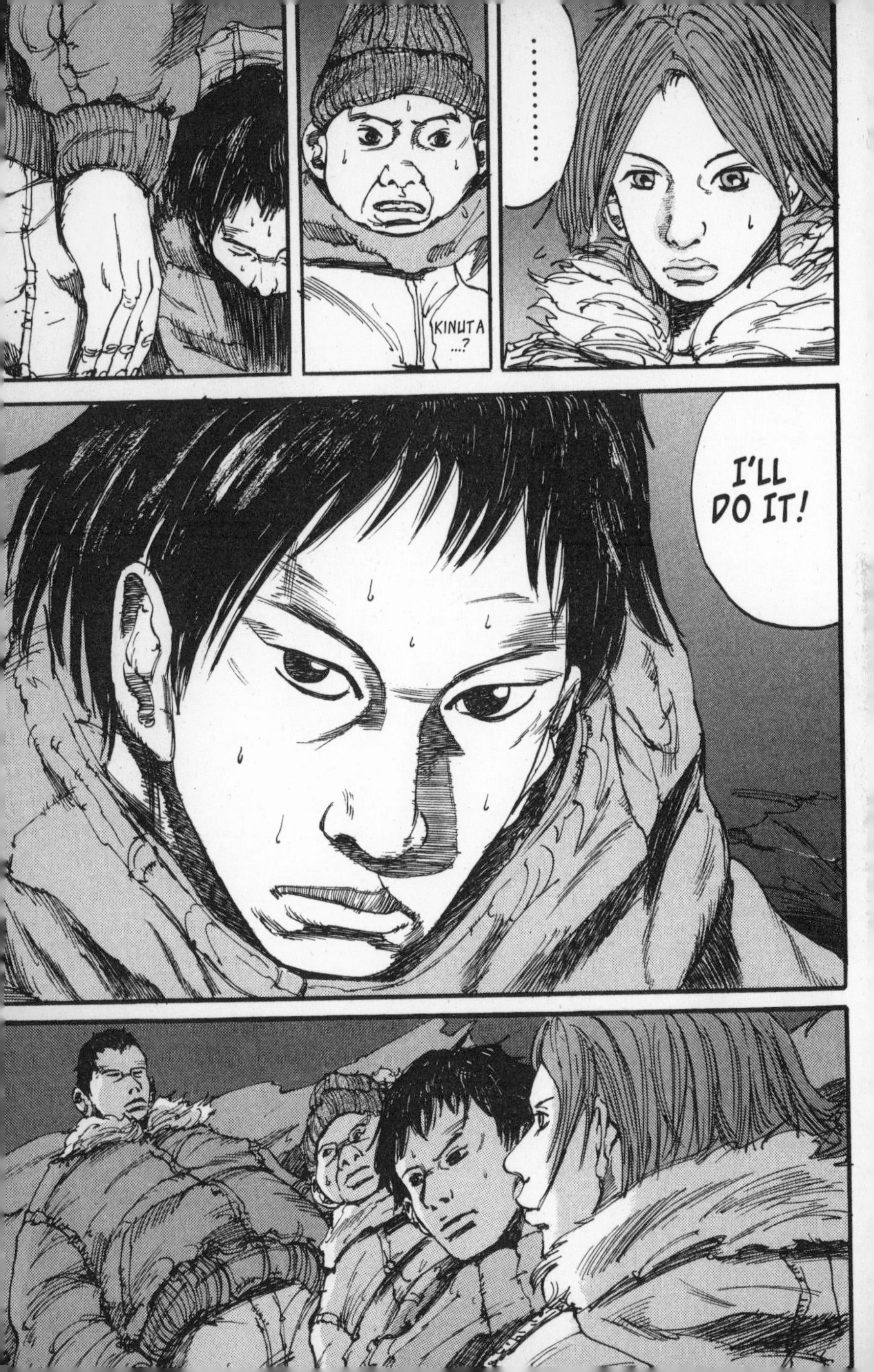
......
KINUTA ...?
I'LL DO IT!

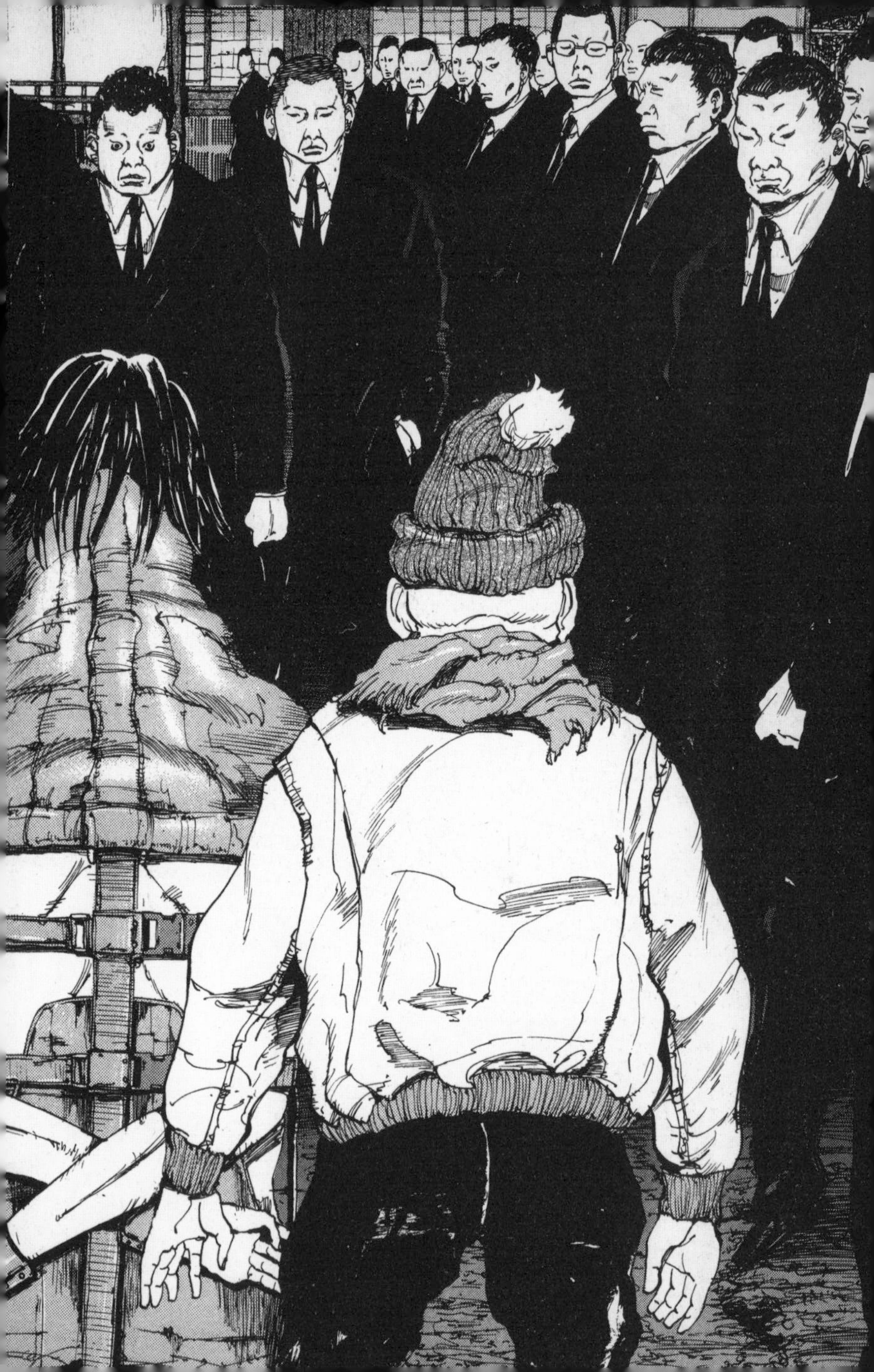

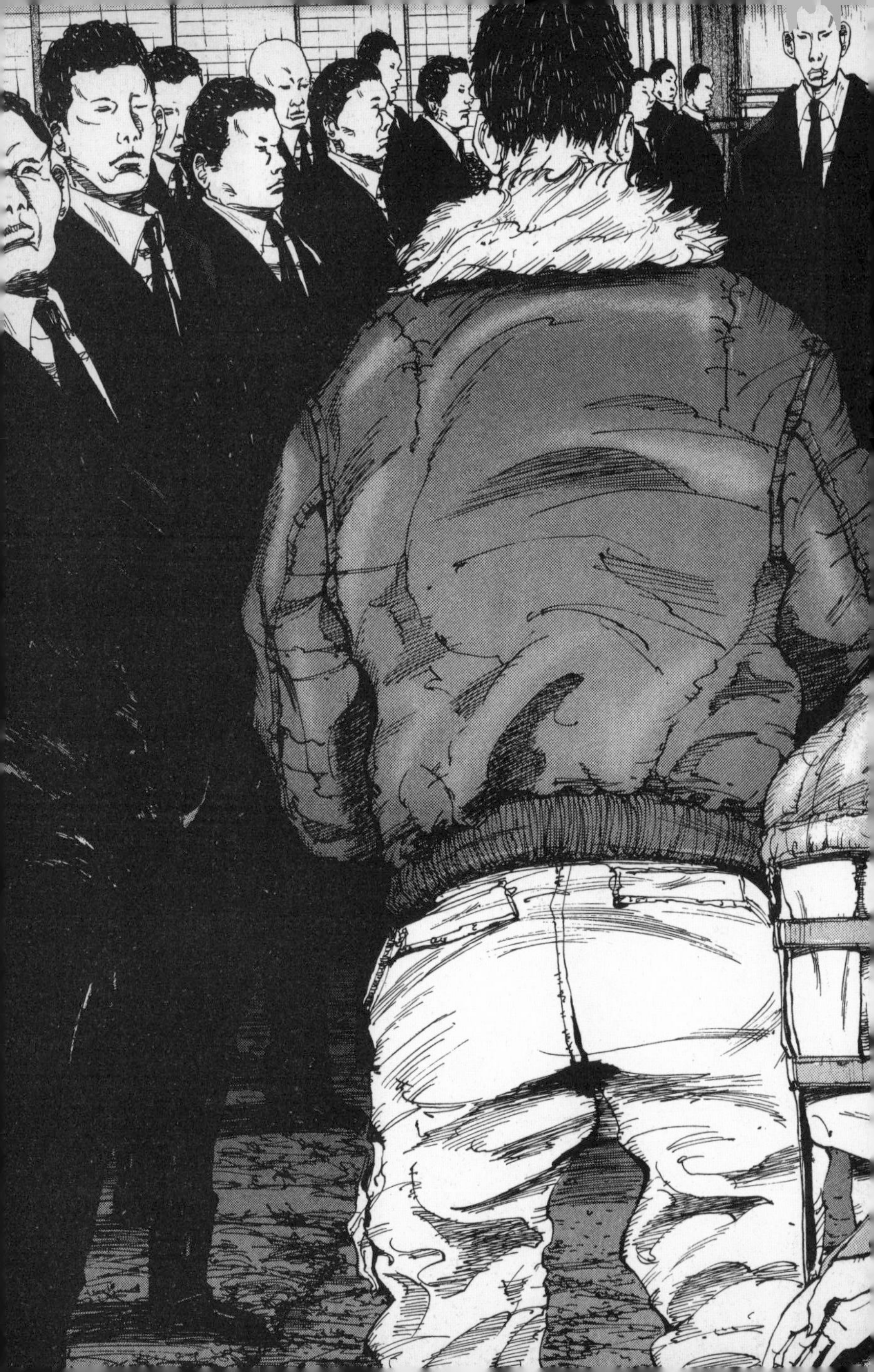

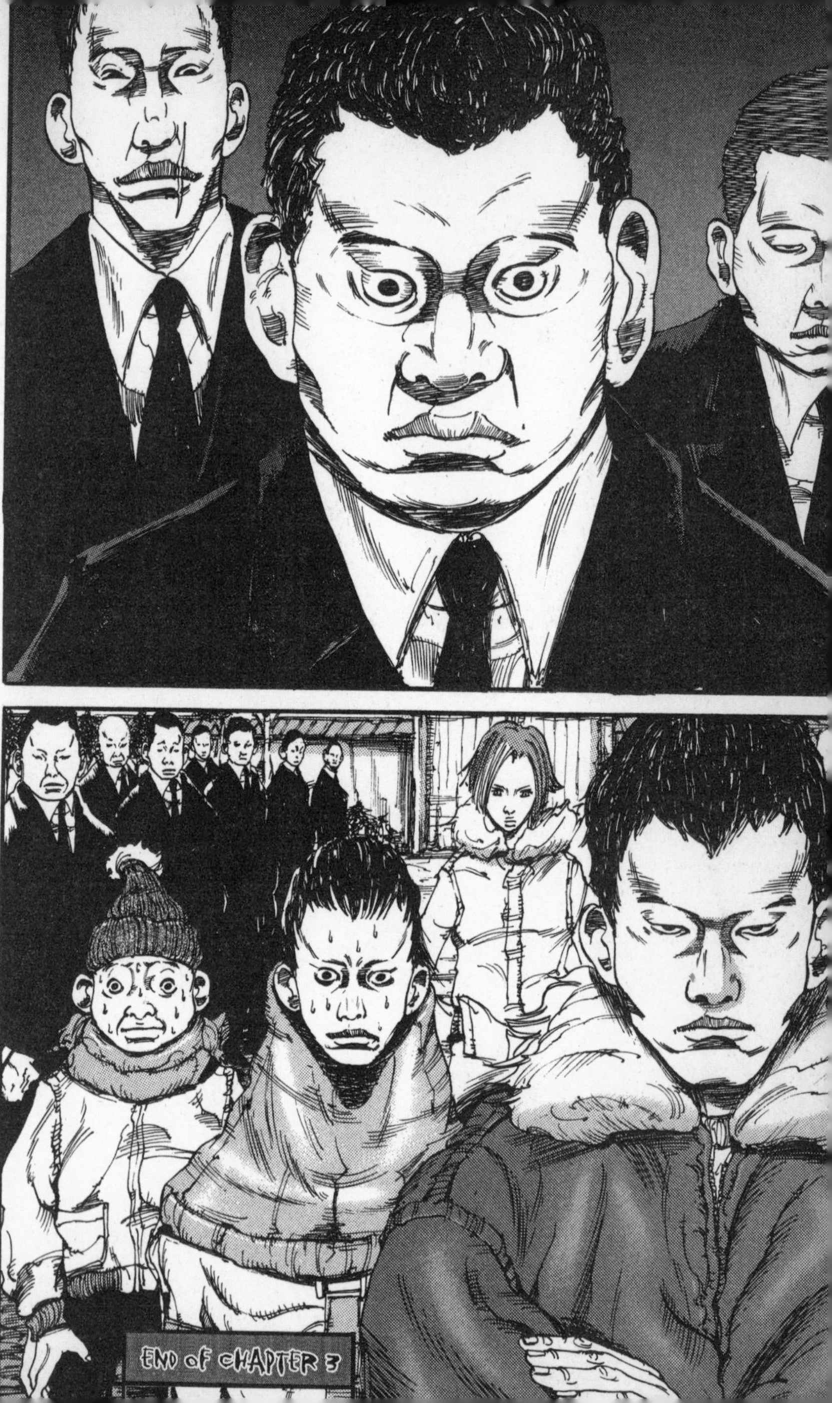
END OF CHAPTER 3

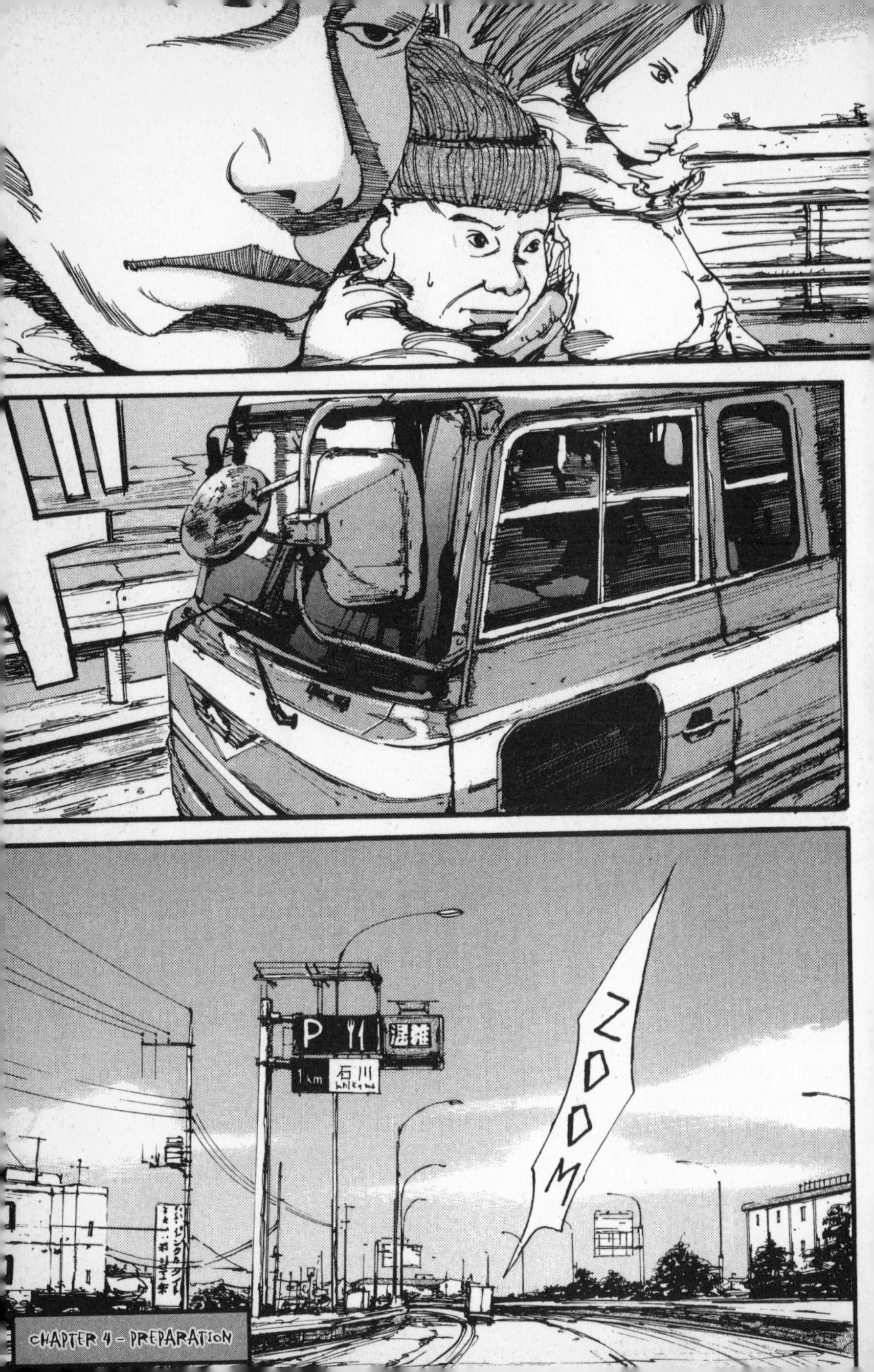
ZOOM
P
混雑
1km 石川
CHAPTER 4 – PREPARATION

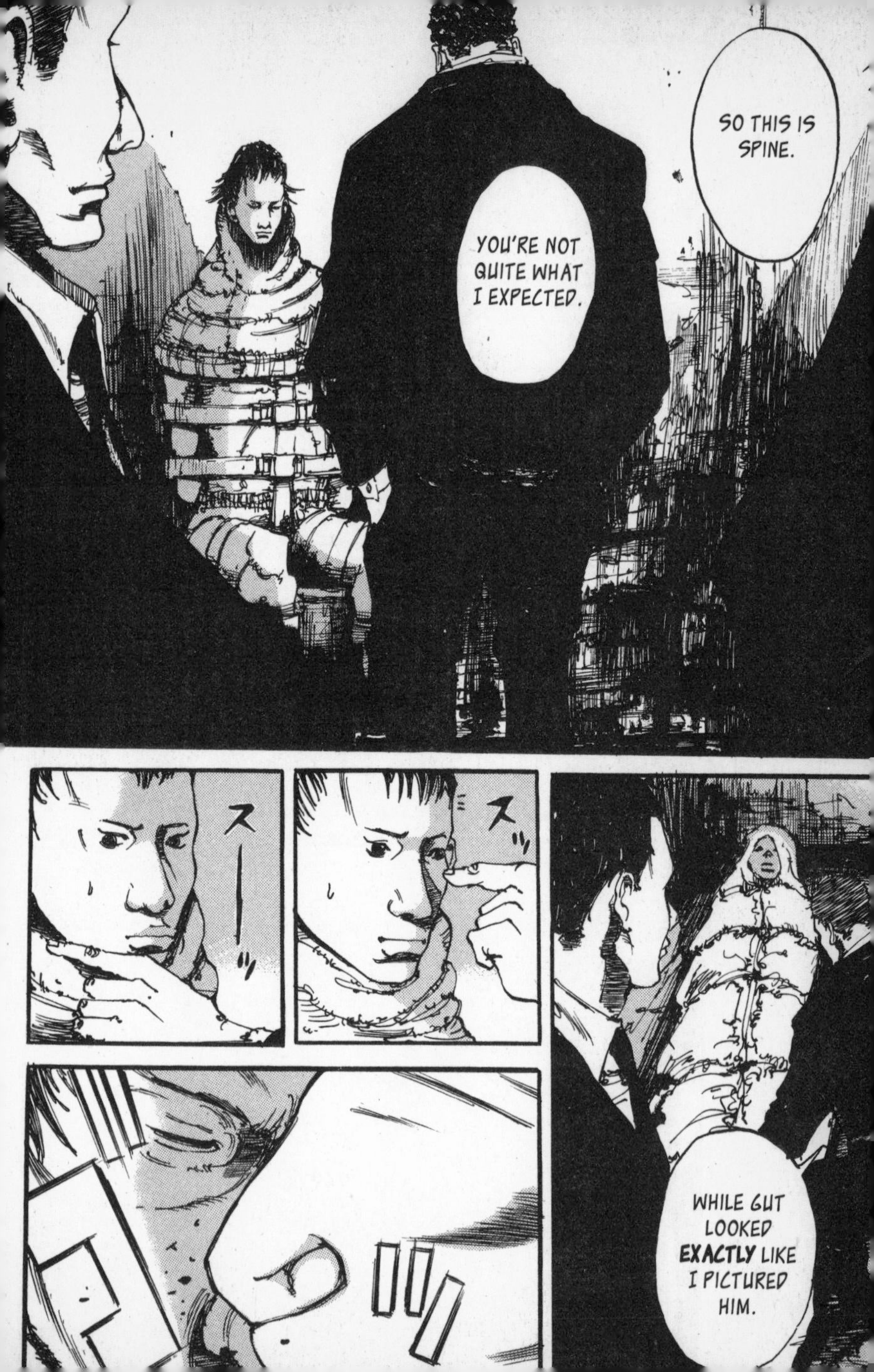
SO THIS IS SPINE.
YOU'RE NOT QUITE WHAT I EXPECTED.
WHILE GUT LOOKED **EXACTLY** LIKE I PICTURED HIM.
スッ
スーッ

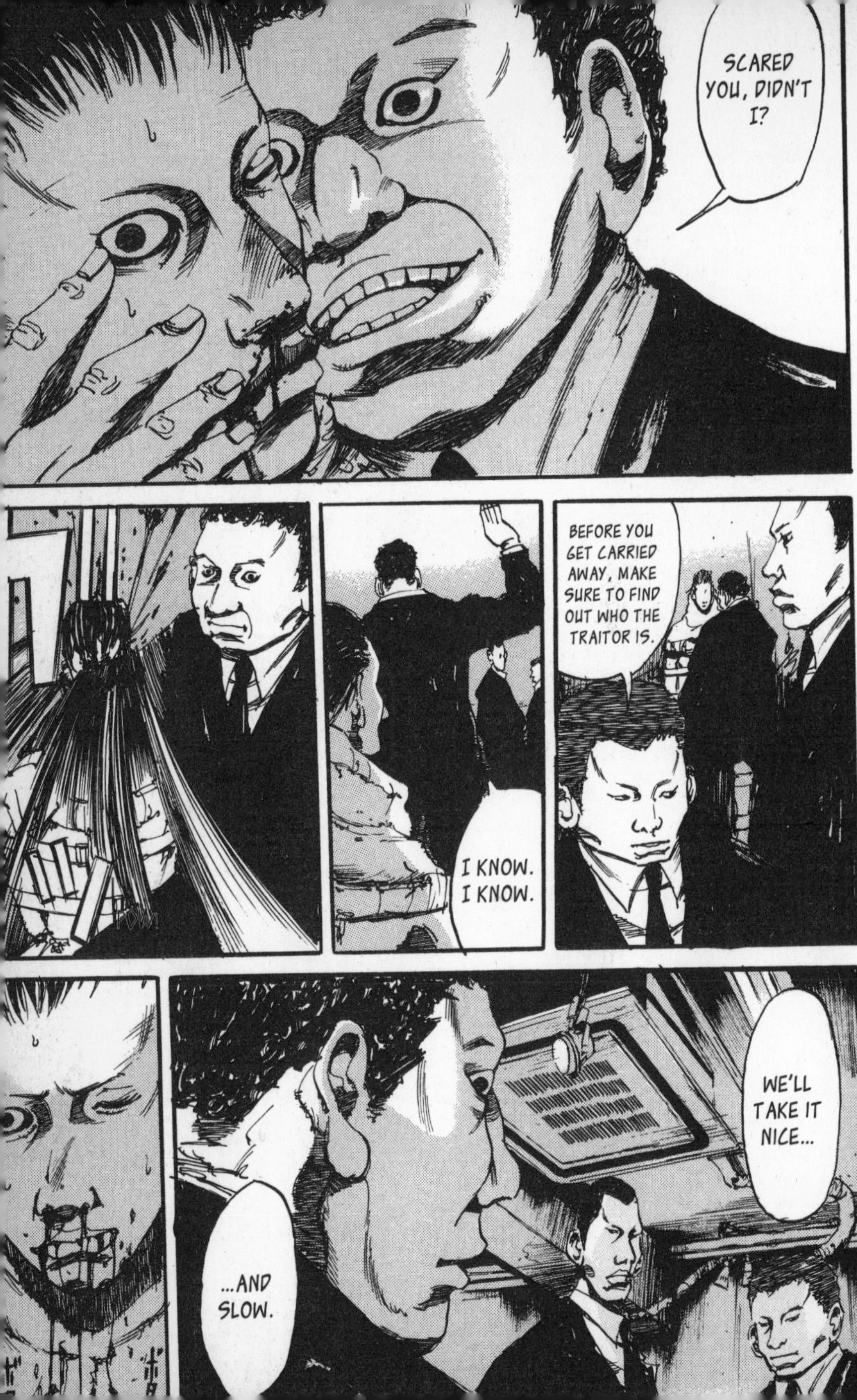
SCARED YOU, DIDN'T I?
BEFORE YOU GET CARRIED AWAY, MAKE SURE TO FIND OUT WHO THE TRAITOR IS.
I KNOW. I KNOW.
WE'LL TAKE IT NICE...
...AND SLOW.

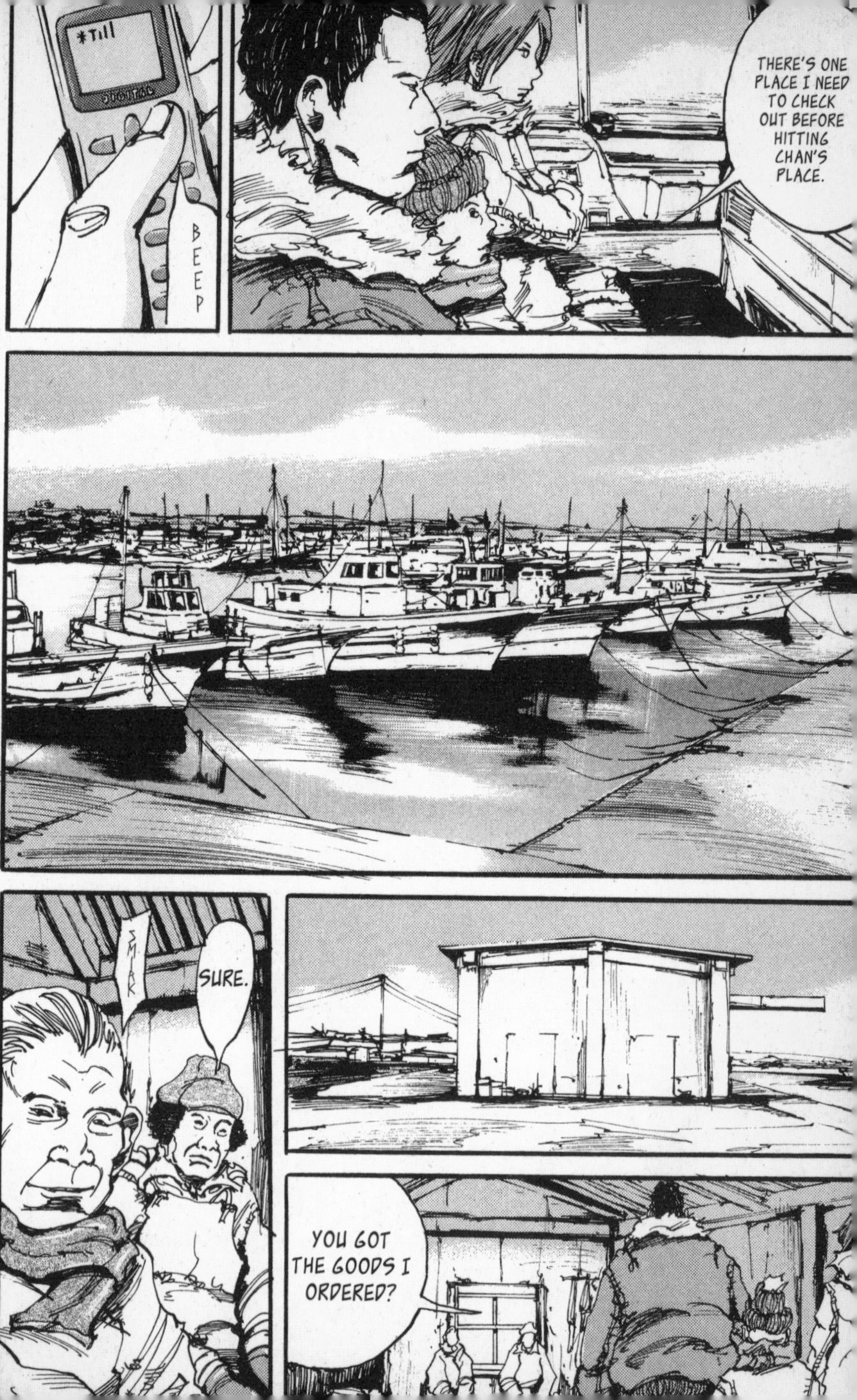
THERE'S ONE PLACE I NEED TO CHECK OUT BEFORE HITTING CHAN'S PLACE.
*Till
BEEP
YOU GOT THE GOODS I ORDERED?
SMIRK
SURE.

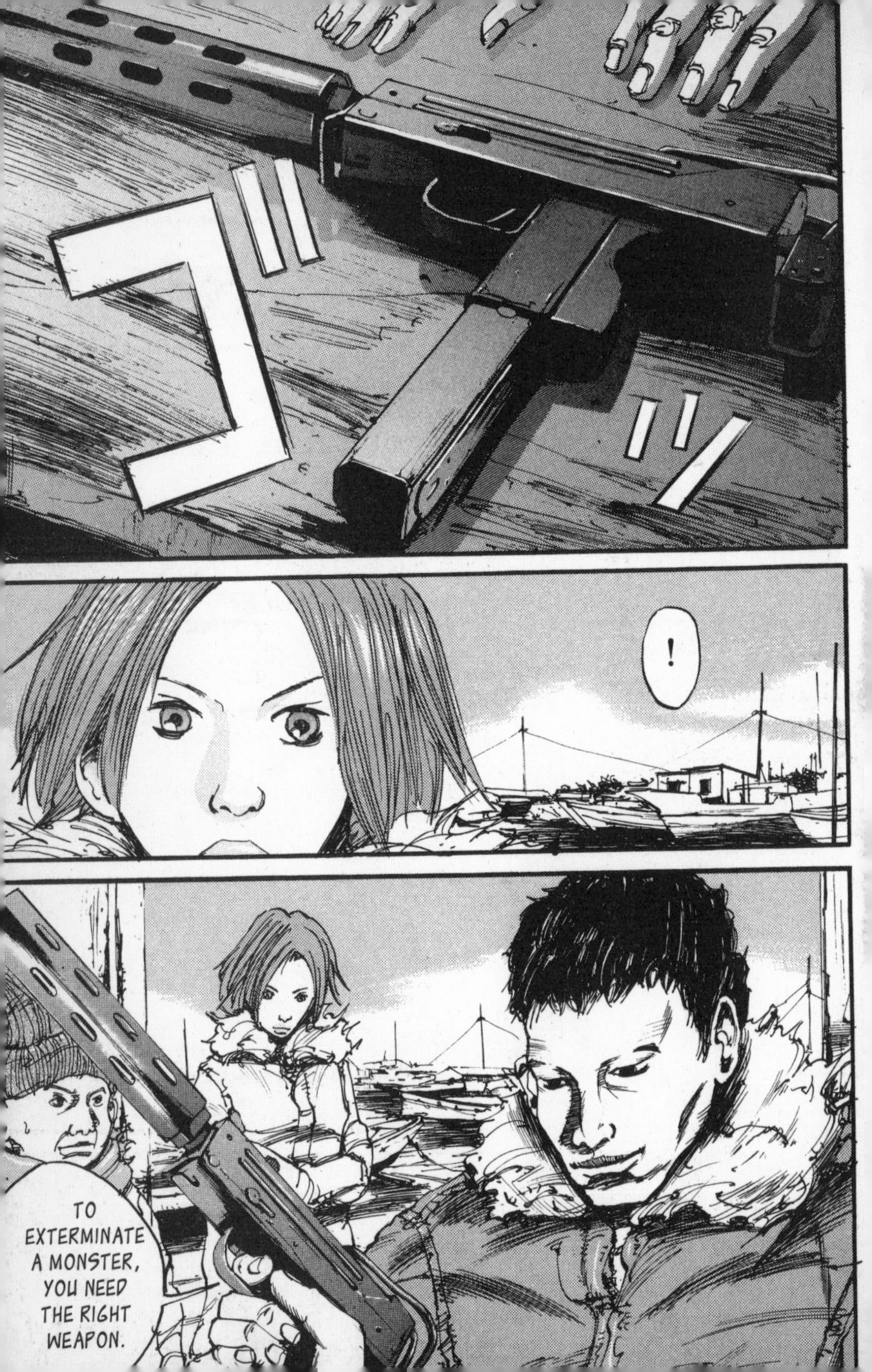
!
TO EXTERMINATE A MONSTER, YOU NEED THE RIGHT WEAPON.

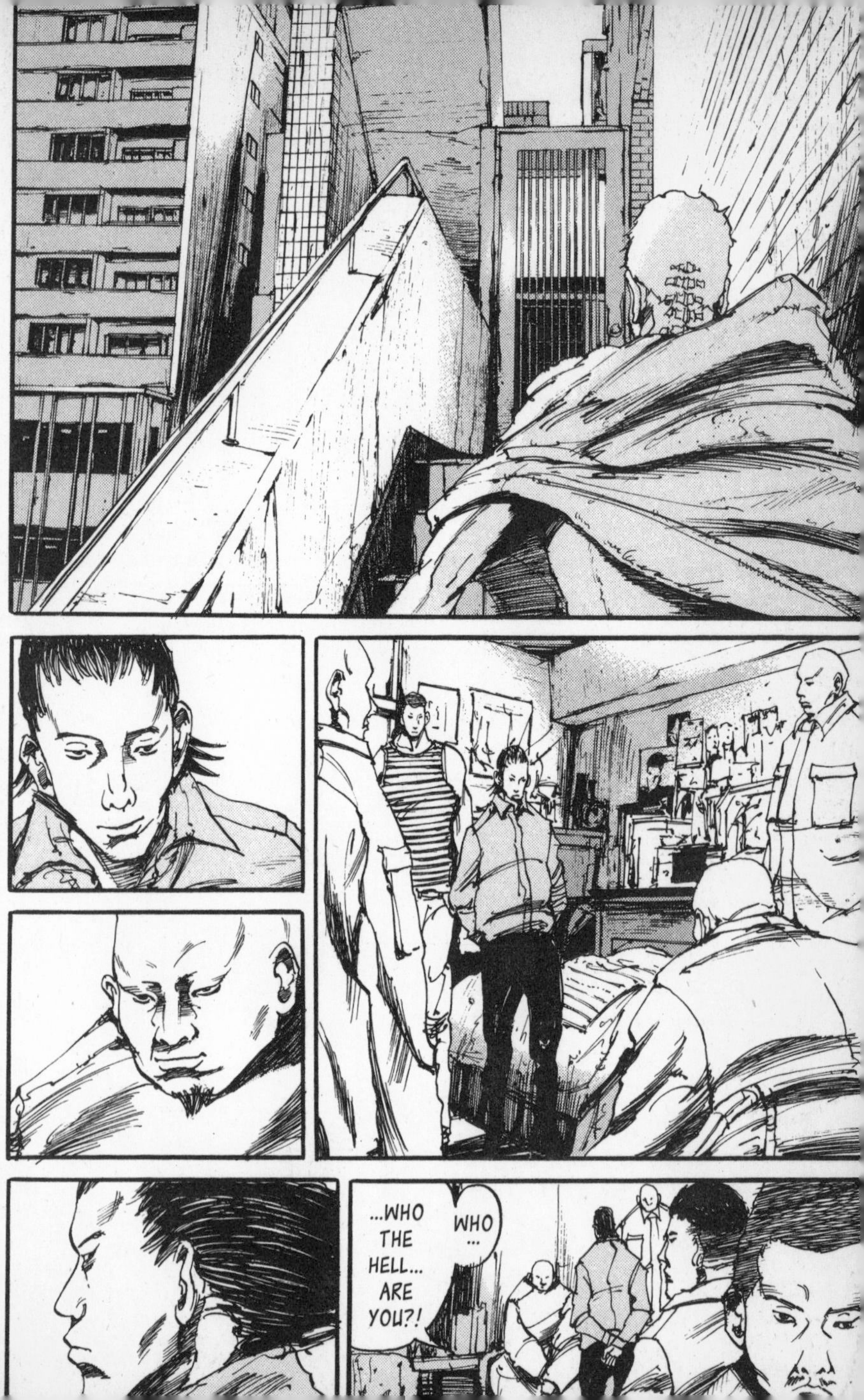
WHO ...
...WHO THE HELL... ARE YOU?!

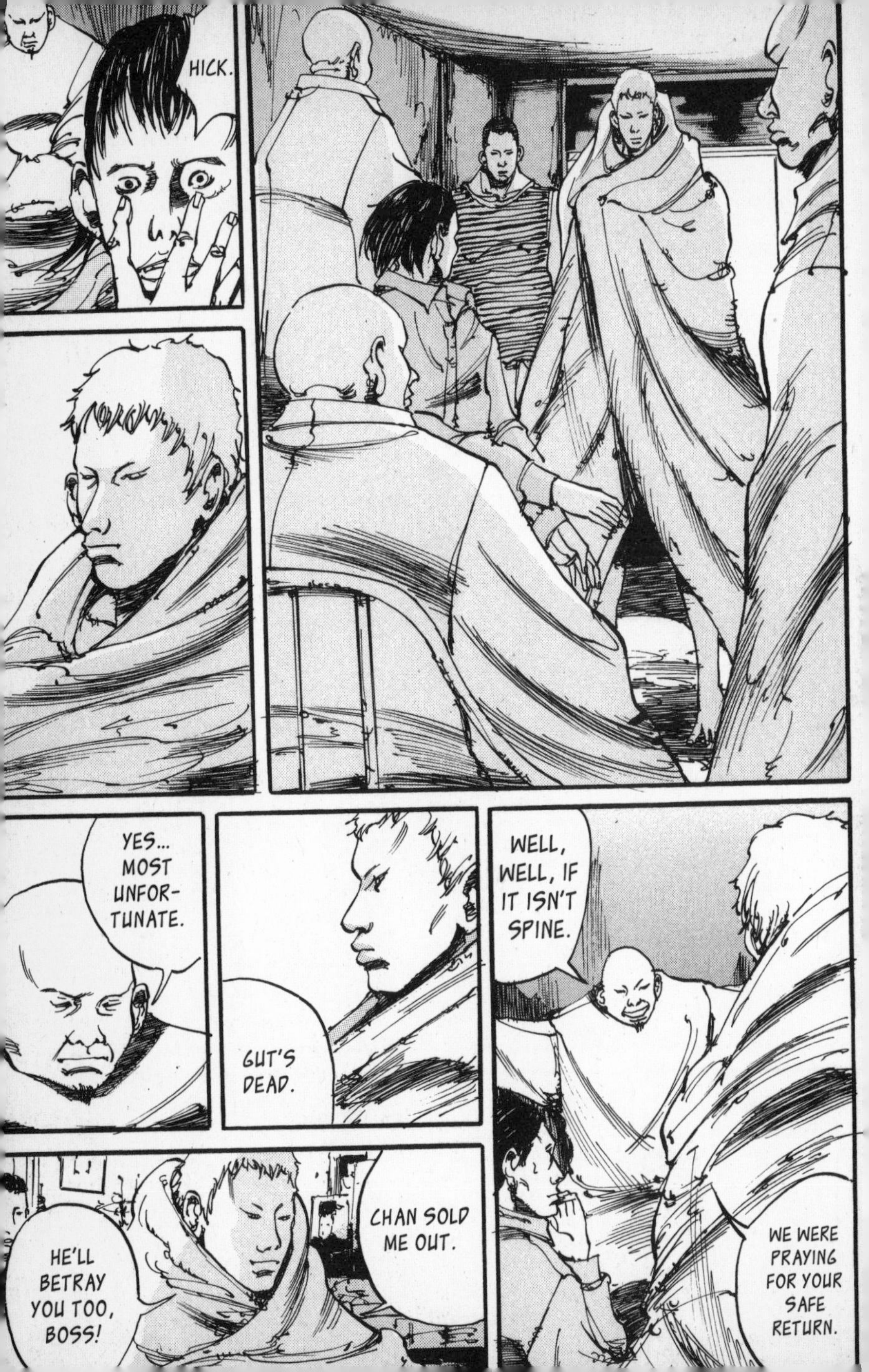
HICK.
WELL, WELL, IF IT ISN'T SPINE.
WE WERE PRAYING FOR YOUR SAFE RETURN.
GUT'S DEAD.
YES... MOST UNFORTUNATE.
CHAN SOLD ME OUT.
HE'LL BETRAY YOU TOO, BOSS!

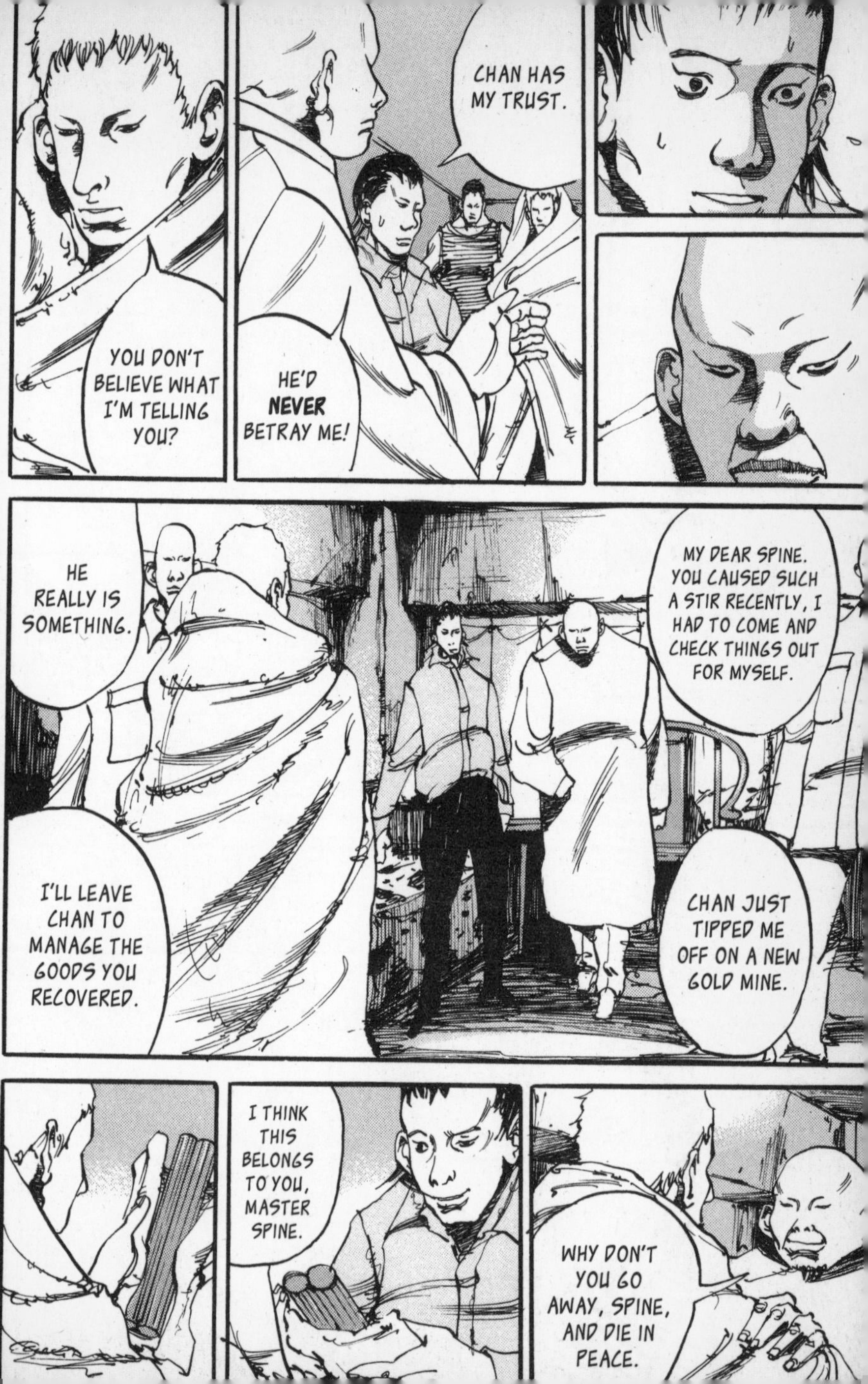
CHAN HAS MY TRUST.
HE'D **NEVER** BETRAY ME!
YOU DON'T BELIEVE WHAT I'M TELLING YOU?
MY DEAR SPINE. YOU CAUSED SUCH A STIR RECENTLY, I HAD TO COME AND CHECK THINGS OUT FOR MYSELF.
CHAN JUST TIPPED ME OFF ON A NEW GOLD MINE.
HE REALLY IS SOMETHING.
I'LL LEAVE CHAN TO MANAGE THE GOODS YOU RECOVERED.
WHY DON'T YOU GO AWAY, SPINE, AND DIE IN PEACE.
I THINK THIS BELONGS TO YOU, MASTER SPINE.

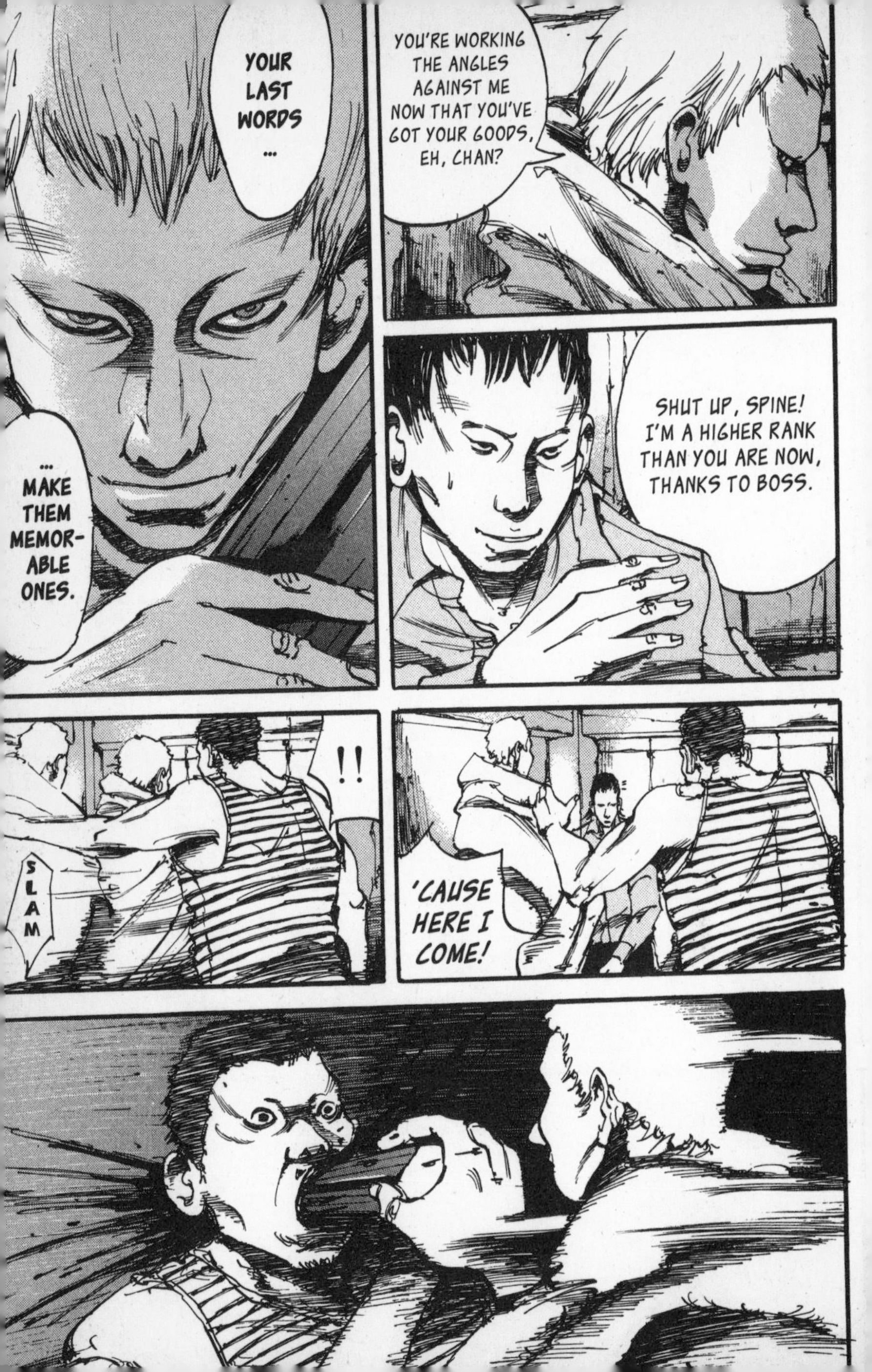
YOU'RE WORKING THE ANGLES AGAINST ME NOW THAT YOU'VE GOT YOUR GOODS, EH, CHAN?
SHUT UP, SPINE! I'M A HIGHER RANK THAN YOU ARE NOW, THANKS TO BOSS.
YOUR LAST WORDS ...
... MAKE THEM MEMORABLE ONES.
'CAUSE HERE I COME!
!!
SLAM

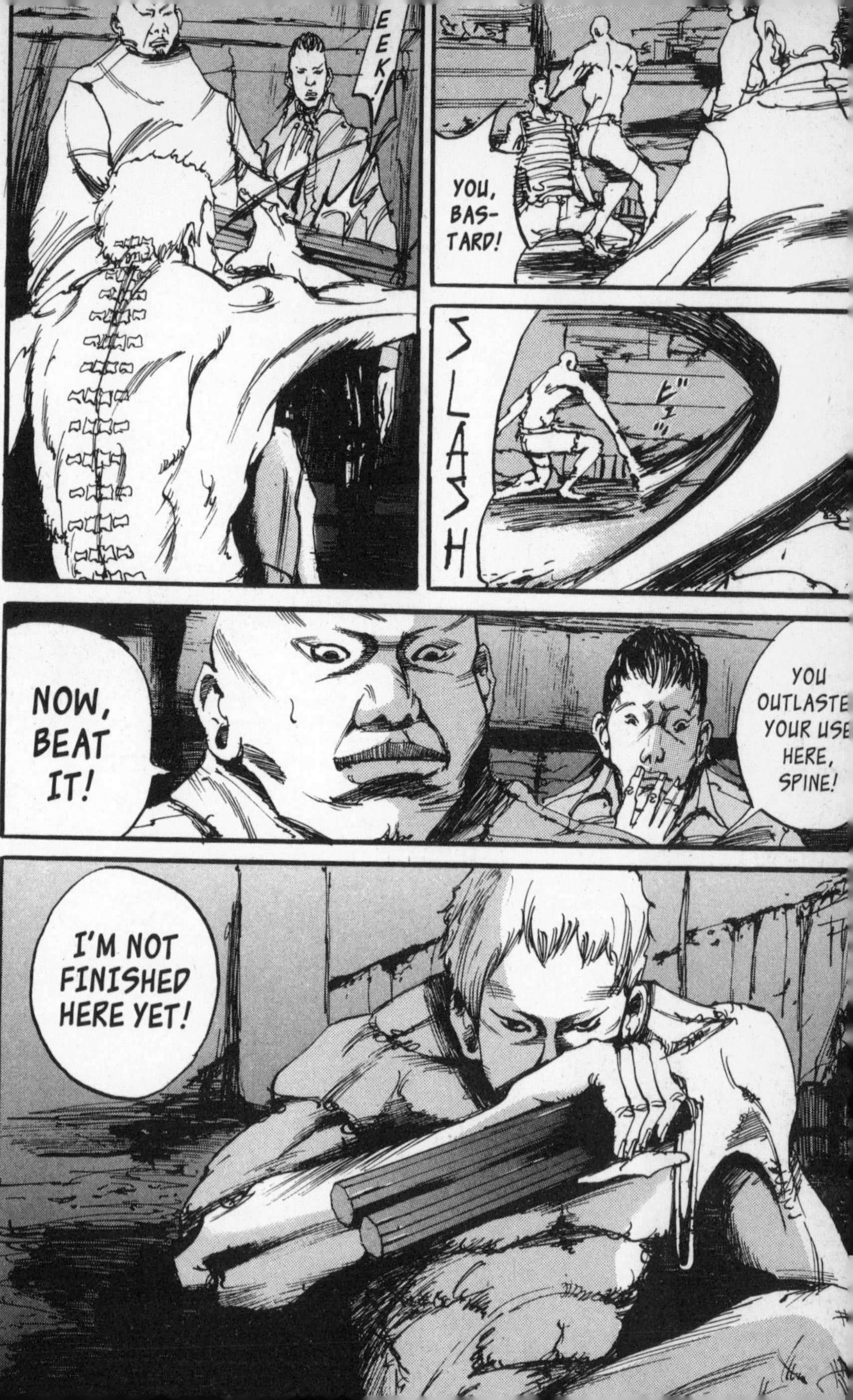
YOU, BAS-TARD!
SLASH
EEK!
YOU OUTLASTE YOUR USE HERE, SPINE!
NOW, BEAT IT!
I'M NOT FINISHED HERE YET!

DOESN'T HE FEEL PAIN?

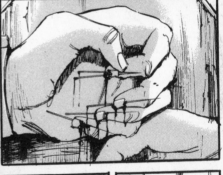

SPLAT

SLUSH

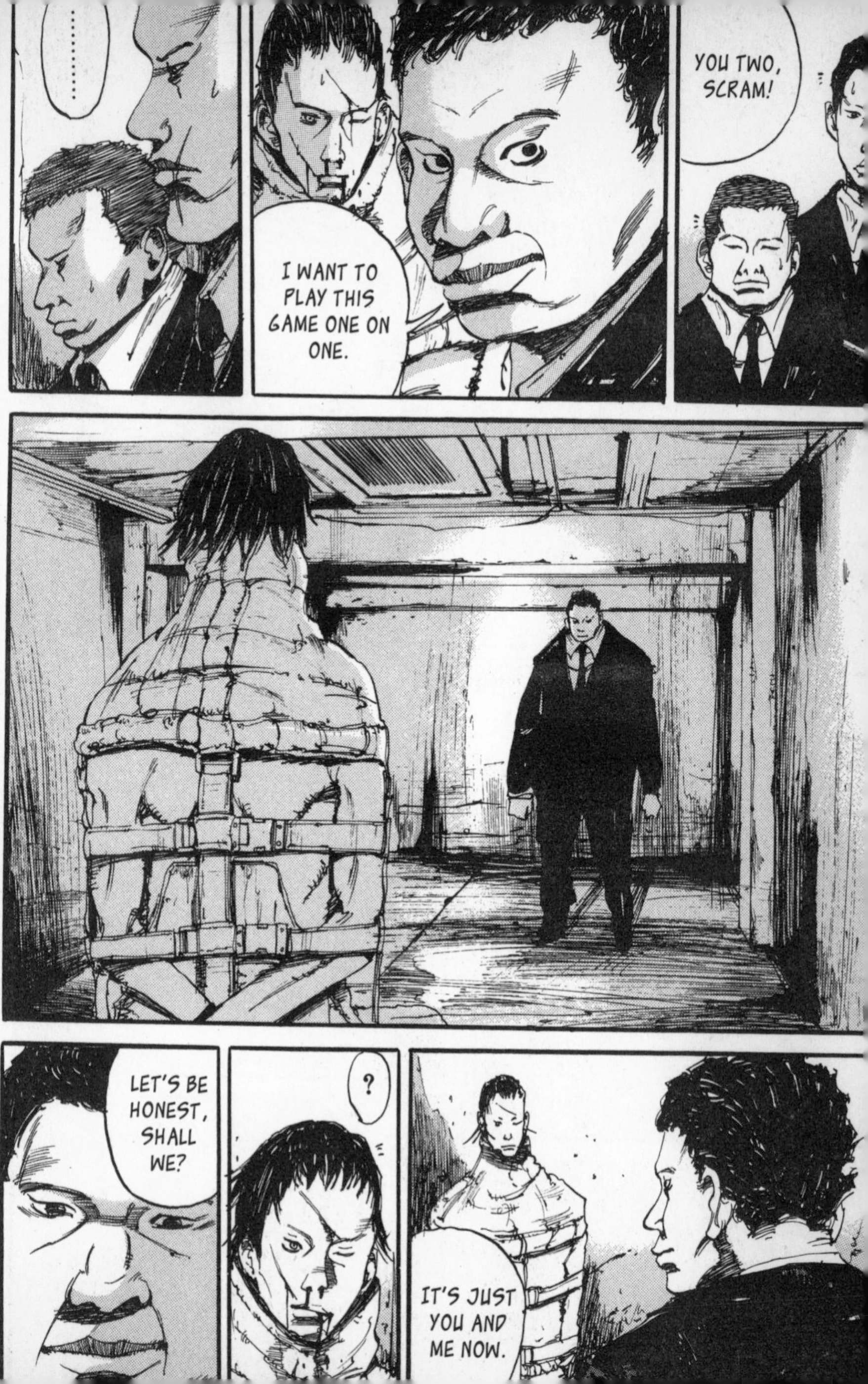
YOU TWO, SCRAM!
I WANT TO PLAY THIS GAME ONE ON ONE.
……
IT'S JUST YOU AND ME NOW.
?
LET'S BE HONEST, SHALL WE?

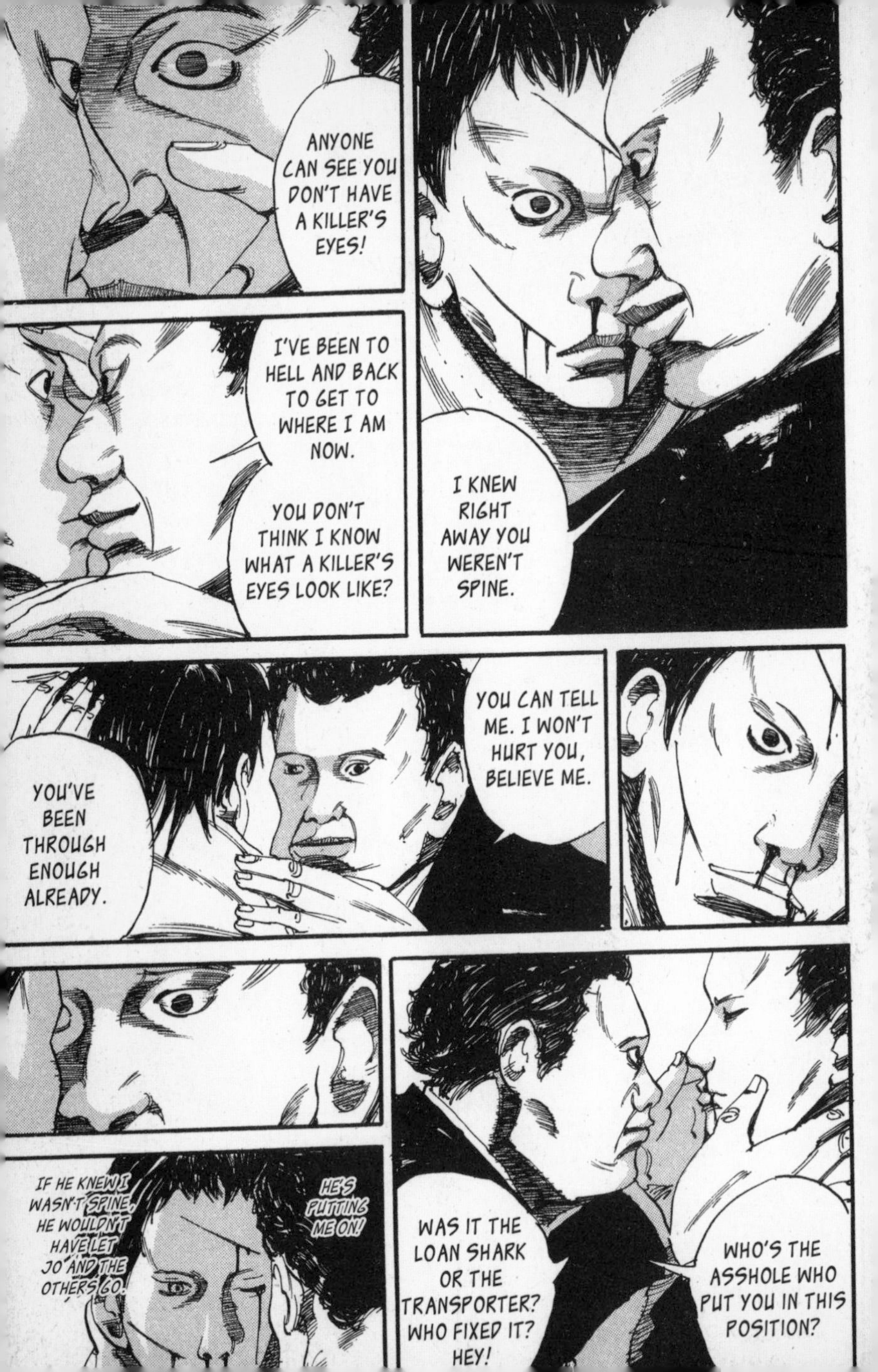
I KNEW RIGHT AWAY YOU WEREN'T SPINE.
ANYONE CAN SEE YOU DON'T HAVE A KILLER'S EYES!
I'VE BEEN TO HELL AND BACK TO GET TO WHERE I AM NOW.
YOU DON'T THINK I KNOW WHAT A KILLER'S EYES LOOK LIKE?
YOU CAN TELL ME. I WON'T HURT YOU, BELIEVE ME.
YOU'VE BEEN THROUGH ENOUGH ALREADY.
WHO'S THE ASSHOLE WHO PUT YOU IN THIS POSITION?
WAS IT THE LOAN SHARK OR THE TRANSPORTER? WHO FIXED IT? HEY!
HE'S PUTTING ME ON!
IF HE KNEW I WASN'T SPINE, HE WOULDN'T HAVE LET JO AND THE OTHERS GO.

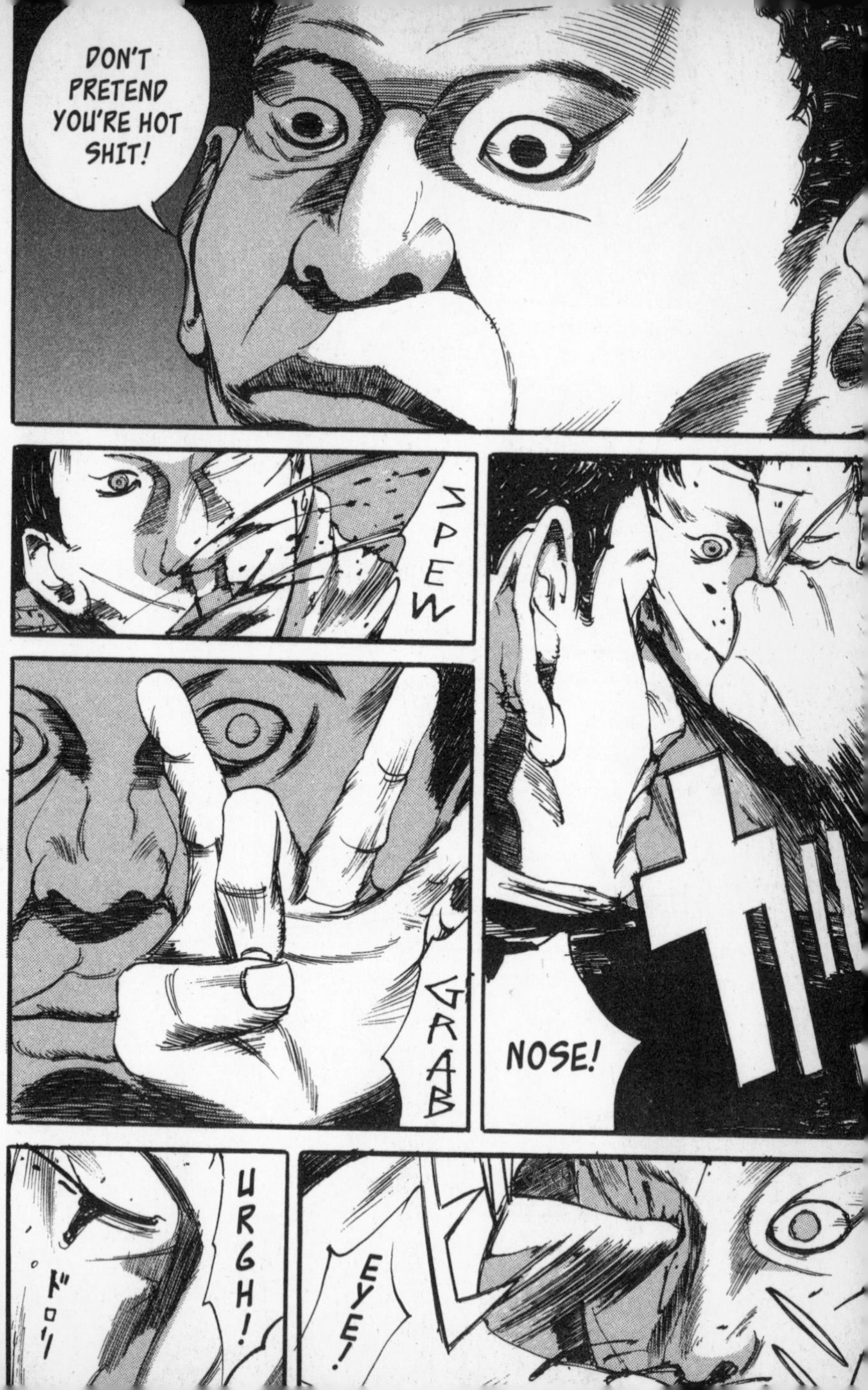
DON'T PRETEND YOU'RE HOT SHIT!
NOSE!
SPEW
GRAB
EYE!
URGH!
ドロリ

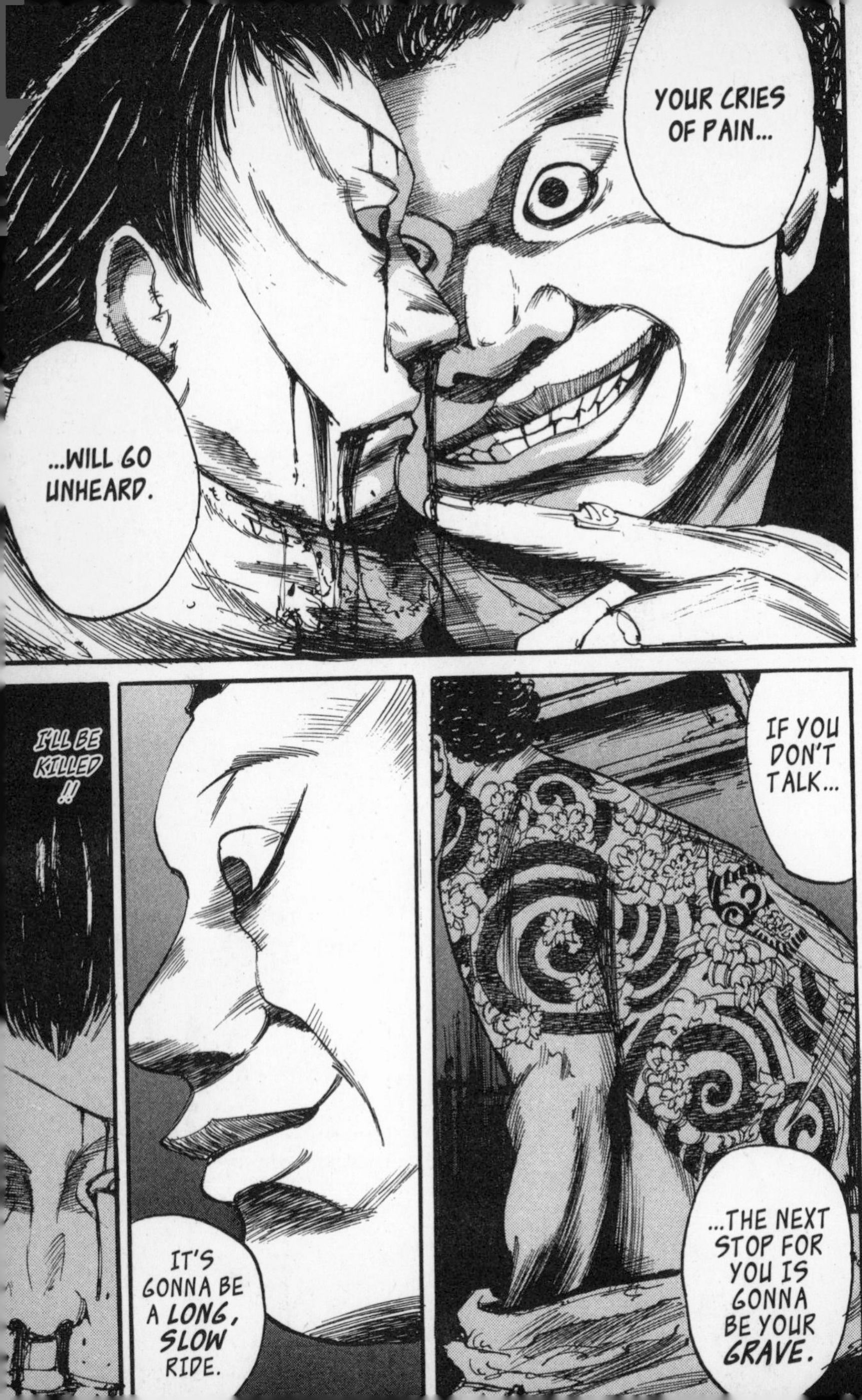
YOUR CRIES OF PAIN...
...WILL GO UNHEARD.
IF YOU DON'T TALK...
...THE NEXT STOP FOR YOU IS GONNA BE YOUR GRAVE.
IT'S GONNA BE A LONG, SLOW RIDE.
I'LL BE KILLED!!

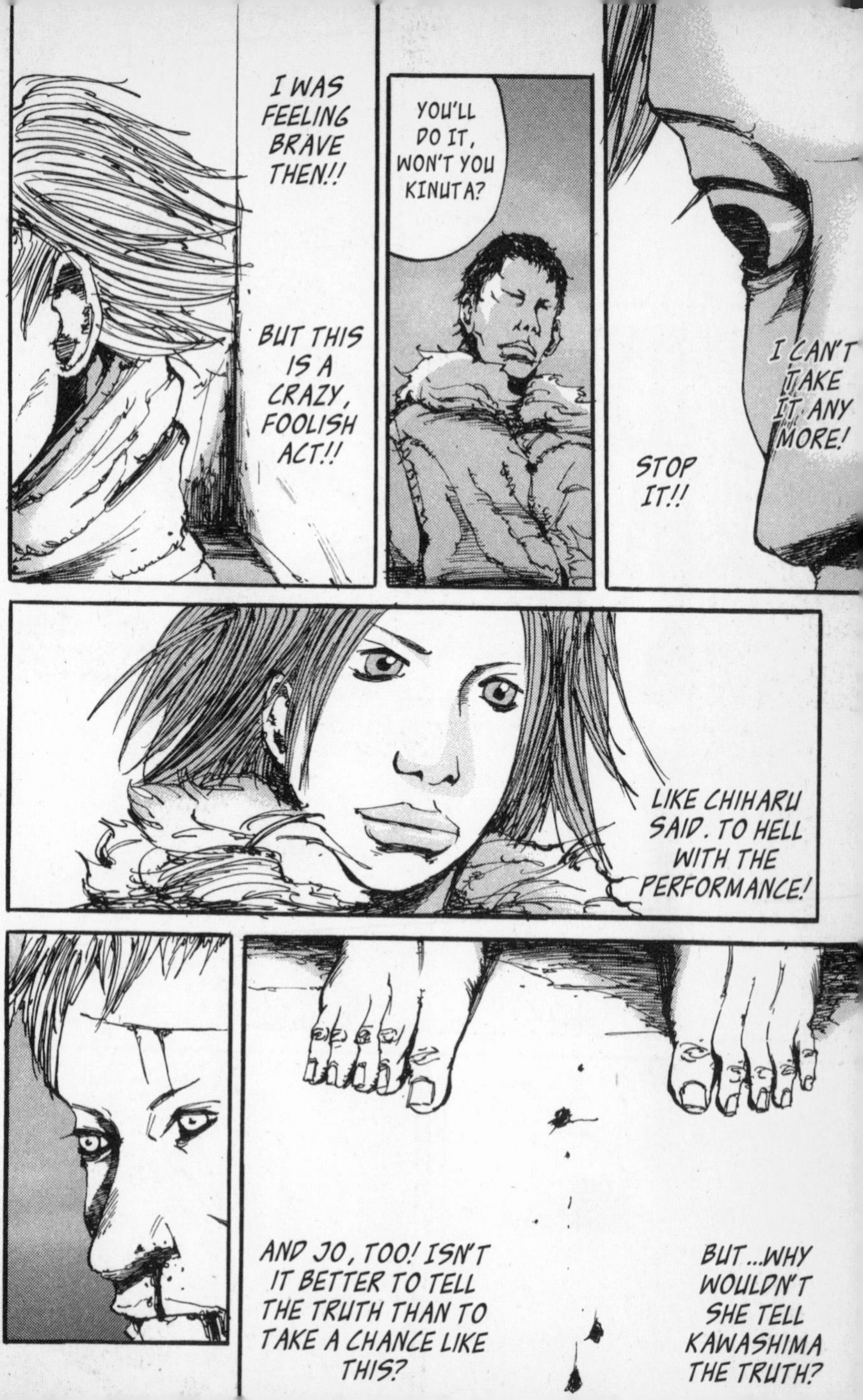
I CAN'T TAKE IT ANY MORE!
STOP IT!!
YOU'LL DO IT, WON'T YOU KINUTA?
I WAS FEELING BRAVE THEN!!
BUT THIS IS A CRAZY, FOOLISH ACT!!
LIKE CHIHARU SAID. TO HELL WITH THE PERFORMANCE!
BUT...WHY WOULDN'T SHE TELL KAWASHIMA THE TRUTH?
AND JO, TOO! ISN'T IT BETTER TO TELL THE TRUTH THAN TO TAKE A CHANCE LIKE THIS?

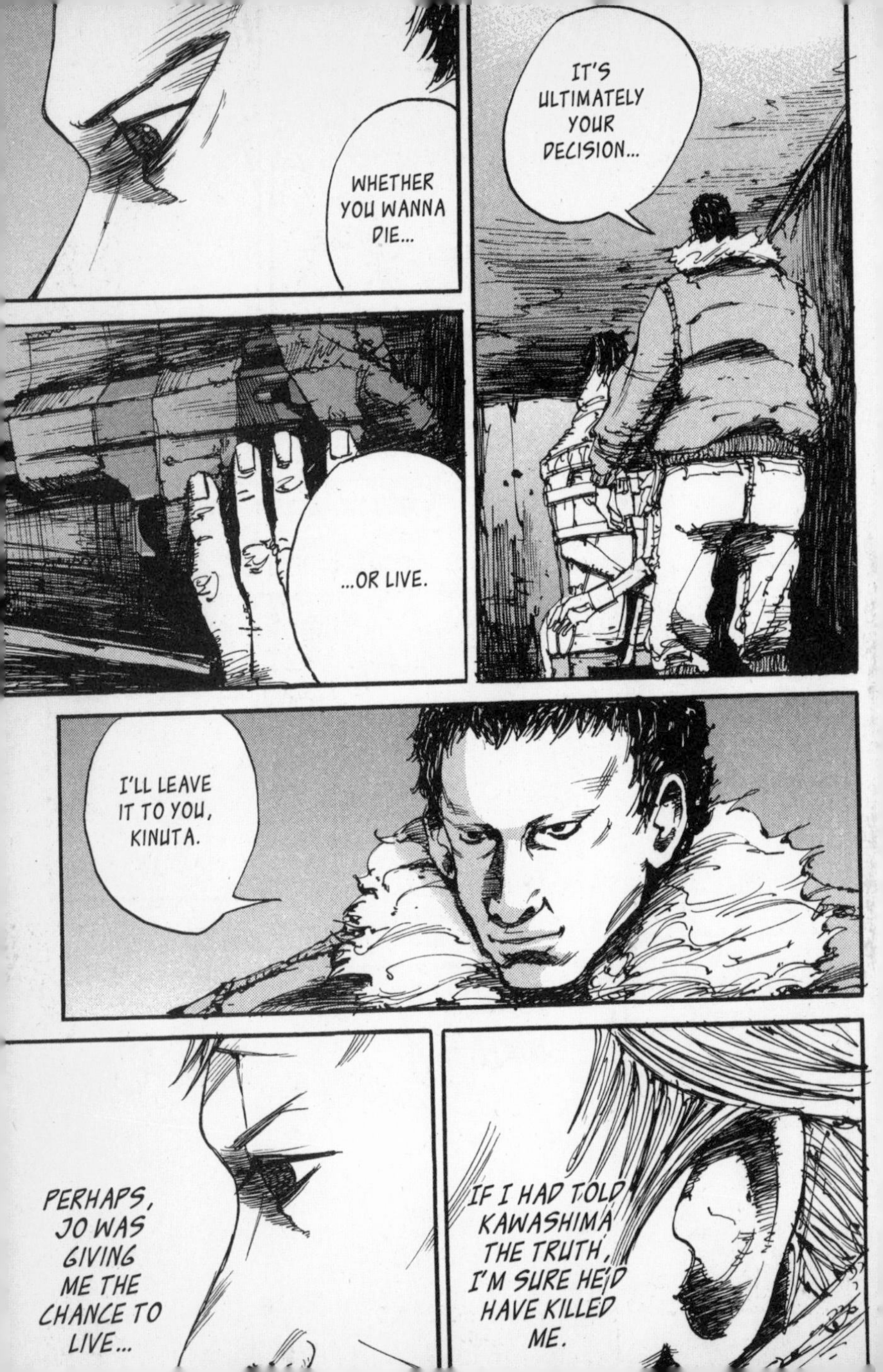
IT'S ULTIMATELY YOUR DECISION...
WHETHER YOU WANNA DIE...
...OR LIVE.
I'LL LEAVE IT TO YOU, KINUTA.
IF I HAD TOLD KAWASHIMA THE TRUTH, I'M SURE HE'D HAVE KILLED ME.
PERHAPS, JO WAS GIVING ME THE CHANCE TO LIVE...

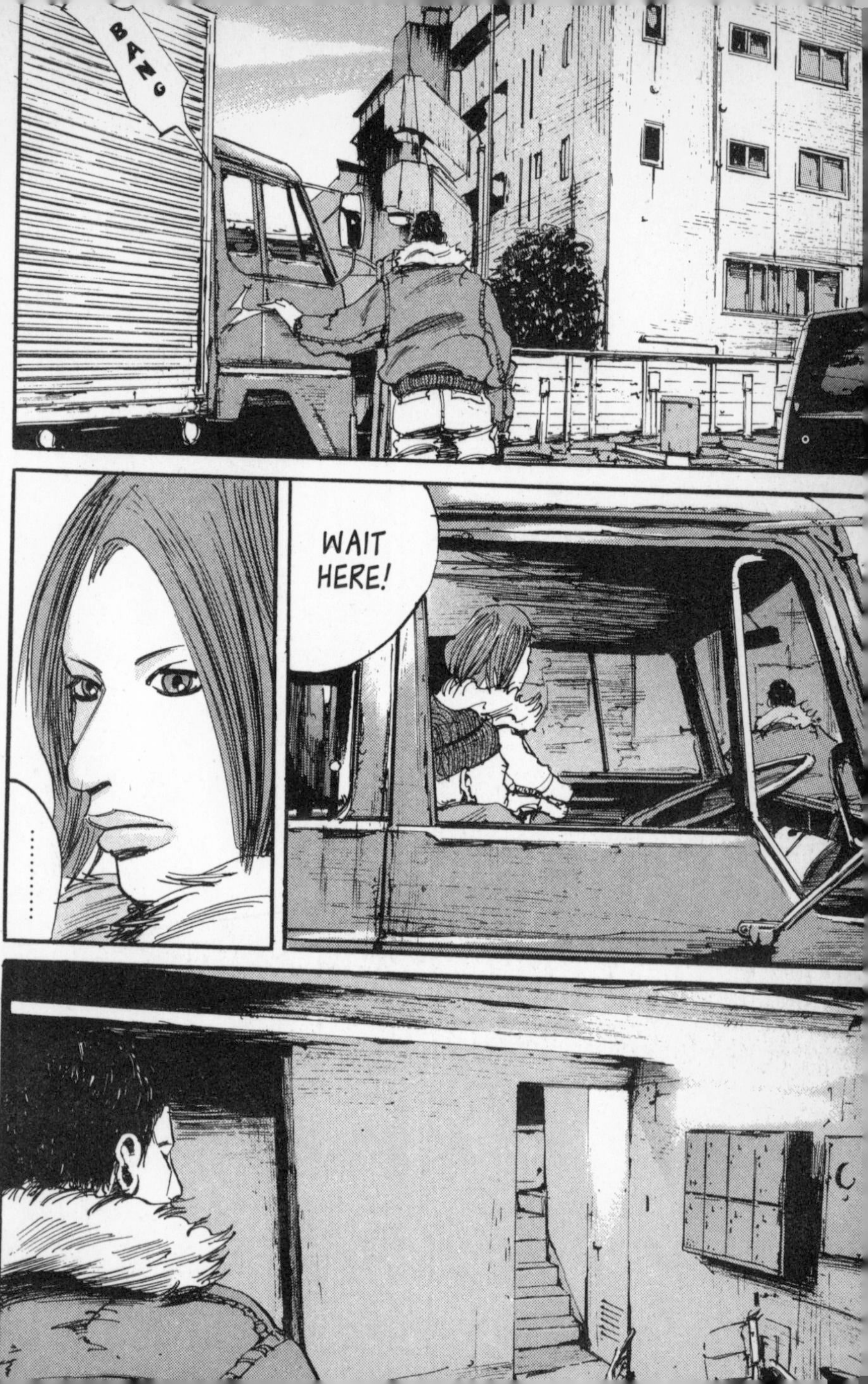
BANG
WAIT HERE!
......

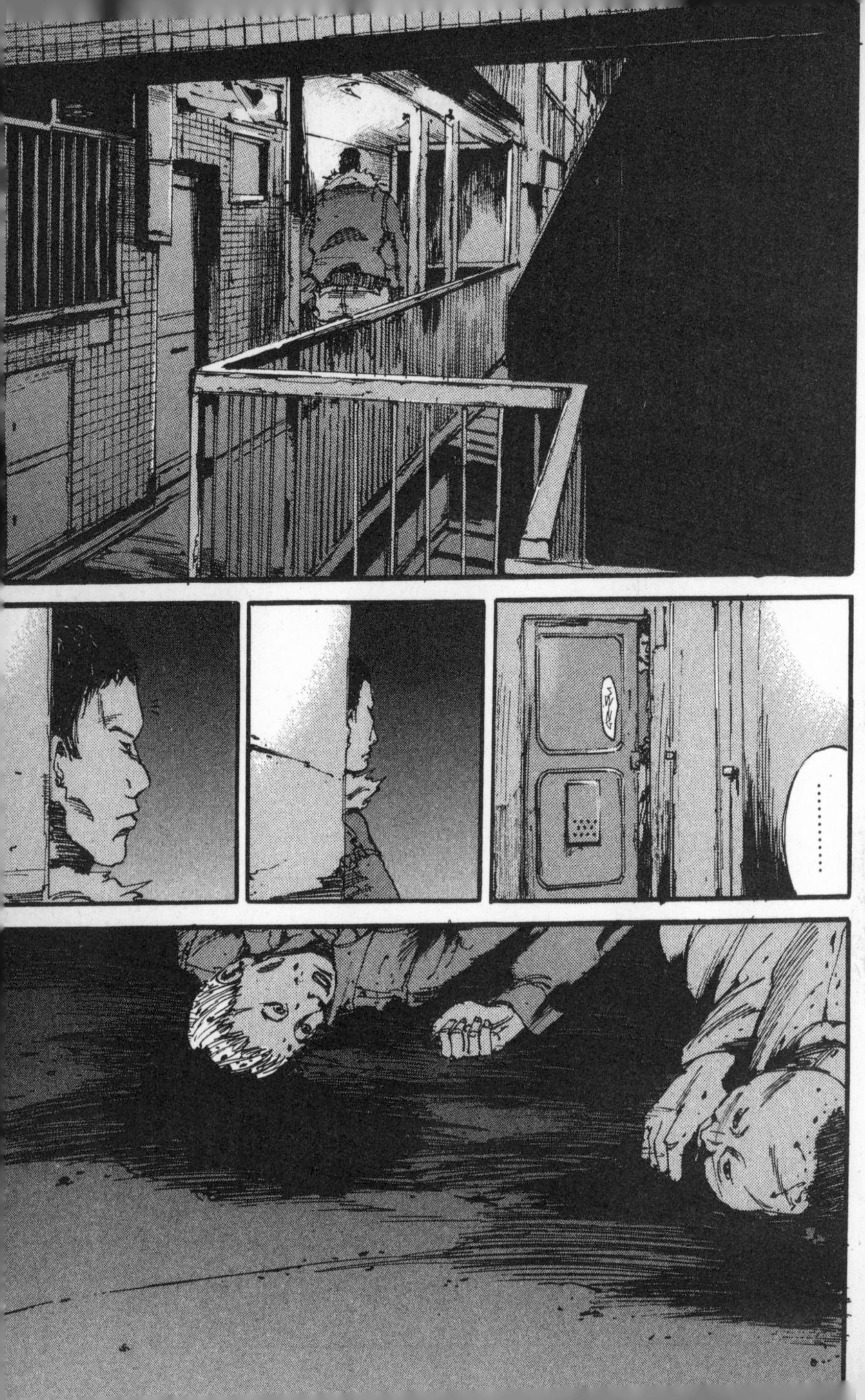
SWING
....

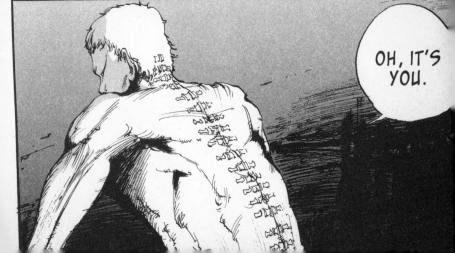

OH, IT'S
YOU.

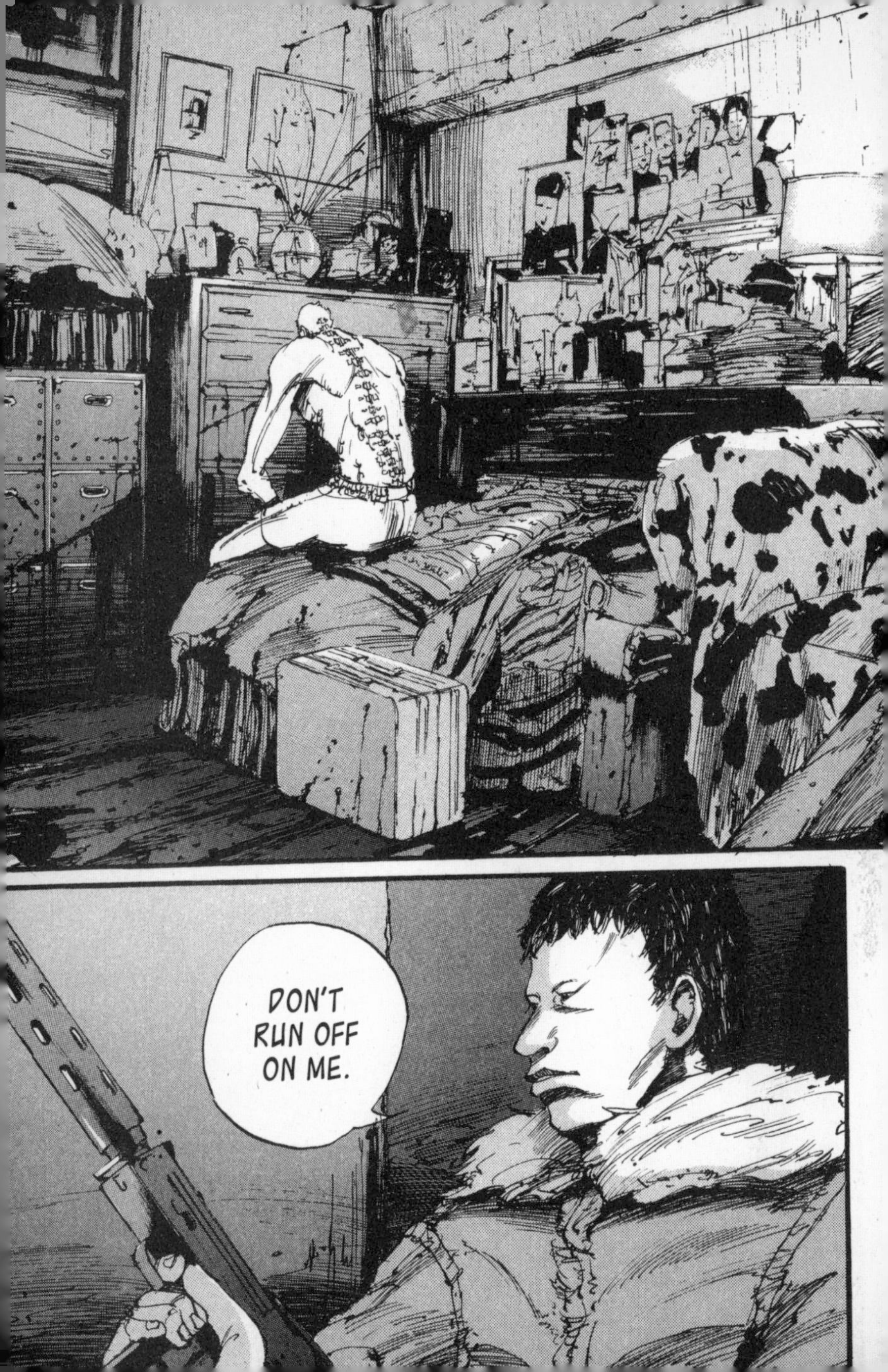
DON'T RUN OFF ON ME.

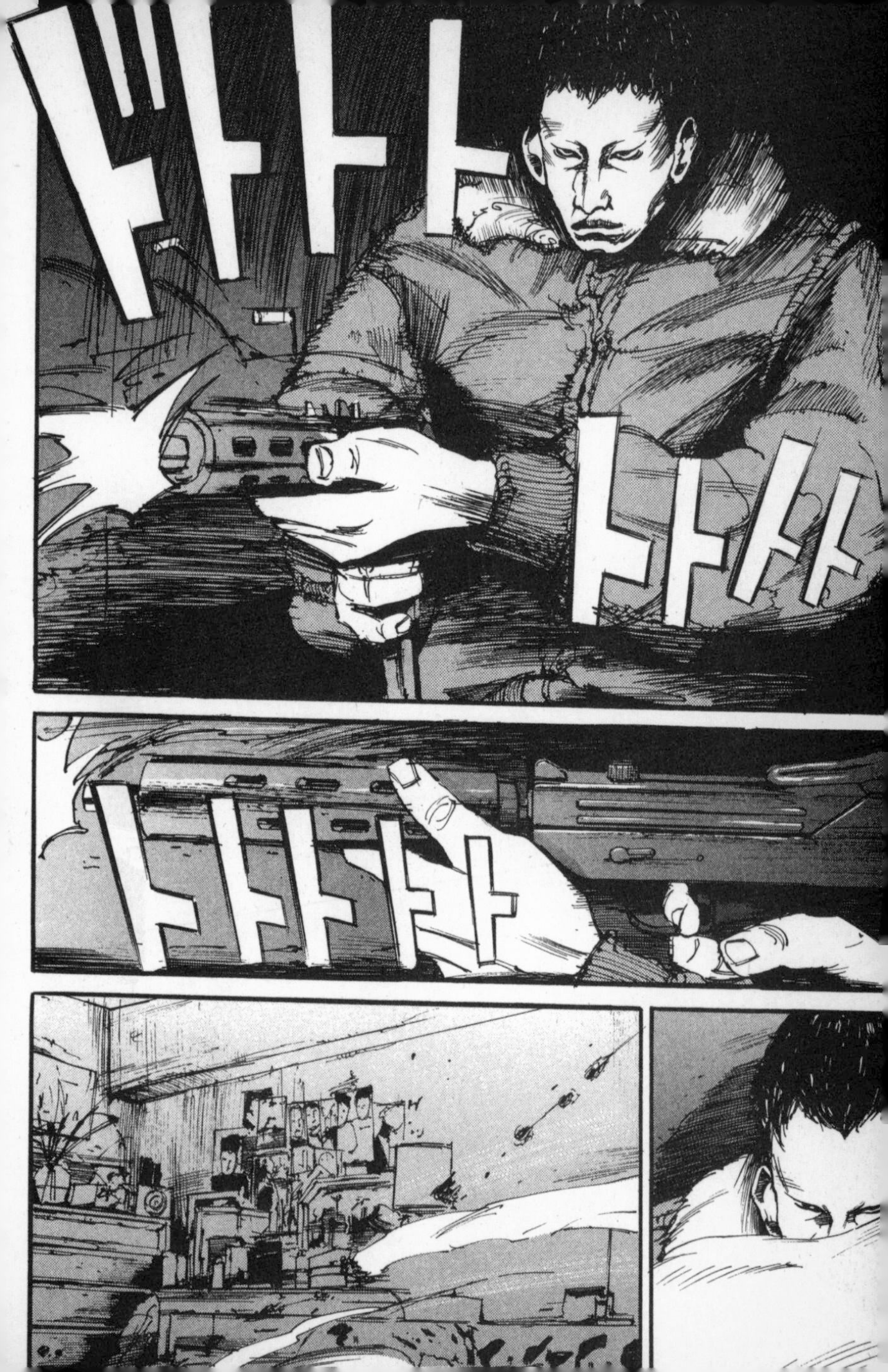
ドトトト
トトトト
トトトトト

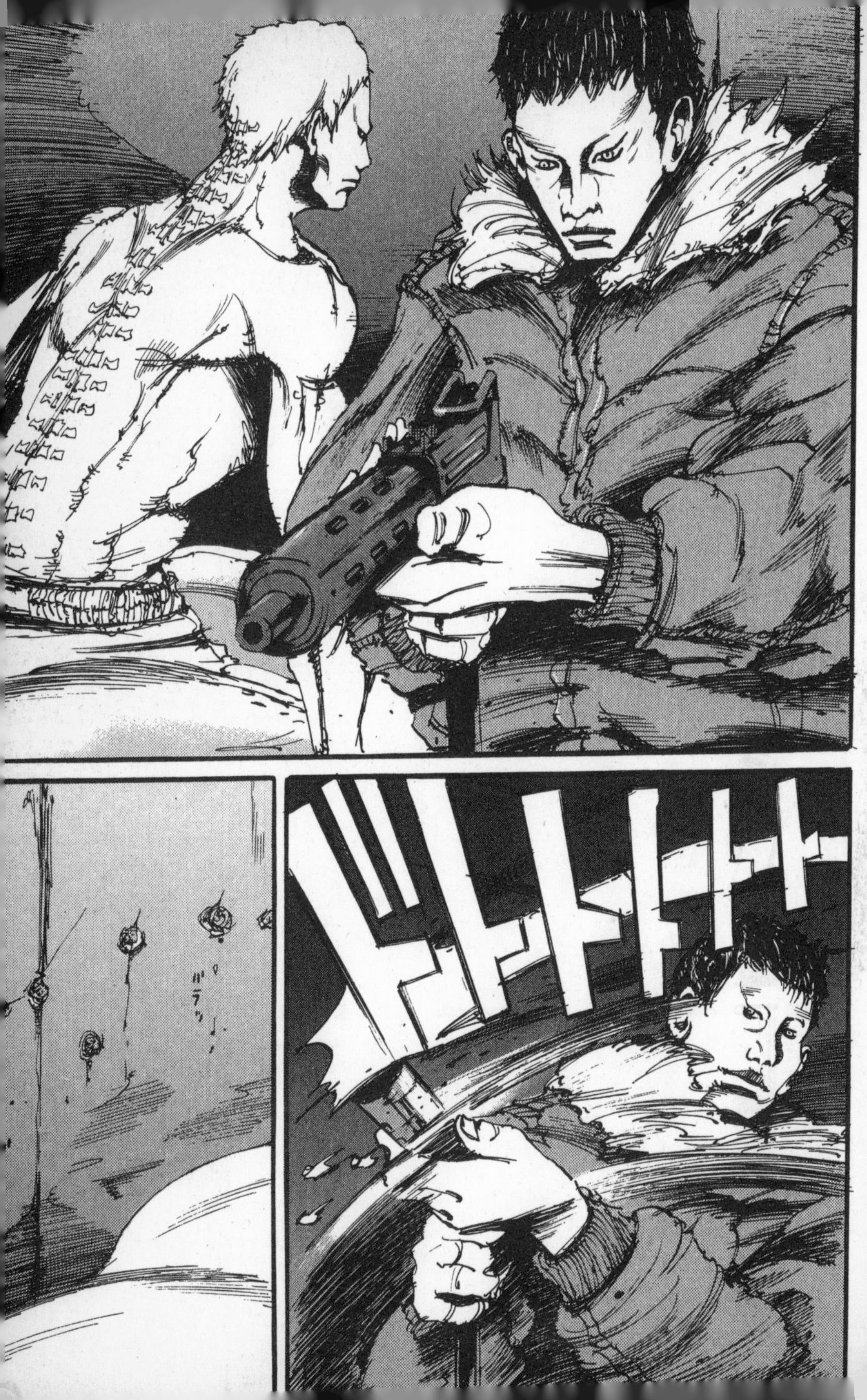
ドドドドドドドー
パラッ

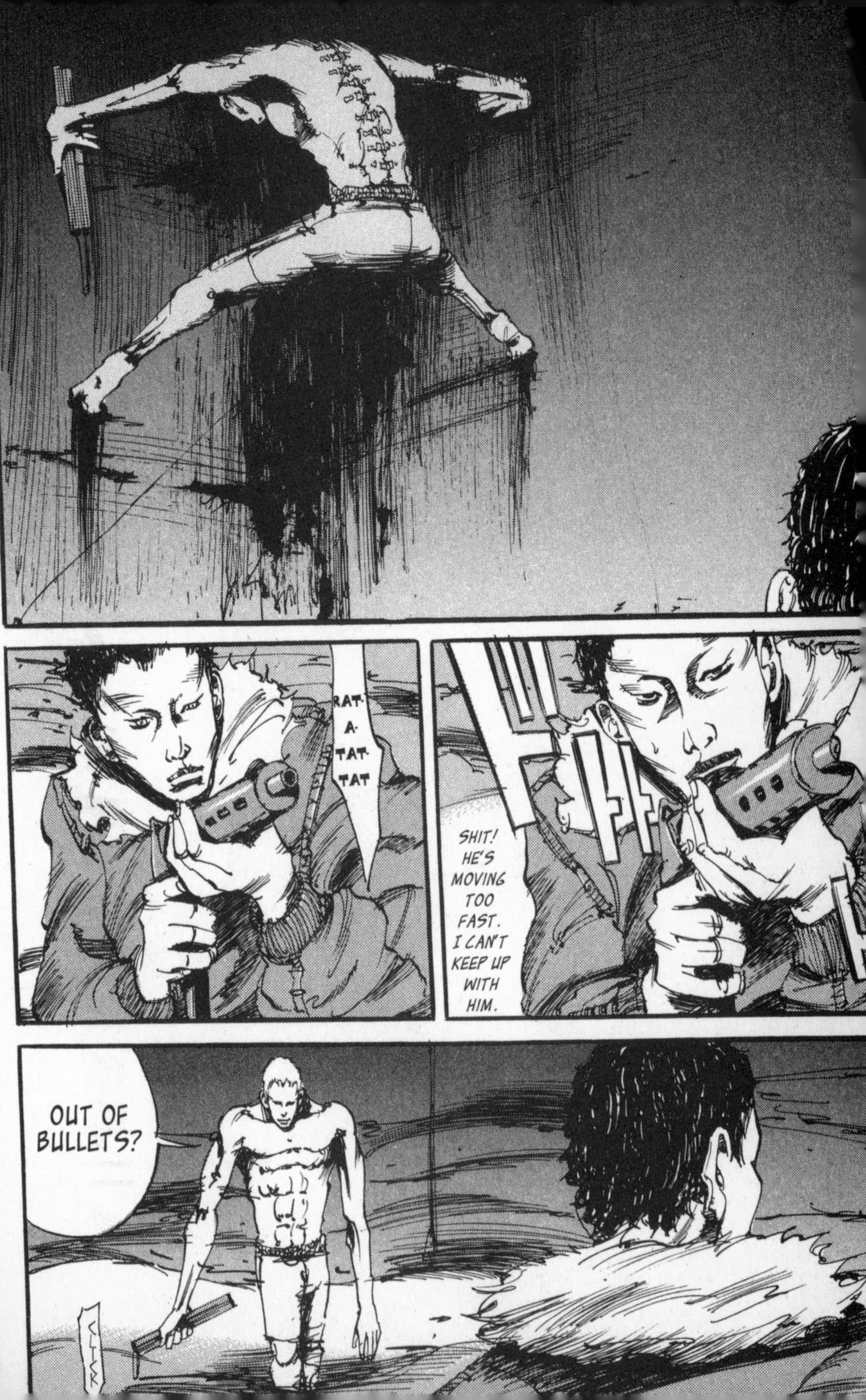
SHIT! HE'S MOVING TOO FAST. I CAN'T KEEP UP WITH HIM.
RAT-A-TAT-TAT
OUT OF BULLETS?
CLICK

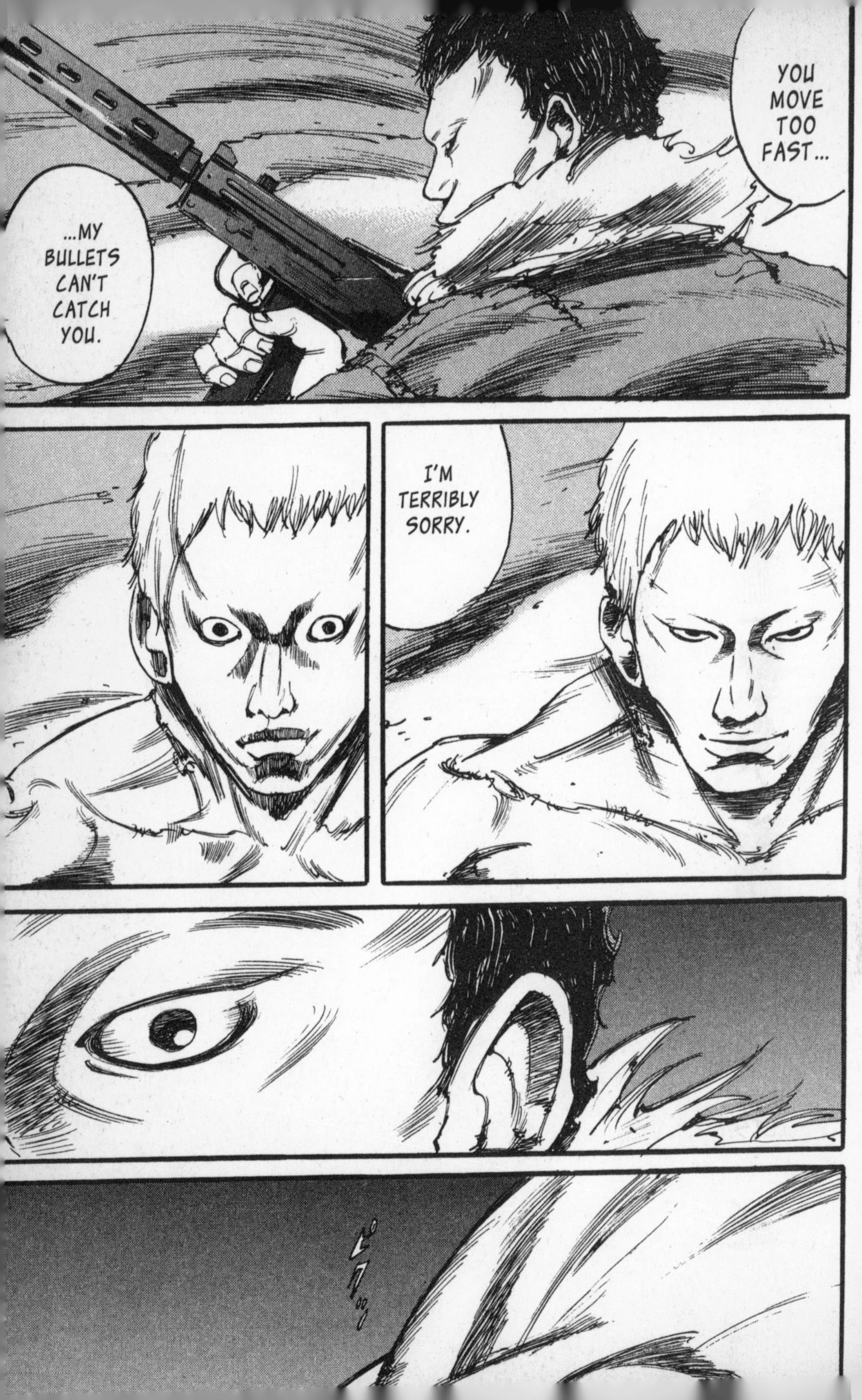
YOU MOVE TOO FAST...
...MY BULLETS CAN'T CATCH YOU.
I'M TERRIBLY SORRY.

SLASH

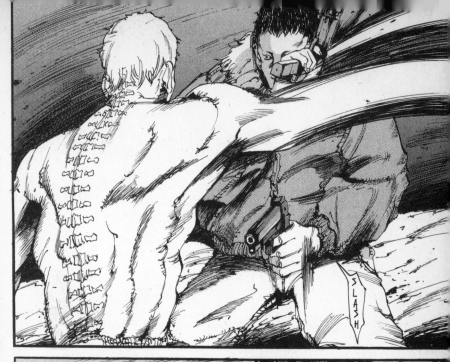

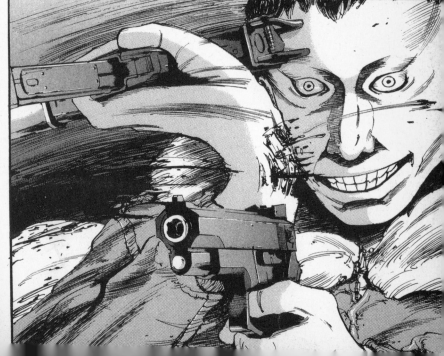

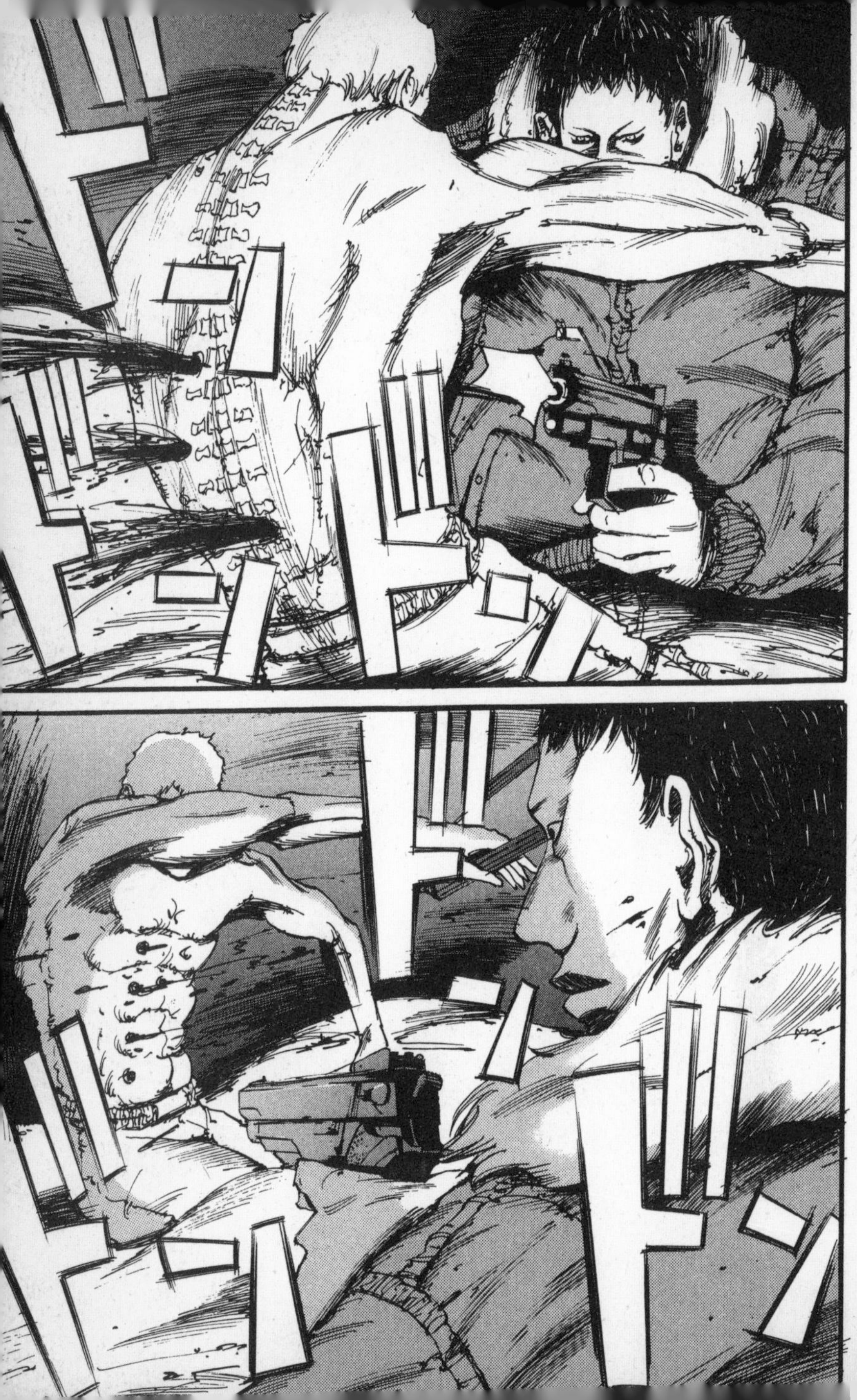

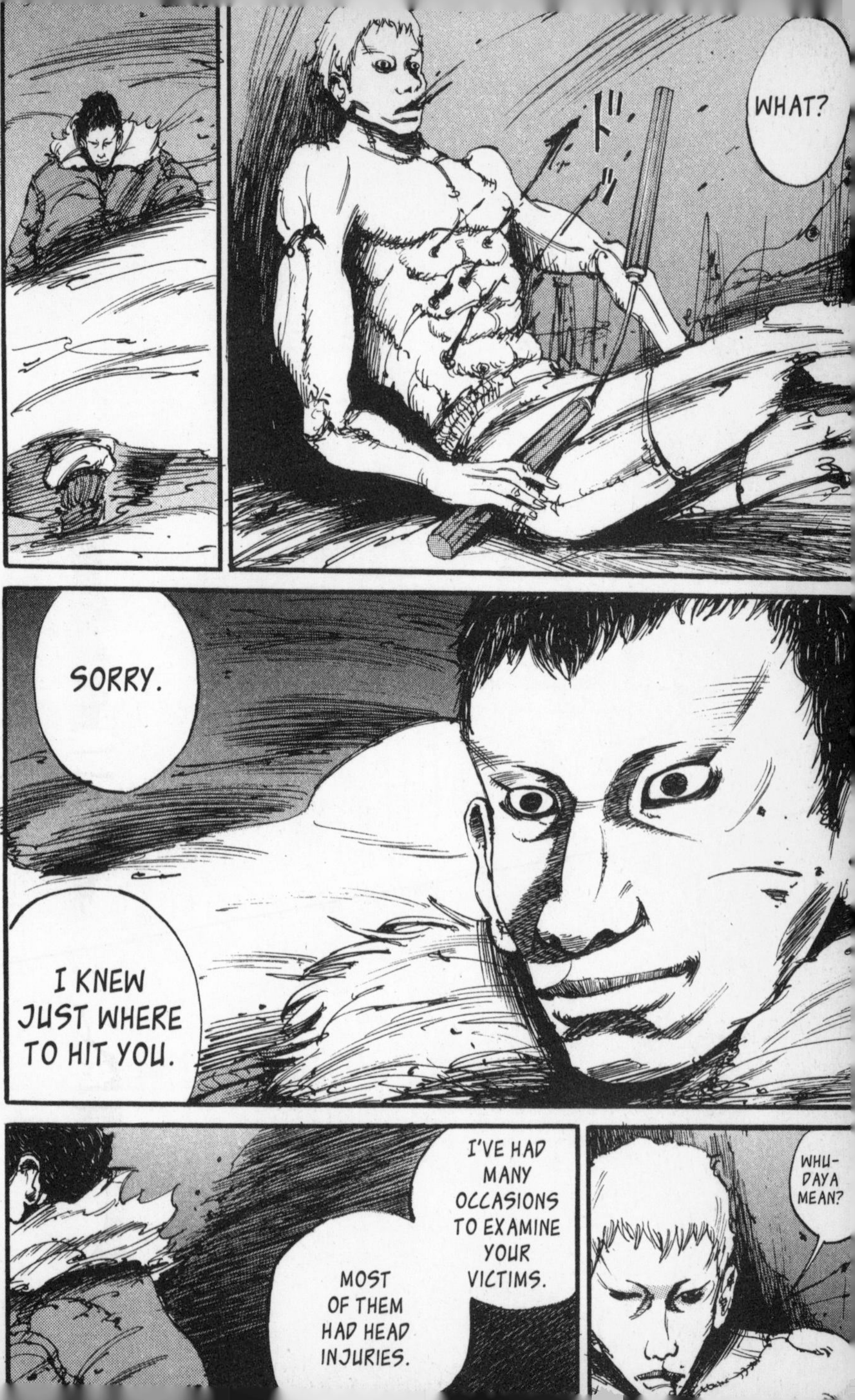
WHAT?
ドッ
SORRY.
I KNEW JUST WHERE TO HIT YOU.
WHU-DAYA MEAN?
I'VE HAD MANY OCCASIONS TO EXAMINE YOUR VICTIMS.
MOST OF THEM HAD HEAD INJURIES.

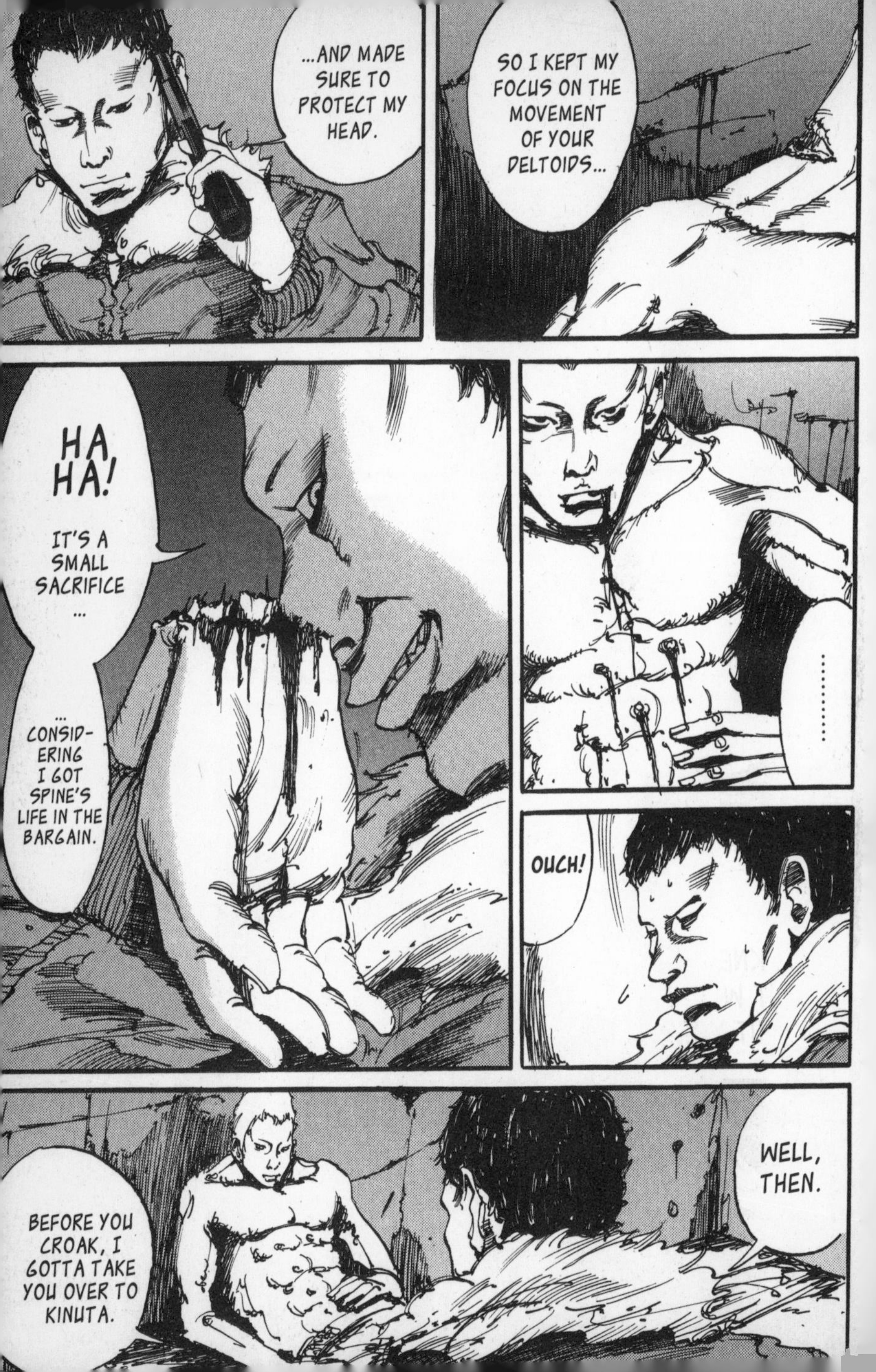
SO I KEPT MY FOCUS ON THE MOVEMENT OF YOUR DELTOIDS...
...AND MADE SURE TO PROTECT MY HEAD.
......
OUCH!
HA HA!
IT'S A SMALL SACRIFICE ...
... CONSID-ERING I GOT SPINE'S LIFE IN THE BARGAIN.
WELL, THEN.
BEFORE YOU CROAK, I GOTTA TAKE YOU OVER TO KINUTA.

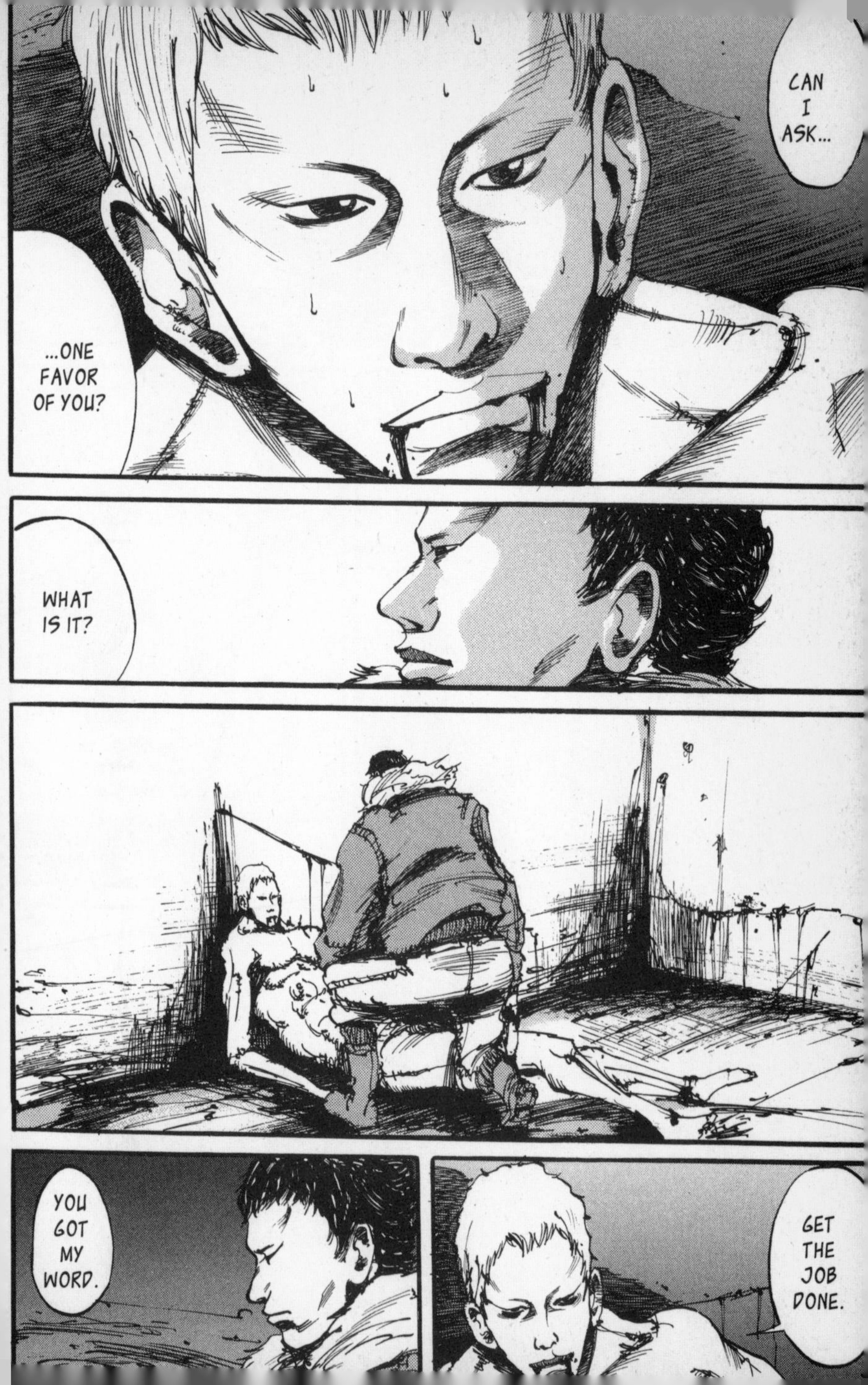
CAN I ASK...
...ONE FAVOR OF YOU?
WHAT IS IT?
GET THE JOB DONE.
YOU GOT MY WORD.

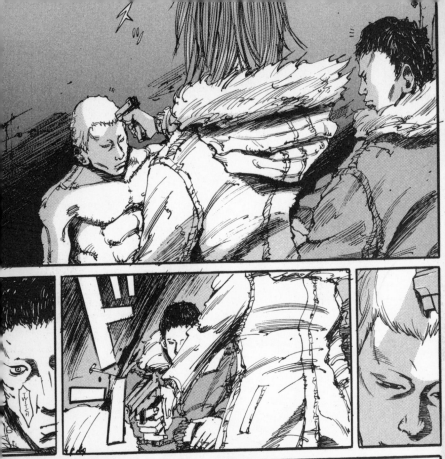

WAS
THAT YOUR
PAYBACK
FOR
KODAMA?

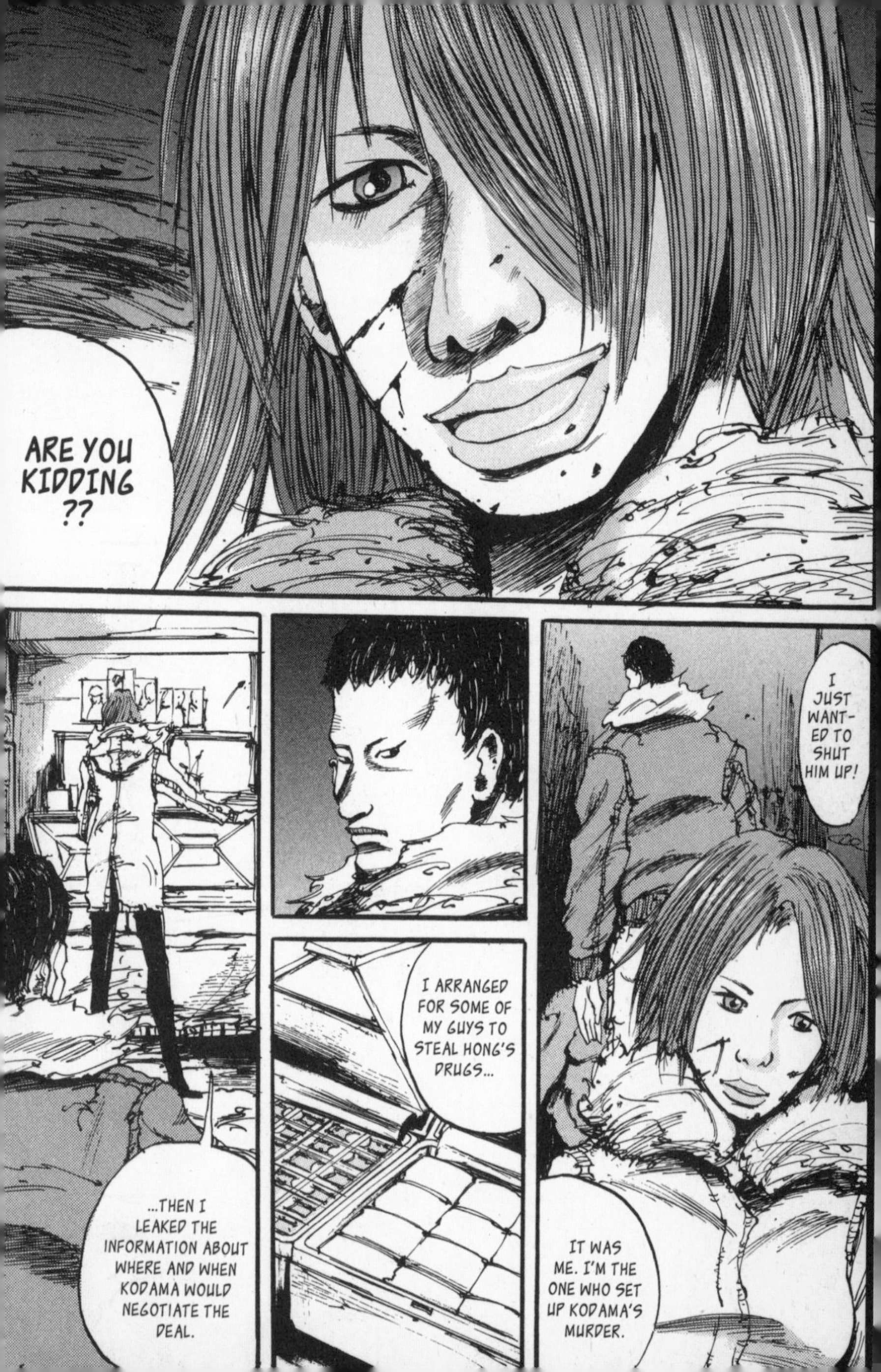
ARE YOU KIDDING ??
I JUST WANTED TO SHUT HIM UP!
IT WAS ME. I'M THE ONE WHO SET UP KODAMA'S MURDER.
I ARRANGED FOR SOME OF MY GUYS TO STEAL HONG'S DRUGS...
...THEN I LEAKED THE INFORMATION ABOUT WHERE AND WHEN KODAMA WOULD NEGOTIATE THE DEAL.

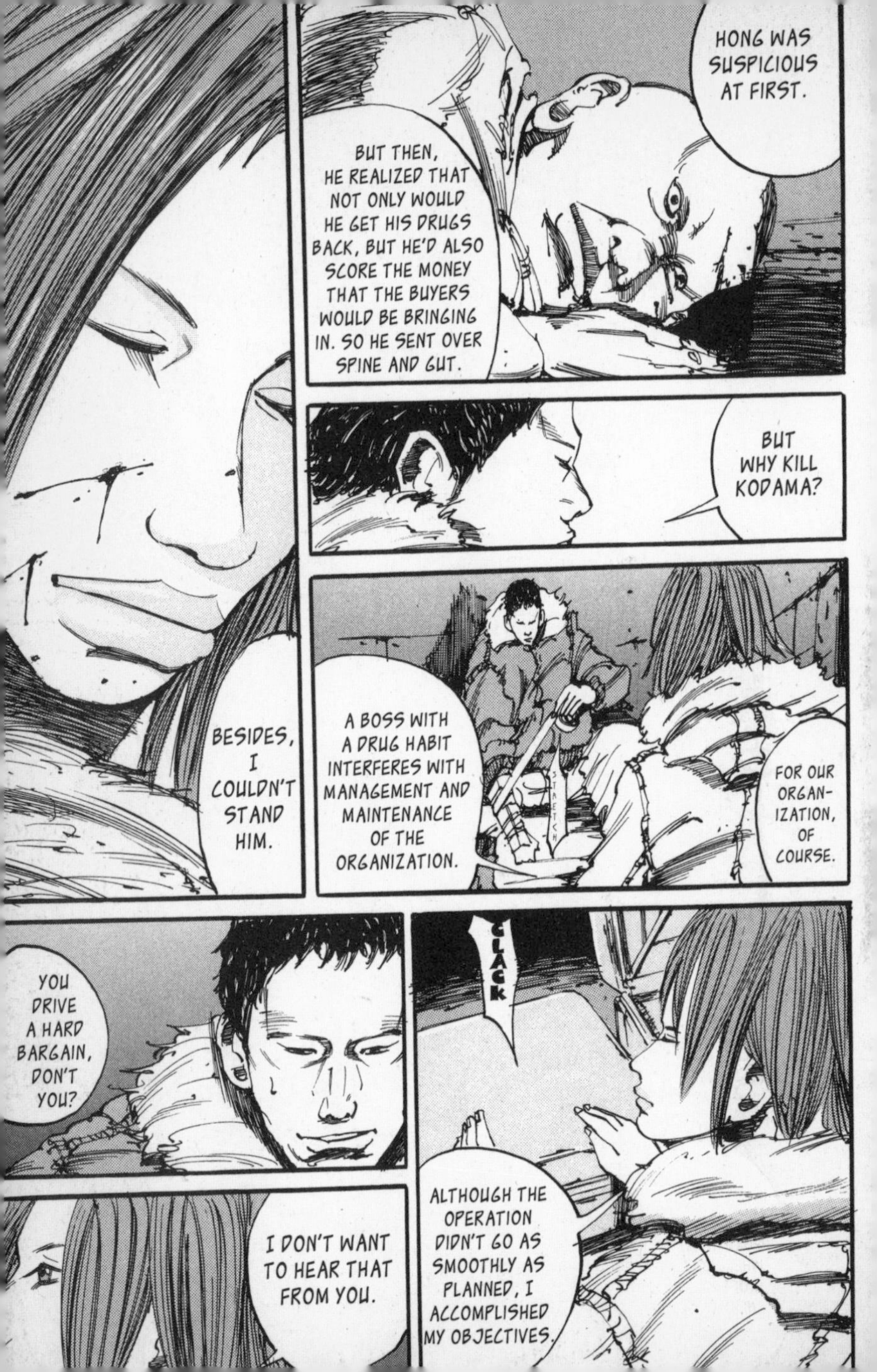
HONG WAS SUSPICIOUS AT FIRST.
BUT THEN, HE REALIZED THAT NOT ONLY WOULD HE GET HIS DRUGS BACK, BUT HE'D ALSO SCORE THE MONEY THAT THE BUYERS WOULD BE BRINGING IN. SO HE SENT OVER SPINE AND GUT.
BUT WHY KILL KODAMA?
FOR OUR ORGANIZATION, OF COURSE.
STRETCH
A BOSS WITH A DRUG HABIT INTERFERES WITH MANAGEMENT AND MAINTENANCE OF THE ORGANIZATION.
BESIDES, I COULDN'T STAND HIM.
CLACK
ALTHOUGH THE OPERATION DIDN'T GO AS SMOOTHLY AS PLANNED, I ACCOMPLISHED MY OBJECTIVES.
YOU DRIVE A HARD BARGAIN, DON'T YOU?
I DON'T WANT TO HEAR THAT FROM YOU.

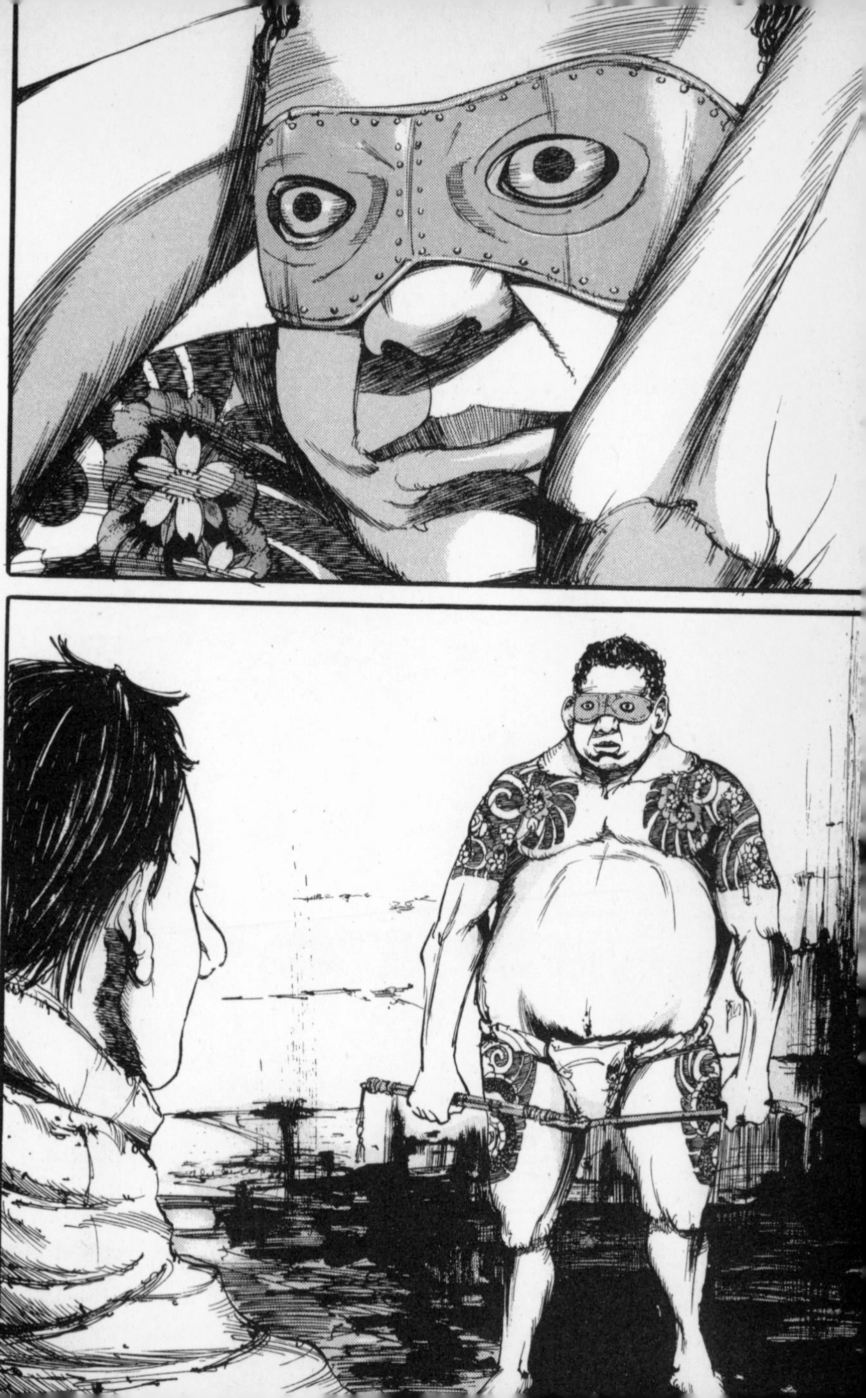

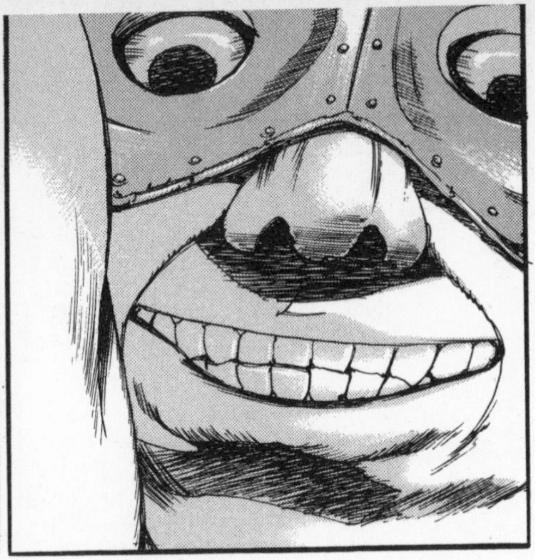

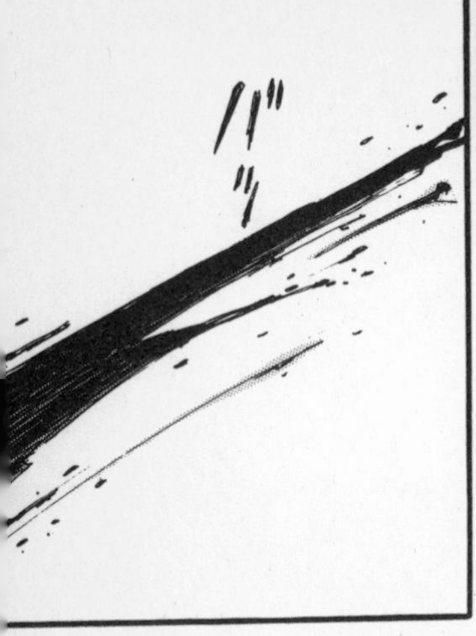

I BELIEVED IN MY POTENTIAL.

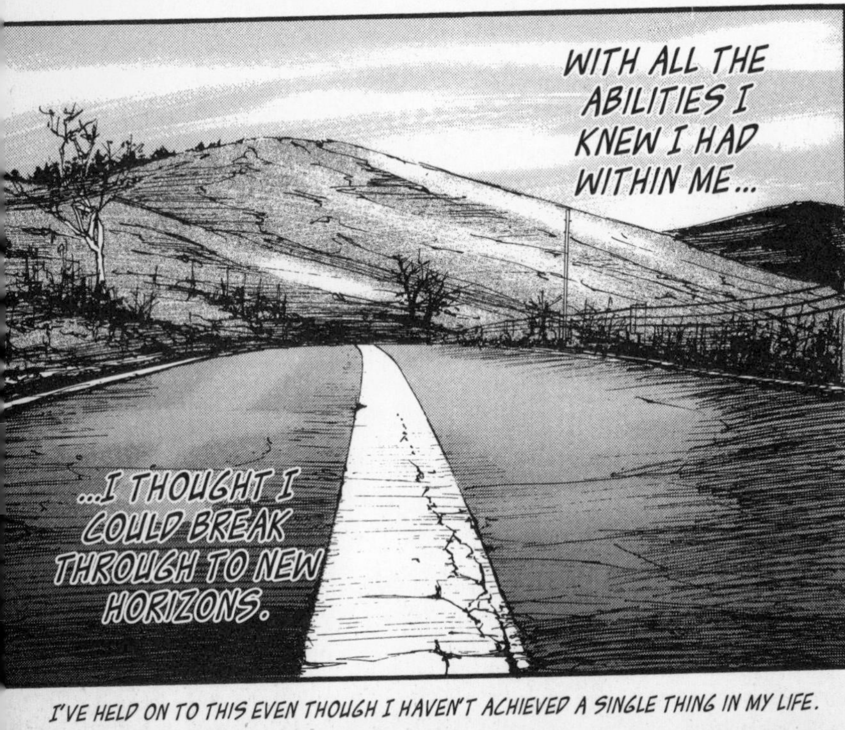
WITH ALL THE ABILITIES I KNEW I HAD WITHIN ME...
...I THOUGHT I COULD BREAK THROUGH TO NEW HORIZONS.

I'VE HELD ON TO THIS EVEN THOUGH I HAVEN'T ACHIEVED A SINGLE THING IN MY LIFE.

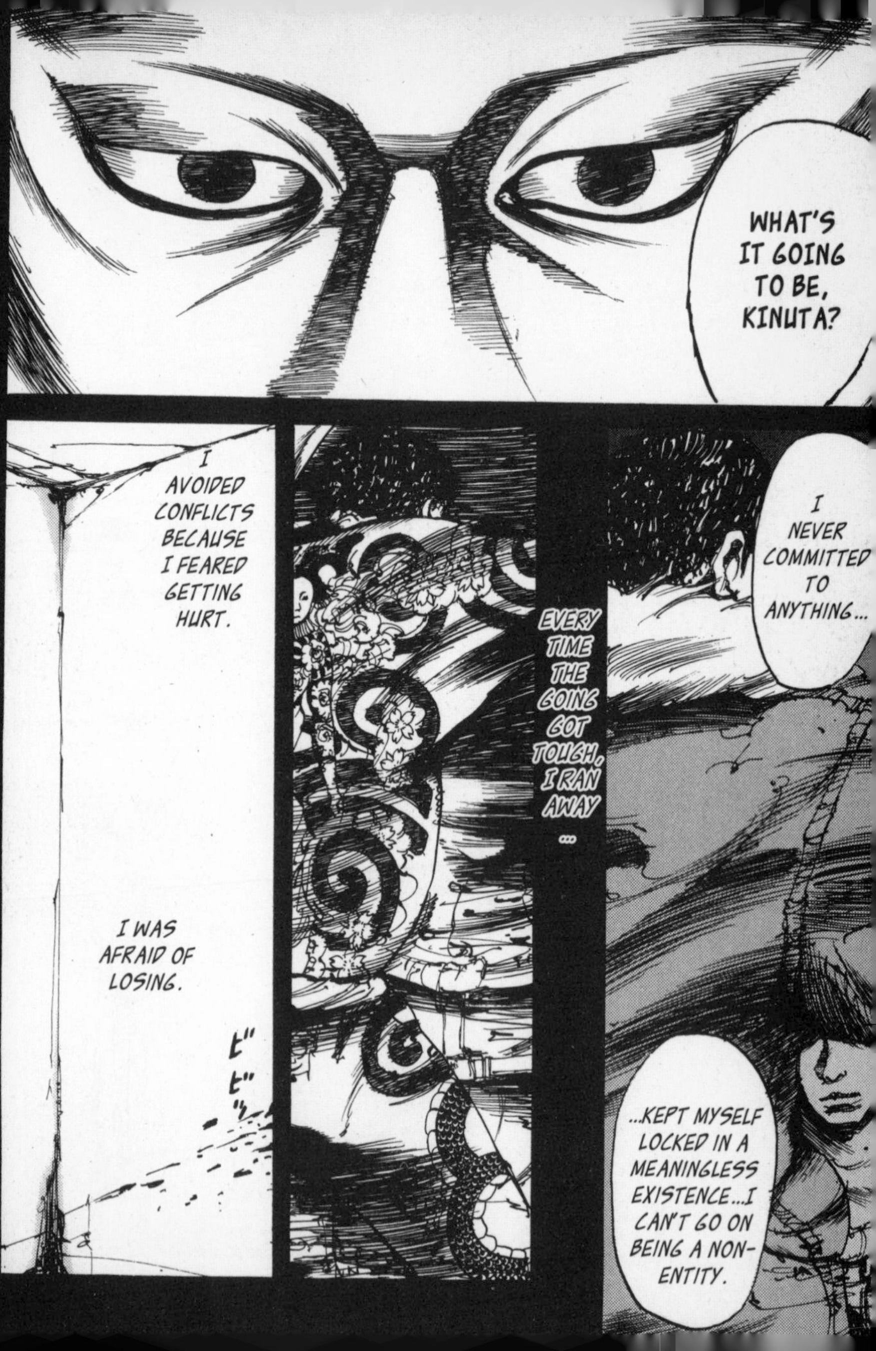
WHAT'S IT GOING TO BE, KINUTA?
I NEVER COMMITTED TO ANYTHING...
...KEPT MYSELF LOCKED IN A MEANINGLESS EXISTENCE...I CAN'T GO ON BEING A NON-ENTITY.
EVERY TIME THE GOING GOT TOUGH, I RAN AWAY ...
I AVOIDED CONFLICTS BECAUSE I FEARED GETTING HURT.
I WAS AFRAID OF LOSING.
ビビッ

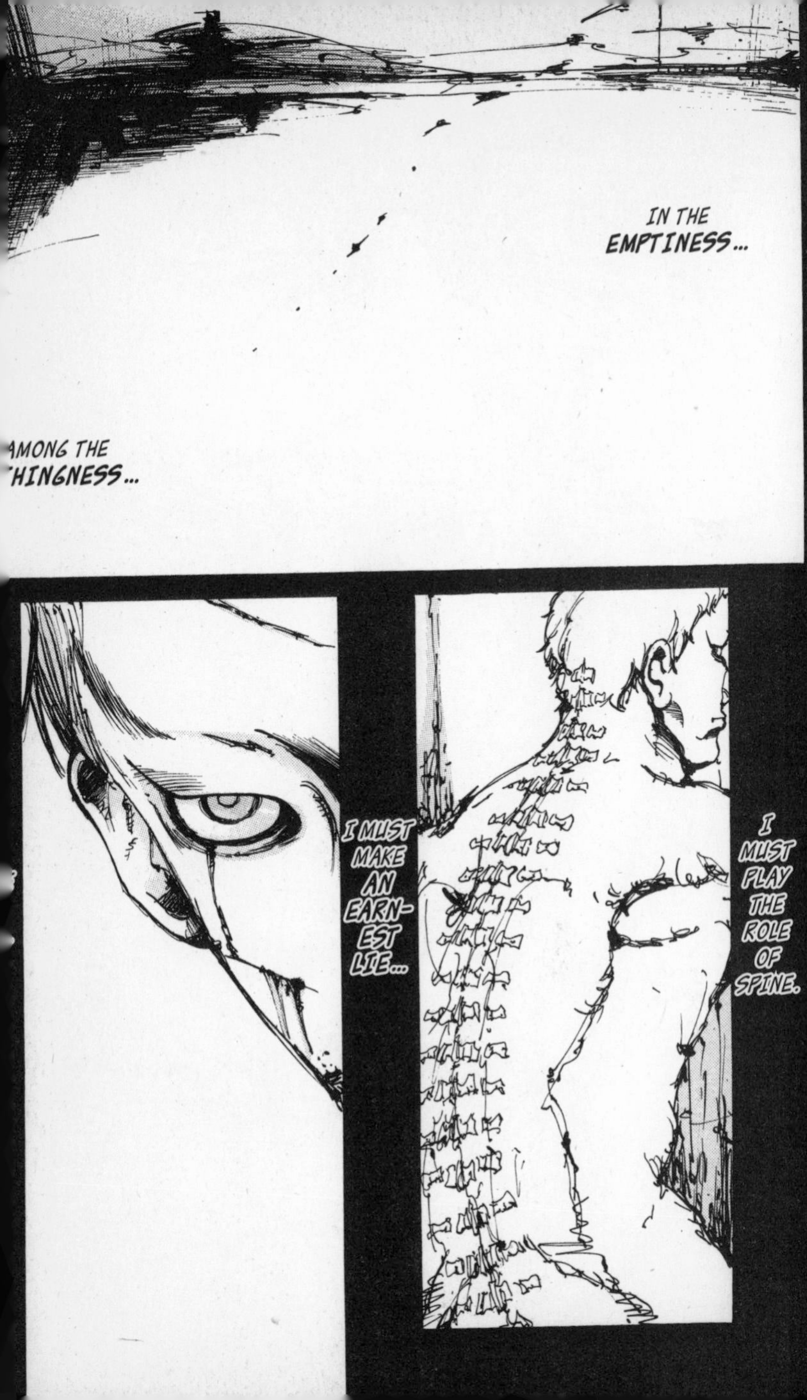
IN THE EMPTINESS...
AMONG THE THINGNESS...
I MUST PLAY THE ROLE OF SPINE.
I MUST MAKE AN EARNEST LIE...

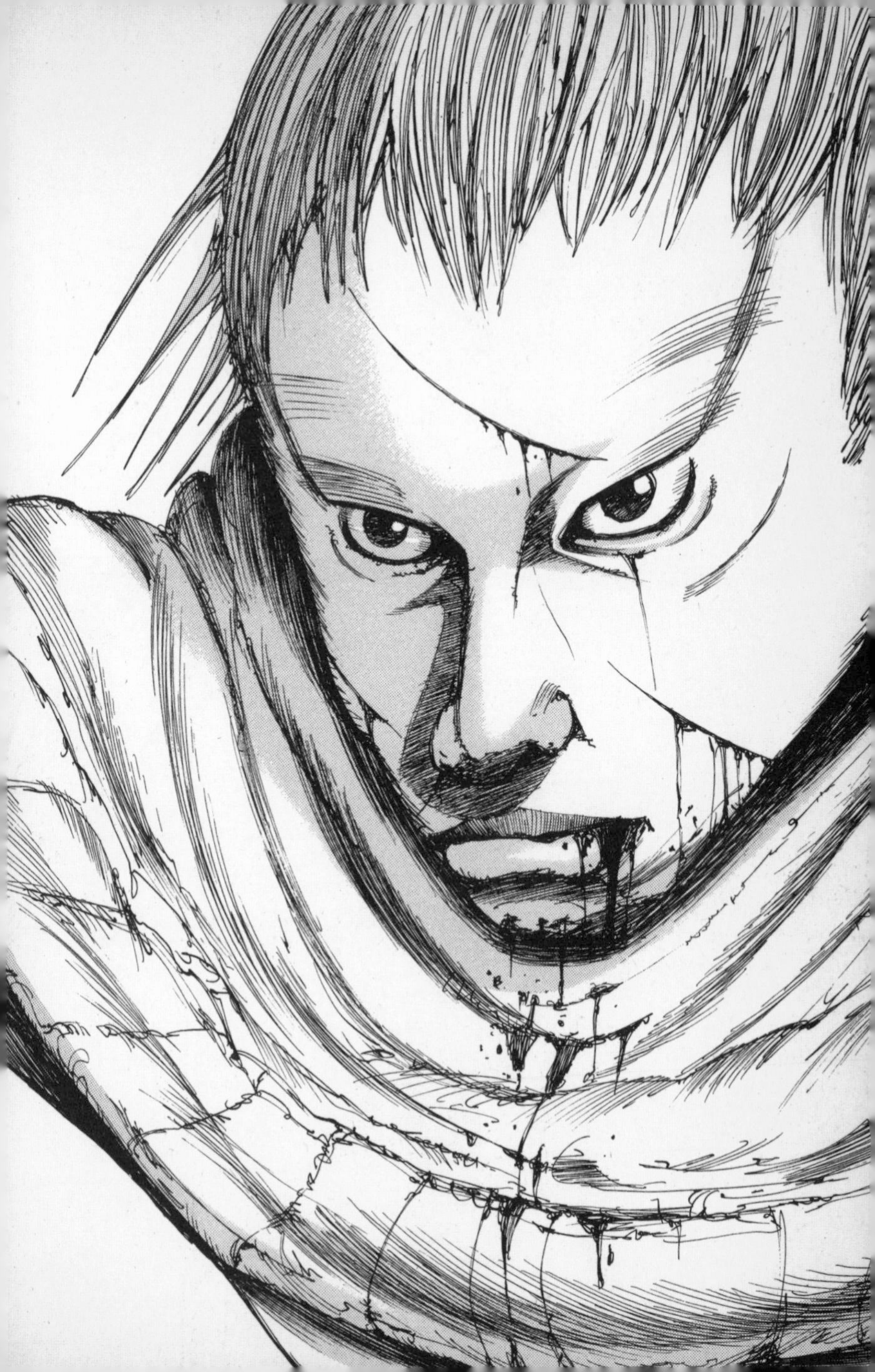

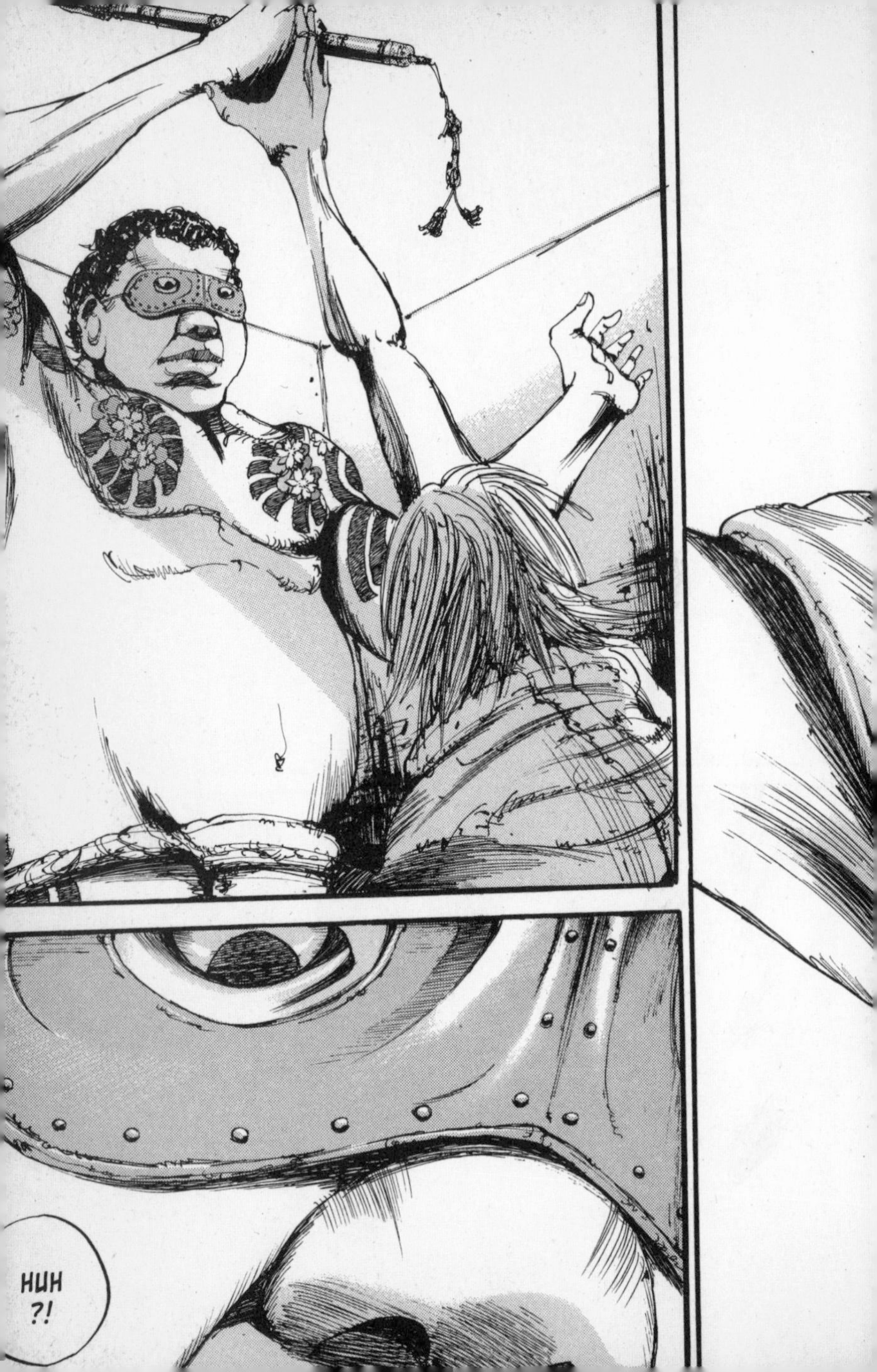
HUH
?!

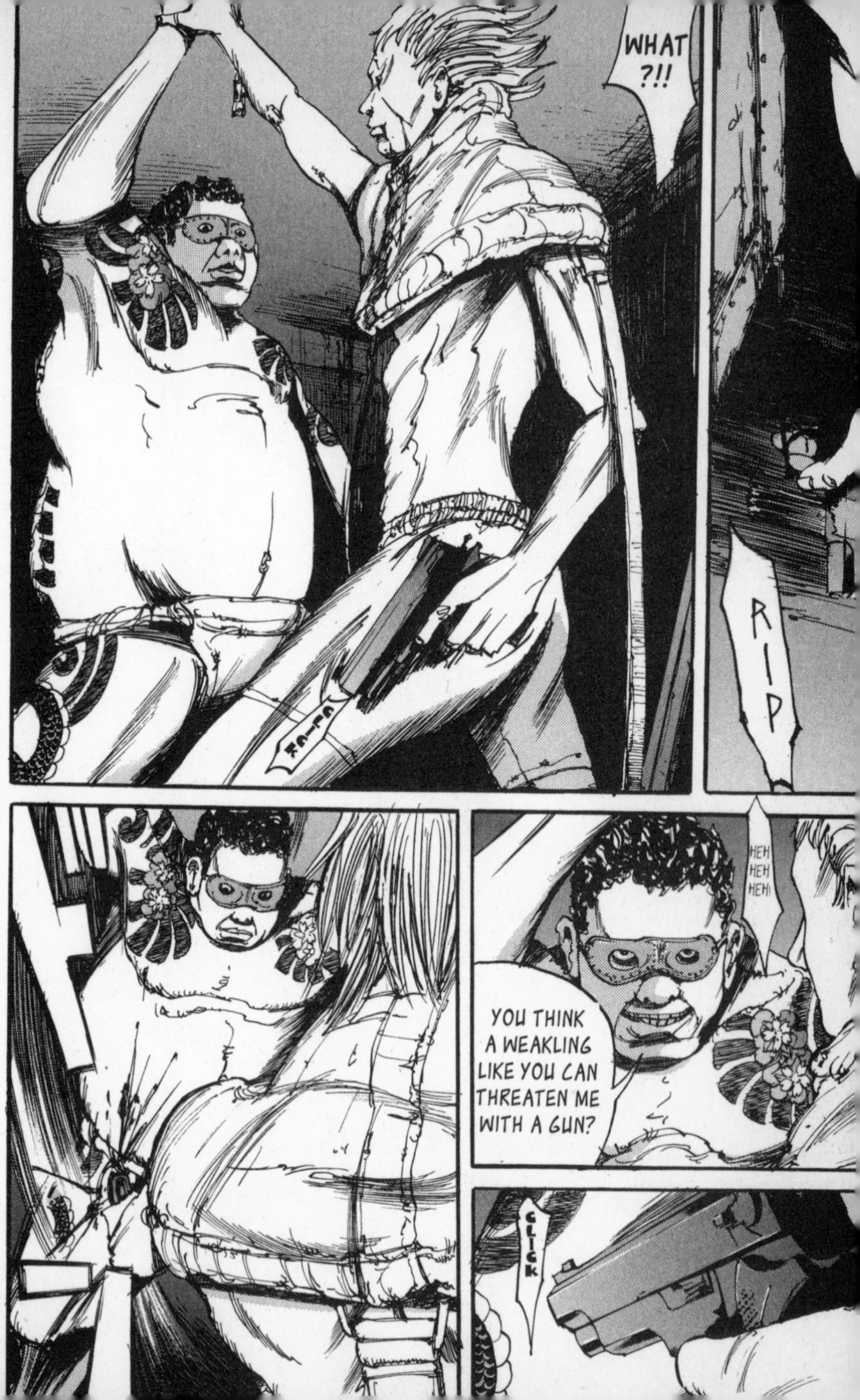
RIP
WHAT ?!!
HEH HEH HEH
YOU THINK A WEAKLING LIKE YOU CAN THREATEN ME WITH A GUN?
CLICK

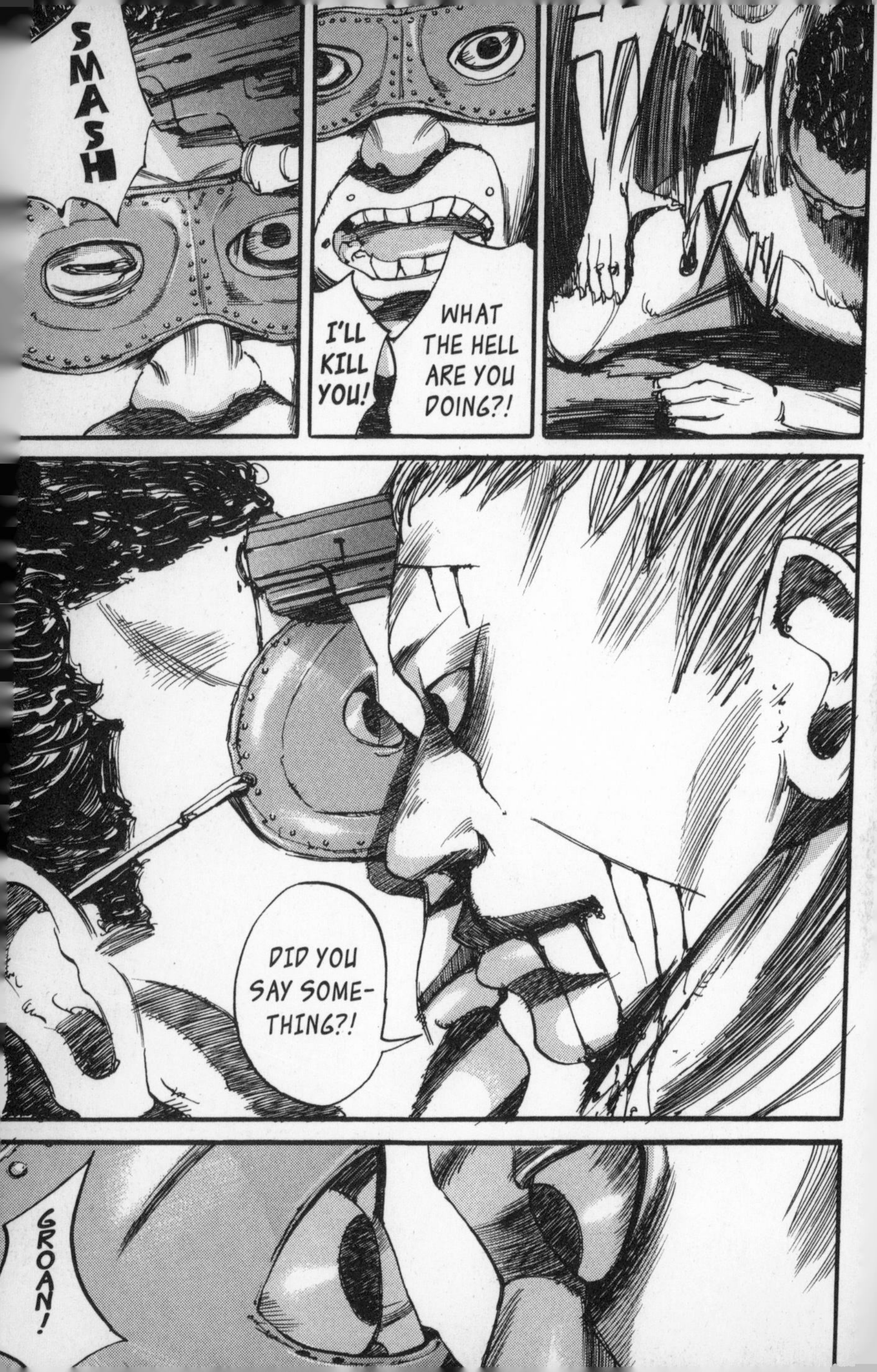
WHAT THE HELL ARE YOU DOING?!
I'LL KILL YOU!
SMASH
DID YOU SAY SOME-THING?!
GROAN!

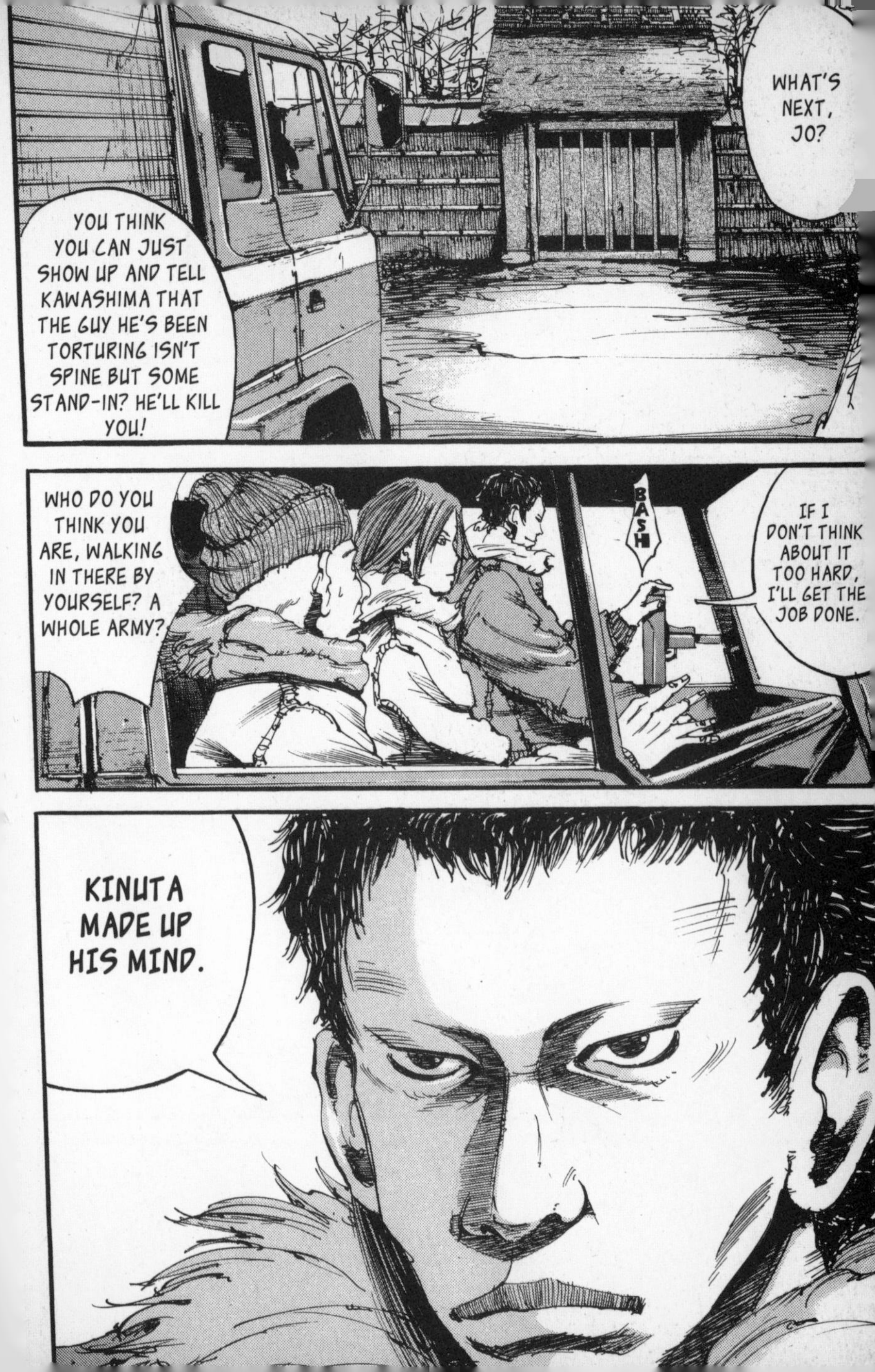
WHAT'S NEXT, JO?
YOU THINK YOU CAN JUST SHOW UP AND TELL KAWASHIMA THAT THE GUY HE'S BEEN TORTURING ISN'T SPINE BUT SOME STAND-IN? HE'LL KILL YOU!
IF I DON'T THINK ABOUT IT TOO HARD, I'LL GET THE JOB DONE.
BASH
WHO DO YOU THINK YOU ARE, WALKING IN THERE BY YOURSELF? A WHOLE ARMY?
KINUTA MADE UP HIS MIND.

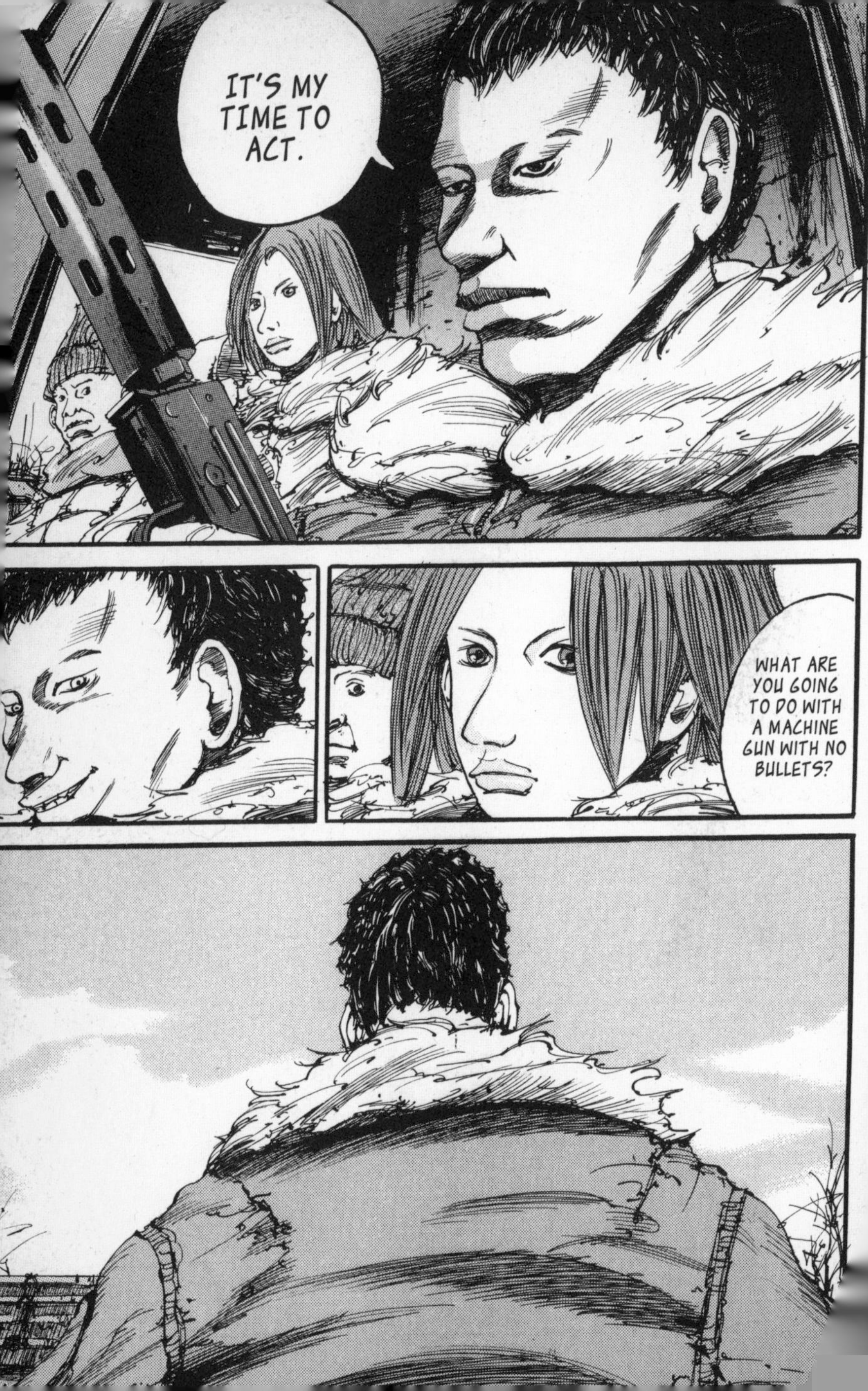
IT'S MY TIME TO ACT.
WHAT ARE YOU GOING TO DO WITH A MACHINE GUN WITH NO BULLETS?

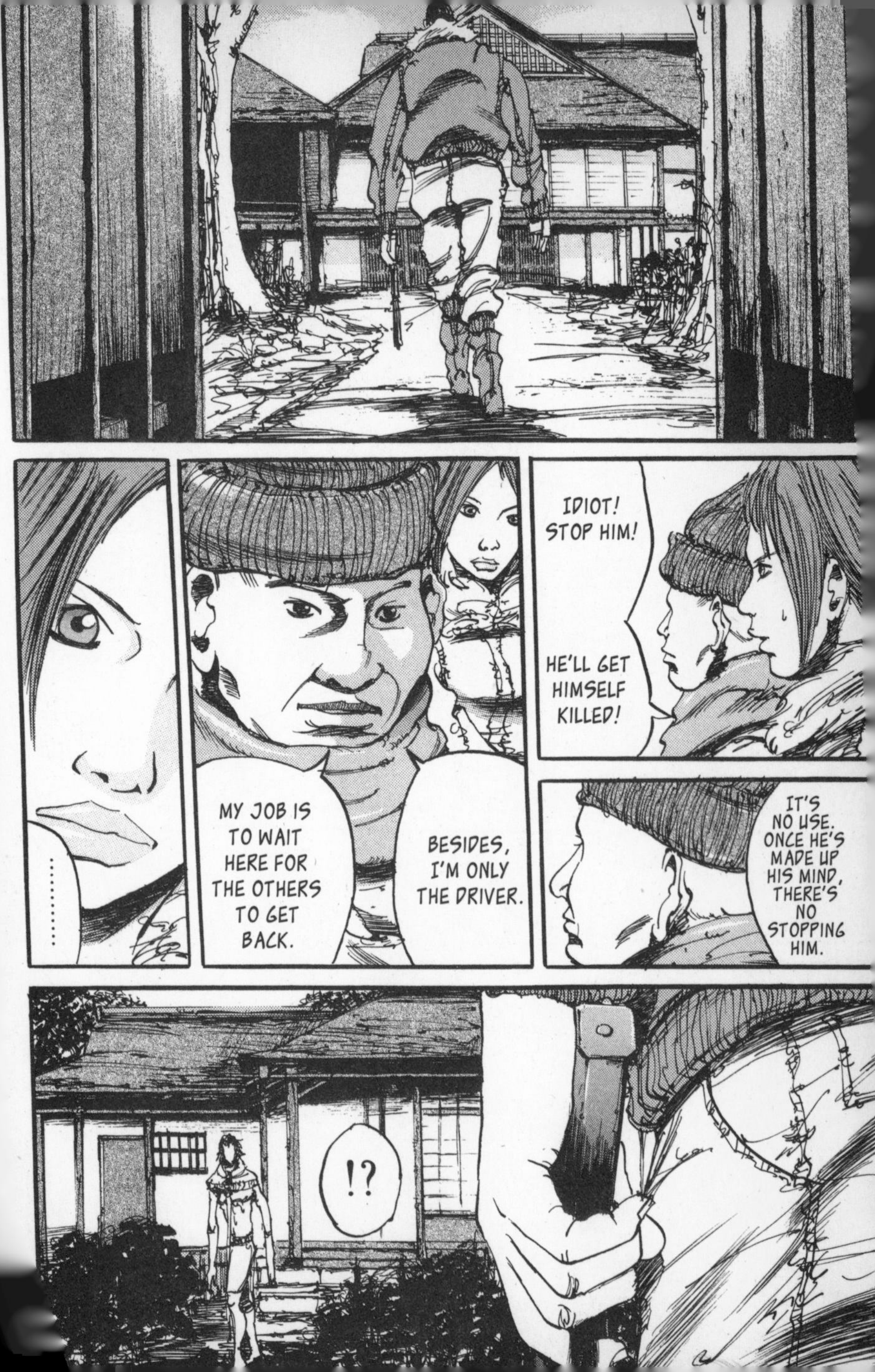
IDIOT! STOP HIM!
HE'LL GET HIMSELF KILLED!
IT'S NO USE. ONCE HE'S MADE UP HIS MIND, THERE'S NO STOPPING HIM.
MY JOB IS TO WAIT HERE FOR THE OTHERS TO GET BACK.
BESIDES, I'M ONLY THE DRIVER.
......
!?

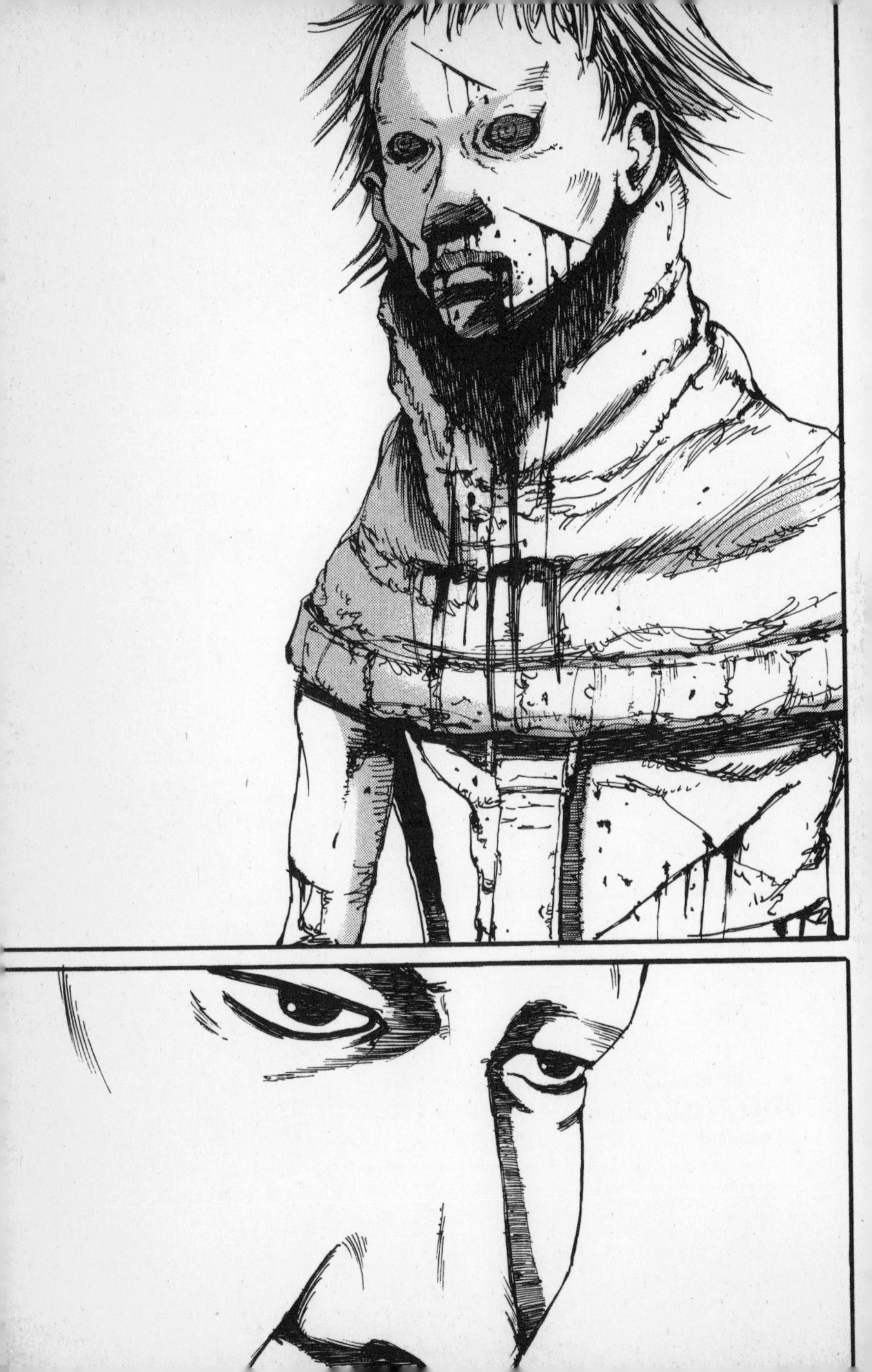

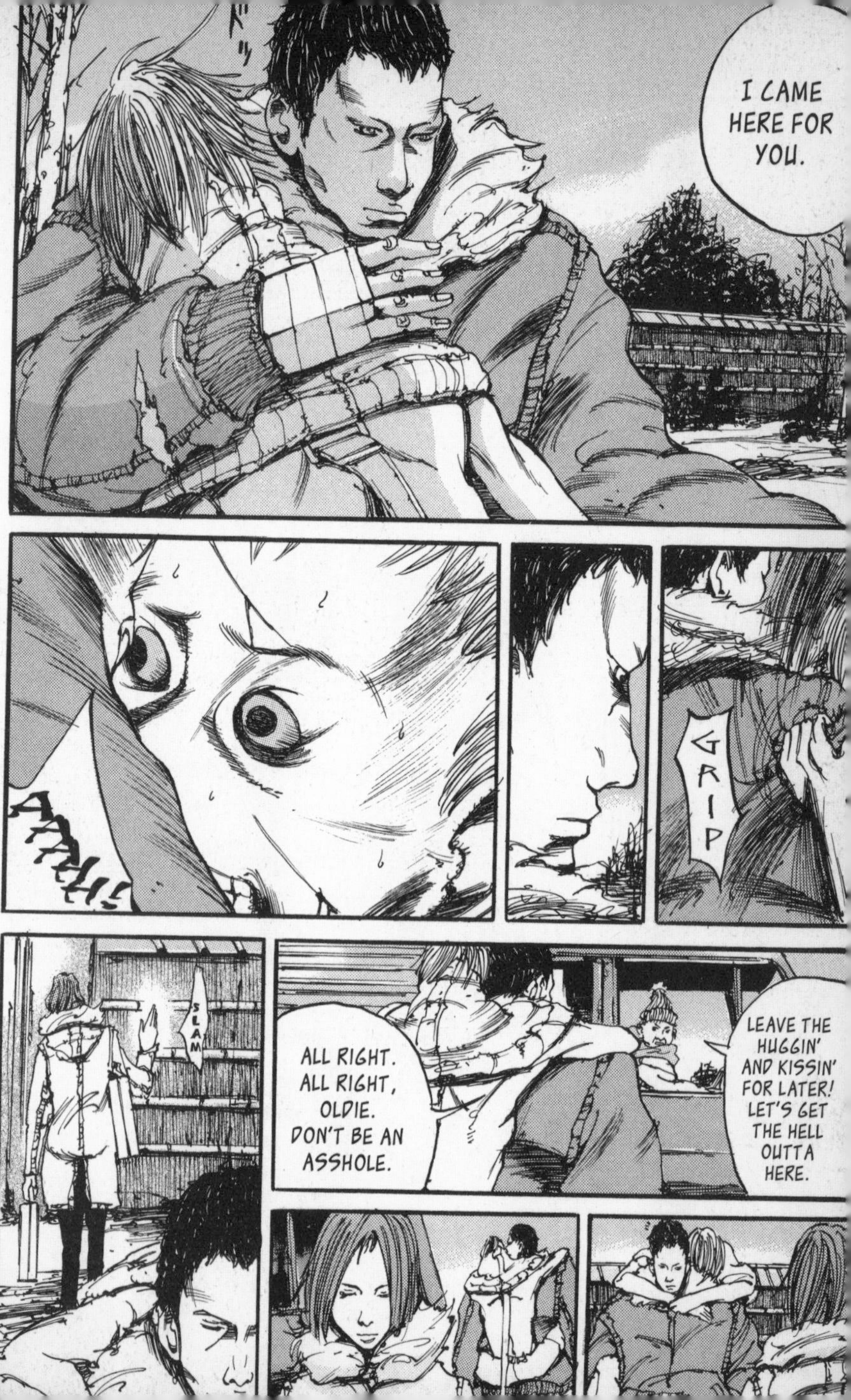
I CAME HERE FOR YOU.
GRIP
AAAAHH!
LEAVE THE HUGGIN' AND KISSIN' FOR LATER! LET'S GET THE HELL OUTTA HERE.
ALL RIGHT. ALL RIGHT, OLDIE. DON'T BE AN ASSHOLE.
SLAM

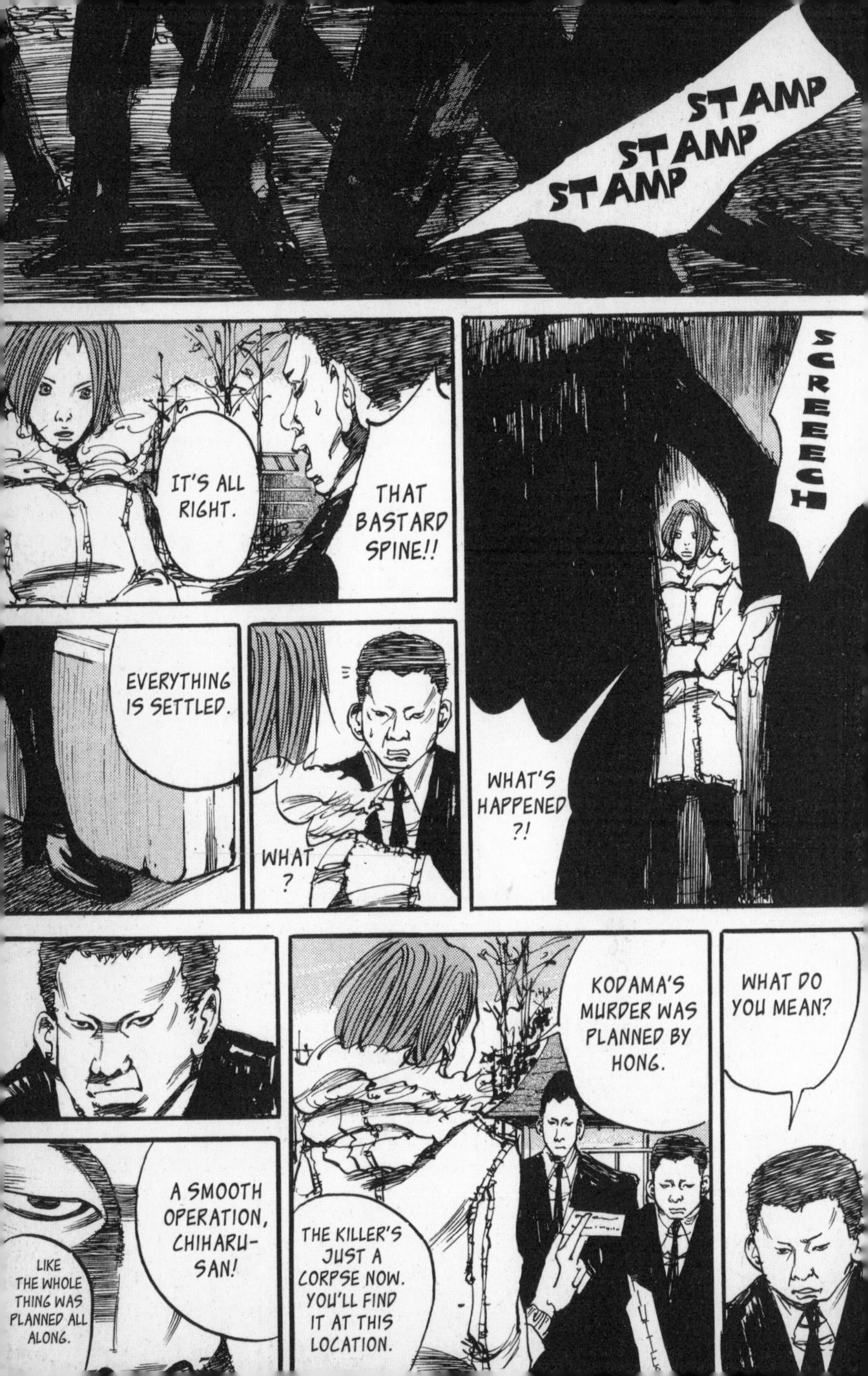
STAMP
STAMP
STAMP
SCREEECH
WHAT'S HAPPENED ?!
THAT BASTARD SPINE!!
IT'S ALL RIGHT.
WHAT ?
EVERYTHING IS SETTLED.
WHAT DO YOU MEAN?
KODAMA'S MURDER WAS PLANNED BY HONG.
THE KILLER'S JUST A CORPSE NOW. YOU'LL FIND IT AT THIS LOCATION.
A SMOOTH OPERATION, CHIHARU-SAN!
LIKE THE WHOLE THING WAS PLANNED ALL ALONG.

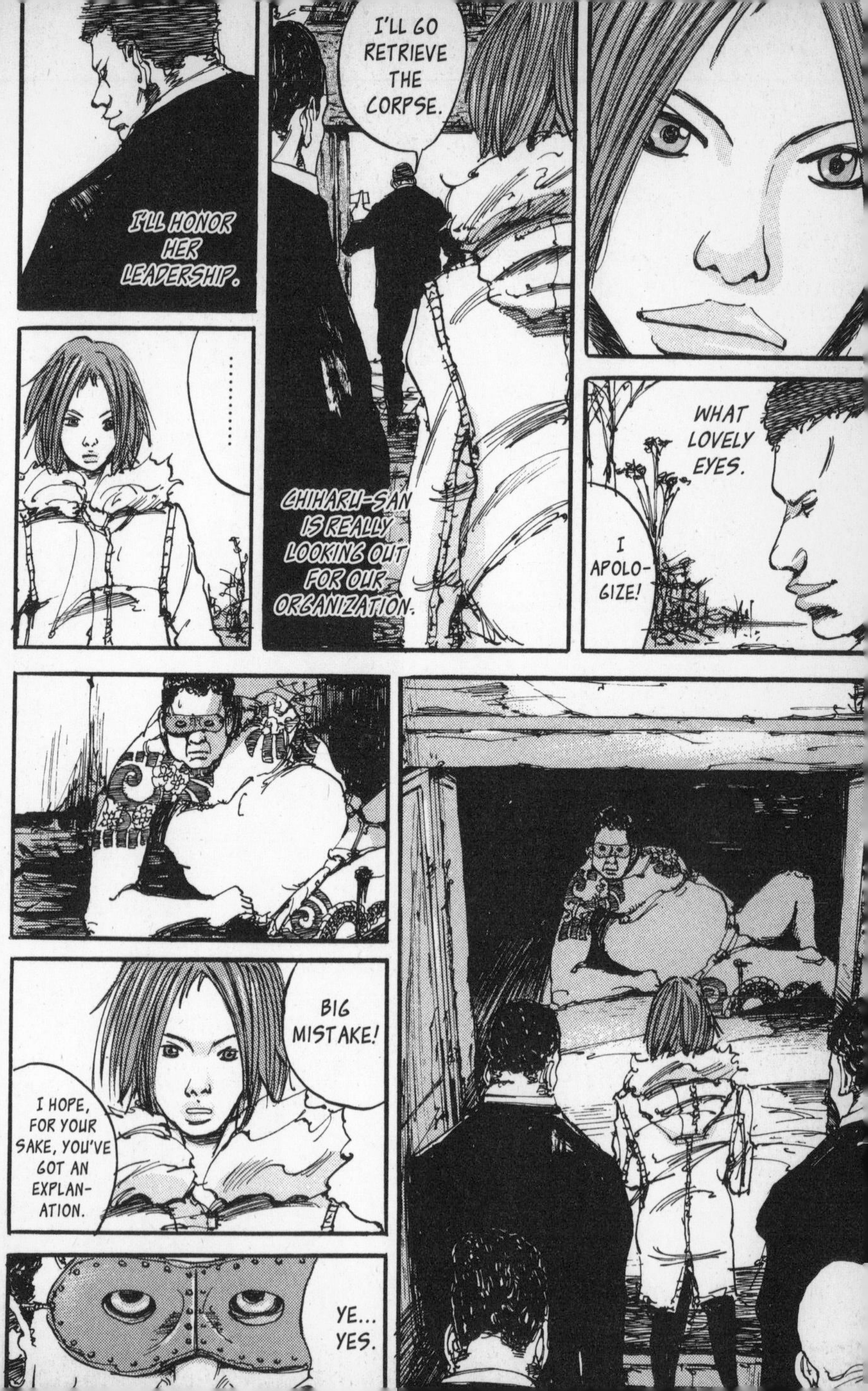
WHAT LOVELY EYES.
I APOLO-GIZE!
I'LL GO RETRIEVE THE CORPSE.
CHIHARU-SAN IS REALLY LOOKING OUT FOR OUR ORGANIZATION.
I'LL HONOR HER LEADERSHIP.
......
BIG MISTAKE!
I HOPE, FOR YOUR SAKE, YOU'VE GOT AN EXPLAN-ATION.
YE... YES.

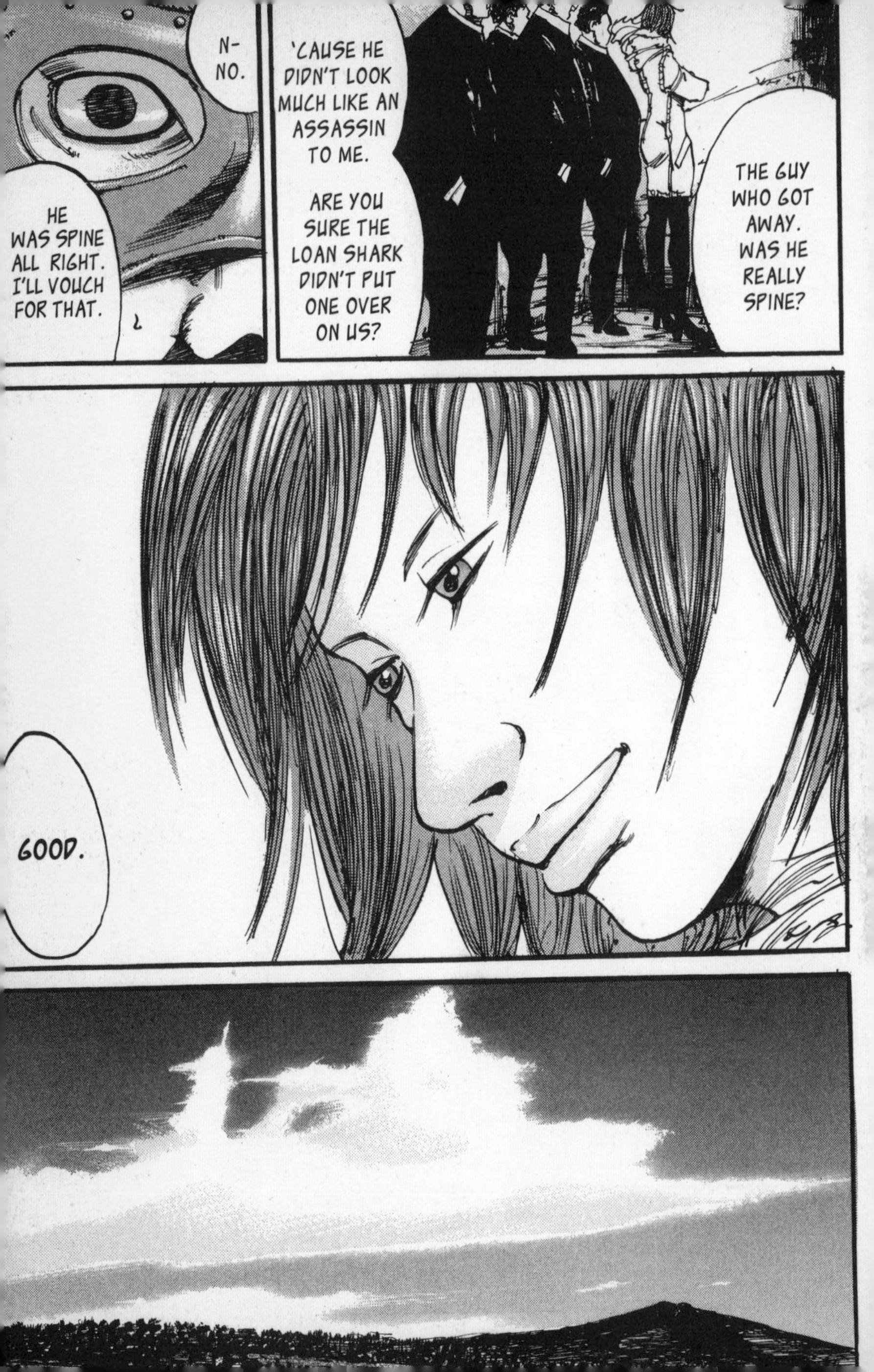
THE GUY WHO GOT AWAY. WAS HE REALLY SPINE?
'CAUSE HE DIDN'T LOOK MUCH LIKE AN ASSASSIN TO ME.
ARE YOU SURE THE LOAN SHARK DIDN'T PUT ONE OVER ON US?
N-NO.
HE WAS SPINE ALL RIGHT. I'LL VOUCH FOR THAT.
GOOD.

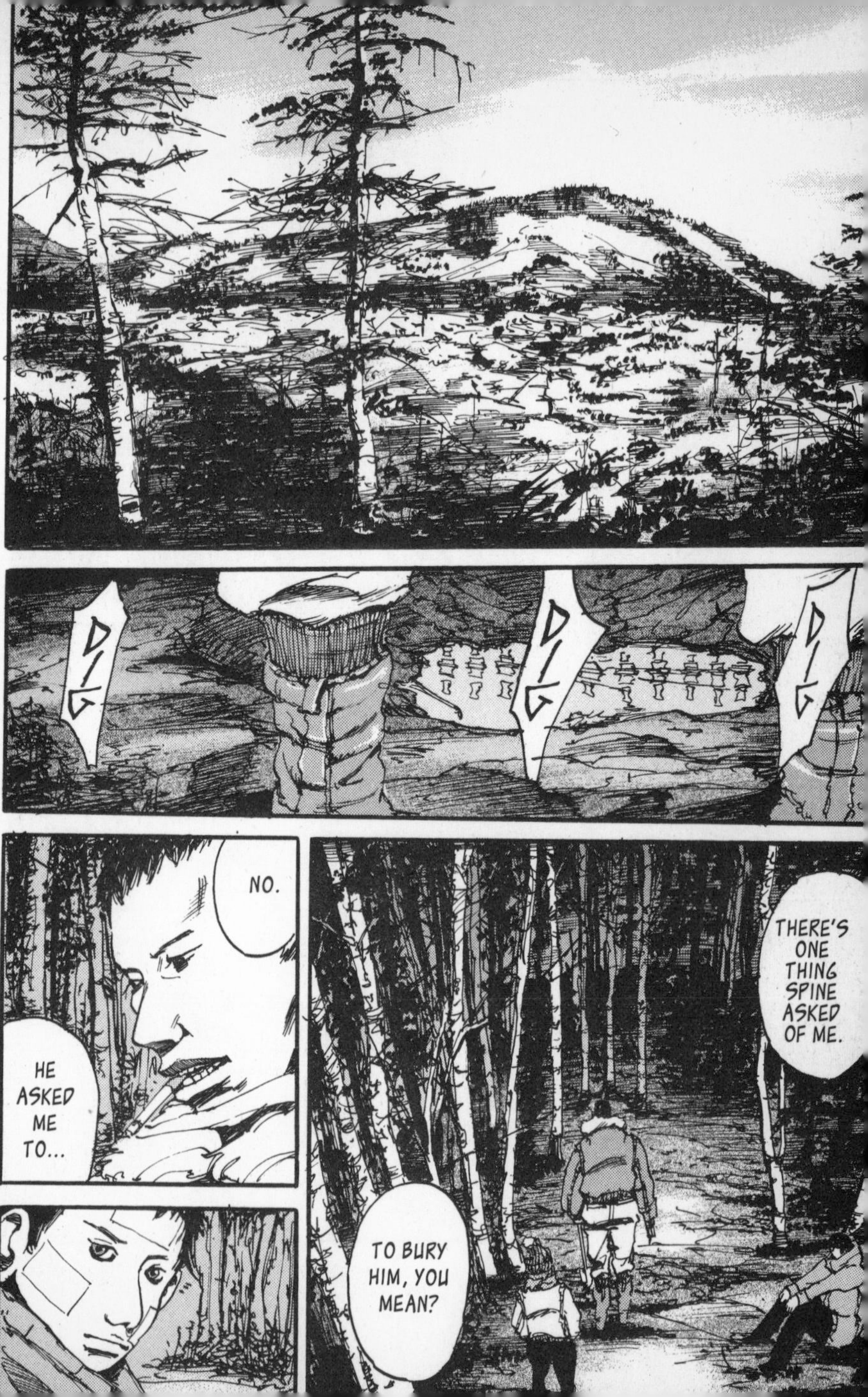
DIG
DIG
DIG
THERE'S ONE THING SPINE ASKED OF ME.
TO BURY HIM, YOU MEAN?
NO.
HE ASKED ME TO...

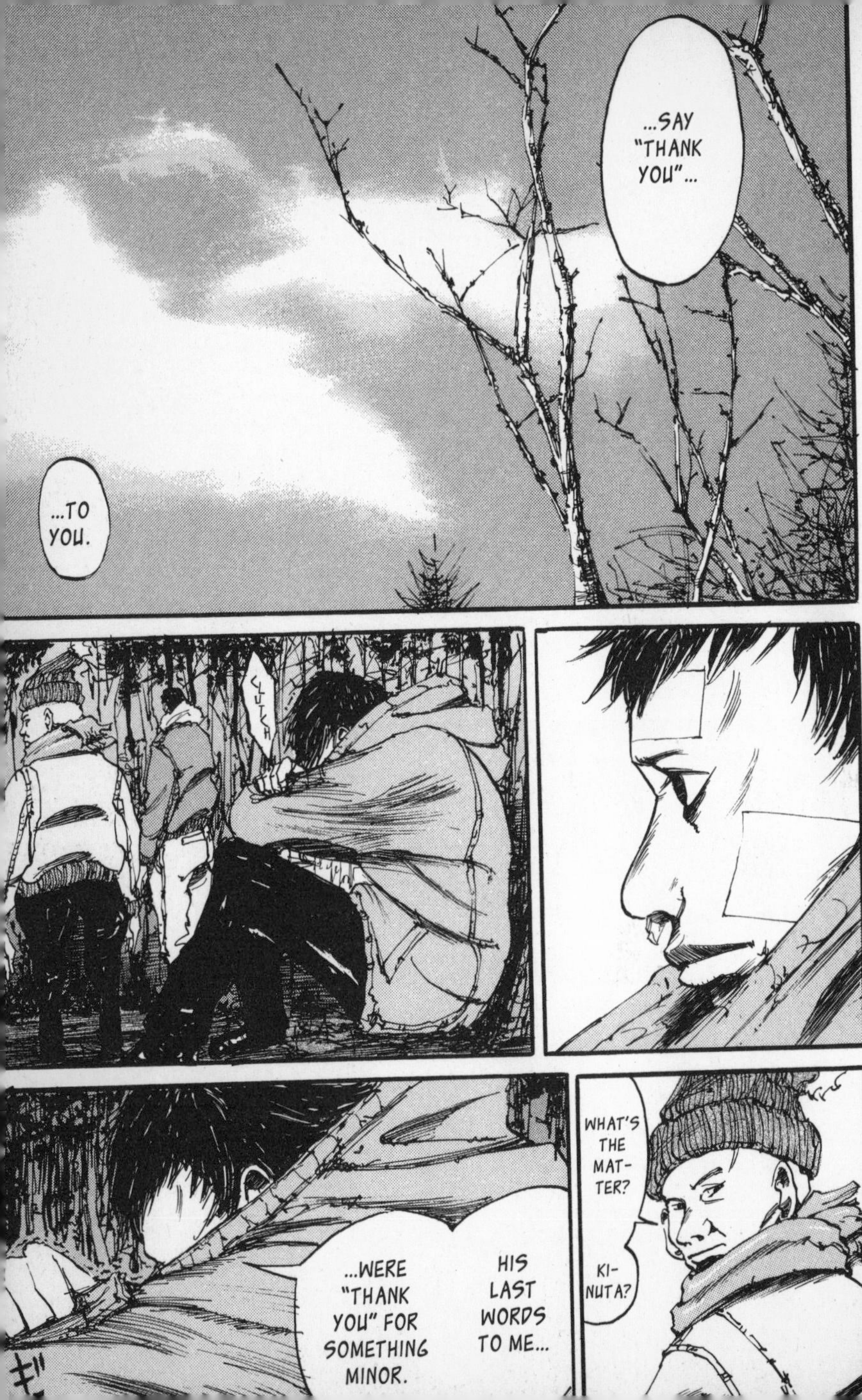
...SAY "THANK YOU"...
...TO YOU.
CLUTCH
WHAT'S THE MATTER?
KI-NUTA?
HIS LAST WORDS TO ME...
...WERE "THANK YOU" FOR SOMETHING MINOR.

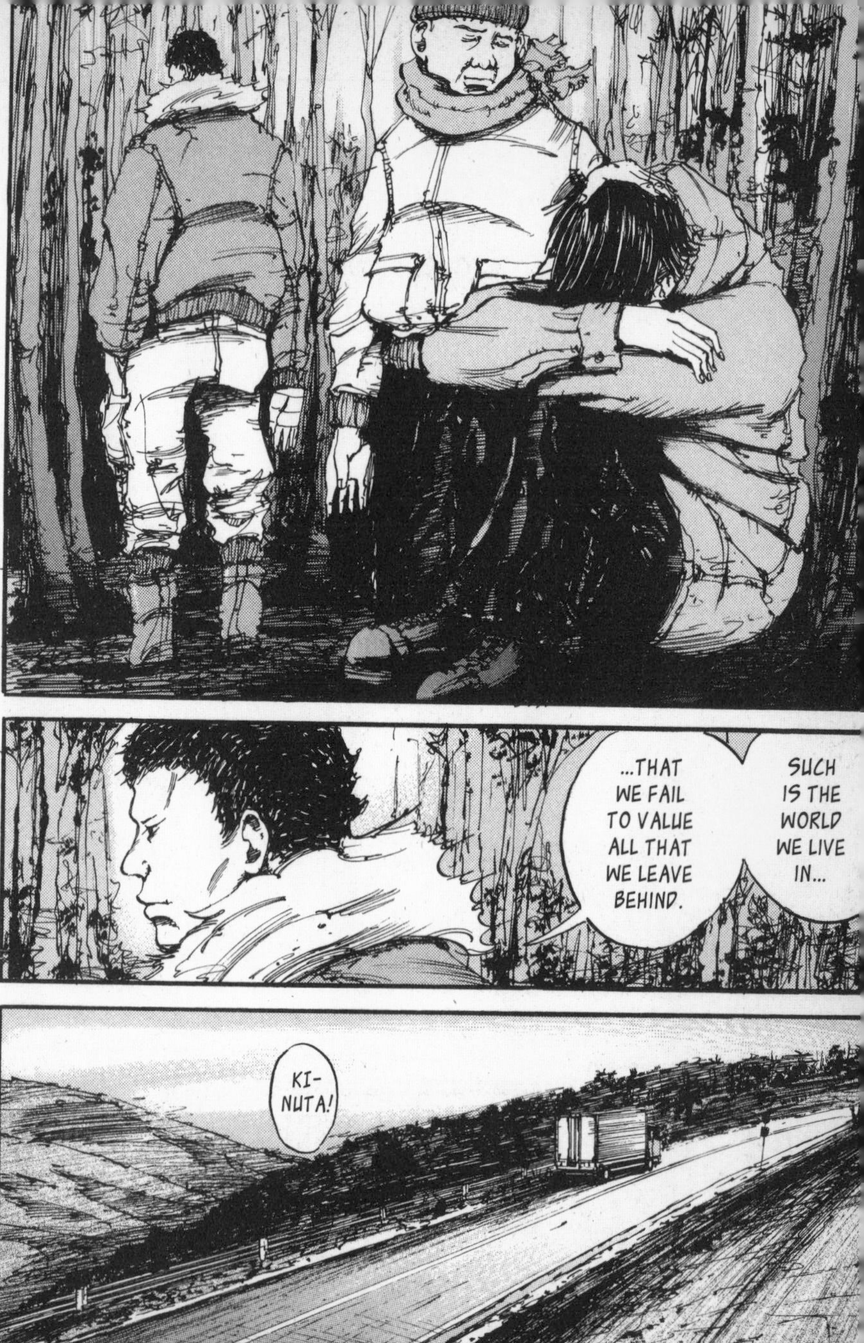
SUCH IS THE WORLD WE LIVE IN...
...THAT WE FAIL TO VALUE ALL THAT WE LEAVE BEHIND.
KI-NUTA!

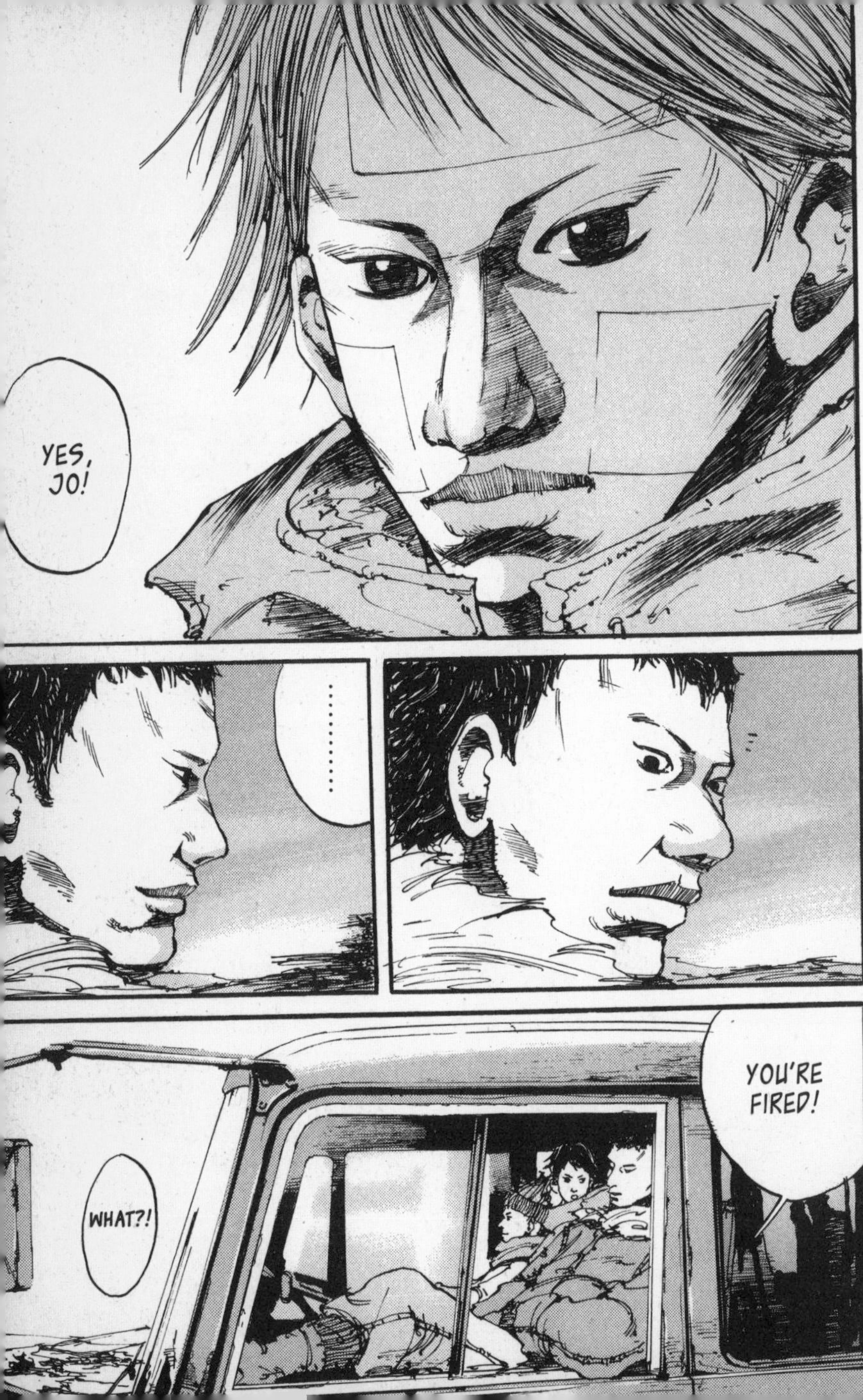
YES, JO!
......
YOU'RE FIRED!
WHAT?!

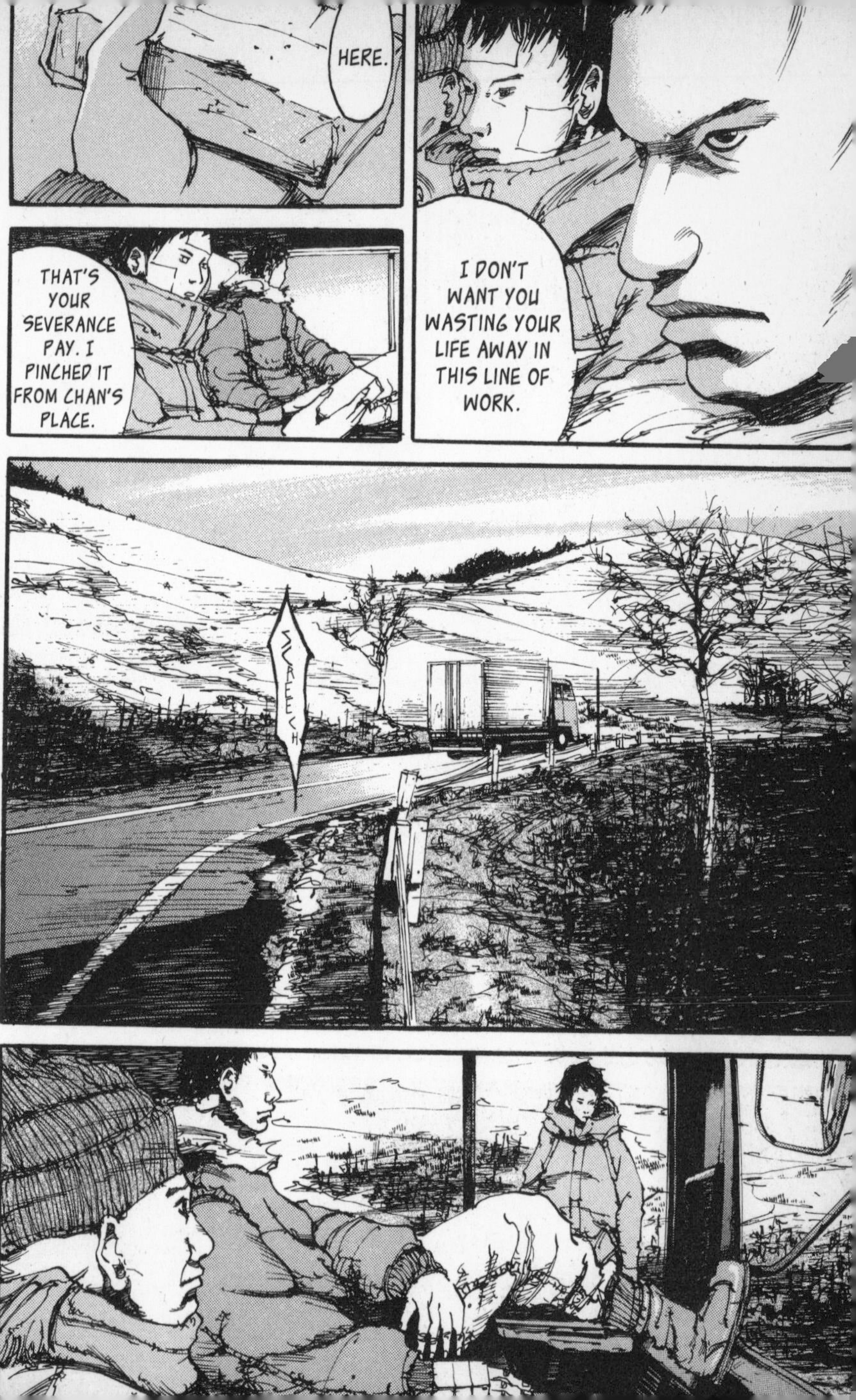
I DON'T WANT YOU WASTING YOUR LIFE AWAY IN THIS LINE OF WORK.
HERE.
THAT'S YOUR SEVERANCE PAY. I PINCHED IT FROM CHAN'S PLACE.
SCREECH

カサ
カサ

ヒュゥ
ワッ

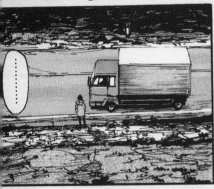

GOOD LUCK TO YOU!

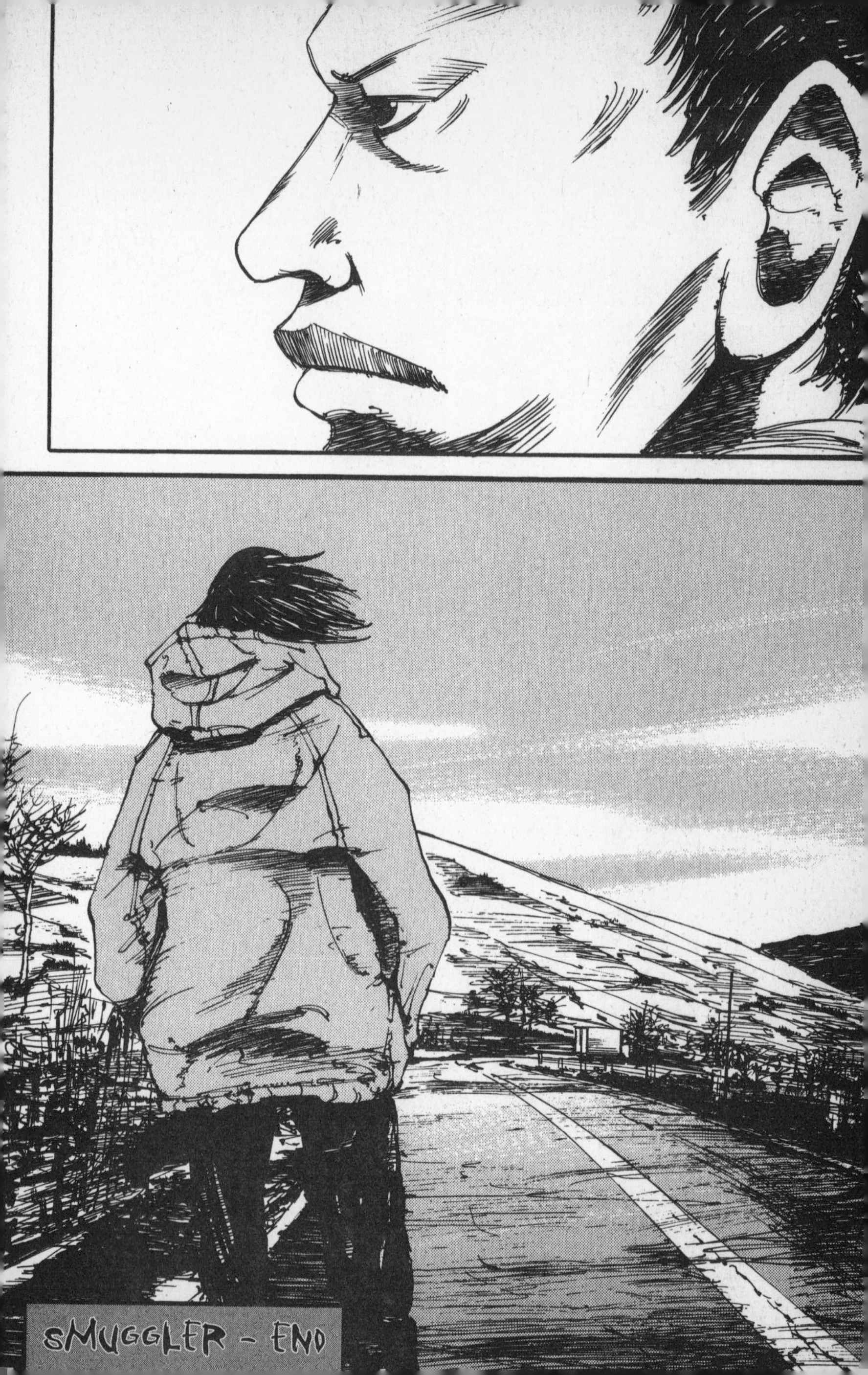
SMUGGLER - END

TOKYOPOP PRESENTS
MANGA 漫画
THE NEW SIZZLING HOT
FREE
MAGAZINE
ZELDA AND FRIEND FROM
WAR ON FLESH
© Justin Boring, Greg Hildebrandt and TOKYOPOP Inc.
SIGN UP FOR FREE WWW.TOKYOPOP.COM

TOKYOPOP SHOP

ROADSONG

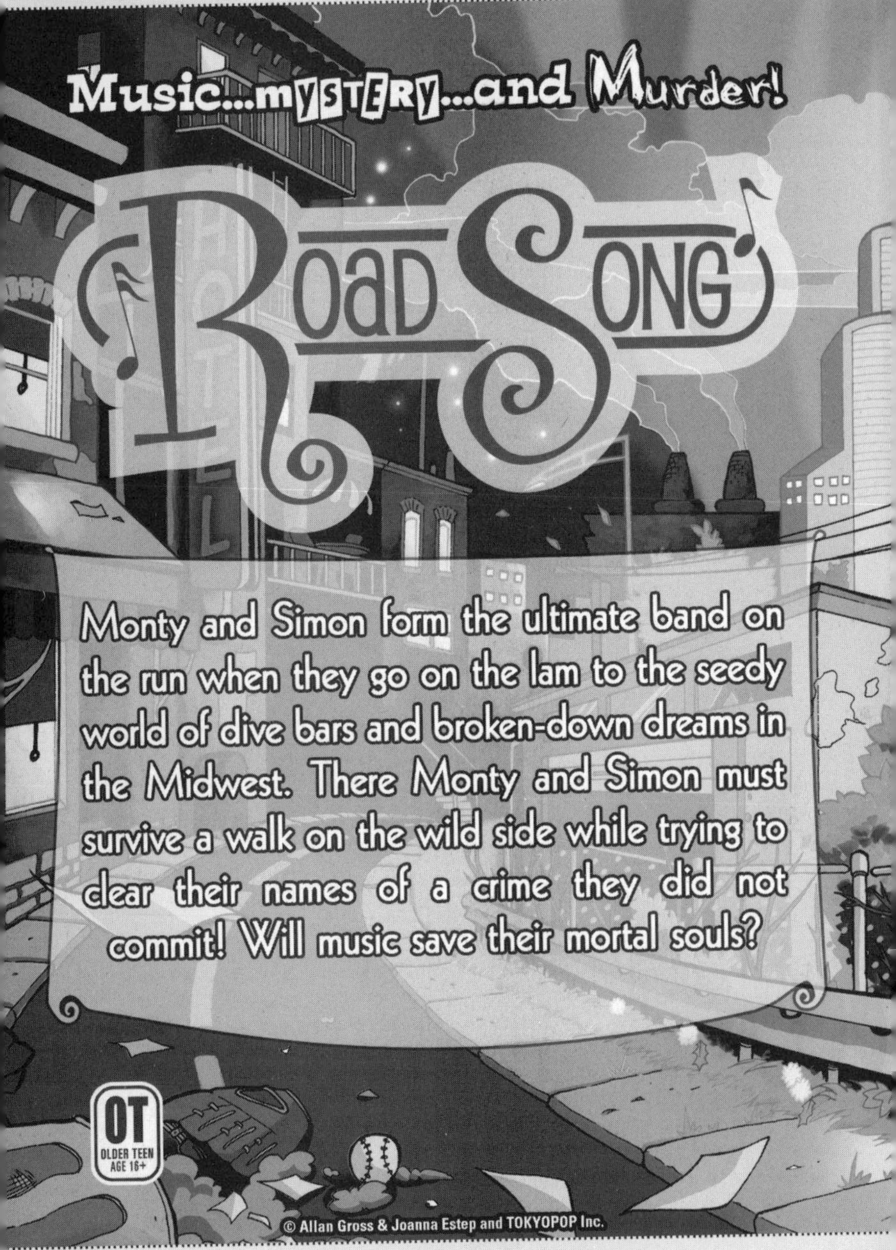

Music...Mystery...and Murder!

RoadSong

Monty and Simon form the ultimate band on the run when they go on the lam to the seedy world of dive bars and broken-down dreams in the Midwest. There Monty and Simon must survive a walk on the wild side while trying to clear their names of a crime they did not commit! Will music save their mortal souls?

OT
OLDER TEEN
AGE 16+

READ A CHAPTER OF THE MANGA ONLINE FOR FREE:

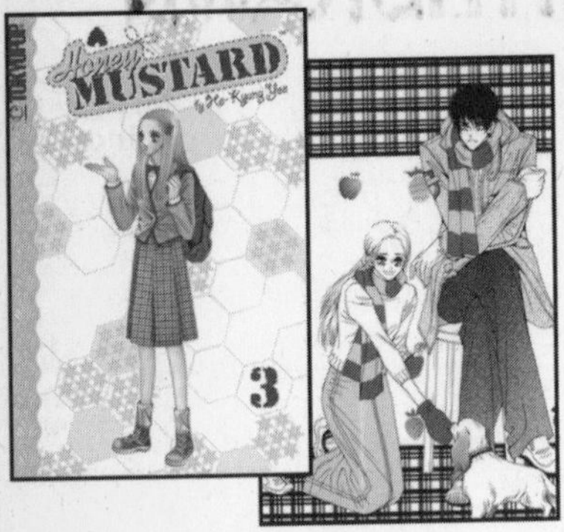
Honey MUSTARD
by Ho-Kyung Yeo
3
TOKYOPOP

BY HO-KYUNG YEO

HONEY MUSTARD

I'm often asked about the title of *Honey Mustard*. What does a condiment have to do with romance and teen angst? One might ask the same thing about a basket of fruits, but I digress. Honey mustard is sweet with a good dose of bite, and I'd say that sums up this series pretty darn well, too. Ho-Kyung Yeo does a marvelous job of balancing the painful situations of adolescence with plenty of whacked-out humor to keep the mood from getting *too* heavy. It's a good, solid romantic comedy...and come to think of it, it'd go great with that sandwich.

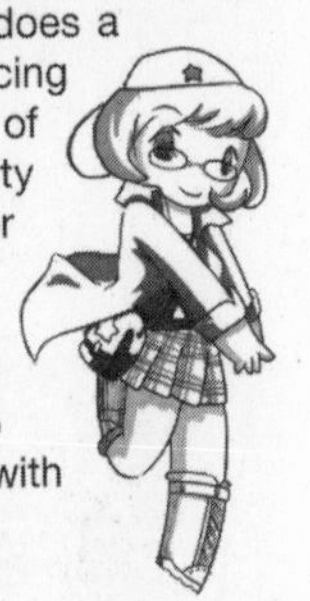

~Carol Fox, Editor

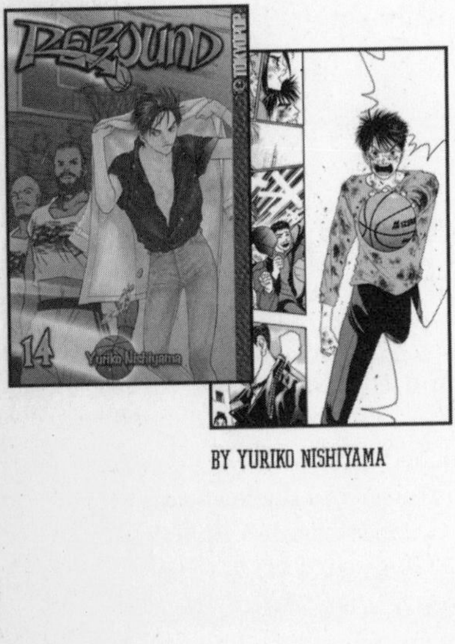
REBOUND
14
Yuriko Nishiyama
TOKYOPOP

BY YURIKO NISHIYAMA

REBOUND

At first glance, *Rebound* may seem like a simple sports manga. But on closer inspection, you'll find that the real drama takes place off the court. While the kids of the Johnan basketball team play and grow as a team, they learn valuable life lessons as well. By fusing the raw energy of basketball with the apple pie earnestness of an afterschool special, Yuriko Nishiyama has created a unique and heartfelt manga that appeals to all readers, male and female.

~Troy Lewter, Editor

DAZZLE
BY MINARI ENDOH

When a young girl named Rahzel is sent off to see the world, she meets Alzeido, a mysterious loner on a mission to find his father's killer. The two don't exactly see eye-to-eye, until Alzeido opens his heart to Rahzel. On the long and winding road, the duo crosses paths with various characters...including one who wants to get a little too close to Rahzel!

An epic coming-of-age story from an accomplished manga artist!

© Minari Endoh/ICHIJINSHA

T TEEN AGE 13+

THE WORLD EXISTS FOR ME
BY BE-PAPAS AND CHIHO SAITOU

Once upon a time, the source of the devil R's invincible powers was *The Book of S & M*. But one day, a young man stole the book without knowing what it was, cut it into strips and used it to create a girl doll named "S" and a boy doll named "M." With that act, the unimaginable power that the devil held from the book was unleashed upon the world!

From the creators of the manga classic *Revolutionary Girl Utena*!

© CHIHO SAITOU and IKUNI & Be-PaPas

T TEEN AGE 13+

TSUKUYOMI: MOON PHASE
BY KEITARO ARIMA

Cameraman Kouhei Midou is researching Schwarz Quelle Castle. When he steps inside the castle's great walls, he discovers a mysterious little girl, Hazuki, who's been trapped there for years. Utilizing her controlling charm, Hazuki tries to get Kouhei to set her free. But this sweet little girl isn't everything she appears to be...

The manga that launched the popular anime!

T TEEN AGE 13+